THE CRIME OF AGGR
AND THE SOLDIER

The international criminality of waging illegal war, alongside only a few of the gravest human wrongs, is rooted not in its violation of sovereignty, but in the large-scale killing war entails. Yet when soldiers refuse to kill in illegal wars, nothing shields them from criminal sanction for that refusal. This seeming paradox in law demands explanation. Just as soldiers have no right not to kill in criminal wars, the death and suffering inflicted on them when they fight against aggression has been excluded repeatedly from the calculation of post-war reparations, whether monetary or symbolic. This, too, is jarring in an era of international law infused with human rights principles. Tom Dannenbaum explores these ambiguities and paradoxes and argues for institutional reforms through which the law would better respect the rights and responsibilities of soldiers.

TOM DANNENBAUM is Assistant Professor of International Law at the Fletcher School of Law and Diplomacy, Tufts University. His article "Why Have We Criminalized Aggressive War?" was awarded the Lieber Prize by the American Society of International Law in 2017.

THE CRIME OF AGGRESSION, HUMANITY, AND THE SOLDIER

TOM DANNENBAUM

Tufts University, Massachusetts

CAMBRIDGE
UNIVERSITY PRESS

University Printing House, Cambridge CB2 8BS, United Kingdom

One Liberty Plaza, 20th Floor, New York, NY 10006, USA

477 Williamstown Road, Port Melbourne, VIC 3207, Australia

314-321, 3rd Floor, Plot 3, Splendor Forum, Jasola District Centre, New Delhi - 110025, India

79 Anson Road, #06-04/06, Singapore 079906

Cambridge University Press is part of the University of Cambridge.

It furthers the University's mission by disseminating knowledge in the pursuit of education, learning and research at the highest international levels of excellence.

www.cambridge.org
Information on this title: www.cambridge.org/9781316620397
DOI: 10.1017/9781316718391

First published 2018

A catalogue record for this publication is available from the British Library

Library of Congress Cataloging in Publication data
Names: Dannenbaum, Tom, author.
Title: The crime of aggression, humanity, and the soldier / Tom Dannenbaum (Tufts University, Massachusetts).
Description: New York, NY : Cambridge University, 2018. | Includes index. | Includes bibliographical references and index.
Identifiers: LCCN 2017054443 | ISBN 9781107169180 (hardback) | ISBN 9781316620397 (pbk.)
Subjects: LCSH: Aggression (International law) | Soldiers–Legal status, laws, etc.
Classification: LCC KZ7140 .D36 2018 | DDC 341.6/2–dc23
LC record available at https://lccn.loc.gov/2017054443

ISBN 978-1-107-16918-0 Hardback
ISBN 978-1-316-62039-7 Paperback

CONTENTS

ACKNOWLEDGMENTS

This book is written in the interstices of international law and normative political theory. I remain grateful to Princeton University and its Department of Politics for recognizing the synergies in my work at the intersection of these two fields and for accommodating my two extended leaves of absence to attend and later teach at Yale Law School during the Ph.D. that led into the book. I was tremendously fortunate during my Ph.D. studies to have advisers in Charles Beitz, Kim Scheppele, and Gary Bass whose patience for my dual pursuits was unending and to whom I was always able to return with thoughts, questions, and drafts.

Chuck has modeled outstanding teaching and mentorship from the first courses I took with him many years ago, throughout my episodes in New Haven, and up to the final dissertation drafts. He combined detailed commentary on each step of the argument and each line of text with an ability to always see the work as a whole. Chuck was always several steps ahead of me in my own arguments, and conversations with him inevitably left me understanding far better what I wanted to argue and the challenges of achieving that objective. I cannot overstate how much I have benefitted from his clarity of thought. As a mentor, he has been simultaneously uplifting and demanding, kind and critical. I could not have asked for a better guide for this journey.

Kim's capacity to transcend fields of research and thought is an inspiration. She has opened my eyes to literatures that I would not have seen, has encouraged me to think about the connections between my project and the work of persons in disciplines with which I was unfamiliar, and has, more than anyone, provided the personal and intellectual link between theory and law that has made this a viable and enjoyable endeavor. Her comments have always been critical and penetrating, but uniquely warm and encouraging. I have left each of our meetings invigorated and with a list of new thoughts and ideas. She has been a rock of support and a true friend. I will be forever grateful.

Gary's course on International Justice was a joy, and it opened my mind to many of the issues that I have since pursued. For that alone, I would be in his debt. Since then, he has been a magnificent mentor. Even when technically on sabbatical, Gary was always willing to meet and discuss drafts with great care and deep thought and to find ways to get together in person despite my bouncing around, even if it meant meeting halfway in New York. Substantively, he has been perhaps the most critical of my advisers – demanding always that I not get lost in the clouds of theory and fail to confront the realities of the subject matter. I have always left our meetings with a stack of readings to pursue and challenges to address. Throughout that process, he has given me great confidence and encouragement. Gary's appreciation for the realities of world politics, combined with a deep commitment to many of the human values immanent in international law, is something to which I aspire. I am thankful for each dimension of his mentorship.

I am immensely grateful to have received the wise and skeptical comments of Alan Patten and Melissa Lane at the early stages of the project. Alan saw immediately the opportunities and also the dangers associated with the project and his comments and criticisms were invaluable in setting me off in the right direction. Melissa exuded energy, encouragement, creativity, generosity, and wisdom in those initial meetings and I am delighted and grateful to have had her return to the project during the final stages of writing.

I owe an enormous debt of gratitude to a number of colleagues and friends from my time at Yale Law School for their sage and penetrating comments. I benefitted in particular from numerous discussions with Bruce Ackerman, Kiel Brennan-Marquez, Amy Chua, Oona Hathaway, Paul Kahn, Itamar Mann, Daniel Markovits, Michael Reisman, Jed Rubenfeld, Scott Shapiro, and John Witt. Paul, Daniel, Jed, and John, in particular, provided the kind of extended advice and mentorship that one could only reasonably expect from dissertation advisers. Amy has been an unrivaled mentor and friend, and Oona has been a tremendous support. I benefitted also from discussions with Anne Alstott, Lea Brilmayer, Heather Gerken, David Grewal, Tracey Meares, Nicholas Parrillo, Robert Post, Jim Silk, Patrick Weil, and Jim Whitman. I owe Dapo Akande a big debt of gratitude for illuminating much of the doctrinal background against which this normative project is set, for penetrating comments on key chapters, and for organizing workshops at Oxford during which I was able to get excellent feedback on the work. The collective wisdom, patience, and generosity among this extraordinary group of scholars is immense.

I have also benefitted greatly from the feedback of discussants and audiences at the Yale Human Rights Workshop, Princeton's Graduate Research Seminar, the Graduate Prize Fellows workshop at Princeton's University Center for Human Values, the Law-Engaged Graduate Students seminar at Princeton's Program in Law and Public Affairs, the Yale Law School Moot Camp, the American Society of International Law's New Voices Session, the Oxford University Public International Law Speaker Series, the European Journal of International Law Workshop on the Crime of Aggression, the Lauterpacht Centre for International Law Speaker Series, and additional invited talks at Columbia Law School, the Fletcher School of Law and Diplomacy, University College London, the University of Miami Law School, the University of Michigan Law School, the University of Pennsylvania Law School, the University of San Diego Law School, and Yale Law School.

I am grateful to Princeton University for funding the first three years of my graduate studies, to the University Center for Human Values for funding my fourth year at Princeton, and to the Robina Foundation for funding my two years of teaching and research at Yale Law School.

For particularly helpful comments, suggestions, and discussions at various stages in the project's development, mention is due to Anu Bradford, Caroline Bradley, Brookes Brown, Cary Coglianese, David Crane, Lori Damrosch, Michael Doyle, William Evans, Dov Fox, Bruce Frier, Michael Froomkin, Michael Glennon, Amanda Greene, Monika Hakimi, Daniel Halberstam, Hurst Hannum, Mark Hewitson, Ian Johnstone, Harold Koh, Christopher Kutz, Cécile Laborde, Michael Lamb, Trevor Latimer, Tamara Rice Lave, Sophia Lee, Ross Lerner, Nan Levinson, Zachary Liscow, Jessica Lowe, Jeff McMahan, Saladin Meckled-Garcia, Frédéric Mégret, Marko Milanovic, Felix Mormann, Julian Mortenson, Melissa Moschella, James Nickel, Sarah Nouwen, Avia Pasternak, David Pozen, Richard Primus, Jonathan Quong, Steve Ratner, Don Regan, David Rodin, Elias Sacks, Padraic Scanlan, Steve Schnably, Henry Shue, Sonja Starr, Kate Stith, and Gideon Yaffe. Philip Pettit and Kwame Anthony Appiah were inspirational leaders of the Center for Human Values workshop. I also owe a special debt to my original cohort of political theorists – Sam Arnold, Brookes Brown, Ryan Davis, Yiftah Elazar, Jessica Flanigan, Rob Hunter, and Joshua Vandiver – for a long series of foundational discussions in the spring and early summer of 2007, as well as for support in the years since.

In the latter stages of the project, I have benefitted greatly from research assistance from María Alvarez-Tolcheff Alarco, Kyra Sanders, Hannah Wheeler, Steven Young, and Marina Ziemian. Thanks are due to Binesh Hass and his colleagues at Editing Press for proofreading. I am also, of course, very grateful to the team at Cambridge University Press, led by Finola O'Sullivan and Emma Collison, for their confidence in the project, their editorial work, and their support throughout. Anne Valentine's editorial work was particularly helpful.

I have spoken to a small number of soldiers over the past few years about the project and their reactions to it in light of their own experiences in the wars in Iraq and Afghanistan. These discussions have occurred always in confidence. However, those conversations have been truly invaluable and I am immensely grateful.

My brothers, Michael, Harry, and Peter, and my parents, Karl and Peggy, have shown tremendous love and patience throughout my research. They are also, of course, responsible for so much that came before.

Finally, it is impossible to articulate how much I owe Keya for this, as for everything else. Her love and companionship are the core of my life and the foundation of everything I do.

TABLE OF CASES

Eritrea–Ethiopia Claims Commission

European Court of Human Rights

Extraordinary Chambers in the Courts of Cambodia

Human Rights Committee

Inter-American Commission on Human Rights

Inter-American Court of Human Rights

International Court of Justice

International Criminal Court

Appeals Chamber

Trial Chambers

Prosecutor v. Katanga and Ngudjolo, Order on the Organisation of Common Legal Representation of Victims, ICC-01/04–01/07 (2009) 32, 333, 334

Pre-Trial Chambers

Prosecutor v. Gbagbo, Second Decision on Issues Related to the Victims' Application Process, ICC-02/11–01/11–86 (2012) 334

Prosecutor v. Gbagbo, Decision on Issues related to the Victims' Application Process, ICC-02/11–01/11–33 (2012) 334

Prosecutor v. Bemba, Confirmation of Charges, ICC-01/05–01/08 (2009) 148

Prosecutor v. Bemba, Sixth Decision on Victims' Participation Relating to Certain Questions Raised by the Office of Public Counsel for Victims, ICC-01/05–01/08–349 (2009) 31

International Criminal Tribunal for the former Yugoslavia

Appeals Chamber

Prosecutor v. Gotovina, Judgment, IT-06–90-A (2012) 248

Prosecutor v. Strugar, Judgment, IT-01–42-A (2008) 148

Prosecutor v. Galić, Judgment, IT-98–29-A (2006) 148

Prosecutor v. Blaškić, Judgment, IT-95–14-A (2004) 140, 148

Prosecutor v. Tadić, Judgment, IT-94–1-A (1999) 54, 229

Prosecutor v. Erdemović, Judgment, IT-96–22-A (1997) 54, 123, 124, 129

Prosecutor v. Tadić, Decision on Defence Motion for Interlocutory Appeal on Jurisdiction, IT-94-1-I (1995) 62, 87, 94, 147, 312, 313

Trial Chambers

Prosecutor v. Perišić, IT-04–81-T (2011) 148

Prosecutor v. Galić, IT-98–29-T (2003) 148

Prosecutor v. Kordić & Čerkez, IT-95–14/2-T (2001) 120

Prosecutor v. Kupreškić, Judgment, IT-95–16-T (2000) 62, 313

Prosecutor v. Erdemović [Second] Sentencing Judgment, IT-96–22-Tbis (1998) 123, 129–30

Prosecutor v. Furundžija, Judgment, IT-95–17/1-T (1998) 94, 260

International Military Tribunal (Nuremberg)

United States v. Göring et al., 22 Trial of the Major War Criminals before the International Military Tribunal 411 (1946) 17, 20, 21, 23, 55, 56, 70, 71, 82, 89, 96, 99, 103, 104, 114, 168, 180–81, 245, 320

International Military Tribunal for the Far East (Tokyo)

Occupying Power Tribunals following World War II

Special Court for Sierra Leone

United Nations Compensation Commission

Domestic Courts

Canada

Germany

Israel

Latvia

Netherlands

United Kingdom

United States

TABLE OF TREATIES AND LEGISLATION

Treaties

European Union Law

Domestic Law

Australia

Germany

Japan

United Kingdom

United States

TABLE OF OTHER AUTHORITIES

Domestic

European Union

Inter-American Commission on Human Rights

International Criminal Court (including preparatory work and submissions to the court)

International Criminal Tribunal for the former Yugoslavia

Institut de Droit International

International Law Association

United Nations General Assembly

United Nations Security Council

United Nations (other)

~

Introduction

We are the ones who have to live
with the memory that we were the instruments
of your pigeon-breasted fantasies.
We are inextricable accomplices
in this travesty of dreams.
But we are not alone.

Vietnam Veteran, WD Ehrhart[1]

I was part of the problem. And I didn't mean to be, and I didn't want to be, but I was there, you know? And that was the crime. The crime was that I was there.

Iraq Veteran, Garett Reppenhagen[2]

Aggressive war entails broad and devastating violence. It is banned peremptorily and criminalized in international law. Its prohibition is in some ways the core premise of the contemporary international order. And yet, those who participate most intimately in the criminal action and those most directly impacted by it appear to be marginalized almost entirely from the international legal framework surrounding the crime of aggression.

International law generally requires that soldiers disobey criminal orders, potentially at profound personal cost. But even high-ranking soldiers who fight enthusiastically for an aggressor force commit no crime by doing so. Quite the opposite. In the vast majority of states, they commit a domestic crime if they *refuse* to fight, and international law

[1] The excerpt from "A Relative Thing" is reprinted from W. D. Ehrhart, Beautiful Wreckage (Adastra Press, 2017), pp. 9–10, by permission of the author.

[2] Matthew Gutmann. Breaking Ranks: Iraq Veterans Speak Out against the War (c) 2010 by the Regents of the University of California (University of California Press, 2010).

offers them no protection from prosecution for that refusal. In other words, these soldiers are required on pain of criminal punishment to kill, maim, and destroy in service of a criminal end.

The legal treatment of soldiers on the other side of such a war is less clearly developed, but at its heart is a similar peculiarity. Assuming no other legal violations, the soldiers killed by an aggressor force are the only human targets of the violence of an aggressive war. These men and women are killed intentionally, by a force that acts without justification, in violation of one of the core legal foundations of the contemporary international order. And yet, international law seems to be unmoved by their deaths. The international human right to life is non-derogable, but *soldiers'* lives, in Gabriella Blum's unsettling description, seem to be "dispensable" from the legal point of view.[3] The leader of an aggressor force perpetrates a grave and criminal wrong by waging an aggressive war, but seemingly not a wrong against *them*. That, at least, is the dominant normative understanding of the law we have.

On its face, this ought to be profoundly jarring. How can international law hold illegal war to be an "accumulated evil" and yet offer soldiers no right whatsoever to refuse to kill in its service? Are soldiers like Ehrhart and Reppenhagen mistaken, from an international legal point of view, when they wrestle with killing in wrongful wars? And can it really be that the lives of soldiers carry so little weight that they can be killed purposefully in furtherance of a criminal enterprise without they or their bereaved families suffering any legally cognizable wrong?

This book is an effort to answer these questions. It seeks to explain the normative posture of international law *vis-à-vis* soldiers, particularly with respect to the criminalization of aggression. As elaborated further in Chapter 2, to offer a normative account of the law here is to take seriously the notion that international law in this domain takes moral positions and that these positions can be articulated and understood in a way that goes beyond the requirements, permissions, and prohibitions of the law as it stands. Understood in this way, the criminalization of aggression is not just a formal prohibition, but also an expression of aggression's *wrongfulness* from the international legal point of view. Exploring the nature of that expressed wrongfulness in a way that remains faithful to the law we have is key to answering the questions posed above.

[3] Gabriella Blum, *The Dispensable Lives of Soldiers*, 2 J. LEGAL ANALYSIS 115 (2010).

On the traditional, and still dominant, normative account of the extant regime, the answers to these questions are relatively straightforward. From that point of view, we ought not be troubled by international law's treatment of soldiers. Endorsing both the criminalization of aggression and the general requirement to disobey criminal orders, this account holds nonetheless that the soldier ordered to fight in an illegal war is not ordered to do anything wrong. In adopting this posture, it recognizes no internal dissonance in the fact that she can be required on pain of criminal punishment to do precisely that. Similarly, on this account, the soldiers fighting against the aggressor force are legitimate targets, and so suffer no wrong when killed by an aggressor force. From that perspective, international systems of recognition and reparation associated with aggression need not, and ought not, focus on soldiers, because they are not the victims of a legal wrong.

This normative marginalization of the soldier in questions about going to war is odd. Much of the work in writing this book has occurred in the United States. It is difficult not to be struck by the normative force of the notion of "supporting our troops" in public discourse here. It is rare to drive any significant distance on a highway without encountering a slogan or icon expressing that sentiment on the bumpers of multiple cars. A virtue of this slogan is that it recognizes that soldiers do not waive their moral status when they put on a uniform. A decision to go to war is thought to require an accounting for the sacrifice those men and women will be asked to make. From this perspective, their lives are not dispensable. They matter as individuals, and they have claims against those whose decisions affect them.

Of course, in domestic public discourse, the recognition of this truth is decidedly partial and partisan. The hint is in the central term of the slogan – "our." Although civilians on all sides are recognized (unequally) as being sources of value, active enemy soldiers hold little or no normative significance in domestic debates.

Panning out to a global perspective on war necessarily breaks down this normative segregation between "our" and "their" troops. However, on the traditional normative account, the result seems to be a leveling down, rather than a leveling up. Waging aggressive war is an international crime with profound consequences for every soldier involved on either side of the conflict. And yet, on the traditional account, soldiers are excluded appropriately, and almost entirely, from the structure of legal rights and responsibilities associated with that crime.

This book offers an alternative vision. It presents a normative account of the law that is more in line with the moral insights of revisionist just war theory than international lawyers or revisionist theorists have thus far recognized. A scrupulous normative account of international law must recognize that the killing and violence performed in an illegal war is profoundly wrongful. In fact, the wrongfulness of that violence is the very reason why aggressive war is a crime. On that account, the soldiers who feel burdened by their participation in that wrongful violence get it right. As such, international law's failure to protect them from being forced to fight ought to be deeply unsettling on the law's own terms. That failure to protect may be defensible, but any defense of it must take seriously the moral burden that such a regime shifts onto the soldier and must account for that displacement.

Recognizing the wrongfulness of the killing and violence performed in an illegal war also requires appreciating that soldiers are wronged when they are killed or harmed by an aggressor force. On this account, their lives are not dispensable from the international legal point of view. The most significant normative function of the criminalization of aggression is precisely to condemn and punish the unjustified taking of soldiers' lives and to offer criminal law protection to their right to life. Moving to the international level does not require dropping the insight of the "support our troops" slogan regarding going to war, it requires globalizing the sentiment, and dropping the possessive. The leader who takes her state into an aggressive war inflicts a direct criminal wrong on the soldiers her forces kill and maim. That must be recognized explicitly in the appropriate legal forms.

The argument is structured as follows. Chapter 1 details the legal framework on aggression, disobedience, and victim status in international criminal law and the relevant related regimes. In so doing, it identifies the normative tension at the heart of international law in this domain and lays the foundation for the puzzle that motivates this book. It also emphasizes that this is not simply a question of doctrinal aesthetics. There is good evidence to believe that soldiers who fight in aggressive war experience real moral pain associated with their participation in its wrongful violence. Equally, there is good reason to believe that those who suffer criminal wrongs without recognition of that wrongfulness suffer a significant second-order harm.

The objective of the book is to provide a normative account of the crime of aggression and the associated treatment of soldiers under international law. Chapter 2 explains what that means and why it is a worthy project. Stated most abstractly, a normative account aims to elaborate a moral framework that would make sense of, and underpin, the law's normative posture on a given issue. To offer such an account is not to start from first principles or to insist that the moral standards articulated ought to be accepted on their own terms. Rather, it is to inhabit the internal legal point of view, and to insist that the moral standards articulated best explain and make sense of the law that we have.

In light of international criminal law's tendency towards the moral expressive, as opposed to coordinative, function of law, giving an account of the crime of aggression means asking what framework of right, wrong, culpability, and innocence would most coherently underpin the existing positive regime. Chapter 2 argues that a candidate account is superior to its alternatives in achieving that objective, to the extent that it better satisfies four criteria. First, it must offer an explanation for what the regime unambiguously requires, permits, and prohibits on the issue at hand. Second, it ought to reflect the law's core purposes. Third, it should cohere with connected or related laws in domains adjacent to that which it explains. Finally, if multiple accounts pass the first three tests, the superior remaining account is that which is most morally plausible. The chapter also defends the project against realist objections and explains the connection between the law and the human experience discussed at the end of Chapter 1.

Chapter 3 answers the first major question of the book. Why have we criminalized aggressive war? It identifies mass killing without the justification of responding to the same as the normative core of the crime of aggression. In so doing, it debunks the traditional normative account of the crime, adopted by both defenders and critics of the criminalization of aggression, which defines it as a macro wrong against a foreign state or people.

To be clear, it is plainly true under current international law that *whether* a war is criminal depends typically, although not exclusively, on which side has violated the other's sovereignty. But that interstate breach is not *why* waging such wars is criminal. It is criminal because waging war in breach of those interstate rules entails widespread killing and the infliction of human suffering without justification. Recognizing this redefines aggression as a crime against humanity perpetrated ordinarily through a violation of sovereignty.

The consequences of these arguments are two. First, the soldier's acts in a criminal war are themselves wrongful from the legal point of view. If soldiers are not wronged by being forced to perform these killings, it can only be because they are innocent of the wrongs they perpetrate. Second, the soldiers killed fighting against a criminal use of force are the primary victims of the criminal wrong. In light of this, Part II of the book considers how to understand international law's posture towards soldiers on both sides.

That task begins in Chapter 4 with a consideration of whether we can make moral sense of the law's posture towards soldiers who fight and kill in criminal wars on the grounds that they are non-culpable for the wrongs they perpetrate due to the duress of being sandwiched between the enemy threat on one side and the legal and social threat from their home government and its people on the other. This theory cannot explain the exclusion of soldiers from victim status, although it might be thought to raise a question as to whether soldiers on the aggressor side would also qualify as victims of the crime. It is true that soldiers forced to fight in aggressive wars are wronged, and that part of that wrong is being subjected to the risk of violence. However, the wrongfulness of that exposure inheres in the domestic coercion that forces them to fight, not in the criminality of aggression. In that sense, it is not a sufficient reason to understand them as direct victims of the crime.

The primary focus of the duress argument is instead on the dissonance of soldiers being forced to kill in criminal wars. For two reasons, it is not a plausible way of making sense of that aspect of the existing regime. First, the level of duress applicable to many soldiers who fight in illegal wars falls far below the threshold ordinarily required for a full excuse for participation in an international crime. Second, and more fundamentally, the duress argument answers the wrong moral question. The crux of the legal dissonance is precisely that a soldier may be punished for refusing to kill in an illegal war. In other words, the duress is the problem; it cannot be the solution. The nature of the duress faced by individuals forced to do wrong in this way may mitigate, and in some cases eliminate, their liability to punishment. It may also remove the standing of many others, especially those connected to the imposition of the duress, to condemn soldiers for that wrongdoing. But to say that it should therefore be easy for such individuals to live with having perpetrated those wrongs misunderstands the first-personal moral perspective.

Chapter 5 considers whether we can instead make moral sense of the law's posture towards soldiers who fight and kill in criminal wars on the grounds that many of them lack access to information essential to defining the *jus ad bellum* status of their wars and are therefore "invincibly" ignorant of the wrongfulness of their acts.

Although superficially attractive, this theory advances implausible moral standards that contradict pervasive legal principles on uncertainty.

It is true that few soldiers *know* their wars to be criminal, but many soldiers fighting in illegal wars lack good reason to believe those wars to be *lawful*. This is crucial. Domestic criminal law, the *jus in bello*, and the *jus ad bellum* all hold it to be wrongful to inflict violence intentionally when uncertain as to whether the justificatory conditions for doing so obtain. Underpinning that bias against the infliction of violence when uncertain about the justificatory conditions is the distinction between killing and letting die, which is also reflected in the law governing both individual and international uses of force.

Of course, the invincible ignorance account does not hold that ignorance itself exculpates. Instead, it holds that the non-culpability of the soldier is a function of his ignorance combined with his trusting deference to the judgment of those with far greater relevant knowledge, namely his leaders. However, three factors undermine the soldier's grounds for presuming the reliability and honesty of the state's official position on the *jus ad bellum* status of a war: multiple, countervailing epistemic authorities; the interestedness of the soldier's leaders; and a global history of state mendacity and mistake on *jus ad bellum* facts. If there is an argument for the soldier to defer on epistemic grounds, it supports deferring not to the soldier's own state, but to the preponderance of uninterested states and international organizations.

This is not to say that soldiers who participate in criminal wars without good reasons to believe their wars to be lawful should be punished for their contributions. For a number of reasons, such punishment would be a mistake. However, the key factor in determining whether the law must accommodate a right to disobey is not whether soldiers ought to be liable to punishment if obedient, but whether or not obedient participation entails the first-personal challenge of living with having done wrong. As introduced in the preceding chapter, the standards on the latter normative dimension are less forgiving.

In attempting to reconcile the seemingly dissonant aspects of the extant regime, the natural response to the cosmopolitan arguments advanced in these early chapters is to argue that soldierly obedience in at least dubious wars is warranted on the grounds of political obligation or associative duty. Chapter 6 considers whether we can make moral sense of the legal posture from either of those perspectives.

The first emphasizes the soldier's obligation to obey domestic law in the absence of an explicit countervailing international legal rule. This argument cannot do the necessary work. Unmoved by the soldier's parochial duty to execute the will of his sovereign, the judges at Nuremberg articulated global cosmopolitan duties under international criminal law. Since Nuremberg, and building on that principle, soldiers have been granted a right to disobey on *jus in bello* grounds even when they would not be criminally liable for following the orders in question. As long as the order was in fact illegal, there is no requirement that the soldier was certain of that illegality at the time of his disobedience. Indeed, this is true of aggression for military's top brass. The unique exclusion of aggression from this principle for all other soldiers, despite the wrongfulness of the killing they are ordered to perpetrate, is one of the core normative peculiarities that the book seeks to explain.

Related to the political obligation argument is the view that soldiers have special duties to protect their co-citizens, their domestic institutions, and the common life that they share. The second half of the chapter considers stronger and weaker forms of this argument. The stronger version, which holds that associative duties excuse soldiers who fight in even clearly criminal wars, stands on a false empirical premise, is morally implausible in holding that the mere possibility of such a response could justify the preemptive killing of innocents, and is inconsistent with the post-Nuremberg regime, which specifically excludes such preventive killing. A more modest alternative holds that the combination of associative duties and the soldier's epistemic limits renders participation in most criminal wars non-culpable. Although more plausible, this applies only to a narrowing range of armed conflicts in which the soldier's home state's security is directly at stake. Even in that class of wars, it can plausibly affect his culpability only when the epistemic balance is close. And even when both of these hurdles are overcome, the associative duties cannot displace the burden of engaging in wrongful killing.

Ultimately, in the wars to which the soldier's associative duties plausibly apply, those ordered to fight in an illegal war may be left with a choice between doing right by their people and doing right by the basic duty not to engage in wrongful killing. In that context, international law cannot coherently deny protection to those who uphold the latter.

Chapter 6 closes by shifting to the situation of those killed fighting against aggression. For many, soldiers have overriding political or associative duties to fight on behalf of their society when it is attacked wrongfully. Typically, this includes a duty to risk their own lives in the protection of that society, or in furtherance of its protection of others – a practice often characterized as sacrifice. However, the fact that soldiers have a duty to risk their lives in this context cannot weaken the wrongfulness of their being killed when they do.

Chapter 7 turns to the importance of the symmetrical application of the law of armed conflict, or *jus in bello*, to both sides. This symmetry is often said to serve the crucial values of limiting the hell of war and facilitating peace. Some argue that this warrants defining the rights and wrongs of conduct in war exclusively in terms of the law of armed conflict and constraining the soldier's responsibilities accordingly in the form of a "warrior's code" role morality. The first move would explain the exclusion of combatant deaths from reparations practice. The second would explain the failure to protect soldiers who refuse to fight in illegal wars. However, neither of these moves withstands scrutiny. Although upholding the *jus in bello* and the warrior's code associated with it is morally important, doing so does not require excluding the *jus ad bellum* completely from the normative space of wartime conduct.

The two kinds of wrong – the violations of the *jus ad bellum* on the one hand and the violations of the *jus in bello* on the other – can be distinguished, criticized in different tones and for different reasons, and prosecuted as different crimes without one undermining or swallowing the other. The fact that the *jus in bello* does not prohibit killing combatants is no reason to exclude their deaths from *jus ad bellum* reparations.

Similarly, accepting the empirical claim that upholding combatant immunity for *jus in bello* compliant acts serves the values of mitigating the hell of war and facilitating peace does not mean accepting that soldiers may fight *non-culpably* in illegal wars. If the soldier is to rely on professional adherence to the warrior's code to dissociate morally from the wrongfulness of killing in a manifestly criminal war, it can only be because the sense of duty rooted in that code has sufficient normative heft to override the presumptive moral duty not to participate. There is no such code-based duty. Soldiers do not enhance or uphold the warrior's code by fighting in illegal wars. *If* they fight, they uphold it by adhering to the *jus in bello*. However, *refusing* to fight in no way undermines or impedes the efficacy of the code. If anything, such refusal would further the objectives of mitigating war's hell and facilitating peace.

Chapter 8 puts forward the best account of international law's failure to protect soldiers who refuse to fight and kill in criminal wars. The deep institutional problem with granting soldiers the right to disobey in an illegal war is that whatever system might be used to vindicate or reject the disobedient soldier's claim would (at the moment of disobedience) almost always need the soldier to make his own judgment on the *jus ad bellum*. The worry is that this would risk military breakdown, *even in lawful wars.*

This is of international concern, because international law depends on strong states capable of fighting lawful wars. Not only is that capacity necessary to push back against aggression when it occurs, it is vital to the military deterrence that limits the incidence of aggression in the first place.

Crucially, however, this does not establish the deeper innocence of those who fight in illegal wars, except, perhaps, on the epistemic margins. Any effort to translate the necessity of enforced obedience into a role morality of obedience would have to show not just that global human security depends on the enforcement of obedience in illegal wars, but also that it depends on soldiers actually obeying orders to fight in illegal wars. For a number of reasons, this translation fails. The result is that international law's dependence on functioning militaries may leave it with no alternative but to empower states to force soldiers to do wrong by its own lights. On this account, soldiers are left bearing the normative remainder of international law's core institutional weakness.

Chapter 8 concludes by considering whether a necessity argument could also underpin the practice of excluding the deaths of those killed fighting against aggression from the wrong redressed by reparations. The strongest argument to that effect is that excluding coerced and deceived soldiers on the aggressor side from any recognition as victims of the wrong of aggression would stoke national resentment of the kind that could prove counter-productive to the reconciliation of former warring parties.

Part III turns to the doctrinal and institutional implications of this account of the law we have. The defining characteristic of a necessity defense of a particular institutional posture is that it endures only as far as the necessity applies and that it implies an enduring imperative to mitigate the harms whenever doing so is consistent with the institutional necessity. Chapter 9 looks at ways in which changing patterns of war-fighting have begun to call into question the enduring application, and even the foundational empirical premises, of the necessity account offered in Chapter 8.

One of the most notable shifts in twenty-first century warfare has been the rise of weaponized unmanned vehicles. This has led to armed conflicts in which the participants on one side do not bear any significant risk. This has two important consequences regarding the situation of soldiers forced to participate in aggression. First, the absence of risk to its soldiers reduces the domestic political cost to a government of going to war without good reason and thus weakens the soldier's basis for trusting his government's claim to be pursuing a lawful action. Second, and more significantly for the argument here, it eviscerates the institutional necessity account, by nullifying the detrimental impact of war on the soldier's *jus ad bellum* judgment, capacity to act, and unit cohesion.

A further notable shift in the conduct of war is the expanding role of private military contractors in contemporary armed conflict. This has broader implications than does the rise of drones and riskless warfare. If strict obedience were truly required to ensure effective institutional performance in war and if the guarantee of such obedience were truly essential to the broader security of the state, one would not expect to see major military powers turn to contractors or other non-military actors for significant security roles in their wars. And yet the practice of major military states has confounded this expectation emphatically. At a bare minimum, this suggests that the empirical premises of the necessity claim must be reexamined, even in the case of wars involving mutual risk.

Chapter 10 explores the internal implications for domestic law and institutions of the normative account developed throughout the book. Uniquely, the burden of killing in a wrongful war transcends the distinction between global moral concerns and domestic, or associative, moral concerns related to waging war. The latter are often framed in terms of a failure to garner democratic authorization or an unnecessary sacrifice of troops. The issue discussed here is different. The violation is a wrong inflicted by a government on its own agents through forcing them to do wrong internationally. It is this multilayered normativity that locates the violation at two levels. On the one hand, the harm is fundamentally international – the lives taken and the political community threatened or destroyed exist outside the soldier's own community; his connection to his victims cuts across the boundaries of any political association. On the other hand, the harm is also fundamentally domestic, because it is the soldier's government (and his broader community) that wrongs him by forcing him to do wrong. It is through this normative intersection that an account of the international crime of aggression underpins domestic doctrinal and institutional imperatives.

The most fruitful domestic reforms would respond to the imperative along one or both of two dimensions: bolstering the soldier's reasons to trust and defer to his state over others (so as to lessen the burden when forced to fight) and alleviating the coercion that drives him to fight in an illegal war. The most viable way to improve the grounds for deference would be to strengthen the influence of the *jus ad bellum* over decision-makers and intelligence agencies in a way that is evident and reliable from the perspective of soldiers. Two institutional steps would combine to advance that objective: the creation of a domestic *jus ad bellum* devil's advocate and the permanent institutionalization of a post-war commission of inquiry. Framework proposals for those kinds of institutions, building on existing institutions in parallel contexts (including, for example, the post-Iraq inquiries in various participating states) are put forward here.

In addition to reform targeted at addressing the soldier's epistemic posture, a second dimension of institutional change offers a limited right for soldiers to refuse to fight in internationally illegal wars whenever such protection is compatible with the preservation of military functioning in lawful wars. The formal classification of wars into low- and high-risk categories is not an implausible ambition. If that were implemented, providing disobedience rights in low-risk wars would be viable without undermining institutional functioning. More ambitiously, a retrospective system of rights vindication has the potential to avoid the institutional danger even in traditional high-risk wars. Under such a system, soldiers who disobey would be punished during the war, regardless of its legality. To make a claim for disobedience protection, the soldier would need to refuse to participate prior to deployment (or redeployment) and outside the theater of conflict, to turn himself in immediately, and to cite the war's illegality at the time of disobedience. If post-war review by the commission of inquiry noted above were to find the war to have been illegal, those who raised that claim at the time of disobedience would be subject to retrospective exoneration, the clearing of their records, and release from any remaining imprisonment. This would maintain the key institution-preserving features of the current system, while encouraging only those highly confident of the illegality of the war to disobey.

Of course, the normative account presented in Parts I and II is an account of international law. As such, its most direct implications arise at the global level. Chapter 11 elaborates on three such implications. The first key interpretive implication of the account presented above is that soldiers who resist participation in illegal war and who face punishment at home should be considered refugees under international law. Thus far, courts have declined to interpret the Refugee Convention this way, despite identifying *jus in bello* resisters as refugees. This chapter draws on existing jurisprudence to establish an interpretation of refugee law that would protect those who refuse to fight in illegal wars and face punishment at home. It also identifies several ways in which existing refugee jurisprudence already demands that asylum authorities reach *jus ad bellum* determinations and otherwise determine the lawfulness of foreign state conduct.

A second reform at the international level would be the development of a human right against being forced to fight in such wars. Like the proposed revision to refugee law, this too could be achieved through the progressive interpretation of existing human rights law. The most promising existing interpretive avenues for the development of such a right are rights of conscience, the developing right to peace, and the rights of rights defenders. Elaborating a right to refuse to participate in aggressive war would give soldiers in states subject to human rights review bodies or courts the possibility of petitioning those institutions when incarcerated for refusing to fight in a wrongful war – a tool most likely to be of significant utility in putting pressure on the state after the war.

Finally, recognizing that the core victims of the crime of aggression are individuals rather than states reframes the normative core of reparations for criminal war. The soldiers killed, injured, and scarred fighting against aggression are the primary victims of an internationally criminal wrong. Indeed, the crime of aggression should be understood to be the core element of international criminal law that protects combatants' right to life. Exploring how a reparations regime associated with aggression might better reflect these normative realities than it has in past cases, this section explores the possibilities and limits of international reparations, and especially the fledgling reparations system of the ICC. It argues for aggression reparations projects that fund veterans' care or reintegration programs, assist dead soldiers' families, and otherwise acknowledge the true wrong at the heart of the crime.

PART I

The Criminalization of Aggression and the Putative Dissonance of the Law's Treatment of Soldiers

1

Soldiers and the Crime of Aggression

Required to Kill for a Criminal End, Forgotten in Wrongful Death

1.1 The Criminalization of Aggression

Nearly seventy years have passed since an international tribunal has convicted a defendant of the crime of aggression, but after decades of the crime's dormancy at the international level, the International Criminal Court (ICC) now has jurisdiction over the crime of waging illegal war.[1] Some have questioned the credentials of the crime.[2] Certainly its inclusion in the chartering statute governing the International Military Tribunal (IMT) at Nuremberg was notable more for its innovation than for its pedigree as a pre-existing international requirement.[3] However, the IMT, its sister tribunal in Tokyo – the International Military Tribunal for the Far East (IMTFE) – and the later Nuremberg Military Tribunals

[1] Assembly of States Parties of the International Criminal Court, Activation of the Jurisdiction of the Court over the Crime of Aggression, Resolution ICC-ASP/16/Res.5 (Dec. 14, 2017).

[2] Harold Hongju Koh and Todd F. Buchwald, *The Crime of Aggression: The United States Perspective*, 109 Am. J. Int'l L. 257 (2015).

[3] Charter of the International Military Tribunal, art. 6(a), Aug. 8, 1945, 59 Stat. 1544, 82 U.N.T.S. 279 [hereinafter IMT Charter] (many have noted the landmark status of this codification). Whitney R. Harris, Tyranny on Trial: The Evidence at Nuremberg 555 (1954); William J. Bosch, Judgment on Nuremberg: American Attitudes toward the Major German War-Crime Trials 14 (1970); Gerhard Von Glahn, Law among Nations 670 (6th edn 1992); R v. Jones [2006] UKHL 16, para. 1 (opinion of Lord Bingham of Cornhill). The American Secretary of War, among others, argued for this reason that the prosecution of aggression would involve retroactive criminalization. *See* Cover letter from Henry L. Stimson to John J. McCloy accompanying Memorandum on Aggressive War by Colonel William Chanler (Nov. 28/30, 1944), *reprinted in* Bradley F. Smith, The American Road to Nuremberg 68–69 (1982) *See, e.g.*, David Luban, *The Legacies of Nuremberg*, 54 Social Research 779, 797–801 (1987); Major Edward J. O'Brien, *The Nuremberg Principles, Command Responsibility, and the Defense of Captain Rockwood*, 149 Mil. L. Rev. 275, 280–81 (1995) (discussing the legal innovation of this crime).

(NMT) run by the American occupying forces accepted the legality of the prohibition and convicted defendants of waging criminal wars.[4]

Since Nuremberg, the criminalization of aggressive wars has been incorporated into the domestic penal codes of a small number of states,[5] is, or has been, under consideration in others,[6] has constitutional status in Germany and Japan,[7] has received formal recognition in other

[4] United States v. Göring et al., Judgment, *in* 22 TRIAL OF THE MAJOR WAR CRIMINALS BEFORE THE INTERNATIONAL MILITARY TRIBUNAL 411, 461–66, 524–26, 528–32, 533–34, 539–40, 544–45, 550–51, 556–57, 561–62, 568–69, 574–76, 580–82 (1948) [hereinafter IMT Judgment]; Ernst von Weizsäcker, *in* 14 TRIALS OF WAR CRIMINALS BEFORE THE NUERNBERG MILITARY TRIBUNALS UNDER CONTROL COUNCIL LAW NO. 10, at 1, 385–89, 399–416, 418–35 (1949); United States v. Araki et al., Judgment of 12 November 1948, *in* 20 THE TOKYO WAR CRIMES TRIAL, at 48, 437–48, 441(John Pritchard & Sonia M. Zaide, eds., 1981) [hereinafter IMTFE Judgment].

[5] Over thirty states have either incorporated the international crime of aggression into their domestic criminal codes, or otherwise criminalized equivalent conduct. *See* Astrid Reisinger Coracini, *Evaluating Domestic Legislation on the Customary Crime of Aggression under the Rome Statute's Complementarity Regime*, *in* THE EMERGING PRACTICE OF THE INTERNATIONAL CRIMINAL COURT 735 (Carsten Stahn & Göran Sluiter, eds., 2009); Astrid Reisinger Coracini, *National Legislation on Individual Responsibility for Conduct Amounting to Aggression*, *in* INTERNATIONAL CRIMINAL JUSTICE. LAW AND PRACTICE FROM THE ROME STATUTE TO ITS REVIEW 547 (Roberto Bellelli, ed., 2010); Aslan Abashidze & Elena Trikoz, *The ICC Statute and the Ratification Saga in the States of the Commonwealth of Independent States*, *in* THE LEGAL REGIME OF THE INTERNATIONAL CRIMINAL COURT: ESSAYS IN HONOUR OF PROFESSOR IGOR BLISHCHENKO 1105, 1108 (José Doria, Hans-Peter Gasser, & M. Cherif Bassiouni, eds., 2009); *Status of Ratification and Implementation*, THE GLOBAL CAMPAIGN FOR RATIFICATION AND IMPLEMENTATION OF THE KAMPALA AMENDMENTS ON THE CRIME OF AGGRESSION [hereinafter GCRIKACA], http://crimeofaggression.info/the-role-of-states/status-of-ratification-and-implementation/ (last visited Aug. 1, 2017).

[6] *See Implementation Documents*, GCRIKACA, http://crimeofaggression.info/resources search/implementation-documents/ (last visited Aug. 1, 2017). *See also* Roger S. Clark, *Complementarity and the Crime of Aggression*, *in* THE INTERNATIONAL CRIMINAL COURT AND COMPLEMENTARITY 721 (Carsten Stahn & Mohamed El Zeidy, eds., 2011) (on ICC complementarity as applied to aggression); *see* Michael P. Scharf, *Universal Jurisdiction and the Crime of Aggression*, 53 HARV. INT'L L.J. 357 (2012) (on the potential for adopting aggression into universal jurisdiction provisions). *See also* Jans Kleffner, *The Impact of Complementarity on National Implementation of Substantive International Criminal Law*, 1 J. INT'L CRIM. JUSTICE 86, 90 (2003). Domestic codification of substantive ICC crimes is arguably an implied obligation under the Rome Statute, though this is not a majority view, and it would clearly not apply to the prosecution of an aggression perpetrated by a foreign state. *Id.* at 92–94; International Criminal Court Assembly of States Parties, Resolution RC/Res.6, Annex III, paras. 4–5 (June 11, 2010) [hereinafter ICC Aggression Amendments].

[7] Grundgesetz für die Bundesrepublik Deutschland (German Basic Law [Constitution]), art. 26 (May 23, 1949). *See also* Strafgesetzbuch [StGB] [Penal Code], BUNDESGESETZBLATT [BGBI] I p. 3322, §§ 80, 80a (Ger.) (Nov. 13, 1998), *available at*

domestic courts[8] (although no successful domestic prosecutions),[9] and has informed the official advice (and resignation) of top government lawyers in the build-up to war.[10]

At the international level, the prohibition on aggressive war has been endorsed repeatedly by the UN General Assembly,[11] has been complemented by the *jus cogens* and *erga omnes* prohibition on the use of force,[12] was included by the International Law Commission (ILC) in its 1996 Draft Code of Crimes against the Peace and Security of Mankind,[13]

www.iuscomp.org/gla/statutes/StGB.htm; Nihonkoku Kenpo (Japanese Constitution), art. 9 (Nov. 3, 1946).

[8] R v. Jones [2006] UKHL 16 at para. 44 (per Lord Hoffman); *id.* paras. 96–98, 103 (where Lords Carswell, Mance, and Rodger of Earlsferry agree in full with Lord Hoffman); Kariņš & Others v. Parliament of Latvia & Cabinet of Ministers of Latvia, Latvian Constitutional Court, Case No. 2007-10-0102, ILDC 884 (LV 2007), para. 10, 25.5–25.6, 64.1 (Latvia).

[9] In 2003, a group of German citizens filed criminal complaints with the Chief Federal Prosecutor alleging that Chancellor Gerhard Schröder and members of his cabinet had prepared for and participated in criminal aggression against Iraq by granting US forces the right to use German airspace, allowing US bases in Germany to be used for activities related to the military operations, and allowing German soldiers to participate in airborne reconnaissance missions to secure the Turkish border with Iraq. The Prosecutor rejected the complaint on the grounds that the specific acts alleged did not amount to German preparation for or participation in the war and there was no risk of deeper German involvement. It did not reach the war's *jus ad bellum* status. Claus Kreß, *The German Chief Federal Prosecutor's Decision Not to Investigate the Alleged Crime of Preparing Aggression against Iraq*, 2 J. Int'l Crim. Justice 245, 247–55 (2004).

[10] Memo from Lord Peter Goldsmith to Prime Minister Tony Blair, Iraq: Resolution 1441, paras. 33–35 (Mar. 7, 2003); Elizabeth Wilmshurst Resignation Letter (Mar. 2003), BBC News (24 March, 2005), *available at* http://news.bbc.co.uk/2/hi/uk_news/politics/4377605.stm.

[11] Declaration on the Inadmissibility of Intervention in the Domestic Affairs of States and the Protection of their Independence and Sovereignty, G.A. Res. 2131(XX), U.N. Doc. A/RES/20/2131(XX) (Dec. 21, 1965); Declaration on Principles of International Law Concerning Friendly Relations and Cooperation among States in accordance with the Charter of the United Nations, G.A. Res. 2625(XXV), U.N. Doc. A/RES/25/2625(XXV) (Oct. 24, 1970); Definition of Aggression, G.A. Res. 3314(XXIX), U.N. Doc. A/RES/3314 (XXIX) (Dec. 14, 1974).

[12] UN Charter, art. 2, para. 4 (1945); Case Concerning Military and Paramilitary Activities in and against Nicaragua (Merits) (Nicar. v. US) [1986] I.C.J. 14 (June 27), para. 190; Case concerning the Barcelona Traction, Light and Power Company, Limited, Second Phase, Judgment, 1970 I.C.J. Rep. 3 (1970), para. 34.

[13] Draft Code of Crimes against the Peace and Security of Mankind with Commentaries, Rep. of the Int'l Law Comm'n on the Work of its Forty-Eighth Session, U.N. Doc. A/51/10, art. 16 (1996) [hereinafter ILC, Draft Code of Crimes], *available at* http://untreaty.un.org/ilc/reports/english/A_51_10.pdf.

and was listed from the start as one of four kinds of crimes that would fall under the jurisdiction of the International Criminal Court (ICC) – jurisdiction that was activated by decision of the Assembly of States Parties in 2017.[14]

Today, aggression stands alongside genocide, crimes against humanity, and *jus in bello* war crimes as the only universal wrongs criminalized at the international level.[15] Indeed, the IMT dictum that it stands *above* those other violations, as "not only an international crime," but "the *supreme* international crime"[16] was endorsed several times during the ICC amendment drafting process.[17] It is worthy of being treated seriously on its own terms.

1.2 The Duty to Disobey Illegal Orders

Also since the post-World War II trials of Nazi and Japanese war criminals, international law has required that subordinates disobey superior orders and domestic laws demanding that they participate in international crimes. This, too, was of ambiguous legal status in 1945.[18] However, the duty to disobey was enshrined in the London Charter governing the IMT,[19] emphasized by the Nuremberg

[14] Rome Statute of the International Criminal Court, U.N. Doc. A/CONF.183/9, 2187 U.N.T.S. 90, art. 5(1)(d) (July 17, 1998) (as amended in 2010 by Doc. C.N.651.2010. TREATIES-8) [hereinafter ICC Statute]. On aggression's activation, *see supra* note 1.

[15] ICC Statute, *supra* note 14, art. 5(1). *See also* R v. Jones, *supra* note 8; IAN BROWNLIE, PRINCIPLES OF PUBLIC INTERNATIONAL LAW 566 (5th edn 1998).

[16] IMT Judgment, *supra* note 4, at 427 [emphasis added]; *see also* IMTFE Judgment, *supra* note 4, at 49,769.

[17] *See, e.g.*, Report of the Informal inter-sessional meeting of the Special Working Group on the Crime of Aggression, Special Working Group on the Crime of Aggression (SWGCA), ICC-ASP/3/SWGCA/INF.1, para. 38 (Aug. 13, 2004); Report of the Informal inter-sessional meeting of the Special Working Group on the Crime of Aggression, SWGCA, ICC-ASP/6/SWGCA/INF.1, para. 56 (July 25, 2007).

[18] Two of the nations at the forefront of the Nuremberg effort, Britain and the United States, had enforced a duty to obey even illegal orders in World War I and in the early stages of World War II before switching to the duty to disobey standard. Gary D. Solis, *Obedience of Orders and the Law of War: Judicial Application in American Forums*, 15 AM. U. INT'L L. REV. 481, 494–514 (1999). Solis observes, "World War II, Nuremberg, and the Subsequent Trials materially altered the legal position of the soldier who pleaded obedience to superior orders in defense of his war crimes." *Id.* at 483–84. *Cf.* GARY JONATHAN BASS, STAY THE HAND OF VENGEANCE 80–81 (1999) (on the success of the superior orders defense in the trials following World War I).

[19] IMT Charter, *supra* note 3, art. 8.

prosecutors,[20] accepted by its judges,[21] applied in its convictions,[22] and re-affirmed in the governing statutory provisions and case law of both the subsequent Nuremberg Military Tribunals (NMT)[23] and the International Military Tribunal for the Far East (IMTFE).[24] In the NMT's seminal articulation, "The obedience of a soldier is not the obedience of an automaton. A soldier is a reasoning agent."[25] The "true test," the IMT insisted, "is not the existence of the order, but whether moral choice was in fact possible."[26]

The doctrine has been in the chartering statute or case law of every international criminal tribunal since,[27] has been affirmed by the General Assembly,[28] appears in most domestic military codes,[29] and has been

[20] Opening Statement at Nuremberg by Robert H. Jackson, Chief Prosecutor for the United States, United States v. Göring et al. (Nov. 21, 1945), 2 TRIAL OF THE MAJOR WAR CRIMINALS BEFORE THE INTERNATIONAL MILITARY TRIBUNAL 98, 151 (1947); Opening statement of M. François De Menthon, United States v. Göring et al. (Jan. 17, 1946), 5 TRIAL OF THE MAJOR WAR CRIMINALS BEFORE THE INTERNATIONAL MILITARY TRIBUNAL 368, 418 (1947).

[21] IMT Judgment, *supra* note 4, at 466.

[22] *See, e.g.*, *id.* at 536. Most defendants at Nuremberg pleaded not guilty on grounds of superior orders. United Nations War Crimes Commission, History of the United Nations War Crimes Commission and the Development of Laws of War, 287 (1948).

[23] Control Council Law No. 10, Punishment of Persons Guilty of War Crimes, Crimes against Peace and against Humanity, art. II(4)(a) (Dec. 20, 1945), *in* 3 OFFICIAL GAZETTE CONTROL COUNCIL FOR GERMANY 50 (1946) [hereinafter Control Council Law No. 10].

[24] Charter of the International Tribunal for the Far East, T.I.A.S. No. 1589, 4 Bevans 20 (Jan. 19, 1946), art. 6.

[25] United States v. Ohlendorf et al., 4 TRIALS OF WAR CRIMINALS BEFORE THE NUERNBERG MILITARY TRIBUNALS UNDER CONTROL COUNCIL LAW No. 10, at 411 (1949) [hereinafter Einsatzgruppen Judgment]. *See also id.* at 470–88.

[26] IMT Judgment, *supra* note 4, at 470.

[27] Statute of the Special Court for Sierra Leone, art. 6(4), U.N. Doc. S/RES/1315 (2000); Statute of the International Criminal Tribunal for Rwanda, art. 6(4), U.N. Doc. S/RES/955 (1994); Statute of the International Criminal Tribunal for the Former Yugoslavia, art. 7(4), U.N. Doc. S/RES/827 (1993); ICC Statute, *supra* note 14, art. 33(1).

[28] Affirmation of the Principles of International Law Recognized by the Charter of the Nürnberg Tribunal, G.A. Res. 95(1), UN GAOR, 1st Sess., U.N. Doc. A/RES/95(I), at 188 (1946).

[29] Mark J. Osiel, *Obeying Orders: Atrocity, Military Discipline, and the Law of War*, 86 CAL. L. REV. 939, 951–52 (1998). The duty to disobey is particularly prevalent in industrialized democracies. *Id.* at 950. *See, e.g.*, US DEPARTMENT OF THE ARMY, YOUR CONDUCT IN COMBAT UNDER THE LAW OF WAR, FM 27–2, 26 (1984). Although it has been somewhat less common in the laws of autocracies (Osiel, *supra* note 29, at 950), certain high-profile Communist states such as the USSR and East Germany did incorporate a rejection of the superior orders defense into their military codes. Solis, *supra* note 18, at 523. *See also* Gabriël Moens, *The German Borderguard Cases: Natural Law and the Duty to Disobey*

applied in domestic prosecutions.[30] In the estimation of the International Committee of the Red Cross (ICRC), it is today a central principle of customary international law.[31] It remains one of the most famous moral achievements and legal legacies of Nuremberg.[32]

The doctrine is striking in its simplicity. It does not matter that genocide, crimes against humanity, and many war crimes are massive collective wrongs over which no lower- or mid-level participant has

Immoral Laws, *in* JURISPRUDENCE OF LIBERTY 146, 149 (Gabriël A. Moens & Suri Ratnapala, eds., 1995).

30 A number of court-martial prosecutions in the Vietnam War involved situations in which the convicted party was acting pursuant to manifestly unlawful superior orders. *See, e.g.*, United States v. Griffen, 39 C.M.R. 586, 590 (1968); United States v. Keenan, 18 C.M.A. 108, 117 (1969); United States v. Schultz, 39 C.M.R 133 (1969); United States v. Schwarz, 45 C.M.R. 852, 856 (1971). Such cases also arose in the American intervention in Korea [United States v. Kinder, 14 C.M.R. 742, 774 (1953)] and outside belligerent contexts [United States v. Cherry, 22 M.J. 284, 286 (C.M.A. 1986)]. The doctrine has been upheld in prosecution for acts in Iraq. *See, e.g.*, United States v. Smith, 68 M.J. 316, 320–21 (C.A.A.F. 2010). *See also* James W. Smith III, *A Few Good Scapegoats*, 27 WHITTIER L. REV. 671 (2006). Israel, France, and Germany have prosecuted soldiers for following illegal orders since Nuremberg. *See, e.g.*, Chief Military Prosecutor v. Malinki (Mil. Ct. Appeal, 1959), 2 PALESTINE Y.B. INT'L L. 69, 104, 109–10 (1985); Craig R. Whitney, *Ex-Vichy Aide is Convicted and Reaction Ranges Wide*, NY TIMES (Apr. 3, 1998) A1; Border Guards Prosecution Case, FED. SUP. CT., GERMANY (Nov. 3, 1992), 100 I.L.R. 366, 369–70, 392–93 (1997); *Germany Reopens Investigations into Nazi Death Camp Guards*, GUARDIAN (Oct. 5, 2011); Helen Pidd, *John Demjanjuk Found Guilty of Nazi War Crimes*, GUARDIAN (May 12, 2011); *Germany Inquiry into Oradour Wartime Massacre in France*, BBC News (Jan. 30, 2013) *available at* www.bbc.co.uk/news/world-europe-21261775.

There have, however, been notable gaps. Of those involved in the My Lai massacre, only former Lt. William Calley was convicted for his obedient participation, and even he was given only a short sentence. United States v. Calley, 46 C.M.R. 1131, 1138 (A.C.M.R. 1973), aff'd 22 C.M.A. 534, 48 C.M.R. 19 (A.C.M.R. 1973), rev'd sub nom. Calley v. Callaway, 382 F. Supp. 650 (M.D. Ga. 1974), verdict reinstated, 519 F.2d 194 (5th Cir. 1975) cert. denied, 425 US 911 (1976). CIA perpetrators of torture authorized under the Bush Administration have not been prosecuted for following those directives.

31 JEAN-MARIE HENCKAERTS & LOUISE DOSWALD-BECK, CUSTOMARY INTERNATIONAL HUMANITARIAN LAW 1, 211 (Rules 151, 154, 155) (2005). Others have argued that the precise contours of the rule regarding the duty to disobey remain a matter of controversy. *See, e.g.*, Andreas Zimmermann, *Superior Orders*, *in* 1 THE ROME STATUTE OF THE INTERNATIONAL CRIMINAL COURT: A COMMENTARY 957, 965 (Antonio Cassese et al., eds., 2002).

32 HARRIS, *supra* note 3, at 557; Telford Taylor, Final Report to the Secretary of the Army on the Nuremberg War Crimes Trials under Control Council Law No. 10, at 109–10 (1949); Martha Minow, *Living up to Rules: Holding Soldiers Responsible for Abusive Conduct and the Dilemma of the Superior Orders Defence*, 52 MCGILL L.J. 1, 4 (2007); Paul D. Marquardt, *Law without Borders: The Constitutionality of an International Criminal Court*, 33 COLUM. J. TRANSNAT'L L. 73, 142 (1995).

personal control. It does not matter that those who refuse to participate in such actions are likely to be punished and replaced, saving no lives through their courageous disobedience.[33] It does not matter that the wrongful acts are required by validly enacted domestic laws or the orders of properly appointed state agents.[34] Cutting through this contextual complexity is an unyielding principle: the harm these subordinates are ordered to inflict is criminally wrongful, and, if they do it, they may be prosecuted. Conditions of duress can mitigate the obedient soldier's punishment, but the duty to refuse stands.[35] In this narrow category of cases, the individual stands as a cosmopolitan citizen who must answer to the global authority of international law.[36] In the words of the IMT, it was the "very essence of the [Tribunal's] Charter . . . that individuals have international duties which transcend the national obligations of obedience imposed by the individual state."[37]

And yet, from the start, one international crime has remained anomalously untouched by this fundamental doctrine. Even high-ranking soldiers ordered to participate in criminal aggression have no duty to disobey. This exception was established at Nuremberg and Tokyo;[38] it is reiterated in the ICC amendment;[39] and it is widely accepted in the popular imagination and in the literature.[40] It is an extremely broad exception. The non-liability of participating in criminal wars applies to those fully aware of the criminal nature of the act, who could refuse to

[33] United States v. Alstötter et al., 3 Trials of War Criminals before the Nuernberg Military Tribunals under Control Council Law No. 10, at 954, 1086–87 (1949 [1947]) (hereinafter Justice Judgment); Einsatzgruppen Judgment, *supra* note 25, at 481. *See also* Section 4.1 of Chapter 4, below; Christopher Kutz, Complicity: Ethics and Law for a Collective Age, 113–15 (2007).

[34] IMT Judgment, *supra* note 4, at 1011; W. Michael Reisman, *The Quest for World Order and Human Dignity in the Twenty-First Century*, 351 Recueil des Cours 368 (2012).

[35] *See* Section 4.1 of Chapter 4 below.

[36] Even for its chief protagonists, Nuremberg was a moment of moral expression as much as legal development. *See* Section 2.1 of Chapter 2 below.

[37] IMT Judgment, *supra* note 4, at 466.

[38] Control Council Law No. 10, *supra* note 23, art. II(2); United States v. von Leeb et al., 11 Trials of War Criminals before the Nuernberg Military Tribunals under Control Council Law No. 10, at 462, 488 (1949) [hereinafter High Command Judgment]. For an example of its application at Tokyo, see IMTFE Judgment, *supra* note 4, at 49,827.

[39] ICC Statute, *supra* note 14, arts. 8 *bis* (1), 25(3bis).

[40] Michael Walzer, Just and Unjust Wars 16, 19 (1977) [hereinafter Walzer, JUW]; Michael Walzer, *The Triumph of Just War Theory (and the Dangers of Success), in* Arguing about War 3, 10–12 (2004); Brian Orend, *War, in* The Stanford Encyclopedia of Philosophy (Edward N. Zalta, ed., 2008) (on Walzer's influence).

participate without facing any personal sanction, and who contributed in essential ways to the war effort, including via the infliction of massive violence.[41]

In short, international law permits unfettered participation in criminal war to everyone except those in "a position effectively to exercise control over or to direct the political or military action of a State."[42] The only actors who have any kind of duty to disobey orders to participate in waging aggressive war are those who are in the chief executive's inner circle – the leadership cabal that formulates the policy and issues the commands.[43] Despite its anomalous nature within international criminal law, this notion that aggression is a "leadership crime" is often considered obvious, and it generated no debate in the ICC's amendment process.[44] Obvious, however, it is not. The distinct structure of aggression requires explanation.

41 On knowledge: High Command Judgment, *supra* note 38, at 488. The main contribution of the high-ranking military officers acquitted in the High Command case was precisely the organization of violence. Twenty-four members of I.G. Farben's managing board were acquitted of *jus ad bellum* crimes on the grounds that they were "followers and not leaders," despite the fact that "Farben largely created the broad raw material basis without which the policy makers could not have even seriously considered waging aggressive war." United States v. Krauch et al., Military Tribunal VI, Opinion and Judgment, 8 TRIALS OF WAR CRIMINALS BEFORE THE NUERNBERG MILITARY TRIBUNALS UNDER CONTROL COUNCIL LAW NO. 10, at 1126 (1949) [hereinafter I.G. Farben Judgment] (follower standard); *id.* at 1216 (Herbert, J., concurring) (on the essential contribution of Farben to the war).

42 This language from the ICC Statute [ICC Statute, *supra* note 14, art. 8 *bis* (1)] is if anything stricter than the language used at Nuremberg, which set the threshold at whether the defendant was "in a position to shape or influence the policy that brings about [the criminal war's] initiation or its continuance after initiation." High Command Judgment, *supra* note 38, at 488.

It should be noted that, at Nuremberg, a lower threshold of direction or control set for criminal liability for *preparing* for war than was set for participating in its initiation or continuation. *Id.* at 489. *See generally* Kevin Jon Heller, *Retreat from Nuremberg: The Leadership Requirement in the Crime of Aggression*, 18 EUR. J. INT'L L. 477 (2007). It does not appear that this distinction will obtain in the ICC context. *Id.*

43 A small number of senior Nazis, such as Field Marshal Wilhelm Keitel, were convicted of crimes against peace despite proffering the superior orders defense. IMT Judgment, *supra* note 4, at 533–36. However, these men were not ordinary subordinates in a chain of command. They were part of the leadership cabal at the top of that chain. *Cf. id. at* 547, 555; I.G. Farben Judgment, *supra* note 41, at 1102.

44 Justice Robert H. Jackson, The United Nations Organization and War Crimes, Address Delivered at the American Society of International Law, Washington DC (Apr. 26, 1952) ("It never occurred to me, and I am sure it occurred to no one else at the conference table, to speak of anyone as "waging" a war except topmost leaders."); HARRIS, *supra* note 3, at 31. On its unchallenged status in the ICC drafting process, *see, for example*, Report of the Informal inter-sessional meeting of the Special Working Group on the Crime of

1.3 The Law of Being Forced to Kill in a Wrongful War

Indeed, the distinctiveness of the crime extends beyond the mere permissibility of fighting in a criminal war. Soldiers and other subordinates have a clear right to disobey illegal orders. This is typically protected in domestic codes, and in the international rights of human rights defenders.[45] Where domestic protections fail, a soldier facing domestic punishment for refusing to perform an illegal order is eligible for refugee status under international law.[46] Importantly, to qualify for these protections, the individual need not have been faced with an order the obedient discharge of which would have rendered him criminally liable.[47] If he would have been sufficiently intimately connected to the legal wrong to have been unable to "wash his hands of guilt," his right to disobey is protected.[48]

Aggression, SWGCA (Aug. 13, 2004), *supra* note 17, paras. 35, 37, 48–49, 53–54, 58–60; Report of the Informal inter-sessional meeting of the Special Working Group on the Crime of Aggression, SWGCA, ICC-ASP/5/SWGCA/INF.1, paras. 88, 91–92 (Sept. 5, 2006); Report of the Special Working Group on the Crime of Aggression, SWGCA, ICC-ASP/6/20/Add.1/Annex II, paras. 17–18 (June 6, 2008); Proposal submitted by Belgium, Cambodia, Sierra Leone & Thailand, Preparatory Commission for the International Criminal Court, Working Group on the Crime of Aggression, PCNICC/2002/WGCA/DP.5 (July 8, 2002).

45 *See, e.g.*, 10 U.S.C., §892 (2000); US Dept. of the Army, Your Conduct in Combat under the Law of War, FM 27-2, at 25 (1984); United States v. New, 55 M.J. 95, 100 (C.A.A.F. 2001); Armed Forces Act 2006 c. 52, art. 12 (U.K.); UK Ministry of Defence, Manual of Service Law 1 (JSP 830 v2.0) ch. 7, at 7-1-40 to 7-1-41 (Jan. 31, 2011). *See also* UN Declaration on the Right and Responsibility of Individuals Groups and Organs of Society to Promote and Protect Universally Recognized Human Rights and Fundamental Freedoms, G.A. Res. 53/144, art. 10, U.N. Doc. A/RES/53/144 (Mar. 8, 1999) [hereinafter UN Declaration on Human Rights Defenders]; Ensuring Protection – European Union Guidelines on Human Rights Defenders, Council of Europe (2008), *available at* http://eur-lex.europa.eu/legal-content/EN/ALL/?uri=LEGISSUM:l33601.

46 UN High Commissioner for Refugees, Handbook on Procedures and Criteria for Determining Refugee Status under the 1951 Convention and the 1967 Protocol Relating to the Status of Refugees, U.N. Doc. HCR/IP/4/Eng/REV.1, para. 171 (1979, Reedited Geneva, January 1992); James C. Hathaway, The Law of Refugee Status 180–81 (1991); Directive 2011/95/EU of the European Parliament and of the Council of 13 December 2011, 337 Official J. E.U. 9 (Dec. 20, 2011) [hereinafter Directive 2011/95/EU].

47 *See, e.g.*, United States v. New, *supra* note 45 (permitting soldiers to challenge the legality of orders that are not patently illegal, though placing the evidentiary burden on the disobedient soldier in the case of orders that are illegal, but not patently so); US Department of Defense, Manual for Courts-Martial United States, para. 14(c)(2)(a)(i), at IV-19 (2008); Mark Osiel, Obeying Orders 242 (1999).

48 Key v. Canada (Min. of Cit. & Immigr.) [2008] F.C. 838, para. 279 (Can.) (citing Zolfagharkhani v. Canada (Min. of Employ. & Immigr.) [1993] 3 F.C. 540 (Can.).

Aggression, again, is different. According to the current body of case law on the matter, those ordered to fight in an aggressive war have no right to disobey. In other words, they can be required, on pain of criminal punishment, to kill, maim, and destroy in a criminal war.[49] Often, domestic courts dismiss the legality of a particular war on procedural grounds, dismissing it as a "political question" that is beyond the scope of judicial review.[50] However, the more interesting decisions have asserted that there is no underlying substantive right to disobey such orders in the first place.

The claimed basis for this position is that lower-level soldiers cannot be held criminally liable for aggression. In US v. Huet-Vaughn, for example, a military appellate court in the United States denied a soldier's claim to a right to refuse to participate in an allegedly illegal war on the grounds that participating in such a war does not entail performing a "'positive act' that would [itself] be a war crime."[51] Similarly, in R v. Lyons, the English and Welsh Court of Appeal limited the right to situations in which the soldier is "ordered to do something which he reasonably believed would be a war crime," finding that this would not be the case if the order merely required participating in an aggressive war.[52] A British court martial similarly denied a claimed right to disobey on the grounds that participating as a soldier in an aggressive war does not entail complicity in the crime of aggression.[53]

[49] The American Uniform Code of Military Justice, for example, provides that crimes like desertion are punishable by death if they occur in war. Uniform Code of Military Justice, 10 U.S.C., § 885(c) (2006), art. 85. The criminality of the war is not a defense to any of these charges. *See infra* notes 50–51 and accompanying text. That said, soldiers who refuse to fight are typically subject to far lighter punishment than the UCMJ permits. *See* Section 4.1 of Chapter 4, below.

[50] Luftig v. McNamara et al., 126 U.S.App.D.C. 4, 373 F.2d 664, 665 (1967); Mitchell v. United States, 369 F.2d 323 (2nd Cir.1966), cert. denied, 386 U.S. 972, reh'g denied, 386 U.S. 1042 (1967); Mora v. McNamara, 128 U.S.App.D.C. 297, 387 F.2d 862 (1967), cert. denied, 389 U.S. 934, 88 S.Ct. 282; United States v. Johnson, 38 C.M.R. 44, 45 (C.M.A. 1967); United States v. Noyd, 40 C.M.R. 195, 203 (C.M.A. 1969); United States v. Wilson, 41 C.M.R. 100, 101 (C.M.A. 1969); United States v. New, 50 M.J. 729, 739–40 (A. Ct. Crim. App. 1999).

[51] United States v. Huet-Vaughn, 43 M.J. 105, 114–15 (1995). *See also* US v. Kabat, 797 F.2d 580, 590 (8th Cir. 1986), cert. denied, 481 U.S. 1030 (1987).

[52] R v. Michael Peter Lyons [2011] EWCA (Crim) 2808, para. 36 (U.K.). *See also id.* at para. 24.

[53] *RAF Doctor Jailed Over Iraq Refusal*, GUARDIAN (April 13, 2006), *available at* www.theguardian.com/uk/2006/apr/13/military.iraq; *RAF Doctor Must Face Iraq Court Martial*, DAILY MAIL (Mar. 22, 2006), *available at* www.dailymail.co.uk/news/article-380677/RAF-doctor-face-Iraq-court-martial.html.

Indeed, this line of thought has applied even when the court would not need to rule on the *jus ad bellum* to uphold the right to disobey. Thus, seized of a case relating to *Unterscharführer* Karl-Heinz Garbe's wartime escape from Nazi custody (pending execution), a post-war appellate court maintained the validity of Garbe's conviction for refusing to fight, even though the IMT had by that time ruled conclusively on the criminality of the wars in question.[54] His right to disobey, the court reasoned, could attach only to orders the discharge of which would have rendered *him* criminally liable, and the order to fight in a criminal war was not such an order.[55] Like Garbe, the vast majority of the more than eight thousand Nazi soldiers who survived the war with desertion convictions lived the rest of their lives as convicted felons; political clemency was not granted until the new millennium.[56]

Perhaps the alleged (or confirmed) aggressor state's courts' dismissal of their own soldiers' efforts to disobey is to be expected. But the picture is little different outside the aggressor state. International human rights law has begun to recognize a *pacifist* right not to fight, as a matter of toleration for those with that minority view.[57] In the few states that allow

[54] *Antifaschistisches Gewissen: Garbe im Kreuzfeuer* [Antifascist Conscience: Garbe in the Crossfire], DER SPIEGEL 7 (Jan. 25, 1947); *In re* Garbe, Süddeutsche Juristen-Zeitung, Jahrg. 2, Nr. 6, cols. 323–30 (June 1947) (Ger.); *see also* Hersch Lauterpacht, *The Limits of the Operation of the Law of War*, 30 BRIT. Y.B. INT'L L. 206, 240–41, n.2 (1953).

[55] *In re* Garbe, *supra* note 54, cols. 324–26.

[56] Tristana Moore, *Nazi Deserter Hails Long-Awaited Triumph*, BBC News (Sept. 8, 2009), *available at* http://news.bbc.co.uk/2/hi/8244186.stm; Gesetz zur Änderung des Gesetzes zur Aufhebung nationalsozialistischer Unrechtsurteile in der Strafrechtspflege vom 23, July 2002 (BGBl. I S. 2714).

[57] Bayatyan v. Armenia, App. No. 23459/03, ECtHR [GC] Judgment (2011); Rep. of the UN Comm'n on Human Rights, Yoon & Choi v. Republic of Korea, Comm. No. 1321–1322/2004, U.N. Doc. A/62/40; GAOR, 62nd Sess., Supp. No. 40, vol. II, annex VII, § 5, at 195 (Nov. 3, 2006); UN Comm'n on Human Rights, General Comment No. 22: The Right to Freedom of Thought, Conscience and Religion under Article 18 of the International Covenant on Civil and Political Rights, U.N. Doc. CCPR/C/21/Rev.1/Add.4/, para. 11 (July 30, 1993); UN Comm'n on Human Rights, Res. 1989/59, 43rd Sess., U.N. Doc. E/CN.4/RES/1989/59 (Mar. 8, 1989); UN Comm'n on Human Rights, Conscientious Objection to Military Service, Res. 1998/77, 54th Sess., Supp. No. 3, 58th mtg., U.N. Doc. E/CN.4/1998/177 (Apr. 22, 1998); UN Office of the High Commissioner for Human Rights, Report: Civil and Political Rights, Including the Question of Conscientious Objection to Military Service, U.N. Doc. E/CN.4/2004/55 (Feb. 16, 2004) (surveying trends in the protection of at least pacifist conscientious objection as a human right). *But see* Cristián Daniel Sahli Vera et al. v. Chile, Case 12.219, Inter-Am. C.H.R., Report No. 43/05, OEA/Ser.L/V/II.124 Doc. 5, paras. 88–100 (2005); Charter of Fundamental Rights of the European Union (2000/C 364/01), art. 15(2), Dec. 18, 2000 ("The right to conscientious objection is recognised, *in accordance with the national laws* governing the

selective conscientious objection or the tiny number that recognize objector status for professional soldiers, the grounding principle is liberal toleration for those with minority views.[58] There is no recognized human right not to be forced to kill in wars that international law itself proscribes and criminalizes.

Eligibility for refugee status has also been denied to applicants who would not be criminally liable for aggression.[59] Perhaps the most detailed explanation for this denial is presented in a Canadian Federal Court decision rejecting the asylum claim of Jeremy Hinzman, an American soldier who had fled to Canada after refusing to fight in Iraq on the grounds that the war was unlawful:

exercise of this right") [emphasis added]. *See generally* Jeremy Kessler, *The Invention of a Human Right*, 44 COLUM. HUM. RTS. L. REV. 753 (2013).

58 On rare allowances for selective conscientious objection, *see, for example*, LEONARD M. HAMMER, THE INTERNATIONAL HUMAN RIGHT TO FREEDOM OF CONSCIENCE 210–14 (2001); Ben. P. Vermeulen, *Conscientious Objection in Dutch Law*, *in* CONSCIENTIOUS OBJECTION IN THE EC COUNTRIES 276 (1992); Defence Legislation Amendment Act 1992, Division 2–5 (June 30, 1992) (Austl.). *See also* The Secretary General, Question of Conscientious Objection to Military Service, U.N. Doc. E/CN.4/Sub.2/1983/30, para. 21 (June 27, 1983) (prepared by Asbjørn Eide & Charna L.C. Mubanga-Chipoya). Rejecting it, *see, for example*, H.C.J. 7622/02 Zonstein v. Judge Advocate General (2002) (Isr.); Gillette v. United States, 401 U.S. 437 (1971); Sepet & another v. Sec'y State Home Dept. [2003] UKHL 15, para. 20 (UK) (per Lord Bingham of Cornhill). On conscientious objector status for professional soldiers, *see* Bart Horeman & Marc Stolwijk, *Refusing to Bear Arms: A World Survey of Conscription and Conscientious Objection to Military Service*, WAR RESISTERS' INT'L (1998) (updated 2005), *available at* www.wri-irg.org/co/rtba/index.html; Army Reg. 600–43, Conscientious Objection (US Army, Aug. 21, 2006); R v. Michael Peter Lyons [[2011] EWCA (Crim) 2808 (Toulson, L.J.), paras. 9–17 (UK).

59 In addition to the reasoning in *Hinzman* discussed in the text, *see also* Hughey v. Canada (Min. of Cit. & Immigr.) [2006] F.C. 421, para. 153 (Can.); Colby v. Canada (Min. of Cit. & Immigr.) [2008] F.C. 805, paras. 11, 15 (Can.). Approving of these rulings, *see* Patrick J. Glen, *Judicial Judgment of the Iraq War*, 26 WIS. INT'L L.J. 965, 1027 (2009). On similar grounds, the German Federal Office for Migration and Refugees recently rejected the asylum application of American soldier André Shepherd, finding that Shepherd would have to prove that he himself would take part in an illegal act. Bundesamt für Migration und Flüchtlinge [Federal Office for Migration and Refugees], Press Release: Kein Asyl für US-Deserteur [No Asylum for US Deserter] (Apr. 4, 2011), www.bamf.de/SharedDocs/Pressemitteilungen/DE/2011/110404-0009-pressemitteilung-deserteur.html?nn=1366068. The EU Directive appears to protect only those for whom obedience would have entailed "commit[ing] a crime against peace," Directive 2011/95/EU, *supra* note 45, arts. 9(2)(e), 12(2). More ambiguously, it also protects those for whom obedience would have entailed "acts contrary to the purposes and principles of the United Nations as set out in the Preamble and articles 1 and 2 of the Charter of the United Nations." *Id.*, art. 12, para. 2.

> 141. [R]efusal to be involved in the commission of a crime against peace could indeed potentially bring a senior member of a government or military within the ambit of [international refugee protection] ... As a result, in the case of a senior official, the legality of the war in issue could well be germane to the claim.
> 158. [T]he ordinary foot-soldier such as Mr. Hinzman ... cannot be held criminally responsible merely for fighting in support of an illegal war, assuming that his or her own personal wartime conduct is otherwise proper.
> 159. [T]he legality of a specific military action could potentially be relevant to the refugee claim of an individual who was involved at the policy-making level in the conflict in question, and who sought to avoid involvement in the commission of a crime against peace. However, the illegality of a particular military action will not make mere foot soldiers participating in the conflict complicit in crimes against peace.
> 160. As a result, there is no merit to the applicants' contention that had Mr. Hinzman participated in the war in Iraq, he would have been complicit in a crime against peace, and should thus be afforded [refugee protection].[60]

As in the domestic cases discussed above, the reasoning here seems to be that the right not to participate in a criminal war attaches only to those who would be criminally liable for waging the war if they were to participate.

This, however, is plainly inadequate to support the holding. It is true, of course, that soldiers ordered to fight in an aggressive war do not face competing legal duties – they are not simultaneously required to obey and to disobey. In that sense, there is no explicit legal contradiction. However, in the context of other illegal orders, soldiers have a right to disobey whether or not they would be personally criminally liable if they were to obey. What matters is whether they can "wash their hands of guilt."[61]

[60] Hinzman v. Canada (Min. of Cit. & Immigr.) [2006] F.C. 420, paras. 141, 158–60 (Can.) [hereinafter Hinzman, Federal Court]. Rather than pointing directly to the Refugee Convention, the judgment discusses refugee protection here through the lens of the UN High Commissioner for Refugees (UNHCR) Handbook – a widely used interpretive guide to Convention rights. On the Handbook (and particularly paragraph 171, which is what is in issue here), *see* Section 11.1 of Chapter 11 below. The Federal Court of Appeal upheld the denial of Hinzman's application for refugee status, though it did not address the relevance of the legality of the Iraq war, instead dismissing the claim on the grounds that the procedural safeguards in US courts were sufficient to ensure that he would not be persecuted even if he were prosecuted for his disobedience. Hinzman v. Minister of Citizenship & Immigration & Hughey v. Canada, [2007] F.C.A. 171, paras. 39–62 (Can.), leave to appeal to the Supreme Court of Canada refused, [2007] S.C.C.A. No. 321 (Can.).

[61] *See supra* note 48 and accompanying text.

Perhaps the judicial denials of the right to disobey are ultimately rooted in the judgment that soldiers ordered to fight in an aggressive war are not tainted by the war's wrongfulness, such that they ought to be able to wash their hands in this way. The lack of any duty to disobey under the *jus ad bellum* (even when the subordinate has full knowledge of the criminality of the war) might be referenced by these courts as a proxy for that deeper claim.

Whatever the reason, the seemingly anomalous exclusion of soldiers ordered to fight aggressive wars from the right to disobey requires explanation. Only in the case of aggressive war do the prospective agents of international criminality have neither a duty to disobey, nor protection against the orders and laws that force them to perpetrate that wrong.

1.4 Victims' Participation and Reparations

The anomalous nature of the soldier's position *vis-à-vis* aggression extends to those on the other side of the war. In the context of any other violent international crime, including collective crimes like genocide, the natural persons harmed or killed as a result of being targeted by the criminal violence are considered the core crime victims.[62] Although much remains uncertain, there is reason to question whether this will be the standard applied in aggression prosecutions.

At stake in this determination are significant participatory and reparative rights and privileges at the ICC. The Rome Statute provides victims the right to gain legal representation before the Court and to submit observations and make representations at the pre-trial stage.[63] It further authorizes the Court to allow victims to present their views and interests during the trial itself, to the extent compatible with the rights of the

[62] On collective crimes, *see* Mothers of Srebrenica v. The Netherlands, ECLI:NL: RBDHA:2014:8748, para. 4.179 Rechtbank Den Haag (July 16, 2014) (Neth.); Redress & Institute for Security Studies [ISS], Victim Participation in Criminal Law Proceedings: Survey of Domestic Practice for Application to International Crimes Prosecutions 9 (Sept. 2015) (crimes against humanity, genocide, and often war crimes, may be collective in one sense, but they also "directly attack the personality and individuality of victims, disrespecting their very 'human existence.'").

[63] ICC Statute, *supra* note 14, arts. 15(3), 19(3), 68; ICC Rules of Procedure and Evidence, Doc. ICC-PIDS-LT-02-002/13_Eng, rules 85–93 (2nd edn 2013) [hereinafter ICC RPE]; ICC Regulations of the Court, Doc. ICC-BD/01-01-04, 79–82, 83(2) (May 2004) [hereinafter ICC Regulations]. *See also* Carsten Stahn et al., *Participation of Victims in Pre-Trial Proceedings of the ICC*, 4 J. Int'l Crim. Justice 219 (2006).

accused.[64] In exercising this authority, the Court has allowed victims to lead evidence pertaining to the accused's guilt, question witnesses, and challenge the admissibility of evidence, among other things.[65] In addition to providing these avenues for participation, the Statute also empowers the Court to order that reparations be paid by a convicted person or persons "to, or in respect of, victims."[66]

In the ICC's first case, the Trial Chamber defined the class of victims eligible for reparations for Thomas Lubanga's conscription of child soldiers as all persons whose harms were proximately caused by the crime, whether directly or indirectly.[67] The Appeals Chamber affirmed this standard in the abstract,[68] but reversed the Trial Chamber's holding that this would encompass those subject to sexual violence as a result of child conscription.[69] Referencing the crime's rationale – the protection of children from the fear and violence of combat and from the trauma of separation from family and school – it defined the "direct victims" of the crime as the conscripted children and defined the harm to which reparations must respond as the physical injury and trauma, psychological trauma, and loss of schooling associated with being conscripted into combat.[70] In the language of an earlier decision on victim participation, this meant defining the direct victims as those the prohibition was

[64] ICC Statute, *supra* note 14, art. 68(3); ICC RPE, *supra* note 63, rules 89–93; ICC Regulations, *supra* note 63, regs. 86–87.

[65] Judgment on the Appeals of the Prosecutor and the Defence against Trial Chamber I's Decision on Victims' Participation of 18 January 2008, Lubanga (ICC-01/04-01/06) Appeals Chamber, paras. 86–105 (July 11, 2008); Judgment, Lubanga (ICC-01/04-01/06) Trial Chamber, paras. 13–14 (Mar. 12, 2012); Sixth Decision on Victims' Participation Relating to Certain Questions Raised by the Office of Public Counsel for Victims, *Bemba* (ICC-10/05-01/08), para. 2 (Jan. 8, 2009); Decision on Victims' Representation and Participation, *Kenyatta* (ICC-01/09-02/11) (Oct. 3, 2012). *See also* T. Markus Funk, Victims' Rights and Advocacy at the International Criminal Court ch. 4 (2015).

[66] *See* ICC Statute, *supra* note 14, art. 75(2). *See also id.*, art. 57(3)(e), 82(4); ICC RPE, *supra* note 63, rules 94–97; ICC Regulations, *supra* note 63, regs. 56, 88, 117.

[67] "Decision Establishing the Principles and Procedures to be Applied to Reparations," Lubanga (ICC-01/04-01/06) Trial Chamber, paras. 249, 180 (Aug. 7, 2012) [hereinafter Lubanga TC: Reparations Principles].

[68] Judgment on the Appeals against the "Decision Establishing the Principles and Procedures to be Applied to Reparations," of 7 Aug. 2012, Lubanga (ICC-01/04-01/06 A A 2 A 3) Appeals Chamber, paras. 1, 124–30 (Mar. 3, 2015) [hereinafter Lubanga AC: Reparations Principles].

[69] Lubanga TC: Reparations Principles, *supra* note 67, paras. 207–09; Lubanga AC: Reparations Principles, *supra* note 68, paras. 196–99.

[70] *Id.*, at paras. 181, 187–91, 196–98.

"clearly framed to protect."[71] "Indirect victims" were those who suffered due to a "close personal relationship" to direct victims or who were harmed protecting them.[72]

This focus on core crime victims and their protectors or close personal relations is both pragmatic and contextually appropriate. The Court is struggling to manage thousands of victims as trial participants in crimes against humanity cases.[73] Reparations are limited initially by the wealth of the convict and secondarily by that of the poorly endowed Trust Fund for Victims, which may loan funds to cover indigent defendants' reparative obligations.[74] Confronted with these challenges, the Court has assigned common legal representatives to facilitate the participation of many victims at trial and has provided for collective reparations to maximize the reach of limited funds.[75] Those techniques depend heavily on relatively coherent victim classes that can be represented and repaired meaningfully in a collective way. Given that those criminally wronged by a given action are more likely to cohere in that way than are all persons harmed foreseeably by the same action, this militates as a pragmatic matter in favor of the "clearly framed to protect" standard.

This definition of victims at the ICC also fits the context. Reparations at the Court are adjudicated in a criminal court, they are attached to a criminal prosecution, and their subject matter is limited to the specific crime(s) of which the relevant defendant was convicted.[76] In other words, ICC reparations are connected inextricably to the condemnation of criminal wrongdoing in a way that other reparative systems are not.[77]

[71] For that earlier language: Decision on "Indirect Victims", Lubanga (ICC-01/04-01/06-1813) Trial Chamber, paras. 45–48, 51 (Apr. 8, 2009). Articulating a similar standard, *see* Broomball, *Commentary on Article 51: Rules of Procedure and Evidence, in* COMMENTARY ON THE ROME STATUTE OF THE INTERNATIONAL CRIMINAL COURT (Otto Triffterer, ed., 2nd edn 2008), 1033–52, at 1033, n. 85. On participation (but not reparations), *see* Valentina Spiga, *Indirect Victims' Participation in the Lubanga Trial*, 8 J. INT'L CRIM. JUSTICE. 183, 186–87 (2010).

[72] Lubanga AC: Reparations Principles, *supra* note 68, paras. 190–91, 196–98.

[73] For a critical appraisal: E. Haslam and I. R. Edmunds, *Common Legal Representation at the International Criminal Court*, 12 INT'L. CRIM. L. REV. (2012) 871.

[74] Lubanga AC: Reparations Principles, *supra* note 68, paras. 106–17.

[75] *Ibid*, paras. 210–15. Order on the Organisation of Common Legal Representation of Victims, *Katanga and Ngudjolo* (ICC-01/04-01/07) Trial Chamber, para. 11 (July 22, 2009); Haslam and Edmunds, *supra* note 73.

[76] Lubanga AC: Reparations Principles, *supra* note 68, paras. 65, 99.

[77] DINA SHELTON, REMEDIES IN INTERNATIONAL HUMAN RIGHTS LAW (2nd edn, 2005), at 237; Andreas O'Shea, *Reparations under International Criminal Law, in* REPAIRING THE

This provides good reason for conceiving of the ICC participation and reparations regime primarily in terms of moral expression,[78] and defining those proximately harmed by the crime as those that suffer the harm "by virtue of which [the crime] is judged to be blameworthy."[79] Understood in this way, the ICC's participatory and reparative features are for the Court to acknowledge the conduct not only to be a violation against the global community, and thus worthy of punishment, but also a wrong against specific persons, whose voices should be heard and with whom the community expresses solidarity via the reparations award. Along these lines, the Court has emphasized that reparations can have a "symbolic" value, that they help to "express" the accountability of the perpetrator to his victims, and that they "must reflect" the context of criminal prosecution.[80]

Understood in this way, ICC victims are those "against whom" the crime is committed.[81] This approach has intuitive appeal. Genocide foreseeably harms tourism in the region in which it occurs, but those harms are not why genocide is a crime and, although tourism business owners may have a valid civil claim, they are not the crime victims. At the very least, there is good reason for the ICC to prioritize those who are criminally wronged when resources cannot stretch to all of those harmed.[82] Analogous domestic systems do precisely that.[83] The focus

PAST? INTERNATIONAL PERSPECTIVES ON REPARATIONS FOR GROSS HUMAN RIGHTS ABUSES, at 189 (M. du Plessis & S. Peté, eds., 2007).

[78] *Cf.* Redress & ISS, *supra* note 62, at 17, 19, 23, 25; CONOR MCCARTHY, REPARATIONS AND VICTIM SUPPORT IN THE INTERNATIONAL CRIMINAL COURT (2012), at 61–62, 133, 188.

[79] The language is borrowed from JOEL FEINBERG, 1 THE MORAL LIMITS OF THE CRIMINAL LAW 123 (1987). On proximate cause, *supra* note 67.

[80] Lubanga AC: Reparations Principles, *supra* note 68, at §§ 202, 70, 65.

[81] This is how they have been defined at other international criminal tribunals. Rule 2, Int'l Crim. Trib. for the Former Yugoslavia Rules of Procedure and Evidence; Judgment, *Duch* (001/18-07-2007-ECCC/SC) Appeals Chamber, para. 416 (Feb. 3, 2012); ILA, Resolution 2/2010: Declaration of International Law Principles on Reparation for Victims of Armed Conflict, art. 3, 15–20 (Aug., 2010).

[82] International Center for Transitional Justice Submission on Reparations Issues, Lubanga (ICC-01/04-01/06) Trial Chamber, paras. 15, 58 (May 10, 2012).

[83] Redress and ISS, *supra* note 78, at 25. *See also id.* at 17, 19, 23. On the genealogical relationship between the ICC victims framework and domestic *partie civilie* proceedings: WILLIAM SCHABAS, AN INTRODUCTION TO THE INTERNATIONAL CRIMINAL COURT 330–31 (2007); McCarthy, *supra* note 78, at 51; Working Paper Submitted by France, *Rights of Victims*, Draft Statute of the International Criminal Court, A/AC.249/L.3, art. 50 (Aug. 6, 1996).

on core crime victims and their loved ones in Lubanga makes sense as a long-term standard.

Assuming the durability of that approach, the first step in determining who counts as a victim of aggression is to identify whose rights its criminalization is "clearly framed to protect." This is where aggression begins to look anomalous. As discussed in greater detail in Chapter 3, criminal aggression tends to be framed primarily as a violation of sovereignty. From that common perspective, if victims are those the law is framed to protect, "the typical victim [of the crime of aggression] is a 'state'," with all of the participatory and reparative rights and privileges that that entails.[84] Indeed, reasoning from the premise that *jus ad bellum* rules "primarily protect the territorial integrity of States," Rainer Hofmann's 2010 International Law Association report questioned whether anyone other than states holds a legal right to *jus ad bellum* reparations.[85]

One of the core arguments of this book debunks that normative premise. Aggression is criminal not because it violates sovereignty, but because it involves unjustified killing. Recognizing this is the platform for resolving much of the normative dissonance introduced in this chapter and for correcting the associated doctrinal errors. But put that argument to one side for the moment. The (mistaken) account of the crime as a crime against sovereignty is commonly held and its implication is indeed that states, and not individuals, are the crime victims of aggression under the "framed to protect" standard.

As acknowledged even by those who endorse the premise and recognize this upshot, this is a problematic implication in the ICC context. Stahn, for example, admits that it may "run against the purpose and

[84] Carsten Stahn, *The "End," The "Beginning of the End" or the "End of the Beginning"?*, 23 LEIDEN J. INT'L L. 875, 877, 880–81 (2010). Taking a similar stance, *see* HANS VAN HOUTTE, HANS DAS, BART DELMARTINO, & IASSON YI, 1 POST-WAR RESTORATION OF PROPERTY RIGHTS UNDER INTERNATIONAL LAW 238 (2008); CARRIE McDOUGALL, THE CRIME OF AGGRESSION UNDER THE ROME STATUTE OF THE INTERNATIONAL CRIMINAL COURT 293 (2013). McCARTHY, *supra* note 78, at 43–44; SCHABAS, *supra* note 83, at 324–25; Aurel Sari, *The Status of Foreign Armed Forces Deployed in Post-Conflict Environments*, *in* JUS POST BELLUM: MAPPING THE NORMATIVE FOUNDATIONS 467, at 483 (Carsten Stahn, Jennifer S. Easterday, & Jens Iverson, eds., 2014). *See also* Erin Pobjie, *Victims of the Crime of Aggression*, *in* THE CRIME OF AGGRESSION: A COMMENTARY 816, at 816–21 (Claus Kreß & Stefan Barriga, eds., 2016).

[85] Rainer Hofmann, Report: Draft Declaration of International Law Principles on Reparation for Victims of Armed Conflict (Substantive Issues), 74th Conference of the International Law Association, The Hague, commentary to art. 3 (Aug. 15–20, 2010).

mandate of the court."[86] Pobjie worries that it would contradict the "spirit of the restorative justice provisions of the Rome Statute."[87] It may also seem to diverge from the widely perceived connection between international criminal justice and human rights,[88] and possibly even from the requirements of the ICC Rules of Procedure and Evidence, which limit victims to natural persons and a specific list of legal persons that suffered particular *jus in bello* harms.[89] Thus, despite viewing the ban on aggression as protecting sovereign rights, Hofmann speculates that its introduction at the ICC may catalyze the development of individual legal rights to *jus ad bellum* reparations.[90]

Ultimately, assuming aggression is a crime against state sovereignty, the Court would find itself in a dilemma. In identifying victims of aggression, it would have either to depart from the "framed to protect" standard in its case law, or to depart from its human-focused Rules and posture.[91] From this perspective, the fact that an obvious opportunity to amend the Rules and clarify matters eschewed in the aggression amendments agreed at Kampala is unfortunate.[92]

If the focus on core crime victims were to be dropped in aggression cases, the question is what standard would take its place. The natural international precedent would be that of the UN Compensation Commission (UNCC), which included as reparable any harm "which, as a matter of objective assessment, would have been expected as a normal and natural consequence" of Iraq's invasion of Kuwait.[93] This broad standard underpinned reparations awards to 1.5 million claimants,[94]

86 Stahn, *supra* note 84, at 881; McDougall, *supra* note 84, at 293; Pobjie, *supra* note 84, at 851–52.

87 Pobjie, *supra* note 84, at 851.

88 Consider how common it is for international criminal law to be framed as a mechanism of accountability for "human rights atrocities." For example: Steven R. Ratner et al., Accountability for Human Rights Atrocities in International Law (3rd edn, 2009).

89 ICC Rules of Procedure and Evidence, *supra* note 63, rule 85. Arguing state victim status *is* viable under Rule 85(b), *see* Pobjie, *supra* note 84, at 847–53.

90 Hofmann, *supra* note 85, commentary to art. 3.

91 Biting the bullet and advocating a departure from the existing focus on the core crime victims, so as to capture the human victims of aggression, *see* Pobjie, *supra* note 84, at 820–22, 826–31.

92 Pobjie, *supra* note 84, at 824.

93 UNCC Governing Council, Report and Recommendations Made by the Panel of Commissioners Concerning the First Instalment of "F3" Claims, S/AC.26/1999/24, § 23 (Dec. 9, 1999).

94 United Nations Compensation Commission, Claims, www.uncc.ch/claims (last visited Sept. 16, 2016).

including *inter alia* those harmed by traffic accidents and property losses caused by the general breakdown of civil order in Kuwait (as distinct from those caused by the violence of conflict) as well as those who suffered losses because the conflict precluded the continuation of a contract.[95]

Whether or not such an approach is appropriate for a civil compensation commission, it sits less easily with the criminal context. Plainly, traffic accidents resulting from the disorder incidental to an illegal invasion are not what the criminalization of aggression was framed to condemn and prevent. It is difficult to imagine the ICC including as victims of genocide or crimes against humanity persons who lost contracting opportunities because of the foreseeable disruption of those crimes. A robust case would need to be made for why such deviation would be appropriate in the context of aggression.[96]

Nonetheless, if the "framed to protect" standard were to be eschewed in the context of aggression, this precedent and perhaps that of the somewhat narrower Ethiopia–Eritrea Claims Commission would provide the most natural existing frameworks for an alternative definition of aggression "victims."[97] It is notable then that both of these commissions excluded almost all combatant deaths and injuries from compensable *jus ad bellum* damages.[98]

On its face, this exclusion ought to strike us as somewhat peculiar. To be sure, large numbers of civilians are almost inevitably killed and injured

[95] UNCC Governing Council, Decision 9, U.N. Doc. S/AC.26/1992/9, §§ 9–10 (Mar. 6, 1992); UNCC Governing Council, Report and Recommendations Made by the Panel of Commissioners Concerning Individual Claims for Serious Personal Injury or Death (Category B Claims), U.N. Doc. S/AC.26/1994/1, at 25 (May 26, 1994); UNCC Governing Council, Report and Recommendations Made by the Panel of Commissioners Concerning the First Instalment of Individual Claims for Damages up to US $100,000 (Category C Claims), U.N. Doc. S/AC.26/1994/3, at 109, 133, 154 (Dec. 21, 1994); UNCC Governing Council, Report and Recommendations Made by the Panel of Commissioners Concerning the First Instalment of "E2" Claims, U.N. Doc. S/AC.26/1998/7, § 147 (1998).

[96] Arguing for a broad approach, while recognizing the "universe of victims" to be "potentially massive," *see* Pobjie, *supra* note 84, at 843.

[97] Final Award: Ethiopia's Damages Claims, Eritrea–Ethiopia Claims Comm'n (Aug. 17, 2009).

[98] *Id.* at para. 338. The UNCC allowed a narrow category of claims on behalf of Kuwaiti soldiers killed or injured during the days of and immediately following the invasion, but excluded combatants killed by Iraqi forces once the coalition was engaged. UNCC Governing Council, Decision 11, U.N. Doc. S/AC.26/1994/1 (May 26, 1994); UNCC Governing Council, Report and Recommendations Made by the Panel of Commissioners Concerning Individual Claims for Serious Personal Injury or Death (Category B Claims), U.N. Doc. S/AC.26/1994/1, at 15 (May 26, 1994).

by the violence of an aggressor force. Some may be targeted in violation of the *jus in bello*, others as an unintentional (albeit foreseeable) consequence of belligerent operations against military targets. As the UNCC recognized, still others may be harmed indirectly, as a result of the disorder or uncertainty incidental to a state's descent into war. A final group may be harmed as a collateral consequence of defensive forces' actions.

Perhaps the UNCC is right that civilians in all of these categories are owed reparations by the aggressor. But only soldiers are the *direct targets* of the criminal violence of aggression. In any other context, that would make them the core victims of the wrong. And yet, despite covering extraordinarily broad victim constituencies, the UNCC and the EECC excluded soldiers without hesitation from victim status and eligibility for reparations.

Of course, the ICC need not follow these examples. It could deviate from its "framed to protect" approach without adopting an alternative that would exclude combatants.[99] However, it is certainly clear that two leading candidates for the approach to victims would focus on states (as the core crime victims) or a broader range of harmed persons that may exclude combatants. And, despite the fact that they are the targets of aggression's criminal violence, I know of no proposal that would place combatants at the *heart* of the class of aggression victims. Just as does the denial of any right to disobey orders to fight in a criminal war, the marginalization of soldiers on the other side demands explanation.

1.5 The Human Stakes: Moral and Physical Wounds

The need to explain the law's anomalous marginalization of soldiers on either side of aggression is not simply a matter of doctrinal aesthetics or the kind of "glib, abstract moralism" produced when normative theory fails to engage with practitioners' experiences.[100] Soldiers bear a heavy and real burden when they inflict wrongful violence. Those killed wrongfully are wronged again when that initial violation goes unrecognized. The complicated connection between these harms and the legality of the war is discussed in the next chapter. First, however, consider the manifestation of those harms in the lives of soldiers.

[99] Pobjie, *supra* note 84, at 840–44.

[100] David Luban, Legal Ethics and Human Dignity 13 (2007) [hereinafter Luban, LEHD].

On the question of whether there is a real human cost to soldiers being forced to fight in aggressive wars, a skeptic might object that soldiers are driven by survival, comradeship, and obedience; they kill enemies readily, irrespective of the wrongfulness or otherwise of the war, and often with apparent zeal.[101] From this, the skeptic might infer that the *jus ad bellum* status of their wars does not weigh on them. If that were right, their being forced to fight in criminal wars would arguably be no more oppressive than is their being forced to comply with any other order.

However, the inference is mistaken. Killing is, for many soldiers, the hardest part of any war.[102] For all but a small minority, the apparent ease with which they kill is an illusion born of the observer's confusion between the roles of context and moral agency.[103] Stanley Milgram's experiments showed how easily we can be nudged by conducive circumstances into obediently performing egregious wrongs.[104] Philip Zimbardo discovered a proclivity to conform to odious role expectations even in the

[101] On zealous killing, *see, for example*, *Collateral Murder*, Wikileaks www.collateralmurder.com/ (last visited Aug. 4, 2017). On the combination of comradeship and zealous killing, *see, for example*, Film: *Restrepo* (National Geographic 2010). On soldiers fighting under little or no duress, *see* Section 4.1, below. *See also* JEFF MCMAHAN, KILLING IN WAR 2 (2009) (describing soldiers as "readily assuaged" by the common view that they "are not blameworthy" for fighting in an unjust war).

[102] LT. COL. DAVE GROSSMAN, ON KILLING, at xxxv, 74, 88, 92, 252 (rev'd edn 2009); S. L. A. MARSHALL, MEN AGAINST FIRE 79 (1947) (University of Oklahoma Press, 2000); DAVID HARDAN, ED., THE MORAL AND EXISTENTIAL DILEMMAS OF THE ISRAELI SOLDIER 35, 41 (1985). There is evidence that many soldiers deliberately miss their targets, do not fire their weapons at all, or pretend to fire and reload (double-loading in the process). GROSSMAN, *supra* note 102, at 4–29. Soldiers who kill often try to deny having done so to themselves and to others. *Id.* at 91, 226.

[103] Dave Grossman reports that only 2 percent of persons kill without difficulty or guilt, and actually enjoy the act. GROSSMAN, *supra* note 102, at 180–84. On our general tendency to underestimate the impact of situational context in determining behavior, *see* JOHN M. DORIS, LACK OF CHARACTER: PERSONALITY AND MORAL BEHAVIOR (2002); Edward E. Jones & Richard E. Nisbett, *The Actor and the Observer: Divergent Perceptions of the Causes of Behavior*, *in* ATTRIBUTION: PERCEIVING THE CAUSES OF BEHAVIOR 79 (Edward E. Jones et al., eds., 1971); Edward E. Jones, *The Rocky Road from Acts to Dispositions*, 34 AMERICAN PSYCH. 107 (1979); RICHARD E. NISBETT & LEE ROSS, HUMAN INFERENCE: STRATEGIES AND SHORTCOMINGS OF SOCIAL JUDGMENT (1980); Lee Ross, *The Intuitive Psychologist and his Shortcomings*, 10 ADVANCES IN EXPERIMENTAL SOC. PSYCH. 173 (Leonard Berkowitz, ed., 1977).

[104] *See generally* STANLEY MILGRAM, OBEDIENCE TO AUTHORITY: AN EXPERIMENTAL VIEW (1974). *See also* LUBAN, LEHD, *supra* note 100, at 240–53 (canvassing some of the most interesting of Milgram's and others' findings in *Obedience to Authority* and subsequent work and discussing how they illuminate the explanation for the powerful tendency towards obedience that Milgram observed).

absence of instruction or command.[105] War exemplifies these phenomena. The extreme deference instilled within the military,[106] intra-unit pressures to stand by one's comrades,[107] legal and social coercion,[108] the gloss of honor and sacrifice,[109] rationalizing propaganda,[110] and a slew of military techniques to enable killing[111] all influence soldiers to inflict violence almost automatically.

However, that automaticity is not indicative of their internal comfort with the resulting acts. The Milgram experiments are jarring precisely because they show how easily we can be nudged to do *what we believe to be deeply wrong*. As Luban observes,

> [M]ost of Milgram's compliant subjects [did not] continue to believe that compliance was the right thing to do once the experiment ended ... In

[105] Philip G. Zimbardo, The Lucifer Effect: Understanding How Good People Turn Evil (2007); Film: *Quiet Rage: The Stanford Prison Experiment* (Philip G. Zimbardo, 2004); C. Haney, W. C. Banks, & Philip G. Zimbardo, *A Study of Prisoners and Guards in a Simulated Prison*, 30 Naval Research Rev. 4 (1973).

[106] Morris Janowitz, The Professional Soldier 39 (1960); Chris Hedges, What Every Person Should Know about War 12 (2003). *See also infra* Section 8.1. On total institutions generally (including in the military), *see* Erving Goffman, Asylums (1961).

[107] Grossman, *supra* note 102, at 88–89.

[108] *See* Section 4.1 of Chapter 4, below. The same phenomenon contributes to contributing to atrocities in theater. Robert Jay Lifton, *Haditha: In an "Atrocity-Producing Situation" – Who is to Blame?* , Editor & Publisher (June 4, 2006), www.editorandpublisher.com/news/haditha-in-an-atrocity-producing-situation-who-is-to-blame/.

[109] Halbertal argues that this gloss can create a false sense of justification – a "dangerous yet common reversal" whereby it is incorrectly assumed that "since it is the mark of the good that it deserves sacrifice, the reverse must be true, too – namely that sacrifice makes something into a good." Moshe Halbertal, On Sacrifice 68 (2012). Indeed, Halbertal contends, "war is not embarked on despite the risk and sacrifice that it involves; it is strengthened and motivated by this aspect." *See also* Mateo Taussig-Rubbo, *Outsourcing Sacrifice: The Labor of Private Military Contractors*, 21 Yale J.L. & Human. 101, 110 (2009); Andrew Fiala, Public War, Private Conscience: The Ethics of Political Violence 50 (2010); McMahan, *supra* note 101, at 2; Ray Monk, Ludwig Wittgenstein: The Duty of Genius 111–12 (1990).

[110] *See infra* note 121.

[111] On the basic aversion to killing, *see infra* note 102. Among the techniques to overcome that aversion are: desensitization training to make killing automatic (Grossman, *supra* note 102, at 252–63; D. Keith Shurtleff, *The Effects of Technology on our Humanity*, Parameters 100–12 (Summer 2002), the dehumanization of enemies (Grossman, *supra* note 102, at 161–68), supervision of killing by a commander (*id.* at 141–48; Marshall, *supra* note 102, at 82. *See also* Milgram, *supra* note 104, at 186–89), physical distance from the victim(s) (Grossman, *supra* note 102, at 97–113, 160, 170.) and the use of multi-person weapons. *Id.* at 153–54.

> fact, they probably never believed that compliance was the right thing to do ... the experiment seemed to corrupt their judgment *temporarily*, disabling their capacity to apply their principles correctly to the situation they found themselves in.[112]

Explaining this, Lifton describes "a type of dissociation ... the formation of a second self" that allows the actor to do things "that would otherwise seem repugnant."[113]

The question, then, is not whether soldiers participate in wrongful wars with apparent readiness, but whether they are at ease with such participation on reflection. Both the anecdotal testimony of individual soldiers and broader psychological studies of returning veterans suggest that soldiers' ultimate comfort with their participation in violence is dependent on whether they can justify it morally.

In that quest, soldiers find the situational factors that enabled the conduct to be normatively impotent.[114] In fact, the ease with which a soldier kills in war can actually *exacerbate* his retrospective struggle to endorse that killing. An American veteran reflects,

> I don't know if it was the training that we had ingrained in us, but ... it wasn't real ... *it was a lot easier then than it is now* ... [T]hat day, I had absolutely no ethical or moral problems with pulling the trigger and taking out as many people as I could ... *[T]hat day it was too easy. That upsets me more than anything else,* how easy it was to pull the trigger over and over again.[115]

[112] LUBAN, LEHD, *supra* note 100, at 287–88. Luban hypothesizes that the corruption of moral judgment may be more permanent when the wrongful conduct and the socialized compliance occur over a long period of time. *Id.* at 288–89. The evidence discussed below suggests that this may not be true for at least some proportion of soldiers.

[113] Lifton, *supra* note 108. Tim O'Brien describes watching a comrade in Vietnam pistol-whipping a civilian woman: "He was numb. *He'd lost himself.* His gyroscope was gone. He didn't know up from down, good from bad." Tim O'Brien, *The Vietnam in Me*, NY TIMES MAGAZINE (Oct. 2, 1994).

[114] JOANNA BOURKE, AN INTIMATE HISTORY OF KILLING 6–7 (1999); Dan Baum, *The Price of Valor*, THE NEW YORKER (July 12, 2004); Brandon Frazier, *The Weight of Violence*, 46 (21) NAT'L CATHOLIC REPORTER 3A (Aug. 6, 2010); TIM O'BRIEN, THE THINGS THEY CARRIED 149 (1990) [hereinafter O'BRIEN, TTTC]. *The Things They Carried* is fictionalized, but appears to communicate what O'Brien (a Vietnam veteran) takes to be a moral reality. *Id.*, at 203; MARK A. HEBERLE, A TRAUMA ARTIST 38 (2001). *See also* the trauma of Vietnam bombers discussed at *infra* note 142.

[115] *Ambush in Mogadishu: Interview Specialist Jason Moore*, PBS FRONTLINE (Sept. 29, 1998) transcript *available at* www.pbs.org/wgbh/pages/frontline/shows/ambush/rangers/moore.html [emphasis added].

To be sure, killings can sit uneasily even with those who are morally certain they did the right thing.[116] However, the burden is greater when the soldier is convinced that he acted wrongfully, as is clearest in the case of those who participated in atrocity.[117] Maj. Peter Kilner argues:

> Conditioning soldiers to reflexively engage targets prepares them to deal with the enemy, but it does not prepare them to deal with their own consciences ... When soldiers kill reflexively ... they morally deliberate their actions only after the fact. If they are unable to justify what they have done, they often suffer guilt and psychological trauma.[118]

For soldiers, the justification for the war is an important part of justifying the killing. Retired US Army Officer Michael Davidson reports that it is precisely because of the difficulty of killing even combatants that "warriors want, and perhaps even need, to believe in the justness of their cause."[119] That need is well understood by military experts,[120] and it is implicit in the universal military effort to affirm for their troops the defensive and just nature of the causes they pursue.[121]

116 AVRAM SHAPIRA, ED., THE SEVENTH DAY: SOLDIERS TALK ABOUT THE SIX-DAY WAR 67–69 (1970). Although arguing that feelings of guilt can arise even when one endorses the specific killing at hand (a reality reflected in the experience of at least some soldiers – *see, for example*, Coming Home, Dateline NBC, May 25, 2008; SHAPIRA, *supra* note 116, at 67–69; WALZER, JUW, *supra* note 40, at 32, 121), Walzer also accepts that the felt psychological burden is far harder to shake if one cannot morally endorse the act in a straightforward way. Michael Walzer, *Political Action: The Problem of Dirty Hands*, 2 PHILOSOPHY & PUB. AFF'S 160, 173–74 (1973).

117 *See, e.g.*, Greg Mitchell, *The US Soldier Who Killed Herself after Refusing to Take Part in Torture*, HUFFINGTON POST (Sept. 15, 2010); Daniel Somers, "*I Am Sorry It Has Come to This*": *A Soldier's Last Words* (June 22, 2013), *available at* http://gawker.com/i-am-sorry-that-it-has-come-to-this-a-soldiers-last-534538357; Gregory L. Vistica, *What Happened in Thanh Phong*, NY Times MAGAZINE 50 (April 29, 2001).

118 Maj. Peter Kilner, *Military Leaders' Obligation to Justify Killing in War*, MILITARY REV. 24 (Mar.–Apr. 2002). *See also* GROSSMAN, *supra* note 102, at 271–73, 295.

119 Michael J. Davidson, *War and the Doubtful Soldier*, 19 N.D. J. L. ETHICS & PUB POL'Y 91, 94–95 (2005).

120 LTC (RET.) LAWRENCE P. CROCKER, ARMY OFFICER'S GUIDE 23 (46th edn 1993); MARSHALL, *supra* note 102, at 162; RICHARD A. GABRIEL, TO SERVE WITH HONOR: A TREATISE ON MILITARY ETHICS AND THE WAY OF THE SOLDIER 62 (1982); HARDAN, *supra* note 102, at 45, 50, 56, 102–04. *But see id.*, at 104 (suggesting the footsoldier (unlike the officer) may not need the same faith in the cause).

121 Military leaders frame the soldier's role as defensive guardian of the state, not enforcer of its interests. *See, e.g.*, BRIG. GEN. AVI BENAYAHU, A SPECIAL SURVEY: THE IDF'S SOCIAL COMMITMENT 2 (Jan. 2010) ("The soldiers of the IDF are obligated ... to *protect* the State of Israel, its citizens and residents") [emphasis added]; Gen. Douglas MacArthur, *Duty, Honor, Country*, Speech to the Corps of Cadets at the US Military Academy at West Point, NY (May 12, 1962) (speaking of "a great moral code ... of those who *guard*

Soldiers who are convinced of the justification for their war report being better able to live with having participated as a result.[122] Others make an effort to ignore reasons to question the war precisely because of the implications those questions would have for the moral meaning of their own acts.[123] The retrospective struggle is greatest when these efforts fail – when the soldier is unconvinced of the basis for using force.[124] The longstanding "presumption of just war theory" has been that such cases are rare – "that all the combatants believe that their country is fighting a just war."[125] But this rings false, and was exposed as such most obviously in the widespread opposition among soldiers and veterans to the American war in Vietnam.[126]

For at least some of those who fight and kill under these conditions, the harm is very much that of having acted culpably and done wrong – of being "morally accountable not just for how they fight but for what they fight for."[127] Soldiers engaged in this struggle report recoiling at being thanked for their service, jarred by the absurdity of receiving gratitude for what they consider wrongdoing.[128] Nancy Sherman writes:

this beloved land of culture and ancient descent"). MATTHEW GUTMANN & CATHERINE LUTZ, BREAKING RANKS: IRAQ VETERANS SPEAK OUT AGAINST THE WAR 51, 53, 91 (2010) (on institutional affirmation throughout training and deployment).

122 An Israeli officer describes having had "a much easier time" participating in wars he understood to be clearly defensive than in other military operations because it alleviated the "need for soul-searching." "Elisha" quoted in SHAPIRA, *supra* note 116, at 165. *See also id.* at 6, 146, 254–55, 262. An American Major describes himself as "offended" by the notion that his war's cause is irrelevant to the moral meaning of his actions, arguing that such a standard equates soldiers to "mafia thugs." Peter Kilner, *Rejecting the Moral Equality of Soldiers*, BLOG: THOUGHTS OF A SOLDIER ETHICIST (Oct. 3, 2005), http://soldier-ethicist.blogspot.com/2005/10/rejecting-moral-equality-of-soldiers.html.

123 GUTMANN & LUTZ, *supra* note 121, at 145; Jacob Diliberto Testimony to: Truth Commission on Conscience in War (Mar. 21, 2010). Manipulating one's truth in this way is difficult to sustain on reflection (*see, for example, infra* note 129) but the felt need for it is revealing.

124 NANCY SHERMAN, THE UNTOLD WAR: INSIDE THE HEARTS, MINDS, AND SOULS OF OUR SOLDIERS 39 (2011).

125 Avishai Margalit & Michael Walzer, *Israel: Civilians and Combatants*, NY REV. BOOKS 21 (May 14, 2001).

126 MURRAY POLNER, NO VICTORY PARADES: THE RETURN OF THE VIETNAM VETERAN 165 (1971); Robert Jay Lifton, *Home from the War: The Psychology of Survival*, *in* THE VIETNAM READER 54, 55 (Walter H. Capps, ed., 1991).

127 SHERMAN, *supra* note 124, at 40. *See also id.* at 45, 47, 63, 92. Nan Levinson, *Mad, Bad, Sad: What Really Happens to US Soldiers*, AL JAZEERA (July 8, 2012).

128 James Jeffrey, *My Military-Industrial Complex: A Veteran's Ambivalence about America's Martial Culture*, GUARDIAN (Sept. 27, 2012); GUTMANN & LUTZ, *supra* note 121, at

> Soldiers are good at compartmentalizing, I've been told over and over. But ... conflicts about complicity and personal responsibility for participation in collective ends don't just disappear. More often, they are displaced, deferred, put on hold until soldiers find the safety and trust needed to express personal doubts and torments ... What soldiers have said over and over ... is that they don't just fight war – they fight specific wars, the wars that it is their luck to be in.[129]

Having complied with the *jus in bello* during the war is not necessarily enough; it matters to soldiers whether the war itself had a legitimate basis.[130] Kilner describes enemy combatants as having a "human right" not to be killed in a wrongful war, and insists that soldiers cannot "abdicate our responsibility" to respect that right.[131]

Perhaps the most iconic articulation of the enduring pain of fighting in a wrongful war is that of Vietnam veteran and novelist, Tim O'Brien. He writes,

> I thought about Canada. I thought about jail. But in the end I could not bear the prospect of rejection: by my family, my country, my friends, my hometown. I would risk conscience and rectitude before risking the loss of love. I have written some of this before, but I must write it again. I was a coward. I went to Vietnam ... Each step was an act of the purest self-hatred and self-betrayal.[132]

O'Brien describes his decision as a "horrid thing" that has demanded "lifelong acts of atonement."[133] He is not alone. Cheyney Ryan observes,

9, 145; Logan Mehl-Laituri, *Veterans' Suicides and Selective Conscientious Objection*, SOJOURNERS (Nov. 8, 2010), http://sojo.net/blogs/2010/11/08/veterans-suicides-and-selective-conscientious-objection. Those not experiencing *jus ad bellum* torment feel differently. Phillip Carter, *For Veterans, Is "Thank You for your Service" Enough?*, WASHINGTON POST (Nov. 4, 2011).

[129] SHERMAN, *supra* note 124, at 63. *See also* GUTMANN & LUTZ, *supra* note 121, at 85, 127, 149.

[130] SHERMAN, *supra* note 124, at 37.

[131] Peter Kilner, *The Justice of the War Does Matter*, BLOG: THOUGHTS OF A SOLDIER ETHICIST (Jan. 25, 2010), http://soldier-ethicist.blogspot.com/2010/01/justice-of-war-does-matter.html.

[132] O'Brien, *supra* note 113. His reference to earlier writing is to a number of passages in quasi-fictional Vietnam novels. *See, e.g.*, O'BRIEN, TTTC, *supra* note 114, at 54–63. Mark Heberle notes the foundational force of this struggle in O'Brien's work. HEBERLE, *supra* note 114, at xxii–xxiii, 204, 290.

[133] HEBERLE, *supra* note 114, at 253. Part of that atonement for O'Brien is writing about Vietnam. *Id.* Vietnam is "the bad war that has forever darkened [O'Brien's] view of himself and his nation." *Id.* at 256.

"Vietnam vets have been more willing to take responsibility for that war than anyone else in our society."[134]

The struggle is not a peculiarity of the era of conscription. Iraq veteran James Jeffrey writes that it has become difficult for him to "look an Iraqi in the eyes" and that he feels burdened as a veteran of the conflict with "a sense of collective guilt."[135] Other Iraq veterans describe being part of "something evil" and the "sickening feeling" of killing in an "illegal and immoral" war.[136]

In the absence of large-scale studies exploring soldiers' sentiments on the legal or moral basis for their wars, and in light of the obstacles to speaking openly about such struggles, direct testimony is inevitably anecdotal.[137] However, statistical evidence on the causes of post-traumatic stress disorder (PTSD) and other trauma among veterans sharpens the reason for taking seriously the notion that soldiers bear a real burden when they fight in wrongful wars.

Consistent with broader recognition of the severity of PTSD arising from perpetrating "acts that transgress deeply held moral beliefs" (so-called "moral injury"),[138] evidence now suggests that killing in war is the

[134] Cheyney Ryan, *Moral Equality, Victimhood, and the Sovereignty Symmetry Problem*, *in* JUST AND UNJUST WARRIORS: THE MORAL AND LEGAL STATUS OF SOLDIERS 131, 134 (David Rodin & Henry Shue, eds., 2008). Taking responsibility in poetic form, *see, for example*, W. D. Ehrhart, The Distance We Travel, *in* THE DISTANCE WE TRAVEL: POEMS BY W. D. EHRHART (1993); W.D. Ehrhart, *Letter*, *in* UNACCUSTOMED MERCY: SOLDIER-POETS OF THE VIETNAM WAR 61, 62 (1989).

[135] James Jeffrey, *"Iraq is Always with You": A Veteran's Memories of the War*, GUARDIAN (Mar. 18, 2013); James Jeffrey, *The Lonely Soldier and the Moral Scars of War*, GUARDIAN (Feb. 17, 2013).

[136] Levinson, *supra* note 127; André Shepherd, Press Conference Statement, Frankfurt, Germany (Nov. 27, 2008), *available at* www.connection-ev.org/article-369 (last visited Aug. 13, 2014). Indeed, most of those cited in the footnotes above and below are volunteer soldiers, as are many of those included in the statistical studies discussed below.

[137] Jeffrey claims the moral pain he articulates is widespread, but also acknowledges the immense difficulty of talking openly about that struggle. Jeffrey, *Lonely Soldier*, *supra* note 135.

[138] Brett T. Litz et al., *Moral Injury and Moral Repair in War Veterans: A Preliminary Model and Intervention Strategy*, 29 CLINICAL PSYCH. REV. 695, 700 (2009). For useful overviews of the concept and the existing research up until 2012, *see* Shira Maguen & Brett Litz, *Moral Injury in Veterans of War*, 23 PTSD RESEARCH QUARTERLY 1 (2012). *See also* RACHEL M. MACNAIR, PERPETRATION-INDUCED TRAUMATIC STRESS: THE PSYCHOLOGICAL CONSEQUENCES OF KILLING 7 (2002) (coining Perpetration-Induced Traumatic Stress (PITS) "as a subcategory of PTSD"); Kent D. Drescher et al., *An Exploration of the Viability and Usefulness of the Construct of Moral Injury in War Veterans*, 17 TRAUMATOLOGY 8, 8 (2011) (defining moral injury). In addition to PTSD

most significant cause of long-term psychological harm among veterans.[139] Studies on Americans who fought in Vietnam or Iraq have shown PTSD, dissociation experiences, functional impairment, violent behaviors, anger, relationship difficulties (including physical violence), substance abuse, and suicidal tendencies to be more tightly correlated with whether a soldier killed in war than with combat exposure, perceived danger, personal life threat, injury, witnessing dying, or witnessing the deaths and injuries of comrades.[140] Indeed, combat exposure, and (in one study) even seeing friends die, has little or no correlation with PTSD when the analysis controls for whether the soldier killed.[141]

symptoms, moral injury produces guilt, shame, demoralization, self-handicapping behaviors, and self-harm. Litz et al., *supra* note 138, at 700–01. *See also* Soul Repair Center, Brite Divinity School, www.brite.edu/programs/soul-repair/ (last visited Aug. 23, 2017).

139 On the incipience of the research in this area, *see* MacNair, *supra* note 138, at 1. On the difficulty of having open conversations on this in the military, *see* Baum, *supra* note 114. *See also* Coming Home, Dateline NBC (May 25, 2008).

140 MacNair, *supra* note 138, at 16–20, 24–26, 155, 175, 178. Shira Maguen et al., *The Impact of Killing in War on Mental Health Symptoms and Related Functioning*, 22 J. Traumatic Stress 435 (2009); Shira Maguen et al., *The Impact of Reported Direct and Indirect Killing on Mental Health Symptoms in Iraq War Veterans*, 23 J. Traumatic Stress 86 (2010); Elizabeth P. Van Winkle & Martin A. Safer, *Killing versus Witnessing in Combat Trauma and Reports of PTSD Symptoms and Domestic Violence*, 24 J. Traumatic Stress 107 (2011); Rachel M. MacNair, *Perpetration-Induced Traumatic Stress in Combat Veterans*, 8 Peace & Conflict 63 (2002); Alan Fontana & Robert Rosenheck, *A Model of War Zone Stressors and Posttraumatic Stress Disorder*, 12 J. Traumatic Stress 111 (1999); Shira Maguen et al., *The Impact of Killing on Mental Health Symptoms jn Gulf War Veterans*, 3 Psychological Trauma 21 (2011).

141 Maguen et al., *The Impact of Killing in War*, *supra* note 140, at 441 (finding no correlation between combat experience and PTSD once killing is accounted for); MacNair, *supra* note 138, 16–17, 174; MacNair, *Perpetration-Induced Traumatic Stress in Combat Veterans*, *supra* note 140 (trauma rates are higher for those who are exposed only to light combat but kill than they are for those that experience heavy combat but do not kill). Among civilians exposed to the Blitz and Allied firebombing in World War II, psychological trauma rates were "very similar to that of peacetime." Grossman, *supra* note 102, at 55. Reconnaissance patrol groups operating behind enemy lines (at high risk, but without orders to kill) and medical personnel deployed in combat areas of extreme risk suffer fewer psychiatric effects than those alongside them who carry the added burden of killing. *Id.* at 59–63. "[C]linical studies that tried to demonstrate that fear of death and injury are responsible for psychiatric casualties have been consistently unsuccessful" (*id.* at 51). PTSD among those who have killed, however, is significant. *Id.* at 225, 249, 286–96. Preliminary research suggests that serving in peacekeeping or relief work in war zones or locations of "ongoing terror" is not associated with PTSD, but participating in combat is. Ellen Connorton et al., *Occupational Trauma and Mental Illness – Combat, Peacekeeping, or Relief Work and the National Co-Morbidity Survey Replication*, 53 J. Occupational & Environmental Medicine 1360 (2011).

Confounding the hypothesis that this is about visual horror, PTSD rates among aerial bombers from Vietnam seem to be "practically indistinguishable" from those of soldiers involved exclusively in the conflict on the ground.[142] Emphasizing the significance of the struggle for moral justification in underpinning this trauma, the only experience more strongly correlated with post-war trauma than having killed combatants is having killed civilians.[143]

The data lack information on soldiers' understanding of the *jus ad bellum* status of their wars.[144] However, four observations are worth emphasizing. First, the variables for which the statistical analyses control rule out the most likely non-moral explanations for the extraordinary

Fontana & Rosenheck, *supra* note 140, at 123 (seeing friends die in combat did not contribute to PTSD once the analysis controlled for its indirect effect via increasing participation in killing others).

142 MacNair, *supra* note 138, at 23. The data on this are imperfect and more work needs to be done. However, even if existing findings were to be reversed, the innovation of drone killing has married increased physical distance with heightened emotional connection to the target. Nicola Abé, *Dreams in Infrared: The Woes of an American Drone Operator*, Spiegel (Dec. 14, 2012). Moreover, as noted above, witnessing dying, and witnessing the deaths and injuries of one's comrades is less tightly correlated with PTSD than is killing, a result that would be difficult to comprehend if the sight of human suffering rather than the feeling of responsibility for it were driving the psychological pain. *See supra* notes 140–41.

143 MacNair, *Perpetration-Induced Traumatic Stress in Combat Veterans*, *supra* note 140; Maguen et al., *The Impact of Killing in War*, *supra* note 140, at 440, 443; Rachel M. MacNair, *The Effects of Violence on Perpetrators*, 14 Peace Rev. 67, 68 (2002). *See also* Richard Strayer & Lewis Ellenhorn, *Vietnam Veterans: A Study Exploring Adjustment Patterns and Attitudes*, 31 J. Social Issues 81, 90 (1975) (participation in atrocities by Vietnam veterans is correlated with guilt, hostility, and severity of maladjustment as compared to those who did not participate in atrocity ["acts of cruelty resulting in death or injury that were both unnecessary and beyond the scope of normal warfare."]). On the impact on PTSD of participation in atrocity killing, *see* Naomi Breslau & Glenn C. Davis, *Posttraumatic Stress Disorder: The Etiologic Specificity of Wartime Stressors*, 144 Am. J. Psychiatry 578 (1987); Fontana & Rosenheck, *supra* note 140; Alan Fontana, Robert Rosenheck, & Elizabeth Brett, *War Zone Traumas and Posttraumatic Stress Disorder Symptomatology*, 180 J. Nervous & Mental Disease 748 (1992).

144 This is unsurprising – the available data-sources are the military's post-conflict surveys of its troops, and "many therapists of war veterans" work for the government. MacNair, *The Effects of Violence on Perpetrators*, *supra* note 143, at 67–68. PITS in general (not just in the *jus ad bellum* domain) is a concept militaries have been traditionally reluctant to examine. *See, e.g.*, MacNair, *supra* note 138, at 162; Peter Marin, *Living in Moral Pain*, *in* The Vietnam Reader, *supra* note 125, 40, 45. *See also* sources cited in *supra* note 139. It was only in 2004 that the Army confirmed that a factor responsible for PTSD was "killing enemy combatants." Baum, *supra* note 114. If killing is "the dead elephant in the room" when discussing PTSD in the military (*id.*), killing when unsure as to the legal and moral justificatory basis for the war is even more taboo.

impact of killing on veterans' psychological injury.[145] Second, the exacerbating effect of killing civilians is precisely what one would expect if the distress were a manifestation of underlying moral torment.[146] Third, the emerging literature on moral injury indicates a strong connection between moral self-assessment, feelings of guilt, and the psychological pain of veterans.[147] One team of researchers concludes, "the moral conflict, shame, and guilt produced by taking a life in combat can be

[145] *See supra* notes 140–42 and accompanying text.

[146] Most civilian killing is either prohibited absolutely, or limited significantly under the *jus in bello*. *See* Section 7.1 of Chapter 7, below. Even when it is permissible, the warrant for such killing is more normatively complex than it is for most other killing in war, and soldiers express greater difficulty in reconciling themselves morally to this form of taking life. SHERMAN, *supra* note 124, at 37, 107–10. Even accepting the arguments presented in the ensuing chapters that killing combatants in a wrongful war is itself wrongful, killing civilians is surely even worse. *See* Chapter 7, below. On the other hand, *see* MACNAIR, *supra* note 138, at 21 (suggesting reasons why we might expect to see higher PTSD rates among atrocity perpetrators other than moral self-assessment, including: "the greater likelihood of seeing the results, the cognitive component, the difference in social support or disapproval, or simply that this is a measure of greater frequency in killing").

[147] On the connection between killing and moral injury, *see, for example*, Alan Fontana & Robert Rosenheck, *Trauma, Change in Strength of Religious Faith, and Mental Health Service Use among Veterans Treated for PTSD*, 192 J. NERVOUS & MENTAL DISEASE 579 (2004). Moral injury includes not just ordinary PTSD symptoms, but also shame, guilt, self-loathing, demoralization, loss of self-worth, self-handicapping behaviors (such as self-sabotaging relationships), and self-harm (such as para-suicidal behaviors). Litz et al., *supra* note 138, at 700–01; Shira Maguen & Brett Litz, *Moral Injury in Veterans of War*, 23 PTSD RESEARCH QUARTERLY 1, 1 (2012); Kent D. Drescher et al., *An Exploration of the Viability and Usefulness of the Construct of Moral Injury in War Veterans*, 17 TRAUMATOLOGY 8, 11 (2011). Charlotte V.O. Witvliet et al., *Posttraumatic Mental and Physical Health Correlates of Forgiveness and Religious Coping in Military Veterans*, 17 J. TRAUMATIC STRESS 269 (2004) (difficulty with forgiveness [by self or by others] is associated with PTSD and depression and that difficulty with self-forgiveness is associated with anxiety). Other studies have found that severity of guilt is related to PTSD severity among Vietnam veterans and that guilt is related to the strength of the subject's belief about personal responsibility, moral integrity, justification, and pre-outcome knowledge. Kris R. Henning & B. Christopher Frueh, *Combat Guilt and its Relationship to PTSD Symptoms*, 53 J. CLINICAL PSYCHOLOGY 801 (1997); Edward S. Kubany et al., *Initial Examination of a Multidimensional Model of Trauma-Related Guilt: Applications to Combat Veterans and Battered Women*, 17 J. PSYCHOPATHOLOGY & BEHAVIORAL ASSESSMENT 353 (1995). *See also* Hillel Glover et al., *Post-Traumatic Stress Disorder Conflicts in Vietnam Combat Veterans: A Confirmatory Factor Analytic Study*, 3 J. TRAUMATIC STRESS 573, 586–89 (1990) (finding guilt [both survivor guilt and perpetrator guilt] as a component of PTSD among Vietnam veterans); Barbara Olaslov Rothbaum et al., *Virtual Reality Exposure Therapy of Combat-Related PTSD: A Case Study Using Psychophysiological Indicators of Outcome*, 17 J. COGNITIVE PSYCHOTHERAPY 163 (2003) (reporting on a therapy case study in which they found that the subject's psychological distress came from acts that he had committed in Vietnam, and this

uniquely scarring across the lifespan."[148] Veteran caregivers provide experiential confirmation of the link between self-blame and psychological harm from their daily work.[149] Fourth, divisions in the soldier's home state over whether the war was justified heighten the rates of psychological trauma among veterans.[150] Some argue that this warrants public support for even bad wars.[151] But evidence from *jus in bello*

distress led to feelings of guilt and anger). *See also* Gregg Zoroya, *Study Suggests Feelings of Guilt May Be a Top Factor in PTSD*, USA TODAY (Nov. 25, 2011). "Personal disintegration," including "self-hatred," also is among one of the strongest PTSD correlates with killing in war. MacNair, *The Effects of Violence on Perpetrators*, *supra* note 143, at 69; MACNAIR, *supra* note 138, at 20. *See also* Maguen et al., *The Impact of Killing in War*, *supra* note 140, at 436, 440–41 (on dissociation as an associated symptom of PTSD and its prevalence among war killers). From her interviews, Sherman writes that in a wrongful war, soldiers' "[p]syches fracture, and self-empathy with warring parts is often in short supply." SHERMAN, *supra* note 124, at 63.

The link between moral self-examination and psychological struggle has been raised in the context of other professions. "Standing as a constant witness," Postema argues, "conscience issues a call to unity and integrity, a warning against the loss of self." When this is denied, he contends, moral disunity is "experienced as psychological dysfunction, suffering." Gerald Postema, *Self-Image, Integrity, and Professional Responsibility*, *in* THE GOOD LAWYER 294, 308 (David Luban, ed., 1983). *See also* MacNair, *The Effects of Violence on Perpetrators*, *supra* note 143, at 70 (emphasizing the need for more study on the relevance of guilt in explaining PITS); MACNAIR, *supra* note 139, at 58 (hypothesizing that both legal and personal moral judgments about the justification for killing are "likely to make a major difference in the psychological aftermath" to police officers who kill in the course of duty).

148 Maguen et al., *The Impact of Killing in War*, *supra* note 140, at 435; Maguen et al., *The Impact of Reported Direct and Indirect Killing*, *supra* note 140, at 90; Kilner, *Military Leaders' Obligation*, *supra* note 118 (soldiers unable to justify their killings in retrospect "will likely, and understandably, suffer enormous guilt [which] manifests itself as post-traumatic stress disorder").

149 Marin, *supra* note 144, at 41; MACNAIR, *supra* note 139, at 25. *See also* Hillel Glover, *Guilt and Aggression in Vietnam Veterans*, 1 AM. J. SOC. PSYCHIATRY 15, 16 (1985). There is growing recognition that treating many veterans' psychological pain may require a moral reparative response rather than a medical approach. Pauline Jelinek, *War Zone Killing: Vets Feel "Alone" in their Guilt*, Associated Press (22 Feb. 2013); Marin, *supra* note 144, at 41, 43–46; SHERMAN, *supra* note 124, at 99; Maj. Peter Kilner, *The Military Ethicist's Role in Preventing and Treating Combat-Related, Perpetration-Induced Psychological Trauma*, JSCOPE (2005), *available at* http://isme.tamu.edu/JSCOPE05/Kilner05.html. *See also* Nenad Paunović, *Cognitive Factors in the Maintenance of PTSD*, 27 SCANDINAVIAN J. BEHAVIOUR THERAPY 167 (1998) (guilt and shame maintain PTSD, so they must be addressed for PTSD symptoms to subside).

150 Psychiatrists, psychologists, and those working in mental health for Veterans Affairs affirm this connection. *See, e.g.*, GROSSMAN, *supra* note 102, at 281, 292, 349 n.6; Baum, *supra* note 114.

151 GROSSMAN, *supra* note 102, at 276 (on the justice of the war), 265–66 (on the impact of popular acclaim for the war), 274–75, 291, 296 (on the need among veterans for

perpetrators suggests platitudinous support would do little to alleviate the pain in the absence of a compelling justification.[152] As Marin observes:

> It is no accident that the war in Vietnam, by far the most morally suspect war America has fought in modern times, has raised the most problems for those who fought it . . . what they now suffer is essentially the result of the bitter reality that caused the schisms here at home – the very nature of the war.[153]

To be sure, caution is required in interpreting the evidence. More data need to be collected and more analysis needs to be done. However, killing seems to be the most traumatic aspect of participating in conflict; the trauma associated with killing appears to be linked to moral self-assessment in a number of ways; at least some soldiers openly connect their post-war pain to the perceived wrongfulness of their wars; others report that a robust belief in the war's cause eases their burden; and the military itself indicates through its actions that soldiers' will to fight (the hardest aspect of which is killing) is dependent in part on a belief in the rectitude of the war. Together, these factors suggest that soldiers experience viscerally the burden of participating in wrongful wars. Affected veterans may be forced to live in "pain and regret for the rest of their lives."[154] In light of the available evidence, taking seriously that burden and evaluating its relationship with the legal status of the war and the law's treatment of soldiers is anything but abstract.

The stakes are more straightforward on the other side of the war. Obviously, the primary harm is tangible, involving physical injury or the

affirmation that they did the right thing). *See also* Lt. Gen. John F. Kelly, *Honor and Sacrifice*, Speech in St. Louis to commemorate Veterans Day (Nov. 23, 2010) (arguing that supporting the troops requires supporting the war).

152 The assumption that platitudinous support dismissing the soldier's moral pain is still pervasive. Baum, *supra* note 114 (quoting Vietnam veteran, Dan Knox); Kilner, *The Military Ethicist's Role*, *supra* note 149 (quoting an infantry commander taking this view). But this cannot overcome the pain, and it may even exacerbate it. Robert Jay Lifton, Home from the War: Vietnam Veterans, Neither Victims nor Executioners 166–67 (1973); Marin, *supra* note 144, at 44, 47. Kilner argues that combatants' need for retrospective justification imposes a duty on leaders to help "soldiers understand that what they learn to do reflexively would be the same choice they would have made reflectively because it is the morally right choice," but recognizes that this relies on the war being a good one. Kilner, *Military Leaders' Obligation*, *supra* note 118. Grossman assumes that the war is justified in describing how PTSD from killing might be addressed, but does not consider what to do if the war is wrongful. Grossman, *supra* note 102, at 299.

153 Marin, *supra* note 144, at 41 [emphasis added].

154 *Id.* at 52.

death of a loved one. At issue here, however, is the cost borne by those who suffer that primary harm *and are denied victim status* in a prosecution of the perpetrator. Whether that denial is justified is the subject of the chapters that follow. What matters here is that for those who claim the status and believe that claim to be warranted, its denial is experienced as a wrongful harm.

Specifically, at the ICC, the harm experienced by a group wrongfully denied victim status can include three distinct elements. First, they are denied the opportunity to make their voices heard in the trial and to ensure that their interests are properly accounted for. Second, they are not eligible for the (admittedly minimal and typically collective) reparations awarded after a conviction. It is surely uncontroversial that those who desire a voice at trial and a stake in post-conviction reparations bear a cost when their claims to that effect are refused. If the denial is unwarranted, that cost is a wrongful harm. A third, deeper harm associated with exclusion from victim status is that those excluded are denied a certain form of moral recognition and global expression of solidarity.

Although less tangible than the reparative or participatory rights themselves, this third dimension of what is at stake in defining the "victims" of aggression is no less significant. The basic human ache for vindication – for the public recognition that a wrong done unto them was in fact wrong – is manifest in the pursuit of human rights litigation in contexts in which there is little or no prospect of significant material gain. It is widely recognized in the literature on transitional justice.[155] And it is manifest in the use and value of "satisfaction" as a reparative response to grave abuses.[156]

Soldiers are sometimes thought to be in a separate category. For some, courageous sacrifice is part of the role. Being killed or harmed in the course of fighting against an aggressor force is part of the duty; it makes one a "hero" not a "victim." This traditional notion of the soldier leaving

[155] *See, e.g.*, MARTHA MINOW, BETWEEN VENGEANCE AND FORGIVENESS: FACING HISTORY AFTER GENOCIDE AND MASS VIOLENCE 93 (1998); Pablo de Greiff, *Justice and Reparations*, *in* REPARATIONS: INTERDISCIPLINARY INQUIRIES 153, 160–67 (Jon Miller & Rahul Kumar, eds., 2007); Brandon Hamber, *The Dilemmas of Reparations: In Search of a Process-Driven Approach*, *in* OUT OF THE ASHES: REPARATION FOR VICTIMS OF GROSS AND SYSTEMATIC HUMAN RIGHTS VIOLATIONS 135, 142, 149 (K. De Feyter et al., eds., 2005).

[156] On the Inter-American Court's focus on satisfaction, *see* Tom Antkowiak, *Remedial Approaches to Human Rights Violations: The Inter-American Court of Human Rights and Beyond*, 46 COLUM. J. TRANS'L L. 351 (2008).

behind his rights upon donning a uniform is, however, increasingly antiquated. The rights of soldiers in battle are being asserted by their families and others, and courts are starting to recognize those claims.[157] This has not yet been asserted on the *jus ad bellum* plane, perhaps because there is no forum for such a suit. But what is clear is that when daughters, sons, wives, and husbands die in combat, those left behind want answers.[158]

Given that the soldier fighting against aggression is injured or killed intentionally in furtherance of a criminal aim, there is a strong *prima facie* basis for concluding that the harms inflicted on the soldier and his loved ones are wrongful from the legal point of view. If that is incorrect, it is important to explain why. If, on the other hand, the harm inflicted is wrongful, but that wrongfulness is not expressed in law, this must be accounted for. The stakes are not at all abstract for those left behind.

157 Smith (No. 2) v. Ministry of Defence [2013] U.K.S.C. 41.

158 This is true of soldiers on both sides (a point discussed further below). *Seats Ballot for Tony Blair's Grilling on Iraq War*, BBC NEWS (Jan. 5, 2010) (one third of the seats for Tony Blair's testimony before the Chilcot Inquiry into the UK's role in the Iraq war were reserved for the families of British soldiers and civilians killed in Iraq); Letters: *Why Did our Sons Die? An Inquiry into the Iraq War is Essential*, GUARDIAN (25 March 2009); *Tony Blair Has "Blood on his Hands", Says Father of Killed Soldier*, TELEGRAPH (10 Oct. 2009).

2

Normative Reasoning and International Law on Aggression

From the discussion thus far, there are two points of putative dissonance in the legal posture towards soldiers. In any other international crime, soldiers (and others) are required on pain of criminal punishment to *disobey* orders to participate in the crime, and are legally protected in various ways when they do so. In diametric opposition, soldiers on the aggressor side of a criminal war are required on pain of criminal punishment to *kill in service of* the criminal end. They receive no legal protection when they refuse. A similar dissonance arises on the other side. Ordinarily, the human targets of internationally criminal violence (and their loved ones) are recognized as victims at the ICC, where they gain a voice in proceedings, access to reparations, and official recognition of the wrongfulness of their suffering. However, leading candidate approaches to victim participation and reparations at the ICC would exclude the only human targets of the violence entailed in an aggressive war.

These two dimensions of dissonance have real stakes for the soldiers involved. And yet, they have received little discussion or pushback. This is almost certainly due to the widely held view that aggression is a normatively unusual crime to begin with. As discussed in Chapter 3, both advocates of the criminalization of aggression and some of the strongest critics of that legal move agree that the criminal wrong of aggression is inflicted on the attacked state. In distancing soldiers on both sides from the interstate crux of the crime, this is the fundamental starting point for their legal marginalization.

The objective of this book is to interrogate that normative account of the crime, present a more powerful alternative that roots the crime in unjustified killing, and to elaborate the legal and institutional implications for soldiers. Before turning to that core argument, it is important to lay the methodological foundations. What does it mean to give a normative account and why is it a valuable endeavor here?

Stated most abstractly, a normative account aims to provide a moral framework that would make sense of, and underpin, the law's posture on a given issue or in a given domain. To offer such an account is not to start from first principles or to insist that the moral standards articulated ought to be accepted on their own terms. Rather, it is to inhabit the internal legal point of view, and to insist that the moral standards articulated best explain and make sense of the law that we have. In addition to the intrinsic value of clarifying the normative message of the law we have, one of the virtues of this endeavor is that it can guide interpretation, both of the law under examination, and of adjacent laws derivative of the former's core meaning.

After describing this normative method and its virtues, this chapter addresses two objections to its application here. First, it responds to the realist claim that seeking normative coherence in a regime created to benefit powerful states' interest is misguided and inevitably futile. Second, it addresses the worry that the normative posture of the law is insufficiently connected to the real moral burdens borne by soldiers on the aggressor side to be salient in dealing with the latter.

2.1 What it Means to Offer a Normative Account[1]

The premise of providing a normative account of a given legal framework is that the laws in that framework do not merely serve to coordinate; they also instantiate what the community in question takes to be important values. The balance between the coordinative and moral expressive functions varies across domains, but criminal law in particular takes a stand on what is right and wrong and on who has acted culpably. It does not provide priced permissions; it prohibits and it condemns.[2]

Some have described international law's adoption of the latter posture as a process of "moralization."[3] It is nowhere clearer than in international criminal law. We cannot make sense of the criminalization of obedient participation in crimes against humanity or genocide as a way of

[1] A version of the argument in this section appears in Tom Dannenbaum, *Why Have We Criminalized Aggressive War?* 126 YALE L.J. 1242, 1249–54 (2017).

[2] This is manifest in particularly sharp form in the moral expressivism and moral education theories of punishment. *See, e.g.*, Elizabeth S. Anderson & Richard H. Pildes, *Expressive Theories of Law: A General Restatement*, 148 U. PA. L. REV. 1503 (2000); R. A. DUFF, TRIALS AND PUNISHMENTS 235–62 (1986); Joel Feinberg, *The Expressive Function of Punishment*, 49 MONIST 397 (1965); Jean Hampton, *The Moral Education Theory of Punishment*, 13 PHIL. & PUB. AFF. 208 (1984).

[3] André Nollkaemper and Dov Jacobs, *Shared Responsibility in International Law: A Conceptual Framework*, 34 MICH. J. INT'L L. 359, 372–74 (2013).

coordinating behavior. Confronting individuals with contradictory obligations under domestic and international law may even muddy coordination and confuse expectations. The criminalization of such obedient participation is instead a moral expression of the wrongfulness of such participation and the blameworthiness of those who engage in it.[4] In David Luban's words, "the law of the Nuremberg Charter criminalized only actions that are morally outrageous."[5]

That expression runs through international criminal practice. In his opening statement of the trial of Revolutionary United Front leaders, Special Court for Sierra Leone Prosecutor David Crane described "evil" and "horror" that descended "into the realm of Dante's inferno."[6] ICTY judge and international criminal law luminary Antonio Cassese identified punishing "morally reprehensible" behavior as the regime's core purpose and a guiding interpretive principle for the tribunal.[7] ICC judge Christine Van den Wyngaert has used the same articulation,[8] and, as is common in domestic law, the ICC has identified "moral blameworthiness" and "cruelty" as factors in sentencing.[9]

[4] On the moral expression of international criminal law, *see* Diane Marie Amann, *Group Mentality, Expressivism, and Genocide*, 2 INT'L CRIM. L. REV. 93, 117 (2002); Margaret M. deGuzman, *Choosing to Prosecute*, 33 MICH. J. INT'L L. 265 (2012); MARK A. DRUMBL, ATROCITY, PUNISHMENT, AND INTERNATIONAL LAW 3, 61, 173–79 (2007); Ralph Henham, *Some Issues for Sentencing in the International Criminal Court*, 52 INT'L & COMP. L. Q. 81, 111 (2003); David Luban, *Fairness to Rightness: Jurisdiction, Legality, and the Legitimacy of International Criminal Law*, *in* THE PHILOSOPHY OF INTERNATIONAL LAW 569, 576 (Samantha Besson & John Tasioulas, eds., 2010); Robert D. Sloane, *The Expressive Capacity of International Punishment*, 43 STAN. INT'L L.J. 39 (2007); Bill Wringe, *Why Punish War Crimes?*, 25 L. & PHIL. 151 (2006); CONOR MCCARTHY, REPARATIONS AND VICTIM SUPPORT IN THE INTERNATIONAL CRIMINAL COURT 132–33 (2012).

[5] Luban, *Fairness to Rightness*, *supra* note 4, 584.

[6] Prosecutor v. Sesay, Case No. SCSL-2004-15-PT, Opening Statement of David M. Crane (Special Court for Sierra Leone) (July 5, 2004).

[7] Prosecutor v. Erdemović, Case No. IT-96-22-A, Appeals Judgment, para. 48 (Int'l Crim. Trib. for the Former Yugoslavia) (Oct. 7, 1997) (Cassese, J., dissenting). *See also* Prosecutor v. Tadić, Case No. IT-94-1, Sentencing Judgment, para. 72 (Int'l Crim. Trib. for the Former Yugoslavia July 14, 1997).

[8] Prosecutor v. Ngudjolo, ICC-01/04-02/12, Judgment pursuant to article 74 of the Statute, para. 23 (Dec. 18, 2012) (Van den Wyngaert, J. concurring).

[9] Prosecutor v. Bemba, ICC-01/05-01/08, Decision on Sentence pursuant to article 76 of the Statute, para. 17 (June 21, 2016); Prosecutor v. Katanga, ICC-01/04-01/07, Decision on Sentence pursuant to article 76 of the Statute, paras. 49, 69–71, 143 (May 23, 2014). The Office of the Prosecutor has suggested that the ICC relies on its "moral presence" to move states to arrest and prosecute most international criminals. The Office of the Prosecutor of the International Criminal Court, *Informal Expert Paper: The Principle of*

The criminalization of aggression is not an anomaly in this respect. The underlying law on the use of force is best understood as "express-[ing] a theory of just war."[10] Signatories to the Kellogg–Briand Pact of 1928 – the first treaty to ban war explicitly, and the key legal hook for the prosecutions at Nuremberg – committed not only to "renounce" the recourse to war, but also to "condemn" it.[11] This followed the unabashedly moralized framing of the issue by the Pact's intellectual forefathers, who described war variously as an "abomination," a violation of the "moral code of mankind," the "greatest of all wrongs," and a "lawful crime," and labeled its orchestrators "super felons among the criminals of the earth."[12] With the signing of the Pact, the notion of war as a global public wrong, rather than a state of bilateral dispute began to take hold.[13]

This moralized legal posture became even more apparent at Nuremberg. In his opening statement before the IMT, chief prosecutor Justice Robert Jackson stressed, "When I say that we do not ask for convictions unless we prove crime, I do not mean mere technical or incidental transgression of international conventions. We charge guilt on planned and intended conduct that involves moral as well as legal wrong."[14] He labeled the pre-Kellogg–Briand legal order "contrary to ethical

Complementarity in Practice, at 5, ICC-01/04-01/07-1008-AnxA (Mar. 30, 2003), www.icc-cpi.int/iccdocs/doc/doc654724.PDF.

10 David Luban, *Just War and Human Rights*, 9 PHIL. & PUB. AFF. 160, 161 (1980).

11 General Treaty for Renunciation of War as an Instrument of National Policy, art. 1, 94 L.N.T.S. 57 (Aug. 27, 1928).

12 John Dewey, *Foreword* to SALMON O. LEVINSON, OUTLAWRY OF WAR 7 (1921); Raymond Robins, *Foreword* to LEVINSON, *supra* note 58, at 14–15. On the prominence of Levinson, Dewey, and Robins in this regard, *see, for example*, William Hard, *The Outlawry of War*, 120 ANNALS AMERICAN ACADEMY POLITICAL & SOCIAL SCIENCE 136, 136 (1925); OONA HATHAWAY & SCOTT SHAPIRO, THE INTERNATIONALISTS: HOW THE RADICAL PLAN TO OUTLAW WAR REMADE THE WORLD, ch. 5 (2017).

13 Henry L. Stimson, *The Pact of Paris: Three Years of Development*, 11 FOREIGN AFF. vii (Supp. 1932); Quincy Wright, *The Meaning of the Pact of Paris*, 27 AM. J. INT'L L. 39, 59 (1933). Identifying this (and not the later UN Charter or the Nuremberg judgments) as *the* transformative moment in the transition of contemporary international law as a whole towards a global system of "outcasting," rather than unilateral enforcement in bilateral relationships, *see* HATHAWAY & SHAPIRO, *supra* note 12.

14 Opening Statement at Nuremberg by Justice Robert H. Jackson, Chief Prosecutor for the United States, United States v. Göring et al. (Nov. 21, 1945), *in* 2 TRIAL OF THE MAJOR WAR CRIMINALS BEFORE THE INTERNATIONAL MILITARY TRIBUNAL 98, 105 (1947). *See also id.* at 147 ("[I]f it be thought that the Charter . . . does contain new law I still do not shrink from demanding its strict application. I cannot subscribe to the perverted reasoning that society may advance and strengthen the rule of law by the expenditure

principles" because it denied the maxim that "unjust wars are illegal."[15] Jackson's colleague Whitney Harris also emphasized the "moral condemnation" underpinning the prosecutions.[16]

The Tribunal itself went to some lengths to establish the positivist credentials for outlawing aggressive war, relying heavily on the Pact in that regard.[17] However, it combined these efforts with moralized claims. In addressing the lack of an explicit criminal prohibition, the IMT held

> the maxim *nullum crimen sine lege* . . . is in general a principle of *justice*. To assert that it is unjust to punish those who in defiance of treaties and assurances have attacked neighboring states without warning is obviously untrue, for in such circumstances the attacker must know that he is doing *wrong* . . . it would be unjust if his wrong were allowed to go unpunished.[18]

It emphasized such wars' wrongfulness in "the conscience of the world," terming aggression "essentially an evil thing" and the "supreme international crime."[19] During IMT deliberations, French judge Donnedieu de Vabres asked his colleagues pointedly, "What are we here for if not to put morals into international law?"[20] The NMT took a similar line.[21] Today, the ban on aggression is widely recognized to be a *jus cogens* norm – international law of such elevated normative weight that states may not derogate, revoke, or otherwise opt out of it.[22]

A normative account seeks to make sense of such a legal posture. What is the moral principle that warrants aggression's status as a "high crime"

of morally innocent lives but that progress in the law may never be made at the price of morally guilty lives").

15 *Id.* at 145.

16 WHITNEY R. HARRIS, TYRANNY ON TRIAL: THE EVIDENCE AT NUREMBERG 529 (1954).

17 United States v. Göring et al., *in* 22 TRIAL OF THE MAJOR WAR CRIMINALS BEFORE THE INTERNATIONAL MILITARY TRIBUNAL 411, 461–66 (1948) [hereinafter IMT Judgment].

18 *Id.* at 462 (emphasis added).

19 *Id.* at 465, 427; *see also* HARRIS, *supra* note 16, at 528. It sourced the law of war not only in treaties, but also in "general principles of justice applied by jurists and practiced by military courts." IMT Judgment, *supra* note 175, at 464.

20 ROBERT E. CONOT, JUSTICE AT NUREMBERG 491 (1983).

21 United States v. von Weizsäcker, *in* 14 TRIALS OF WAR CRIMINALS BEFORE THE NUERNBERG MILITARY TRIBUNALS UNDER CONTROL COUNCIL LAW NO. 10 at 1, 318–19 (1949) (aggressive war was "essentially wrong" even before the Kellogg–Briand Pact).

22 On the *jus cogens* status of the prohibition on the use of force, *see* Section 1.1 of Chapter 1 above. On the significance of the concept in international criminal law, *see* Cherif Bassiouni, *International Crimes: Jus Cogens and Obligatio Erga Omnes*, 59 L. & CONTEMP. PROBS. 63 (1996).

rather than a "mere tort" in international law?[23] To hold that such questions have answers is not to hold that any particular individual must accept the moral posture underpinning the law in all cases. Rather, it is to recognize the law's internal claim to normativity – its claim to lay out a schedule of obligations, as distinct from commands or social habits.[24]

In other words, to give a normative account of a law is to endeavor to inhabit the internal legal point of view.[25] This means starting not from first principles, but from an analysis of the current law. However, it also means seeking to account for that law's underlying normative claims, rather than seeking merely to describe or interpret the rule.

In the context of this book, this means accounting for why aggression is worthy of the condemnation that attaches to criminal punishment, and for which (if any) features of participating in, or being affected by, the criminal wrong have implications for one's legal punishment, protection, vindication, or reparation.

Given the moral expression of international criminal law, there is a strong presumption that the scope of criminal liability does not extend beyond the form of culpable wrongdoing at the core of the crime.[26] However, importantly, the reverse is not true. In other words, on the moral theory underpinning the crime in question, a particular actor may be culpable for the core wrong and yet not be criminally liable. By the law's own normative lights, an agent in that situation would be unable to "wash her hands of guilt."[27]

23 Harry F. Cunningham, Note, *Meaning of "Aggression" in the United Nations Charter*, 33 Neb. L. Rev. 606, 608 (1954).

24 *Cf.* H. L. A. Hart, The Concept of Law 40, 55–57 (2nd edn 1994); Scott J. Shapiro, *What Is the Internal Point of View?*, 75 Fordham L. Rev. 1157, 1157 (2006); Scott J. Shapiro, Legality 214–17 (2011) (on the law's moral aim).

25 *See, e.g.*, Hart, *supra* note 24, at 89–91; Shapiro, *Internal Point of View*, *supra* note 24.

26 The detachment of pure deterrence theory from that principle is perhaps its most universally recognized flaw. *See, e.g.*, David Boonin, The Problem of Punishment 41–52 (2008); H. J. McCloskey, *Utilitarian and Retributive Punishment*, 64 J. Philosophy 91, 93–102 (1967). As a result, many of those sympathetic to deterrence argue that it is only because of the individual's culpability for wrongdoing that punishing him in service of a deterrent (or other) aim can be justified at all. *See, e.g.*, H. L. A. Hart, *Prolegomenon to the Principles of Punishment*, *in* Punishment and Responsibility: Essays in the Philosophy of Law 1, 8–13 (H. L. A. Hart & John Garner, eds., 2nd edn 2008); Alan. H. Goldman, *Toward a New Theory of Punishment*, 1 Law & Philosophy 57 (1982); Christopher Heath Wellman, *The Rights Forfeiture Theory of Punishment*, 122 Ethics 371 (2012).

27 *See* Section 1.3 of Chapter 1 above.

The most obvious example is that of an individual shielded from legal liability by a robust immunity. But that is far from the only case. Those culpable for the underlying wrong may be shielded from criminal liability due to the risks of creating perverse effects, of collateral harm on innocent parties, of exacerbating the propensity for wrongdoing, and of draining resources better spent in other ways.[28] Punishment could also be precluded on the grounds that the potential punitive authority lacks standing to condemn the culpable perpetrator.

This distinction between the scope of criminal liability and the underlying culpable wrongdoing emphasizes why the issues raised in Chapter 1 come apart. Soldiers' non-liability for aggression does not itself explain why they have no right not to fight in such wars. Similarly, those legal aspects of soldiering on the aggressor side do not themselves explain why the harms suffered by soldiers on the other side do not underpin their victim status at the ICC. Instead, these phenomena require a deeper normative account, starting with a normative account of the criminalization of aggression itself.

The methodological starting point of the argument that follows is that a normative account is superior to its alternatives in charting the moral underpinnings of the law to the extent that it better satisfies four criteria. First, it must offer an explanation for what the regime unambiguously permits and prohibits concerning the issue at hand. Second, it ought to be compatible with the law's core purposes, as evinced in the law's structure and in the articulations of its framers. Third, it should cohere with connected or related laws in domains adjacent to that which it explains. Finally, if multiple accounts pass the first three tests with equal strength, the superior remaining account is that which is most morally plausible.

The first is a straightforward and inflexible threshold criterion. The essential feature of any normative account is that it explains morally the law that we have, not the law that we ought to have. The second and third criteria are more flexible. They do much of the work in distinguishing between better and worse accounts, but they are not minimum essential

[28] Reasons related to creating the optimal incentives for peace and limiting the hell of war militate against punishing soldiers for fighting in criminal wars, even when they are culpable for doing so. *See* Chapter 7 below. As I discuss in *Crime Beyond Punishment*, there are good reasons associated with moral expression, the creation of positive incentives, and the encouragement of reconciliation to eschew punishment in the aftermath of atrocity, even when the perpetrators are deserving of it. Tom Dannenbaum, *Crime Beyond Punishment*, 15 U.C. Davis J. Int'l L. & Pol'y 189, 203–19 (2009).

criteria. At their core is the basic observation that the law's credibility as a normative system is dependent on the schedule of imperatives it issues and purposes it serves cohering together in a structure of mutual support, rather than collapsing into discord or internal contradiction.[29] When the normative messages of different laws conflict, the law's authority to condemn or to demand action decreases.[30] Given the fragmented nature of international law's enforcement, the rarity of credible coercive backing, and thus the premium on normative acceptance, this premium on internal coherence is particularly acute at the global level.[31]

However, although coherence is an important trait of a good normative account of the law, it cannot be an essential criterion. Law is created and revised by the cumulative efforts of different agents acting at different times with different objectives. It is the product of compromise and sometimes of deliberate efforts by competing lawmakers to create internal contradictions. As a result, it may be impossible in a given case to provide a normative account that both explains the moral core of a particular law and fits with the regime's purpose or with adjacent rules. In that scenario, the best normative account of the law in question will be dissonant with the regime as a whole. When no more coherent alternative is viable, work on normative underpinnings can be valuable in helping to identify such dissonance.

The final criterion is that the normative account should be morally plausible. This is not an exercise in redefining the law through moral discovery. Moral plausibility is a tiebreaker when two normative accounts

[29] On the role of coherence in legal reasoning generally, *see* RONALD DWORKIN, LAW'S EMPIRE (1986); Robert Alexy & Aleksander Peczenik, *The Concept of Coherence and its Significance for Discursive Rationality*, 3 RATIO JURIS 130 (1990); Barbara Baum Levenbook, *The Role of Coherence in Legal Reasoning*, 3 LAW & PHIL. 355 (1984); Ronald Dworkin, *Law as Interpretation*, 9 CRITICAL INQUIRY 179 (1982); Ken Kress, *Coherence*, *in* A COMPANION TO PHILOSOPHY OF LAW AND LEGAL THEORY 533 (Dennis Patterson, ed., 2nd edn 2010); Neil MacCormick, *Coherence in Legal Justification*, *in* THEORY OF LEGAL SCIENCE: PROCEEDINGS OF THE CONFERENCE ON LEGAL THEORY AND PHILOSOPHY OF SCIENCE, LUND, SWEDEN, DECEMBER 11–14, 1983, at 235 (Aleksander Peczenik et al., eds., 1984); Joseph Raz, *The Relevance of Coherence*, *in* ETHICS IN THE PUBLIC DOMAIN 277 (1994).

[30] *Cf.* Hersch Lauterpacht, *The Limits of the Operation of the Law of War*, 30 BRIT. Y.B. INT'L L. 206, 209 (1953).

[31] THOMAS M. FRANCK, THE POWER OF LEGITIMACY AMONG NATIONS 14, 135–82, 481 (1990). *See* particularly *id.* at 153 (on the "relationship, not only between a rule, its various parts, and its purpose, but also between the particular rule, its underlying principle, and the principles underpinning other rules of that society").

satisfy the first three criteria equally well.[32] If one of two accounts that explain a law in a way that is consistent with its aims and adjacent legal rules is morally untenable, the other account better comports with the law's basic claim to normativity.

In sum, to give a normative account of the crime of aggression and the regime around it means to explain the rules we have in a way that comports with their purpose and coheres with the broader legal context. If multiple alternatives do that, the more morally plausible has the edge. By accounting for the regime on aggression in this way, we can begin to understand the soldier's position within it. That understanding can shed light on how we ought to interpret the law. By clarifying the law's moral expression, it can also inform external evaluation and critique.

2.2 The Realist Objection

For realists, this approach is likely to seem misguided. Their starting premise is that international law is fundamentally a tool of powerful states' interests.[33] Since state interests are not determined by a coherent moral theory, it would be an analytic error to expect various of their aggregate outputs to be explicable with reference to one. In other words, the realist objection is not that the putative dissonance of soldiers' normative marginalization in the law around aggression does not exist, but that it is unworthy of attention.

It would be a mistake to refrain from exploring the normative underpinnings of aggression on this basis. First, the premise is empirically dubious. Second, the unambiguously moral language of the law in this domain warrants being engaged on its own terms. Third, the view that the legal posture described above *can* be rooted effectively in a morality of states' rights is sufficiently common to require examination, whatever the empirical explanation for the law we have.

[32] Dworkin goes further, demanding that morality be brought to the forefront of international legal interpretation. Ronald Dworkin, *A New Philosophy for International Law*, 41 PHIL. & PUB. AFF. 2, 7, 13 (2013).

[33] For a recent statement of legal realism in this realm, *see* JACK GOLDSMITH & ERIC POSNER, THE LIMITS OF INTERNATIONAL LAW 13, 170 (2005). For Posner and Goldsmith, international law is not *only* a tool of power – within limited circumstances, it can also be a useful tool of coordination and cooperation when power and interest allow. For a classic statement, *see, for example*, ROBERT D. SCHULZINGER, THE MAKING OF THE DIPLOMATIC MIND 94 (1975) quoting Ellery C. Stowell, Lecture at the Foreign Service School (1926).

A forensic analysis of the empirical merits of realism is not necessary here. It is sufficient to note that there are good reasons to be highly skeptical of the assertion that international law is either *simply* a function of state power or *entirely* impotent in the face of state interest. Power and interest are plainly important in determining both the content of the law and the degree of compliance with its requirements. However, an international legal regime is not merely the set of rules that states agree during treaty negotiations. Rules require interpretation, and regimes adjust to address issues within their scope as those issues arise over time.[34] Even when states have total control over treaty-making, this process of adjustment involves a much broader range of players, including international organizations, international and domestic courts, and transnational and domestic social movements.[35] Indeed, several such actors have already been involved in elaborations of the crime of aggression to date.[36]

To be sure, these other actors have their own interests. However, for courts and international organizations in particular, engaging in normatively infused reasoning often serves those interests. Courts expand their asserted authority when they affirm the force and develop the scope of international law.[37] Given at least some of the mechanisms by which they may gain compliance with the resulting rulings – mechanisms like facilitating domestic political mobilization, persuading executive branch officials normatively, and gaining buy-in from domestic judges – interpretations that are normatively coherent are more likely to advance institutional interests.[38] Similarly, social movements and others seeking

[34] *See, e.g.*, ABRAM CHAYES & ANTONIA HANDLER CHAYES, THE NEW SOVEREIGNTY 228–29 (1995). On the institutional "discourse" through which this adjustment occurs, *see id.* at 110.

[35] The likes of Simmons, and Risse, Ropp, and Sikkink have emphasized the role of both non-state actors and interpretive bodies in performing such elaboration. *See, e.g.*, THE POWER OF HUMAN RIGHTS: INTERNATIONAL NORMS AND DOMESTIC CHANGE (Thomas Risse, Stephen C. Ropp, & Kathryn Sikkink, eds., 1999); THE PERSISTENT POWER OF HUMAN RIGHTS: FROM COMMITMENT TO COMPLIANCE (Thomas Risse, Stephen C. Ropp, & Kathryn Sikkink, eds., 2013); BETH A. SIMMONS, MOBILIZING FOR HUMAN RIGHTS: INTERNATIONAL LAW IN DOMESTIC POLITICS (2009).

[36] The IMT, NMT, and IMTFE all contributed to defining the leadership element of aggression, domestic courts continue to elaborate the implications for disobedience rights. Social movements were crucial in driving the Kampala Amendments, and the ICC and domestic courts will chart the contours of the crime going forward.

[37] *See, e.g.*, Anne-Marie Burley & Walter Mattli, *Europe before the Court: A Political Theory of Legal Integration*, 47 INT'L ORG'N 41 (1993).

[38] On the mechanisms of compliance, *see infra* note 44.

to use courts have an interest in pushing for change by appealing to the latter's interest in reconciling the law to its core normative principles.

Judicial reasoning of that kind is especially notable in domains that have an overt moral aim, like human rights, humanitarian law, and international criminal law,[39] as well as in examinations of customary international law, where the lack of a text diminishes direct state control over doctrine.[40] Exemplifying this approach, the ICTY rooted its expansion of a number of key *jus in bello* rules for international armed conflict to non-international armed conflict in the common normative foundation of the two bodies of law, reasoning, "what is inhumane in international armed conflict cannot but be inhumane in non-international armed conflict."[41] Similarly, in one of the earliest decisions on the extraterritorial application of human rights law, the Human Rights Committee held, "it would be unconscionable" for the jurisdiction clause of the International Covenant on Civil and Political Rights "to permit a State party to perpetrate violations . . . on the territory of another State, which violations it could not permit on its own territory."[42] To be sure, the European Court of Human Rights has taken a more tortuous path, but it has progressively expanded its jurisprudence on extraterritoriality in the same direction.[43]

[39] Ruti Teitel, Humanity's Law 35, 61 (2011); Louis Henkin, The International Bill of Rights: The Covenant on Civil and Political Rights 15 (1981); Louis B. Sohn, *The New International Law: Protection of the Rights of Individuals Rather than States*, 32 Am. U. L. Rev. 1 (1982); Yoram Dinstein, *The Interaction of International Law and Justice*, 16 Israel Y.B. Hum. Rts. 9, 41–42 (1986).

[40] Anthea Elizabeth Roberts, *Traditional and Modern Approaches to Customary International Law: A Reconciliation*, 95 Am. J. Int'l L. 757 (2001); John Tasioulas, *In Defence of Relative Normativity: Communitarian Values and the Nicaragua Case*, 16 Oxford J. Legal Studies 85 (1996); John Tasioulas, *Customary International Law and the Quest for Global Justice*, *in* The Nature of Customary Law: Philosophical, Historical and Legal Perspectives 307 (Amanda Perreau-Saussine & James B. Murphy, eds., 2007); Brian D. Lepard, Customary International Law: A New Theory with Practical Applications (2010); Jean-Marie Henckaerts & Louise Doswald-Beck, 1 Customary International Humanitarian Law xlviii (2005).

[41] Prosecutor v. Tadić, Decision on Defence Motion for Interlocutory Appeal on Jurisdiction, Int'l Crim. Trib. for the Former Yugoslavia Case No. IT-94-1-I, para. 19 (Oct. 2, 1995) [hereinafter Tadić Interlocutory Decision on Jurisdiction]. *See also* Prosecutor v. Kupreškić (Judgment), Int'l Crim. Trib. for the Former Yugoslavia Case No. IT-95-16-T, paras. 525–27 (Jan. 14, 2000).

[42] Sergio Euben Lopez Burgos v. Uruguay, Communication No. R.12/52, U.N. Doc. Supp. No. 40 (A/36/40), at 176, para. 12.3 (1981).

[43] *See, e.g.*, Jaloud v. Netherlands, ECtHR App. No. 47708/08, para. 152 (Nov. 20, 2014).

Such developments have not been sought or welcomed by powerful states. However, once the specific content of the doctrine has escaped states' control in this way, a range of forces at the domestic and international levels contribute to compliance, even when the specific rule runs against the relevant states' interests.[44] Among these forces is the use of international law to mobilize politically, to persuade normatively, and to reason in domestic courts. As noted above, in each of these contexts, international law is more effective when rooted in coherent principles that bolster the legitimacy of the actors who use it in these ways. In short, power is important, but the impact of the law's moral underpinnings on its evolving content is sufficient to warrant normative evaluation.

Putting the empirical question to one side, there is also an inherent value to engaging international law on its own terms. When it frames issues in a moralized way, it may be interrogated and held to account according to that framing. If it cannot stand on its own terms in that respect, that is a failing worthy of note. If, on the other hand, a coherent and plausible normative account can be given, that would be worthy of note for the opposite reasons and may raise further questions for realism.

[44] On the multilayered mechanisms of compliance with international law, *see, for example*, sources cited at *supra* note 33, 35; THOMAS M. FRANCK, FAIRNESS IN INTERNATIONAL LAW AND INSTITUTIONS (1995); ANDREW T. GUZMAN, HOW INTERNATIONAL LAW WORKS: A RATIONAL CHOICE THEORY (2008); Martha Finnemore & Katherine Sikkink, *International Norm Dynamics and Political Change*, 52 INT'L ORG. 887 (1998); Thomas M. Franck, *Legitimacy in the International System*, 82 AM. J. INT'L L. 705 (1988); Ryan Goodman, *The Difference Law Makes: Research Design, Institutional Design, and Human Rights*, 98 AM. SOC. INT'L L. PROC. 198 (2004); Ryan Goodman & Derek Jinks, *How to Influence States: Socialization and International Human Rights Law*, 54 DUKE L.J. 621 (2004); Harold Hongju Koh, *Why Do Nations Obey International Law?*, 106 YALE L.J. 2599 (1997). On the power and efficacy of non-state actors in international law, *see, for example*, sources cited at *supra* note 35. Although not focused on "law" explicitly, the likes of Axelrod, Keohane, and Young also contributed to understanding the institutional mechanisms of compliance. ROBERT M. AXELROD, THE EVOLUTION OF COOPERATION (1984); ROBERT O. KEOHANE, AFTER HEGEMONY: COOPERATION AND DISCORD IN THE WORLD POLITICAL ECONOMY (1984); ROBERT O. KEOHANE, INTERNATIONAL INSTITUTIONS AND STATE POWER (1989); ORAN R. YOUNG, COMPLIANCE AND PUBLIC AUTHORITY: A THEORY WITH INTERNATIONAL APPLICATIONS (1979); ORAN R. YOUNG, INTERNATIONAL COOPERATION: BUILDING REGIMES FOR NATURAL RESOURCES AND THE ENVIRONMENT (1989). Liberal international relations scholars argue that compliance depends partly on domestic regime type. *See, e.g.*, Anne-Marie Slaughter, *International Law in a World of Liberal States*, 6 EUR. J. INT'L L. 503 (1995); Andrew Moravcsik, *Taking Preferences Seriously: A Liberal Theory of International Politics*, 51 INT'L ORGANIZATION 513 (1997).

The value of such interrogation is particularly pronounced in a scenario in which there is a widely held moral view that might seem to make sense of the law we have. As elaborated in the ensuing chapters, precisely that is the case here. In asserting the innocence of fighting in a wrongful war and the permissibility of killing soldiers even in an aggressive war, the dominant moral theory (and a popular view in society more broadly) rejects the notion that the existing treatment of soldiers is in tension with the criminalization of wrongful war. The fact that this traditional just war theory might be thought to make sense of and underpin the current legal posture heightens the importance of subjecting it to critical scrutiny on those terms.

2.3 Why the Legal Status of Soldiers' Wounds Matters

A second objection to the project would focus on the relationship between the moral burden of fighting in a wrongful war and the legal status of the war. The lived struggle described at the end of the previous chapter is rooted in soldiers' personal moral judgments about the justice of the war, not in international law. Why should this self-relational struggle be part of the motivation for exploring the normative underpinnings of the law? After all, it is not only soldiers forced to fight in *illegal* wars that feel moral pain; so too does anyone forced by law to do anything that *they deem* morally wrongful. Indeed, some significant proportion of soldiers forced to do wrong by the law's own lights will *not* be burdened precisely because they do not find the action to be morally problematic.

This much is plainly true. But whether the soldier is *right* to be burdened matters. The law's position on that question goes directly to whether it can coherently rely on the soldier's capacity to "wash her hands of guilt" in denying her the right to refuse to fight in a criminal war. As such, it goes to how the soldier ought to be treated on the law's own terms. In other words, it informs whether the soldier's burden is of a nature to ground at least a *pro tanto* legal claim.

The distinction between private moral pain and legally cognizable moral pain is obvious when applied to soldiers on the other side. The sting of injustice associated with being denied recognition, voice, and access to reparations after being wrongfully harmed or having a loved one wrongfully killed is contingent on the victim feeling that the harm was in fact wrongful. But the legal distinction between those who suffer that pain in contexts in which the felt wrong is a legal wrong and those who suffer that pain in contexts in which it is not is so obvious as to be uncontroversial.

The same point obtains on the aggressor side. A moral burden rooted in the moral judgments that underpin the law is qualitatively different from a burden rooted in the bearer's own moral judgment. Translating the latter burden into a legal claim depends on accepting a liberal pluralist premise.[45] Even having accepted that premise, determining whether to protect the individual from the burden involves gauging whether to accommodate her dissenting group given considerations of fairness, equality, feasibility, reasonableness, and the presumptive commitment to uphold the rule of law.[46] When those factors weigh against accommodation, there is no internal dissonance. Instead, there is a normative impasse.[47] The subject may feel compelled to disobey, but from the legal point of view, she is mistaken in her moral pain, and may be coherently punished for her disobedience.[48]

Debates about whether to protect conscientious objection (pacifist and selective) occur in precisely this liberal frame. The overriding question in these discussions is how far to protect and nurture the commitments of individuals when those commitments conflict with the law.[49] Wherever

[45] MICHAEL WALZER, OBLIGATIONS: ESSAYS ON DISOBEDIENCE, WAR, AND CITIZENSHIP 12 (1970).

[46] For examples of this kind of accommodation, *see, for example*, Religious Freedom Restoration Act, Pub. L. No. 103–41, 107 Stat. 1488 (Nov. 16, 1993); White House Office of the Press Secretary, Fact Sheet: Women's Preventive Services and Religious Institutions (Feb. 10, 2012). In the military context, selective conscientious objector rights are denied due to the difficulty of determining whether a genuine integrity threat actually obtains (Gillette v. US, 401 U.S. 437, 456 (1971)), the concern that exemptions would be unfair or arbitrary (*id.*; Zonstein v. Judge Advocate General [2002] H.C.J. 7622/02, para. 16 (Israel)), and the importance of upholding the authority of the initial decision and maintaining national unity (*id.* para. 14).

[47] WALZER, OBLIGATIONS, *supra* note 45, at 18.

[48] *Cf.* Simon Cabuela May, *Principled Compromise and the Abortion Controversy*, 33 PHIL. & PUB. AFF. 317, 336 (2005); Elizabeth Ashford, *Utilitarianism, Integrity and Partiality*, 97 J. PHILOSOPHY 421, 424 (2000).

[49] *See, e.g.*, WALZER, OBLIGATIONS, *supra* note 45, at 117–18, 136–38, 140–41; Leonard Hammer, *Selective Conscientious Objection and International Human Rights*, 36 ISR. L. REV. 145 (2002); David Malamet, *Selective Conscientious Objection and the Gillette Decision*, 1 PHIL. & PUB. AFF. 363 (1972); A CONFLICT OF LOYALTIES (James Finn, ed., 1968); JOHN RAWLS, A THEORY OF JUSTICE 323–26 (rev'd edn. 1999) (*but see* discussion on *id.*, at 331–35, discussed in *infra* notes 50–51); James Dao, *War and Conscience: Expanding the Definition of Conscientious Objection*, NY TIMES BLOG: AT WAR (Nov. 10, 2010); JOHN RAWLS, JUSTICE AS FAIRNESS: A RESTATEMENT 23, 111 (Erin Kelly, ed., 2001). *See also* sources cited at *supra* note 46.

one draws the line in those cases, the key point here is that there is no inherent dissonance in denying or limiting such rights by law.[50]

The situation of the soldier forced to fight in a criminal war is different. If the arguments of this book hold, the soldier who feels the pain of killing in such a war gets it *right* from the legal point of view. The imperative to take seriously her moral burden is not contingent on accepting the liberal pluralist premise. It does not depend on whether her view falls within the scope of reasonable views accepted as part of the legitimate plurality of moral postures. And the imperative to refrain from imposing that moral burden on her is not contingent on the internally defined limits of liberal toleration and accommodation. The argument of this book is that a coherent normative account of the law must recognize that such a soldier's burden is grounded in the very moral principles that lie at the heart of the international criminal regime. In that sense, when she refuses to fight in a criminal war, international law "upholds" the righteousness of her refusal.[51] When it allows her criminal punishment for doing so, the result is a profoundly dissonant moral expression.

To recognize this connection between certain soldiers' burdens and the law is not to prioritize doctrinal aesthetics. The soldier's struggle is personal. It is that of being able to live with herself. However, when that struggle is rooted in the same moral principles that underpin the law, the threat to her integrity entailed by a law that would force her to do wrong by the law's own lights is simultaneously a threat to the normative integrity of international law. The legal imposition of her moral injury cannot be solved with revised laws that better reflect the overlapping consensus of plural groups. It cannot be solved with accommodations or exemptions. It cannot be solved by persuading her and others in her position of moral principles that they currently reject. It cannot be solved with a legal rejection of her views as unreasonable and therefore not worthy of accommodation. Such responses fail because her moral burden is *internal* to the law.

Of course, not all soldiers share international law's position on the use of force. Many are driven by nationalist commitments,

[50] There is none at all if the regime does not place liberal pluralism at its normative core, and, even if it does, liberalism is internally limited on this issue. *See, e.g.*, RAWLS, *supra* note 49, 325, 333–34.

[51] This is the language used by Rawls, but without an extended assessment of the issue under discussion here. RAWLS, THEORY OF JUSTICE, *supra* note 49, at 335.

compartmentalized professionalism, or a military code of "honor."[52] Some will bear personal burdens in lawful wars. Others will fight unburdened in an illegal war. But none of this resolves the dissonance associated with the treatment of those whose burden is rooted in the moral substance of the law.

There would be a normative dishonesty in defending the existing legal regime on the grounds that its subjects reject its core normative principles, or that an all-volunteer force can solve the problem.[53] It would also be false. The long relationship of interaction and mutual influence between the law and morality of war is such that illegal wars are, on most moral understandings, also wrongful wars. This is part of what Walzer terms the "triumph" of just war theory.[54] On the rare occasions on which this is not the case, such as the so-called "illegal but legitimate" 1999 NATO intervention in Kosovo, this throws the legal standard into a state of flux, as alternative interpretations gain traction by seeking to reconcile the two normative orders.[55] The tight connection between the

[52] Gen. Douglas MacArthur, *Duty, Honor, Country*, Speech to the Corps of Cadets at the US Military Academy at West Point, NY (May 12, 1962) (combining all three in the military slogan "Duty, Honor, Country"). On nationalism here, *see* Paul W. Kahn, *American Hegemony and International Law Speaking Law to Power: Popular Sovereignty, Human Rights, and the New International Order*, 1 Chi. J. Int'l L. 1, 18 (2000); Paul W. Kahn, *Balance of Power: Redefining Sovereignty in Contemporary International Law*, 40 Stan. J. Int'l L. 259, 263, 273 (2004); John Keegan & Richard Holmes, Soldiers: A History of Men in Battle 49 (1985). On the capacity for professional compartmentalization, *see, for example*, Richard Strayer & Lewis Ellenhorn, *Vietnam Veterans: A Study Exploring Adjustment Patterns and Attitudes*, 31 J. Soc. Issues 81, 91 (1975). On masculinity and honor, *see, for example*, Keegan & Holmes, *supra*, at 21, 259, 267, 276; James H. Toner, True Faith and Allegiance 119–20 (1995); Richard A. Gabriel, To Serve with Honor: A Treatise on Military Ethics and the Way of the Soldier (1982); Parker v. Levy, 417 U.S. 733, 765 (1974) (Blackmun, J., concurring); *id.*, at 789 (Stewart, J., dissenting). *But see* Steven Pinker, The Better Angels of our Nature: Why Violence Has Declined, at ch. 8 (2011) (on its decline).

[53] *Cf.* Secretary of Defense, Robert Gates, Remarks by Secretary Gates at Duke University, North Carolina (Sept. 29, 2010). Relatedly, Walzer considers the need to use "unscrupulous or morally ignorant soldiers" when an extreme emergency demands violating the *jus in bello.* He laments, "we must look for people who are not good, and use them, and dishonor them." Michael Walzer, Just and Unjust Wars 325 (1977) [hereinafter Walzer, JUW].

[54] Michael Walzer, *The Triumph of Just War Theory (And the Dangers of Success), in* Arguing about War 3, 10–12 (2004); Walzer, JUW, *supra* note 53, at 16, 19.

[55] Kosovo catalyzed revised legal thinking on humanitarian intervention, including the articulation of the progressively developing legal doctrine of the Responsibility to Protect. *See* discussion in *infra* Section 3.3. A similar phenomenon has occurred in the realm of anticipatory self-defense. Read plainly, the text of the UN Charter clearly precludes

two is also reflected in the frequent cross-references between law and morality in this domain.[56] Many soldiers are likely to judge their wars morally using standards that closely reflect those enshrined in international law. If the arguments that follow hold, when such soldiers feel the moral burden of killing in a wrongful war, this is a pain that sounds in international law's own normative register.

anticipatory self-defense. However, most international lawyers interpret the Charter to allow for some degree of anticipatory force. This is touched on in Section 5.3 of Chapter 5, below. For a recent claim regarding a case in which law and morality might diverge, *see* Ian Hurd, *Bomb Syria, Even If It Is Illegal*, NY TIMES A27 (28 Aug., 2013).

56 The use of moral language by legal authorities in asserting the lawful or unlawful status of a war is canvassed above. Soldiers upset by the perceived wrongfulness of their wars regularly interlace claims and judgments about immorality and illegality. *See, e.g.* Kevin Tillman, After Pat's Birthday, Truthdig (Oct 19, 2006); Lt. Ehren Watada, Speech, Veterans for Peace 2006 National Convention, Seattle WA (Aug. 12, 2006); MATTHEW GUTMANN & CATHERINE LUTZ, BREAKING RANKS: IRAQ VETERANS SPEAK OUT AGAINST THE WAR 145, 165–66 (2010).

3

What Is Criminally Wrongful about Aggressive War?*

The starting point for trying to make sense of international law's posture towards soldiers is to consider what makes aggression a crime. On the orthodox normative account, aggression's criminality is rooted in a macro wrong against a foreign state, not a compound of minor wrongs against a population of individual human persons. If correct, this account might be thought to shed light on some of the issues discussed in Chapter 1. Straightforwardly, on this view, the direct crime victim would be the attacked state, not its killed or injured troops (or collaterally harmed civilians). Perhaps an argument could be made from the same premise that soldiers on the aggressor side are too far removed from that macro wrong to bear criminal liability, or even to bear any normative burden for it from the legal point of view.

The premise, however, is false. It is true that whether a war is criminally aggressive is determined ordinarily by whether it involves a particular form of interstate wrong. But that is not *why* such wars are criminal. Aggressive war is a crime because it entails killing without justification. Five reasons explain why this is so. First, banning aggression *restricts* states from using force to protect their core sovereign rights, including even their rights of political independence and territorial integrity. Those core states' rights cannot make sense of the move to ban aggression. Second, what distinguishes aggression from any other sovereignty violation – what makes *it* criminal, when no other sovereignty violation is – is not that it involves an especially egregious violation of territorial integrity or political independence, but that it involves killing without justification. Third, the unjustified killing account makes sense of aggression's standing alongside genocide, war crimes, and crimes against humanity. The traditional notion that aggression is a crime against sovereignty instead isolates aggression as the inexplicably odd crime out. Fourth, this is

* Much of the content of this chapter was previously published as the core of: Tom Dannenbaum, *Why Have We Criminalized Aggressive War?*, 126 Yale L.J. 1242 (2017).

compatible with the public reasons for restricting *jus ad bellum* rights in the early twentieth century, which focused not on infringements of states' rights but on the infliction of death without justification. Finally, references to aspects of sovereignty notwithstanding, the significance of wrongful killing to the criminality of aggression was apparent in the first prosecutions of the crime. This chapter elaborates each of these arguments in detail. First, however, it is essential to get to grips with both the contours of the orthodox account and why it is so widely held.

3.1 The Orthodox Account: The Moral Value of States

The doctrinal starting point for the orthodox account is clear. The IMT and IMTFE articulated the crime as that of waging "aggressive wars" against other "countries" or "nations," and the latter tribunal described states as the "intended victims."[1] In line with that posture, both tribunals arranged their findings regarding aggression into individual criminal wars, identified and separated by victim state.[2] On its face, the ICC amendment seems to continue that tradition, following the General Assembly's 1974 articulation in defining an aggressive war as one that violates the "sovereignty, territorial integrity or political independence of another State" or otherwise runs contrary to the UN Charter.[3]

[1] United States v. Göring et al., Judgment, *in* 22 TRIAL OF THE MAJOR WAR CRIMINALS BEFORE THE INTERNATIONAL MILITARY TRIBUNAL 411, 433 (1948) [hereinafter IMT Judgment]; United States v. Araki et al., Judgment of 12 November 1948, *in* 20 THE TOKYO WAR CRIMES TRIAL, at 49,136, 48,922, 48,936 (John Pritchard & Sonia M. Zaide, eds., 1981) [hereinafter IMTFE Judgment]. Control Council Law No. 10, Punishment of Persons Guilty of War Crimes, Crimes against Peace and against Humanity (Dec. 20, 1945), *in* 3 OFFICIAL GAZETTE CONTROL COUNCIL FOR GERMANY 50, art. II(1)(a) (1946) [hereinafter Control Council Law No. 10].

[2] *See, e.g.*, IMT Judgment, *supra* note 1, at 439–58; JULIUS STONE, AGGRESSION AND WORLD ORDER: A CRITIQUE OF UNITED NATIONS THEORIES OF AGGRESSION 136 (1958) (noting that the IMT found "that Germany had been guilty of aggression against no less than twelve States").

[3] Definition of Aggression, G.A. Res. 3314(XXIX), art. 1 (Dec. 14, 1974); Rome Statute of the International Criminal Court, U.N. Doc. A/CONF.183/9, 2187 U.N.T.S. 90, art. 8 *bis* (2) (July 17, 1998) (as amended in 2010 by Doc. C.N.651.2010.TREATIES-8) [hereinafter ICC Statute]. *See also* ICC, Elements of Crimes, ICC-PIOS-LT-03-002/15_Eng. 30 (2013), www.icc-cpi.int/resource-library/Documents/ElementsOfCrimesEng.pdf (defining the elements of the crimes of aggression, one of which is "the use of armed force by a State against the sovereignty, territorial integrity or political independence of another State"); Draft Code of Crimes against the Peace and Security of Mankind with Commentaries, Rep. of the Int'l Law Comm'n on the Work of its Forty-Eighth Session, U.N. Doc. A/51/10,

Against this background, Michael Walzer describes international law on this issue as rooted morally in a "domestic analogy," in which aggression is an infringement upon the attacked state akin to the infringement of burglary on a human person.[4] Under this "legalist paradigm," states "possess rights more or less as individuals do."[5] After all, he contends, it is "the state that claims against all other states the twin rights of territorial integrity and political sovereignty" – the rights that the crime of aggression seeks to protect.[6] Understood in this way, aggression is a morally unique international crime. Whereas genocide, war crimes, and crimes against humanity are all rooted in wrongs against human beings, the normative heart of aggression is a wrong against states. With notable exceptions,[7] precisely that assumption is reflected across the legal academic literature.[8]

art. 16(4) (1996) [hereinafter ILC, Draft Code of Crimes] ("The rule of international law which prohibits aggression applies to the conduct of a State in relation to another State").

4 MICHAEL WALZER, JUST AND UNJUST WARS 58 (1977) [hereinafter WALZER, JUW]; On the relationship between Walzer's work and the law, *see infra* note 9.

5 WALZER, JUW, *supra* note 4, at 58, 61. Identifying "'the traditional theory' of the just war, the law of war, and common-sense thought about war" as all sharing this view which McMahan himself rejects, *see* Jeff McMahan, *What Rights May Be Defended by Means of War?*, *in* THE MORALITY OF DEFENSIVE WAR 115, 118 (Cécile Fabre & Seth Lazar, eds., 2014). Using the analogy at Nuremberg, *see* Telford Taylor, Statement of the Prosecution, United States v. Göring et al., Judgment (Aug. 30, 1946), *in* 22 TRIAL OF THE MAJOR WAR CRIMINALS BEFORE THE INTERNATIONAL MILITARY TRIBUNAL 271, 280 (1948).

6 Michael Walzer, *The Moral Standing of States: A Response to Four Critics*, *in* THINKING POLITICALLY 219, 221 (David Miller, ed., 2007). *Cf.* ICC Statute, *supra* note 3, art. 8 *bis* (2) (defining an act of aggression as a "use of armed force by a State against the sovereignty, territorial integrity or political independence of another State, or in any other manner inconsistent with the Charter of the United Nations").

7 Two pieces published approximately contemporaneously with the article on which this chapter draws (Tom Dannenbaum, *Why Have We Criminalized Aggressive War?*, 126 YALE L.J. 1242 (2017) take loosely related positions, although for different reasons and with notable differences. Frédéric Mégret, *What is the Specific Evil of Aggression?*, *in* THE CRIME OF AGGRESSION: A COMMENTARY 1398 (Claus Kreß and Stefan Barriga, eds., 2016); Jens David Ohlin, *The Crime of Bootstrapping*, in *id.* 1454. A third has several passages that are also loosely in line with this way of thinking. ADIL AHMAD HAQUE, LAW AND MORALITY AT WAR (2017).

8 Carsten Stahn, *The "End," the "Beginning of the End" or the "End of the Beginning"? Introducing Debates and Voices on the Definition of "Aggression,"* 23 LEIDEN J. INT'L L. 875, 877 (2010); Jens Iverson, *Contrasting the Normative and Historical Foundations of Transitional Justice and Jus Post Bellum*, *in* JUS POST BELLUM: MAPPING THE NORMATIVE FOUNDATIONS 80, 96 (Carsten Stahn, Jennifer S. Easterday, & Jens Iverson, eds., 2014); Gerhard Werle, *Principles of International Criminal Law*, at 395, n. 1170 (2005); Oscar Solera, *Defining the Crime of Aggression*, at 427 (2007); Erin Pobjie, *Victims of the Crime of*

Seeking to make moral sense of this idea,[9] Walzer argues that it captures the genuine wrong that an aggressive war inflicts on the attacked political collective – a collective that is defined imperfectly, but, all things considered, optimally, by state borders. For him, "[t]he state is constituted by the union of people and government,"[10] and the *jus ad bellum*'s relationship to individual human beings is in its protection of their "communal rights" of self-determination.[11] "Break into the [state] enclosures," Walzer explains, "and you destroy the communities. And that destruction is a loss to the individual members."[12] In other words, if individuals are wronged when their state is invaded illegally, that wrong is suffered only indirectly, through the wrong to the political collective of which they are part.

Emphasizing the priority status of the collective here, Walzer insists that the wrong of aggression obtains irrespective of the responsiveness of the state to its members – in other words, it obtains whether or not the state is democratic or respectful of human rights and the rights of minorities. Only "when a government turns savagely upon its own people" does the morality of states that underpins the crime lose its force, because in that context the state ceases to be a viable forum for collective self-determination of any kind.[13] Notably, on that last point, Walzer is clear that his philosophical position departs from what he takes

Aggression, *in* The Crime of Aggression, *supra* note 7, 816, at 816–17, 821–22, 825–26. *See also* Section 1.4 of Chapter 1 above.

9 *Just and Unjust Wars* engages with the interstices of the law, history, and morality of Nuremberg and its legacy. Although Walzer writes that such trials "by no means exhaust the field of [moral] judgment" on the *jus ad bellum* (Walzer, JUW, *supra* note 4, at 288), the text frequently engages with the specifics of the Nuremberg cases, and is replete with moral analysis that uses the term crime rather than wrong. His starting paradigm is the "legalist paradigm." *Id.*, at 61. Here, in particular, Walzer offers a normative account of the regime. He then tweaks that account at the margins to accommodate moral concerns that he believes are inadequately addressed by that framework. On the links between Walzer's work and the law, *see, for example*, Haque, *supra* note 7, at 21. Walzer's account has achieved such influence that he has been termed the "dean of contemporary just war theorists." Brian Orend, *War*, *in* The Stanford Encyclopedia of Philosophy (Spring 2016 edn) (Edward N. Zalta, ed., 2008).

10 Walzer, *The Moral Standing of States*, *supra* note 6, at 221.

11 *Id.*, at 230. *See also* Walzer, JUW, *supra* note 4, at 61, 90, 96 (discussing aggression's violation of the "communal autonomy" of the state and the "right of men and women to build a common life").

12 Walzer, *The Moral Standing of States*, *supra* note 6, at 234.

13 Walzer, JUW, *supra* note 4, at 101. *See generally id.*, at 101–08 (discussing humanitarian intervention). It is in this scenario that the law's equation of political collective and state is, for Walzer, imperfect.

to be the moral underpinnings of the law.[14] With that caveat, Walzer not only identifies in international law on this issue an unequivocally statist normative posture, he defends that posture as morally appropriate.[15] For him, the crime of aggression captures a real wrong – a wrong against the state, the moral value of which is derived from its function as a site of collective self-determination.

This view of the wrong of aggression occurring at the interstate level is widely shared both as a premise of doctrinal work and among legal theorists.[16] Paul Kahn, for example, contends that the criminalization of aggression at Nuremberg represented and initiated a "new legal regime founded on protecting state sovereignty."[17] Like Walzer, Kahn sees this prohibition as an effort to ban and condemn violations of "positive sovereignty, understood as the self-formation of a people" in a state whose boundaries allow that people to function as "a single, collective actor."[18] Similarly, Christopher Kutz argues that aggression's wrong is in denying the target state's people the chance to make "their politics on their own" – a denial that Kutz argues wrongs non-democratic peoples no less than democratic ones.[19] Although each of these theorists identifies the political collective as the sovereign that is wronged by aggression, the key point is that for each, that macro wrong cannot be "reduced," in David Rodin's words, to an aggregation of harms against individuals.[20]

Larry May arrives at a similar conclusion without relying on self-determination. He argues that "aggression is morally wrong because it

[14] *Id.*, at 86.

[15] Walzer, JUW, *supra* note 4, at 51–108. *See also* David Luban, *Preventive War*, 32 Phil. & Pub. Aff. 207, 211–13, 211 n.2 (2004) (noting that Walzer's core normative account of the legalist paradigm "represent[s] [Walzer's moral] baseline, not his final position [which accommodates humanitarian intervention, for example]. But the [sovereignty-focused] baseline captures the core of the Charter system"); Charles R. Beitz, *Bounded Morality: Justice and the State in World Politics*, 33 Int'l Org. 405, 408–09 (1979) (discussing Walzer's theory in relation to other theories about the "morality of states").

[16] On the connection to doctrinal work, *see supra* note 8.

[17] Paul W. Kahn, Sacred Violence: Torture, Terror, and Sovereignty 54–55 (2008).

[18] Paul W. Kahn, *The Question of Sovereignty*, 40 Stan. J. Int'l L. 259, 262–63 (2004).

[19] Christopher Kutz, *Democracy, Defence, and the Threat of Intervention*, *in* The Morality of Defensive War, *supra* note 5, at 229, 231, 236. Unlike Walzer and Kahn, Kutz does not link this moral theory to the law. However, by locating the moral violation at the heart of aggression in its negation of collective autonomy through its infringement of states' rights, he buttresses Walzer's dominant account of the legal regime. *Id.*, at 237, 241–42.

[20] David Rodin, War and Self-Defense 6, 127–32 (2002).

destabilizes States that generally protect human rights more than they curtail them."[21] For May, then, the state's value lies in its service to human beings, rather than in its approximation of the political collective. Nonetheless, on his theory, the wrong of aggression remains a wrong against the state. This, he argues, has implications not just for how we understand the victim, but also how we define the perpetrator. Precisely because the wrong at the core of the crime of aggression occurs on the macro level, "the acts of individuals that make up war are conceptually and normatively distinct from the State aggression."[22] For May, this raises a question about how we can hold even high-ranking individuals, "criminally liable for invading Poland," since the core interstate wrong is simply not something that they can commit.[23]

Of course, crimes against humanity and genocide have collective elements of their own: the former involves a widespread and systematic attack; the latter, an intent to destroy a group. But what distinguishes aggression for May is that the micro contributions of the participants in an aggressive war "are not themselves criminal,"[24] and, indeed, are "not themselves wrong independent of what is going on at the State level."[25] Accordingly, he contends that rooting the wrong of aggression in the component killings and destruction would provide "no relevant moral distinction between aggressive wars and defensive wars."[26] The result, May explains, is that aggression is not a wrong that individuals ("even lots of them") can commit, unless they control the state itself.[27] High-ranking officials can be morally connected to that interstate wrong only if they combine the right level of control over the state with the intention to shape state action.[28] From this perspective, the macro nature of the crime is two-dimensional.[29] The moral wrong at the core of aggression is a wrong inflicted on a victim state (or at least the collective it represents) by individuals acting through a perpetrator state.[30]

Setting aside their differences for the moment, as a broad matter, the theories advanced by the likes of Walzer, Kutz, Kahn, and May are potentially attractive as candidate normative accounts of the law we have,

[21] LARRY MAY, AGGRESSION AND CRIMES AGAINST PEACE 6–7 (2008). [22] *Id.*, at 15.
[23] *Id.*, at 250–51. [24] *Id.*, at 229. [25] *Id.*, at 256. [26] *Id.*, at 339. [27] *Id.*, at 256.
[28] *Id.*, at 254.
[29] Walzer, too, suggests the macro feature of the crime is two-dimensional – with the wrong inflicted *on a victim state* by individuals acting *through a perpetrator state*. *See supra* note 6 and accompanying text.
[30] ILC, Draft Code of Crimes, *supra* note 3, at 43, para. 4, cmt. to art. 16; STONE, *supra* note 2, at 141.

because they seem to make sense of important features of the crime. Most notably, they explain why the crime occurs only when there is an interstate violation and why individual criminal liability turns on holding the power and influence to act through an aggressor state. They also offer the beginnings of an explanation of why the law takes the posture it does towards soldiers on either side of an aggressive war.

The appeal of something like this normative account of the crime is emphasized by the fact that it is accepted also by many who oppose the criminalization of aggression. Those in this position agree that the crime is rooted in a purported moral wrong "against a state" as opposed to "violations against individuals."[31] It is just that for them, this is precisely why it ought not to be an international crime.

Along these lines, David Luban argues that the inclusion of aggression in the Nuremberg prosecutions "compromised" the trial's key achievements.[32] Whereas other elements of the trial, such as the inclusion of crimes against humanity, the removal of official immunity, and the duty to disobey internationally illegal domestic laws, promised a limit on sovereignty "in the name of 'humanity,'" the criminalization of aggression pushed in the other direction, "fortif[ying]" sovereignty against outside interference.[33] The trials' "central achievement" of recognizing crimes against humanity was thus undermined, leaving "a legacy that is at best equivocal and at worst immoral."[34] Ultimately, Luban considers the criminalization of aggression to have been "a major moral enemy of the human rights movement."[35]

Reacting to ICC amendments, Erin Creegan has offered an updated version of this sentiment. She contends, "Without adversely affected

[31] Letter from Aryeh Neier, President, Open Society Institute et al. to Foreign Ministers, "Regarding the Crime of Aggression" (May 10, 2010), www.opensocietyfoundations.org/sites/default/files/icc-aggression-letter-20100511.pdf [https://perma.cc/G9GX-2FSX]. *See also International Criminal Court: Amnesty International's Call for Pledges by States at the 13th Session of the Assembly of States Parties*, AMNESTY INT'L 5, n.18 (Oct. 29, 2014), www.amnesty.org/download/Documents/8000/ior530102014en.pdf [https://perma.cc/PW47-HZGA]; David Luban, *Just War and Human Rights*, 9 PHIL. & PUB. AFF. 160, 164, 166 (1980); DAVID LUBAN, LEGAL MODERNISM, 335, 337 (1994); Erin Creegan, *Justified Uses of Force and the Crime of Aggression*, 10 J. INT'L CRIM. JUSTICE 59, 62 (2012).

[32] LUBAN, LEGAL MODERNISM, *supra* note 31, at 335. *See also id.*, at 337 (arguing that the General Assembly cast aggression as "the violation of sovereignty" in 1974, in keeping with the "spirit of Nuremberg").

[33] LUBAN, LEGAL MODERNISM, *supra* note 31, at 337–39. [34] *Id.*, at 335–37.

[35] *Id.*, at 341.

human victims, it is hard to put a crime like aggression in a category similar to war crimes or crimes against humanity or genocide. And it does not seem to belong next to them; it almost demeans them."[36] She describes human beings' rights not to be subject to the wrongs of genocide, war crimes, and crimes against humanity as "infinitely more" powerful than the right of states not to be the victims of aggression.[37]

The interesting point here is the internal premise shared by both defenders of the criminalization of aggression such as Walzer, and critics of its criminalization such as Luban. Despite disagreeing morally on what position the law ought to take, they agree fundamentally on a shared normative account of the crime we have.[38] If they are right, perhaps the positions discussed in Chapter 1 are coherent. After all, if aggression is in fact a crime of state against state, the natural conclusion would be that the attacked state is indeed the core crime victim. Any alternative victim focus in an ICC aggression prosecution would require a significant shift in the Court's jurisprudence on crime victims.[39] Similarly, if the criminal wrong of aggression occurs exclusively on this macro level, perhaps it makes sense that only those with control over the aggressor state can be held criminally liable. For other participants, including the vast majority of the military, the criminal wrong would fall outside their "sphere of activity."[40] Although more would need to be said on this, soldiers' remoteness from that macro criminal wrong might also be thought to mean, from the legal point of view, that they ought to be able to "wash their hands of guilt" when they participate in a criminally aggressive war.[41]

[36] Creegan, *supra* note 31, at 63. [37] *Id.*, at 68.

[38] Notably, Luban describes Walzer's as "the best defense I know" of the crime of aggression and the focus on sovereignty at its moral core. LUBAN, LEGAL MODERNISM, *supra* note 31, at 342–43 n.19.

[39] Recognizing that the inclusion of persons other than the state would require a deviation from existing ICC jurisprudence, but arguing for such a shift, *see* Pobjie, *supra* note 8, at 816–22, 826–31.

[40] WALZER, JUW, *supra* note 4, at 39, 304. Taking that view as a matter of normative theory, *see* Paul W. Kahn, *The Paradox of Riskless Warfare*, 22 PHILOSOPHY & PUB. POL'Y 2, 2 (2002); Dan Zupan, *A Presumption of the Moral Equality of Combatants: A Citizen-Soldier's Perspective, in* JUST AND UNJUST WARRIORS: THE MORAL AND LEGAL STATUS OF SOLDIERS 214, 214 (David Rodin & Henry Shue, eds. 2008). Articulating the view in legal context, *see* Robert H. Jackson, The United Nations Organization and War Crimes, Address Delivered at the American Society of International Law, Washington DC (Apr. 26, 1952); United States v. von Leeb, 11 TRIALS OF WAR CRIMINALS BEFORE THE NUERNBERG MILITARY TRIBUNALS UNDER CONTROL COUNCIL LAW NO. 10 , at 462, 488 (1949) [hereinafter High Command Judgment].

[41] *See* Section 1.3 of Chapter 1 above.

3.2 The Wrong of Criminal Aggression: Unjustified Killing and Violence

The premise, however, is false. The normative core of the crime of aggression is not a morality of states' or political collectives' rights, but a morality that condemns the unjustified killing of human persons. To be clear, the position advanced here is not that sovereignty is irrelevant to the crime of aggression. Under current international law, *whether* a war is criminal is determined in part by whether it violates the "sovereignty, territorial integrity or political independence of another State" or is otherwise "inconsistent with the Charter of the United Nations."[42] In other words, *which* wars are wrongful is a macro-level question that depends typically, although not exclusively, on which side has violated the other's sovereignty.

But that interstate breach is not *why* waging such wars is criminal. Waging war in breach of those interstate rules is a crime because it entails widespread killing and the infliction of human suffering without justification. Seen in this way, aggression is a modified form of crime against humanity, perpetrated ordinarily through a violation of sovereignty.[43]

To understand why this must be the case, consider the point from five perspectives. First, the concept of sovereign rights is indeterminate as a normative guide on the issue of aggression. The criminalization of such wars is as great a restraint on state sovereignty as it is a protection of it. Moreover, interstate violations that more effectively and severely infringe core sovereign rights than does aggressive war are not criminal. Second, what distinguishes aggression from any other sovereignty violation is that it involves killing without the justification of responding to human violence or its immediate threat. Other forms of killing without justification are criminal in another form. By protecting combatants' and

[42] ICC Statute, *supra* note 3, art. 8 *bis* (2).

[43] Arguing that aggression could be prosecuted as a crime against humanity under the "other inhumane acts" provision of article 7 of the Rome Statute, *see* Benjamin B. Ferencz, *The Illegal Use of Armed Force as a Crime against Humanity*, 2 J. USE OF FORCE & INT'L L. 187 (2015); Benjamin B. Ferencz, *Aggressive War: The Biggest Crime against Humanity*, 43 STUD. TRANSNAT'L LEGAL POL'Y 31 (2011). There is, however, a key difference between aggression and the formal category of crimes against humanity – a difference that is crucially important as a matter of the law's normative expression. The latter involves the perpetration of wrongs against a *civilian* population, whereas the former is concerned centrally with wrongs perpetrated against combatants. *Cf.* ICC Statute, *supra* note 3, art. 7; *infra* note 94 and accompanying text and Section 3.2.2 below.

collateral civilians' right to life, the criminalization of aggression fills a crucial gap in that broader criminal-law approach to unjustified killing. Third, understanding aggression in this way reconciles its criminalization to the so-called "humanization" of international law – the rise of the human being as a normative focal point in legal interpretation and doctrinal development. This phenomenon is manifest especially clearly in international criminal law. Fourth, the claimed imperative to incorporate a restrictive *jus ad bellum* into twentieth-century international law was articulated not in terms of sovereignty, but in terms of human suffering. Finally, wrongful killing was normatively central to the reasoning of the judges and prosecutors at Nuremberg and Tokyo on the crime of aggression. Ultimately, states' rights are important in structuring when the use of force is permitted, but aggression is a crime about the infliction of human death and suffering without justification.

Recognizing the criminal wrong of aggression to be the infliction of unjustified human violence suggests that legal interpretation and thinking in this domain might be better illuminated by a recent, revisionist tranche of just war theory than has thus far been recognized. A growing cohort of moral theorists has countered the longstanding Walzerian orthodoxy that the *jus ad bellum* can be restricted morally to the macro level, with no implications for the rights or wrongs of the constituent actions.[44] Led by Jeff McMahan, these revisionists have for the most part avoided engagement with international law, criticizing Walzer for what they consider to be a conflation of the law and the morality of war.[45] One

[44] *See generally* many of the contributions to the edited volume JUST AND UNJUST WARRIORS, *supra* note 40, which is structured around the moral equality of combatants question, with voices on both sides. In addition to Jeff McMahan, *infra* note 45, who has been particularly prolific on this issue, *see, for example*, David Rodin, *Two Emerging Issues of Jus Post Bellum*, *in* JUS POST BELLUM: TOWARDS A LAW OF TRANSITION FROM CONFLICT TO PEACE, 53, 68–75 (Carsten Stahn & Jann K. Kleffner, eds., 2008); RODIN, *supra* note 20, at 165–73; David R. Mapel, *Response to War and Self-Defense: Innocent Attackers and Rights of Self-Defense*, 18 ETHICS & INT'L AFF'S 81 (2004).

[45] JEFF MCMAHAN, KILLING IN WAR 105 (2009) (describing a "ubiquitous tendency to conflate the morality of war with the law of war"); *id.*, at 112 (on Walzer); Jeff McMahan, *Killing in War: A Reply to Walzer*, 34 PHILOSOPHIA 47, 51 (2006) ("Walzer believes that what he calls the war convention is just an adaptation, developed over many centuries, of our ordinary morality to the circumstances of war. But again I have doubts"). Walzer, for his part, argues, "What Jeff McMahan means to provide . . . is a careful and precise account of individual responsibility in time of war. What he actually provides, I think, is a careful and precise account of what individual responsibility in war would be like if war were a peacetime activity." Michael Walzer, *Response to McMahan's Paper*, 34 PHILOSOPHIA 43, 43 (2006).

of the upshots of the arguments in this chapter is that these philosophical critics may have more to say about the internal normativity of the existing legal regime than they or international lawyers have understood.

3.2.1 Sovereignty Cannot Explain Why Aggression Is Criminal

When it comes to war, sovereignty cuts both ways. Although banning aggressive war has protected certain sovereign rights, it has also limited the sovereign's capacity to assert and protect many of its other rights. Indeed, despite his framing of Nuremberg and the UN Charter as moves towards protecting sovereignty,[46] Kahn recognizes that on a maximal vision of sovereignty in international affairs, "there is no difference between protection and assertion: To protect the state is to assert its power to defend its 'vital interests.'"[47]

Prior to Nuremberg, and certainly prior to Kellogg–Briand, international law reflected precisely that principle: states had the power and authority to use violence to punish or seek to end non-violent infringements of their legal rights.[48] They could wage war to settle a dispute, reverse a wrongful seizure, or otherwise retake what was rightfully theirs.[49] Capturing this core doctrine, Vattel wrote simply, "Whatever

[46] *See supra* notes 17–18 and accompanying text. [47] Kahn, *supra* note 18, at 263.

[48] Hans Kelsen, General Theory of Law and State 331 (Anders Wedberg trans., 1945); Oona Hathaway & Scott Shapiro, The Internationalists chs. 1–4 (2017); Stephen C. Neff, War and the Law of Nations: A General History 225–39 (2005); 3 Robert Phillimore, Commentaries upon International Law 18–22 (2nd edn 1873); *Le Régime de Représailles en Temps de Paix*, Annuaire Institut de Droit International 708–711 (Institut de Droit International 1934); Linos-Alexander Sicilianos, *The Relationship between Reprisals and Denunciation or Suspension of a Treaty*, 4 Eur. J. Int'l L. 341, 351–52 (1993).

[49] Hathaway & Shapiro, *supra* note 48, chs. 1–4. *See, e.g.*, Convention Respecting the Limitation of the Employment of Force for the Recovery of Contract Debts, art. 1, Oct. 18, 1907, 36 Stat. 2241 (prohibiting the recourse to armed force for the recovery of contractual debts *only if* the debtor state submits to an offer of arbitral settlement and complies with the subsequent award); Convention for the Pacific Settlement of International Disputes, art. 1, July 29, 1899, 32 Stat. 1799 (requiring only that signatories "use their *best efforts* to insure the pacific settlement of international differences" (emphasis added)); Emmer de Vattel, The Law of Nations, or, Principles of the Law of Nature, Applied to the Conduct and Affairs of Nations and Sovereigns, §§ 333, 342 (Béla Kapossy & Richard Whatmore, eds., Liberty Fund rev. edn 2008) (1758). Even the Covenant of the League of Nations allowed states to resolve international disputes with force, as long as they first submitted the dispute to the League of Nations Council (or arbitration or judicial settlement), and waited for a cooling off period of nine months (six awaiting the ruling and three following the ruling). In the case of a

strikes at [a sovereign state's] rights is an injury, and a just cause of war."[50] The use of force was the key tool of law enforcement and sovereignty *vindication* in an international regime focused on interstate relations and state rights.[51] In the absence of a system of global institutions by which the "right" in any dispute could be verified, states also had the sovereign authority to determine whether such vindication was called for.[52]

In one sense, this system rendered states vulnerable to armed attack. But this was not because state's rights were unimportant. Rather, the animating premise was that it was inconceivable that the state's authority to determine whether force was necessary to protect its legal rights could be abrogated.[53] The sovereign stood above international law.[54] From that position of priority, what was truly defensive of its rights was necessarily something "that a state had to judge for itself."[55] Understood in this way, sovereignty "resists [the] universalization" upon which any genuinely restrictive *jus ad bellum* depends.[56]

Recognizing this assertive dimension of sovereignty is crucial. Precisely because it lacked any meaningful *jus ad bellum* restraint, the pre-Nuremberg/pre-Kellogg–Briand era was the high-water mark of sovereignty in international law. Thus, rather than asserting that banning war

Council referral, force would only be banned if the Council were unanimous and the other state complied with its ruling. *See* League of Nations Covenant, arts. 12–16.

50 VATTEL, *supra* note 49, at § 26. *See also* Francisco Suárez, *On War (Disputation XIII, De Triplici Virtue Theologica: Charitate)* (1610), in SELECTIONS FROM THREE WORKS, § IV.4 (at p. 817) (Gladys L. Williams, Ammi Brown, & John Waldron, trans., Clarendon Press 1944).

51 HANS KELSEN, PRINCIPLES OF INTERNATIONAL LAW 33–34 (1st edn 1952); CHARLES G. FENWICK, INTERNATIONAL LAW 4 (3rd edn 1948); WILLIAM EDWARD HALL, A TREATISE ON INTERNATIONAL LAW 61 (7th edn 1917).

52 HERBERT WHITTAKER BRIGGS, THE LAW OF NATIONS: CASES, DOCUMENTS, AND NOTES 976 (2nd edn 1952); YORAM DINSTEIN, WAR, AGGRESSION AND SELF-DEFENCE 78–79 (5th edn 2012); HALL, *supra* note 88, at 61–62; W. Michael Reisman, Editorial Comment, *Coercion and Self-Determination: Construing Charter Article 2(4)*, 78 AM. J. INT'L L. 642 (1984).

53 FRANCIS LIEBER, GENERAL ORDER NO. 100: INSTRUCTIONS FOR THE GOVERNMENT OF ARMIES OF THE UNITED STATES IN THE FIELD 18 (New York, D. Van Nostrand 1863) ("The law of nations allows every sovereign government to make war upon another sovereign state"). On one reading, states retained the authority to wage war not only to enforce their existing legal rights, but also to initiate legal change in the absence of a global legislature. Josef L. Kunz, Editorial Comment, *Bellum Justum and Bellum Legale*, 45 AM. J. INT'L L. 528, 528 (1951).

54 Channeling Carl Schmitt, *see* Kahn, *supra* note 18, at 263.

55 *Id.*, at 263 n.18.

56 *Id.*, at 276.

would erect "a wall around sovereignty,"[57] Salmon Levinson – a vanguard advocate for what ultimately became the Kellogg–Briand Pact – felt compelled to rebut the allegation that allowing this "check upon [the state's] original unlimited power" would unjustifiably "invade" and "impair" core sovereign rights.[58] Accepting that adopting the prohibition would limit sovereignty, Levinson insisted that the retention of the sovereign right to use force at its own discretion was morally indefensible.[59] Along similar lines, Frank Kellogg acknowledged in a public address after the signing of the Pact that the key obstacle facing the drafters had been the longstanding notion that waging war was simply "a nation's legal right."[60]

Of course, although the criminalization of aggression and the prohibition against the use of force have limited sovereignty in this way, the new regime has also enhanced states' legal protection against armed attack.[61] However, that newly protected dimension is just one element of sovereignty. Precisely because of the elevation of that element, all other aspects of sovereignty lost the unilateral vindication mechanism upon which they had depended.[62] The assertion and protection of those other rights have been taken away from the sovereign and transferred to the global collective.[63]

The obvious defense of the traditional account here would be to argue that the ban on aggression prohibited and criminalized the *most severe* violation of state sovereignty in exchange for eliminating lesser sovereign rights. Had that been the exchange, a sovereignty-focused account could

57 *Cf.* Luban, Legal Modernism, *supra* note 31, at 337.

58 Salmon O. Levinson, Outlawry of War 12, 21 (1921). On Levinson's role in the move to ban war, *see* William Hard, *The Outlawry of War*, 120 Annals Am. Acad. Pol. & Soc. Sci. 136, 136 (1925); Hathaway & Shapiro, *supra* note 48, ch. 5.

59 Levinson, *supra* note 58, at 22 ("A sovereign nation that would set itself up above all the laws of justice in its dealings with other nations is unworthy to retain its sovereignty").

60 Frank B. Kellogg, Former US Sec'y of State, The Pact of Paris and the Relationship of the United States to the World Community, Address Delivered over the Columbia Broadcasting System (Oct. 30, 1935), http://avalon.law.yale.edu/20th_century/kb1935.asp [https://perma.cc/AUF5-MKAX].

61 In that narrow sense, despite the restrictions that this legal shift placed on a slew of sovereign rights, Kahn and Luban are not wrong to use the language of protection to describe the relationship between sovereignty and the criminalization of aggression. *See supra* notes 17, 31.

62 On the role of the ban on war in transforming war from a system of unilateral enforcement to a system of collective enforcement, *see* Hathaway & Shapiro, The Internationalists, *supra* note 48.

63 *Id.*

explain why aggression, alone among sovereignty violations, is an international crime and a violation of *jus cogens*.[64] The explanation would be that aggression has this special status because it is the interstate violation most profoundly detrimental to the essential elements of sovereignty.

This, however, is not the case. Put to one side all of the sovereignty rights given up in the ban on the use of force and consider in isolation the sovereign rights at the crux of today's *jus ad bellum*: political independence and territorial integrity.[65] On these issues alone, aggression is not uniquely harmful. A criminal use of force can be far more modest in its diminution, and even intended diminution, of these rights than would be non-belligerent, non-criminal infringements of the same rights.

Consider, for example, the non-belligerent installation of a puppet regime in a foreign state through the manipulation of its elections.[66] Puppet regimes create principal–agent problems for the intervening state, and democratic manipulation will not always work flawlessly, but such illegal actions would infringe on political independence and self-determination profoundly, and often to a greater extent than is even *intended* by an illegal military attack.[67] And yet such non-violent

[64] *Cf.* Military and Paramilitary Activities in and against Nicaragua (Nicar. v. US), Judgment, 1986 I.C.J. 14 (June 27), para. 205 (the use of force is a "particularly obvious" violation of sovereignty, but the category extends to any intervention in a state's "choice of a political, economic, social and cultural system" and "foreign policy," among other things). Detailing various non-violent sovereignty violations, *see* Respect for the Principles of National Sovereignty and Non-Interference in the Internal Affairs of States in their Electoral Processes, G.A. Res. 52/119 (Feb. 23, 1998); Declaration on the Inadmissibility of Intervention and Interference in the Internal Affairs of States, G.A. Res. 36/103, annex (Dec. 9, 1981); and Declaration on Principles of International Law Concerning Friendly Relations and Co-operation among States in Accordance with the Charter of the United Nations, G.A. Res. 2625(XXV), 122–23 (Oct. 24, 1970) [hereinafter Friendly Relations Declaration].

[65] *See* UN Charter, art. 2, para. 4; ICC Statute, *supra* note 3, art. 8 *bis*.

[66] On the installation of a puppet regime as a sovereignty violation, *see* sources cited in *supra* note 64. The Nuremberg judges knew well how effectively the installation of a puppet regime can eviscerate a state's political independence. *See* IMT Judgment, *supra* note 1, at 433–36, 573. For brief discussions of historical cases and future dangers of foreign electoral manipulation, *see, for example*, Jack Goldsmith, *What is Old, and New, and Scary in Russia's Probable DNC Hack*, LAWFARE (July 25, 2016), https://lawfareblog.com/what-old-and-new-and-scary-russias-probable-dnc-hack [https://perma.cc/R35B-A7DW]; and Bruce Schneier, *By November, Russian Hackers Could Target Voting Machines*, WASHINGTON POST (July 27, 2016), www.washingtonpost.com/posteverything/wp/2016/07/27/by-november-russian-hackers-could-target-voting-machines/ [https://perma.cc/FHU9-UML9].

[67] Cécile Fabre has argued correctly that, to be consistent, Walzerian just war theory would need to classify such action as an aggression warranting defensive force. Cécile Fabre,

interventions are clearly not internationally criminal, since they lack "the use of armed force."[68]

The same applies to non-violent violations of territorial integrity. Failing to hand over territory to a lawfully seceding entity, holding another state's territory following a misguided handover from a departing former colonial power, or illegally manipulating an independence referendum in a way that triggers an effective secession are all severe infringements of another state's territorial integrity.[69] However, without an armed attack, none would be internationally criminal.[70]

In contrast, examples of criminal aggression listed in the ICC amendment, such as aerial bombardment or an attack on a foreign state's naval fleet, may do very little to undermine the victim state's self-determination, territorial integrity, or political independence.[71] The same is true of drone strike campaigns against non-state actors in a foreign territory, which are perfectly compatible with leaving intact the political independence and territorial integrity of the host state.[72] The point is not just that such belligerent acts may prove unsuccessful in taking territory or overthrowing the government.[73] More fundamentally, it is that

Cosmopolitanism and Wars of Self-Defence, *in* THE MORALITY OF DEFENSIVE WAR, *supra* note 5, at 90, 103–04. Asserting precisely such a claim in moral theory (but not as a matter of law), *see* Kutz, *supra* note 19, at 242–43.

68 ICC Statute, *supra* note 3, art. 8 *bis* (2). This exclusive focus on *armed* force, explicit in the criminal provision, is also generally understood to apply to article 2, para. 4 of the UN Charter. *See, e.g.*, Washington Conference Use of Force Committee, *Report on Aggression and the Use of Force*, INT'L L. ASS'N, §§ A.2, C.3 (2014), www.ila-hq.org/en/committees/index.cfm/cid/1036 [https://perma.cc/QM4M-MAPE].

69 For an example of the first case, *see* Land and Maritime Boundary between Cameroon and Nigeria (Cameroon v. Nigeria), Judgment, 2002 I.C.J. 303 (Oct. 10).

70 Whether actions like Russia's role in the 2014 Crimean referendum qualify as criminal aggressions is discussed in Sections IV.A and V.A, *infra*. The best interpretation is that they do not, but they are marginal cases. Crucially, however, if they are criminal, it is because of their latent human violence.

71 ICC Statute, *supra* note 3, art. 8 *bis* (2).

72 *Cf.* H. of Lords H. of Commons Joint Comm'n on Human Rights, The Government's Policy on the Use of Drones for Targeted Killing, Second Report of Session 2015–16, HL Paper 141 HC 574, para. 3.40 (May 10, 2016) (UK), https://publications.parliament.uk/pa/jt201516/jtselect/jtrights/574/574.pdf (indicating that an assertion of the right to target "any member of ISIL/Da'esh anywhere" in the world is incompatible with the *jus ad bellum*).

73 Consider, for example, Iraq's failed aggression against Iran. *See* Further Report of the Secretary-General on the Implementation of Security Council Resolution 598 (1987), U.N. SCOR, 46th Sess., paras. 5–7, U.N. Doc. S/23273 (Dec. 9, 1991), *reprinted in* R. K. Ramazani, *Who Started the Iraq–Iran War?: A Commentary*, 33 VA. J. INT'L L. 69, 84–85, 87–89 (1992) [hereinafter Further Report of the Secretary-General]; *see also*

criminal aggression need not even pursue the *objective* of undermining significantly those core elements of sovereignty.[74]

The fact that belligerent actions with minimal impact or intended impact on sovereignty are criminal, while non-violent infringements of political independence and territorial integrity are not, cannot be explained with reference to the *degree* to which each action violates those core sovereignty rights. If that were the standard, the outcomes would be reversed. The crime as currently constituted must be explained by something else.

3.2.2 *Unjustified Killing Makes Sense of Aggression's Criminality*

Far more robust as a normative explanation of the crime than the fact or degree of aggression's violation of sovereignty or states' rights is the *form* of that violation, the *means* by which it is perpetrated.[75] What is unique about illegal war among violations of states' rights – what makes *it* criminal, when no other sovereignty violation is – is the fact that it entails the slaughter of *human* life, the infliction of *human* suffering, and the erosion of *human* security. To qualify as aggression, those harms must occur ordinarily (although not exclusively) in an unjustified attack in which one state infringes the core sovereign rights of another. However, it is the unjustified killing and infliction of human suffering, and not the violation of sovereignty, that are the wrongs at the heart of aggression. Consider three ways in which this is so.

First, even within the category of violent interstate interactions, the *reason* that a particular aggressive attack is unjustified is not that it infringes the target state's territorial integrity or political independence. Assuming no Security Council authorization, what determines that one side of an international armed conflict is in violation of the *jus ad bellum* is that it does not

Ige F. Dekker, *Criminal Responsibility and the Gulf War of 1980–1988: The Crime of Aggression*, *in* THE GULF WAR OF 1980–1988: THE IRAN–IRAQ WAR IN INTERNATIONAL LEGAL PERSPECTIVE 249, 268 (Ige F. Dekker & Harry H. G. Post, eds., 1992) (arguing that Iraq engaged in a criminal war of aggression).

74 A proposal to limit criminal aggression to uses of force seeking to take territory or overthrow a government was rejected. Proposal Submitted by Germany: Definition of the Crime of Aggression, 30 July 1999, U.N. Doc. PCNICC/1999/DP.13. Consider also the Security Council's finding that Israeli airstrikes in Tunis in 1985 amounted to aggression, even though the target was the PLO headquarters, not Tunisian governmental targets, and there was no effort to take territory. S.C. Res. 573 (Oct. 4, 1985); *see also infra* notes 95–106 and accompanying text.

75 *Cf.* McMahan, *supra* note 5, at 117 (on the importance of the means–ends distinction in understanding what makes aggressive war morally wrong).

respond to an *armed* attack.[76] Therefore, the use of force seeking to *remedy or prevent* a severe but non-violent infringement of political independence or self-determination, such as the manipulation of its elections through hacking, would be illegal and could qualify as an act of criminal aggression.[77] Similarly, according to the Ethiopia–Eritrea Claims Commission, it is a *jus ad bellum* violation, and thus at least potentially criminal, for a state to use force to *recover* its own territory, if that retaking does not respond to an armed attack.[78] Indeed, even when one state controls another's territory following an armed attack by the former, if the latter's forcible response is sufficiently delayed, it too would be illegal and potentially criminal.[79]

On the other hand, a defensive use of force that has a significant and intended impact on the aggressor's internal structures of government or its territory would be lawful as long as that force were necessary and proportionate to stopping the armed attack. The paradigmatically lawful wars against Germany and Japan in World War II each led to long-term occupations and regime changes, not to mention Germany's territorial and political fragmentation for half a century.

Moreover, using force in response to a foreign armed attack is lawful, even if that attack does not threaten the victim's territorial integrity or political independence.[80] Indeed, according to the Ethiopia–Eritrea ruling, such defensive uses of force are lawful even if the objective is merely to defend the attacked state's personnel while they are exercising peaceful control over the aggressor's *own* sovereign territory.[81]

[76] UN Charter, art. 2(4) & ch. VII (especially art. 51). *See also* sources cited *supra* note 64.

[77] *Cf.* Fabre, *supra* note 67, at 104–05 (analyzing the morality of hypothetical forcible responses to interference with the right to vote).

[78] Partial Award: *Jus ad Bellum* – Ethiopia's Claims 1–8 (Eri. v. Eth.), 16 R.I.A.A. 457, 464–67 (Eri.–Eth. Claims Comm'n 2005); *cf.* Friendly Relations Declaration, *supra* note 64, at 122. The Claims Commission did not find this particular action to be a criminal aggression. However, since it was a violation of the UN Charter, it could have qualified as aggression under the ICC Statute, had it been of the requisite character, gravity, and scale (thresholds it may well have surpassed had Badme not been a tiny, low-population border town). ICC Statute, *supra* note 3, art. 8 *bis* (1–2). Criticizing the Claims Commission's approach to the fact that Eritrea's armed attack was inflicted on Ethiopian forces on Eritrean territory, *see* Christine Gray, *The Eritrea/Ethiopia Claims Commission Oversteps its Boundaries: A Partial Award?* 17 EUR. J. INT'L L. 699, 710–18 (2006).

[79] *See* DINSTEIN, *supra* note 52, at 230–33.

[80] *See, e.g.*, Case Concerning Oil Platforms (Iran v. US), Judgment, I.C.J. 161, para. 72 (Nov. 6, 2003) ("The Court does not exclude the possibility that the mining of a single military vessel might be sufficient to bring into play the 'inherent right of self-defence'").

[81] *See* sources cited *supra* note 78 (Ethiopia was found not to have violated the *jus ad bellum* in defending itself against Eritrea's effort to retake Badme).

What unifies these cases is that a lawful use of force must respond to an international attack on, or threat to, the lives of its human subjects; that is what it means for an attack to be *armed*.[82] Of course, territorial integrity and political independence are often protected by defensive war and violated by aggressive war. But the legal realities discussed above indicate the overriding importance of human life and physical integrity. Severe violations of territorial integrity or political independence are not internationally criminal, and do not trigger a right to use remedial force, unless they also involve a severe threat of violence to human beings. At the same time, uses of force that do little or nothing to protect core sovereign rights are lawful as long as they respond to an armed attack. Conversely, it *is* criminally aggressive to inflict violence on human beings in a foreign state even if there is no intention or significant prospect of harm to territorial integrity or political independence as a result of the attack. Indeed, this holds even if that infliction of violence aims merely to recover the aggressor's own sovereign territory.

There are, of course, marginal *jus ad bellum* cases in which human life seems to play a less central role and core sovereignty rights appear to come to the fore. The most notable such case is that of the so-called "bloodless invasion." This case is examined at greater length in Section 3.3, below. However, by way of brief preview, whether bloodless invasions are criminal at all is at least debatable. Moreover, even if they are criminal, the key to understanding their criminality is not the fact that such invasions infringe sovereignty, but rather that they do so by imposing the immediate threat of lethal violence against anyone who might resist.

The second reason in favor of the unjustified killing account of aggression is that it fits with the broader legal posture on violence to human beings. Whereas aggression is unique among sovereignty violations in its criminal status, it is decidedly not unique in that respect

[82] The threat to life need not necessarily be consummated for an action to count as an armed attack and thus generate a right to defensive force, but even in that case, the latter right hinges on the fact of latent human violence. Offering such a position in moral philosophy, *see, for example*, Fabre, *supra* note 67, at 109–13; Thomas Hurka, *Proportionality in the Morality of War*, 33 PHIL. & PUB. AFF. 34, 54–55 (2005) (the lethal threat of a wrongful (but potentially bloodless) aggressor at least increases significantly the amount of force that may be used in response, even if it does not justify the same quantum of force as would an aggression aimed at causing death). At the individual level, *cf.* MODEL PENAL CODE, § 3.06(3)(d)(ii) (AM. LAW INST., Proposed Official Draft 1962). Similar issues are discussed in the analysis in § 3.3, below, on bloodless invasion.

among forms of large-scale killing and human harm that do not respond defensively to the threat or infliction of such killing and harm. On the contrary, such non-defensive killing is generally criminal in one form or another.

Perhaps the most important element of sovereignty is the state's monopoly on the legitimate use of internal force. However, that authority is not unlimited. When state agents inflict widespread killing or human harm internally, without responding to some form of attack or imminent internal threat, they commit a crime against humanity.[83] State militaries may use force against insurgents in a non-international armed conflict, but until such insurgents have formed (and thus have begun to pose an internal belligerent threat), the state cannot initiate such an attack. To do so would be to engage in a widespread and systematic attack on a civilian population.[84] If non-state actors coalesce into a military response to such an attack by the state, then, from that point on, such actors would become combatants, and state forces may target them without committing a crime.[85] But that transformation would not change the criminality of state actors' initial attack on human life.

Similarly, when non-state actors inflict widespread death or human harm against civilians, they too commit crimes against humanity.[86] When they inflict harms of this kind on state armed forces or other combatants, they commit murder and other universally applicable domestic crimes without the international law privileges of belligerency.[87] Although the latter harms are not internationally criminal, they are domestically criminal in all states, and international law offers no

[83] ICC Statute, *supra* note 3, art. 7.

[84] Unlike state armed forces, non-state "combatants" do not exist until the protracted hostilities necessary to trigger a non-international armed conflict are underway. *See* Protocol (II) Additional to the Geneva Conventions of 12 August 1949, and Relating to the Protection of Victims of Non-International Armed Conflicts, art. 5, 1125 U.N.T.S. 609 (June 8, 1977); Prosecutor v. Tadić, Decision on Defence Motion for Interlocutory Appeal on Jurisdiction, Case No. IT-94-1-I, para. 70 (Int'l Crim. Trib. for the Former Yugoslavia) (Oct. 2, 1995) [hereinafter Tadić Interlocutory Decision on Jurisdiction]; Nils Melzer, *Interpretive Guidance on the Notion of Direct Participation in Hostilities under International Humanitarian Law*, INT'L COMMITTEE OF THE RED CROSS 27, 33, 36 (2009), www.icrc.org/eng/assets/files/other/icrc-002-0990.pdf [https://perma.cc/D3R8-HD9F].

[85] For a discussion on combatant status for non-state actors, *see* MELZER, *supra* note 84, at 31–35.

[86] ICC Statute, *supra* note 3, art. 7.

[87] *See* Richard R. Baxter, *So-Called "Unprivileged Belligerency": Spies, Guerrillas and Saboteurs*, 28 BRIT. Y.B. INT'L L. 323 (1951); Knut Dörmann, *The Legal Situation of*

immunity to those who perpetrate such crimes on behalf of non-state actors.

On a smaller scale, other forms of killing not justified on defensive grounds are war crimes.[88] Classic examples include killing civilians or prisoners of war.[89] And, outside the context of armed conflict, killings that do not protect persons or the broader community are criminalized domestically as murder; international human rights law demands as much.[90]

Thus, whether perpetrated by the state, a non-state group, or an individual, killing cannot be used to change even an illegal or unjust status quo unless it responds to human violence or the threat thereof. Of course, the point at which such violence becomes criminal, and the criminality of threatening such violence, varies depending on the actors and contexts involved.[91] There is a presumption in favor of the legitimacy of internal uses (and especially threats) of force by the state and a strong presumption against the use or threat of force by non-state actors. Similarly, the context of war changes the flexibility of what constitutes defensive action and the attribution of responsibility for unjustified killing.

In that sense, the differentiation across these crimes is important. Indeed, it helps to make sense of the interstate element of aggression (which typically involves a sovereignty violation). Rather than being the core criminal wrong, as the traditional account would have it, that interstate infringement identifies a particular form of unjustified killing and enables the thresholds of criminality to reflect the presumptions of

"Unlawful/Unprivileged Combatants," 85 INT'L REV. RED CROSS 45 (2003); *see also, e.g.*, Military Commissions Act, 10 U.S.C., §§ 948a(6)–(7), 948c, 950t (2009).

88 For relevant war crimes involving killing and human suffering, *see* ICC Statute, *supra* note 3, art. 8.

89 *See, e.g.*, *id.*, arts. 8(a)(i), 8(b)(i, vi).

90 On the human rights law requirement that the unjustified takings of life be met with criminal sanction, *see, for example*, Osman v. United Kingdom, App. No. 87/1997/871/1083 (1998), para. 115; and Human Rights Comm'n, *General Comment 31: The Nature of the General Legal Obligation Imposed on States Parties to the Covenant*, U.N. Doc. CCPR/C/21/Rev.1/Add.13, para. 8 (May 26, 2004). The only non-protective killing that need not trigger criminal sanction is the death penalty in states where it remains legal; however, its permissibility in international human rights law is fragile and awkward. UN Secretary-General, *Report of the Special Rapporteur on Extrajudicial, Summary or Arbitrary Executions*, U.N. Doc. A/67/275 (Aug. 9, 2012); Protocol No. 13 to the Convention for the Protection of Human Rights and Fundamental Freedoms, Concerning the Abolition of the Death Penalty in All Circumstances, 2002, C.E.T.S. No. 187.

91 HAQUE, *supra* note 7, at 9.

legitimacy and contextual considerations appropriate to that form. The state has a lower presumption of legitimacy using (or threatening) force internationally than it does domestically, and a higher presumption of legitimacy than do non-state actors. But this differentiation *among crimes* ought not obscure the common trait that makes them all crimes. The non-defensive use of lethal force by any actor is generally criminally prohibited, even if its purpose is to remedy an unjust status quo. Aggression extends that fundamental principle to the interstate context.[92]

Viewing aggression in this way spotlights why it is its own crime. The other provisions described above prohibit rebels' killing of civilians and combatants; they prohibit state forces' killing of civilians or groups yet to form a lethal rebellious threat; and they prohibit non-defensive killing outside armed conflict. What no provision other than the crime of aggression prohibits is a state's forces' unjustified killing of a foreign state's combatants and collateral civilians in an illegal war.[93] In the absence of a crime of aggression, the unjustified infliction of death and suffering in such interstate contexts would have been the normative anomaly in which such harms could be inflicted without any prospect of criminal liability. Aggression fills a crucial gap, providing otherwise missing criminal law protection to the right to life of combatants and collateral civilians.[94]

The third aspect of the unjustified killing account's explanatory superiority is that at least one type of criminally aggressive war involves the infliction of human violence, but no violation of sovereign rights. Article 8 *bis* includes a category of criminal war *alternative* to uses of armed force "against the sovereignty, territorial integrity or political independence of another State," namely the "use of armed force by a State . . . in any other manner inconsistent with the Charter of the United Nations."[95] As in the UN Charter, the more specific categories serve as

[92] Opening Statement at Nuremberg by Justice Robert H. Jackson, Chief Prosecutor for the United States, United States v. Göring et al. (Nov. 21, 1945), *in* 2 Trial of the Major War Criminals before the International Military Tribunal, Nuremberg, 14 November 1945–1 October 1946: Proceedings 98, 149 (1947).

[93] Combatants' right to life is granted narrow protections in the *jus in bello*. *See, e.g.*, ICC Statute, *supra* note 3, arts. 8(2)(b)(vi, xi), 8(2)(c), 8(2)(d)(ix). However, that regime does not protect combatants from the illegal and non-defensive violence of an aggressor.

[94] Haque, *supra* note 7, at 3. *Cf. supra* note 90, *infra* note 146. As the "supreme crime," it is perhaps fitting that aggression protects the right of life, which is sometimes termed the "most fundamental human right, or the supreme right." H. of Lords H. of Commons Joint Comm'n on Human Rights, *supra* note 72, para. 3.56.

[95] ICC Statute, *supra* note 3, art. 8 *bis* (2) (emphasis added).

points of emphasis.[96] However, for the broader category of armed force used "in any *other* manner inconsistent with the Charter" to make sense, it must include wrongful wars that do *not* infringe another state's "sovereignty, territorial integrity or political independence."

One obvious example of a use of force fitting that description would be a war waged by a state in its own territory against a UN-authorized force deployed to prevent the host state from engaging in atrocity. A recent example was the use of force by Libya in its own territory against the UN-authorized NATO coalition in 2011.[97]

In that particular war, NATO engaged only aerially and suffered little damage and zero casualties, so the Libyan action against NATO would almost certainly not surpass the character, gravity, and scale threshold requirements of article 8 *bis* (1).[98] However, for the reasons outlined below, the little force that Libya did muster was plainly "inconsistent with" the UN Charter, as required by 8 *bis* (2). Counterfactually, had Libya caused sufficient NATO casualties to exceed the 8 *bis* (1) threshold, its action in doing so would have been a criminal aggression. Since the conflict took place exclusively within universally recognized Libyan territory and the subject of dispute was Libyan domestic policy, this is explicable only in light of the lack of justification for the violence against coalition troops, not in light of any infringement of sovereignty or self-determination.

The inconsistency of such action with the UN Charter is established by three elements. First, the Charter prohibits states from using force in their "international relations" – including on their own territory – in any way contrary to the Charter's "purposes."[99] Interactions between a host

96 *Cf.* Ian Brownlie, International Law and the Use of Force by States 267 (1963); Dinstein, *supra* note 52, at 89–90.

97 On the authorization, *see* S.C. Res. 1973 (Mar. 17, 2011). On Libyan force against the NATO intervention, *see, for example, US Navy Drone Missing over Libya was "Shot Down" by Gaddafi's Forces*, Daily Mail (Aug. 5, 2011), www.dailymail.co.uk/news/article-2023069/U-S-Navy-drone-missing-Libya-shot-Gaddafis-forces.html [https://perma.cc/V2TQ-Y9UV].

98 *Cf.* Dannenbaum, *supra* note 7, Section V.A (on why bloodless invasions should not count as criminally aggressive).

99 UN Charter, art. 2(4). On the application of article 2(4) to uses of force on a state's own territory, *see* Tom Ruys, *The Meaning of "Force" and the Boundaries of the* Jus ad Bellum*: Are "Minimal" Uses of Force Excluded from UN Charter Article 2(4)?*, 108 Am. J. Int'l L. 159, 180–88, 209 (2014), for a discussion of article 2(4)'s applicability and relevant examples of state practice and legal opinion; and Indep. *Int'l Fact-Finding Mission on the Conflict in Georgia*, 1 Report 23–25, paras. 20–24 (2009), for an argument that Georgia's use of force against Russian troops in South Ossetia (Georgian territory) was an illegal armed attack triggering a Russian right to use force in self-defense (a

state like Libya and a UN-authorized force clearly fall in the category of international relations, and the furtherance of the Security Council's work under Chapter VII is clearly a UN purpose.[100] Second, the only exception to the Charter's prohibition on the use of force (other than acting pursuant to a Security Council authorization), is self-defense. Under Article 51 of the Charter, however, self-defense applies only "until the Security Council has taken the measures necessary to maintain international peace and security" and self-defensive measures "shall not in any way affect the authority and responsibility of the Security Council" to act under Chapter VII.[101] Third, the authorization of forces to prevent domestic atrocity is now widely recognized as part of the Security Council's authority, and indeed responsibility, under Chapter VII, as part of its activity in maintaining international peace and security.[102] As such, it overrides any affected state's right of self-defense.

The upshot is clear. When states fight back against UN-authorized forces on their territory, their action in doing so meets the core requirement of article 8 *bis* (2). As long as the action is of sufficient character, gravity, and scale, it is a criminal aggression.[103]

right that Russia exceeded in its response). *See also* INT'L LAW ASS'N USE OF FORCE COMM., REPORT ON AGGRESSION AND THE USE OF FORCE, § A.2 (2014) [hereinafter ILA USE OF FORCE COMM. REPORT] (concluding that the UN Charter prohibition was meant to be an "all-inclusive" ban on the use of force in international relations, with "no loopholes"). For a contrary view, *see* Oliver Dörr, *Use of Force, Prohibition of*, *in* 10 MAX PLANCK ENCYCLOPEDIA OF PUBLIC INTERNATIONAL LAW 607, 612, paras. 23, 25 (2012), who argues that "to come under the prohibition, the use of armed force by a State must be directed against the territory of another State."

[100] Compare UN Charter, arts. 1(1), 24, 25, 39.

[101] *Id.*, art. 51. ILA USE OF FORCE COMM. REPORT, *supra* note 99, § B.2 (interpreting article 51 to mean that a state's right to use force in self-defense *ceases* when the Security Council steps in).

[102] The interpretation of internal human rights abuses as threats to international peace and security capable of triggering Chapter VII is long established. *See, e.g.*, S.C. Res. 418 (Nov. 4, 1977); S.C. Res. 181 (Aug. 7, 1963). The 2011 authorization to use force in Libya rested on the internal atrocities and anticipated atrocities of the Gaddafi regime. S.C. Res. 1973 (Mar. 17, 2011). On the Security Council's claimed *responsibility* to authorize such forces, *see* World Summit Outcome, G.A. Res. 60/1, paras. 138–39 (Sept. 16, 2005); S.C. Res. 1674, para. 4 (Apr. 28, 2006); UN Secretary-General, *Implementing the Responsibility to Protect* 8–9, U.N. Doc. A/63/677 (Jan. 12, 2009); INT'L COMM'N ON INTERVENTION AND STATE SOVEREIGNTY, THE RESPONSIBILITY TO PROTECT, paras. 6.13–6.28 (2001) [hereinafter ICISS REPORT]; Anne Peters, *The Security Council's Responsibility to Protect*, 8 INT'L ORG. L. REV. 15 (2011).

[103] Some have argued that, in addition to meeting the *chapeau* of article 8 *bis* (2), an action must also fall into one of the examples listed in the ensuing sub-paragraphs (a)–(g). DINSTEIN, *supra* note 52, at 139; Kai Ambos, *The Crime of Aggression after Kampala*, 53

Thus understood, "aggression" is a term of art; its meaning is defined not by which state struck first, but by which engaged in an illegal and grave use of force.[104] As the Institut de Droit International resolved in 1971, "the party opposing the United Nations Forces has committed aggression," irrespective of whether it acted first or crossed a border to do so.[105]

This bears on the question at hand. Reference to core states' rights cannot explain the criminality of waging war against a UN-authorized humanitarian intervention force operating exclusively in the attacking state's own territory.[106] But the criminality of killing UN personnel in order to defend an ongoing atrocity *can* be explained with reference to killing and inflicting human suffering without justification.

Of course, humanitarian intervention without Security Council authorization is generally thought to be illegal. The notion that fighting against a humanitarian intervention within one's own borders could itself be criminal

GERMAN Y.B. INT'L L. 463, 487 (2010); Marina Mancini, *A Brand New Definition for the Crime of Aggression: The Kampala Outcome*, 81 NORDIC J. INT'L L. 227, 234–35 (2012). Even if this were correct, an attack on UN-authorized forces within a state's territory would be an attack on "the land, sea or air forces, or marine and air fleets of another State." ICC Statute, *supra* note 3, art. 8 *bis* (2)(d). In any event, the dominant view is that the list is illustrative, with 8 *bis* (1) and the *chapeau* of 8 *bis* (2) sufficient to define the crime. *See, e.g.*, Rep. of the Special Working Grp. on the Crime of Aggression, at 14, para. 34, I.C.C. Doc. ICC-ASP/6/20/Add.l (2008); AM. BRANCH OF THE INT'L LAW ASS'N INT'L CRIMINAL COURT COMM., THE CRIME OF AGGRESSION: THE NEW AMENDMENT EXPLAINED, QUESTIONS AND ANSWERS 6–7 (2011); CARRIE MCDOUGAL, THE CRIME OF AGGRESSION UNDER THE ROME STATUTE OF THE INTERNATIONAL CRIMINAL COURT 103–05 (2013); Roger S. Clark, *Amendments to the Rome Statute of the International Criminal Court Considered at the First Review Conference on the Court, Kampala, 31 May–11 June 2010*, 2 GOETTINGEN J. INT'L L. 689, 696 (2010); Matthew Gillett, *The Anatomy of an International Crime: Aggression at the International Criminal Court*, 13 INT'L CRIM. L. REV. 829, 844–45 (2013); Claus Kreß & Leonie von Holtzendorff, *The Kampala Compromise on the Crime of Aggression*, 8 J. INT'L CRIM. JUSTICE 1179, 1191 (2010); Astrid Reisinger, *Defining the Crime of Aggression*, *in* FUTURE PERSPECTIVES ON INTERNATIONAL CRIMINAL JUSTICE 425, 440 (Carsten Stahn & Larissa van den Herik, eds., 2010).

104 DINSTEIN, *supra* note 52, at 140 (the criminal aggressor need not have opened fire);

105 INSTITUT DE DROIT INT'L, CONDITIONS OF APPLICATION OF HUMANITARIAN RULES OF ARMED CONFLICT TO HOSTILITIES IN WHICH UNITED NATIONS FORCES MAY BE ENGAGED, art. 7 (1971).

106 In defense of the traditional account of aggression, one might argue that an attack on the UN-authorized troops would be a violation of those troops' states' rights. *Cf.* Ruys, *supra* note 99, at 180. However, this would require articulating the relevant sovereign rights in a way that renders them either derivative of the human cost of the attack or detached from what Walzerian and related accounts have in mind.

therefore applies most plausibly only when the intervention has Security Council backing.[107] Nonetheless, even if limited to that scenario, this further supports an account of aggression as a crime rooted in wrongful killing, not the severe violation of states' rights. The special case of unauthorized humanitarian interventions is addressed in Section 3.3 below.

Ultimately, the non-defensive killing in an illegal war is why waging such a war is criminal. This explanation best accounts for why the state's right to protect itself from armed attack survived Nuremberg and the UN Charter, whereas its right to use force to vindicate each of its other legal rights was discarded comprehensively. It is consistent with the criminalization of unjustified killing more generally. And it is what clarifies why using force against an invading UN-authorized humanitarian intervention would itself involve waging a criminally aggressive war.

3.2.3 *The Humanization of International Law*

An additional virtue of the unjustified killing account is that it reconciles the criminalization of aggression to the broader normative context. In recent decades, the very foundations of international law have shifted away from a regime rooted exclusively in state sovereignty and towards a regime that privileges human rights and human values – a transformation often termed the "humanization" of international law.[108] This phenomenon is most explicit in the contemporary notion that sovereignty is at some level

[107] On the legal status of humanitarian intervention, *see infra* notes 169–70 and accompanying text.

[108] Louis Henkin, The Age of Rights 2–10 (1990); Theodor Meron, The Humanization of International Law (2006); Ruti G. Teitel, Humanity's Law 27 (2011); W. Michael Reisman, Editorial Comment, *Sovereignty and Human Rights in Contemporary International Law*, 84 Am. J. Int'l L. 866, 872 (1990); Yoram Dinstein, *The Interaction of International Law and Justice*, 16 Israel Y.B. Hum. Rts. 9, 41–42 (1986); Tom Farer, *Remarks on "Bombing for Peace: Collateral Damage and Human Rights,"* 96 Proc. Ann. Meeting Am. Soc'y Int'l L. 104, 106 (2002); Louis B. Sohn, *The New International Law: Protection of the Rights of Individuals Rather than States*, 32 Am. U.L. Rev. 1, 1 (1982); *see also* Paul W. Kahn, *American Hegemony and International Law: Speaking Law to Power: Popular Sovereignty, Human Rights, and the New International Order*, 1 Chi. J. Int'l L. 1, 5–6, 10–16 (2000) (identifying the trend, but also picking out some of the challenges associated with it); Madeleine K. Albright, *Opinion, The End of Intervention*, NY Times (June 11, 2008), www.nytimes.com/2008/06/11/opinion/11albright.html [https://perma.cc/MN58-ZWMD] (describing the debate on this as rooted in a dispute over whether international law is a "living framework of rules intended to make the world a more humane place," or merely "a collection of legal nuts and bolts cobbled together by governments to protect governments").

conditional on the state discharging its "responsibility to protect" the basic human rights of those within its control.[109] The account presented here identifies the initial criminalization of aggression as an early step in this trajectory and makes sense of its ongoing customary criminality and its incorporation into the Rome Statute in the more deeply humanized contemporary international legal context.

The humanization process has been especially prominent and consequential in international criminal law. At the vanguard of that regime's revival, the International Criminal Tribunal for the former Yugoslavia (ICTY) wasted no time in framing its interpretive approach in precisely such terms, reasoning that "[a] State-sovereignty-oriented approach has been gradually supplanted by a human-being-oriented approach. Gradually the maxim of Roman law *hominum causa omne jus constitutum est* (all law is created for the benefit of human beings) has gained a firm foothold in the international community as well."[110]

This notion is manifest throughout the framework of international criminal law. Crimes against humanity, war crimes, and genocide focus on the most severe harms to human beings.[111] The Office of the Prosecutor at the ICC selects cases with a view to surpassing the gravity threshold for admissibility based on the severity of the human harms they involve.[112] And, in perhaps the most obvious privileging of humanity over sovereignty, international criminal law requires subjects to

[109] ICISS Report, *supra* note 102, paras. 1.3, 2.14–2.15, 2.30–2.32; UN High-Level Panel on Threats, Challenges & Change, *A More Secure World: Our Shared Responsibility*, paras. 29–30, U.N. Doc. A/59/565 (Dec. 2, 2004). *See also* Carsten Stahn, *Responsibility to Protect: Political Rhetoric or Emerging Legal Norm?*, 101 Am. J. Int'l L. 99, 118 (2007) ("The core tenet of the concept (sovereignty entails responsibility) enjoys broad support among states, and in the United Nations and civil society"); Kofi Annan, *Two Concepts of Sovereignty*, Economist 49–50 (Sept. 16, 1999) ("States are now widely understood to be instruments at the service of their peoples, and not vice versa"); Lee Feinstein & Anne-Marie Slaughter, *A Duty to Prevent*, Foreign Aff. (Jan./Feb. 2004), www.foreignaffairs.com/articles/2004-01-01/duty-prevent [https://perma.cc/KE8K-A4RB] (describing R2P as "nothing less than the redefinition of sovereignty itself").

[110] Tadić Interlocutory Decision on Jurisdiction, *supra* note 84, para. 97. The Tribunal later insisted that human dignity had "become of such paramount importance as to permeate the whole body of international law." Prosecutor v. Furundžija, Case No. IT-95–17/1-T, Judgment, para. 183 (Int'l Crim. Trib. for the Former Yugoslavia) (Dec. 10, 1998).

[111] *See* ICC Statute, *supra* note 3, arts. 6–8; cf. the start of Section 1.4, of Chapter 1, above (discussing how mass crimes, like genocide, also have an individual impact).

[112] *See* Office of the Prosecutor, Policy Paper on Preliminary Examinations, Int'l Crim. Ct., paras. 61, 63 (Nov. 2013), www.legal-tools.org/uploads/tx_ltpdb/OTP_-_Policy_Paper_Preliminary_Examinations_2013-2.pdf [https://perma.cc/2DGA-9D7Q]; *see also* ICC Statute, *supra* note 3, art. 17(1)(d) (providing the gravity threshold).

disobey domestically authoritative sovereign commands in order to protect other human beings.[113]

The traditional account suggests that the criminalization of aggression is in tension with, or even opposition to, this "humanization," and thus with international criminal law itself.[114] The account presented here, in contrast, locates aggression at the heart of that process.[115] Criminalizing aggression constrains the sovereign's previously unlimited authority to vindicate its rights with force, preserving that authority only when necessary to protect human beings from the illegal infliction of violence or to respond to the illegal threat of such human violence.[116] Seen in this light, the classification of aggression (and no other sovereignty violation), alongside genocide, crimes against humanity, and war crimes, makes sense.

A legal regime's core claim to normativity is strengthened when it coheres internally.[117] The traditional account renders international criminal law "equivocal" and self-undermining – simultaneously a major step forward in human rights and "a major moral enemy of the human rights

[113] *E.g.*, Charter of the International Military Tribunal, art. 8, Aug. 8, 1945, 59 Stat. 1544, 82 U.N.T.S. 279 [hereinafter IMT Charter]; Control Council Law No. 10, Punishment of Persons Guilty of War Crimes, Crimes against Peace and against Humanity (Dec. 20, 1945), *in* 3 OFFICIAL GAZETTE CONTROL COUNCIL FOR GERMANY 50 (1946), art. II(4)(b) [Control Council Law No. 10, *supra* note 1]; Charter of the International Tribunal for the Far East, T.I.A.S. No. 1589, 4 Bevans 20 (Jan. 19, 1946), art. 6 [hereinafter IMTFE Charter]; ICC Statute, *supra* note 3, art. 33(1); IMT Judgment, *supra* note 1, at 466, 470 (discussing the duty to disobey domestic laws that violate international laws and providing examples of those international laws that unambiguously protect human beings); Statute of the Special Court for Sierra Leone, art. 6(4), Jan. 16, 2002, www.rscsl.org/Documents/scsl-statute.pdf [https://perma.cc/DX4E-9UAJ]; Statute of the International Tribunal for Rwanda, S.C. Res. 955, annex, art. 6 (4) (Nov. 8, 1994); Updated Statute of the International Criminal Tribunal for the Former Yugoslavia, art. 7(4) (May 25, 1993), www.icty.org/x/file/Legal%20Library/Statute/statute_sept09_en.pdf [https://perma.cc/CCC3-TTZ5]; 4 TRIALS OF WAR CRIMINALS BEFORE THE NUERNBERG TRIBUNALS UNDER CONTROL COUNCIL LAW NO. 10, NUERNBERG, 1946–APRIL 1949, at 470–88 (1949); 1 JEAN-MARIE HENCKAERTS & LOUISE DOSWALD-BECK, CUSTOMARY INTERNATIONAL HUMANITARIAN LAW 551–55, 563–67 (2009).

[114] *Cf. supra* notes 32–37 and accompanying text.

[115] In more recent work, Luban seems to have sympathy for something similar to this account, writing, "The decision to ban the use of force except in self-defense represented a judgment, emerging from the smoldering ruins of Europe and Japan, that treating war as an instrument of policy poses an intolerable threat to 'fundamental human rights' and 'the dignity and worth of the human person.'" Luban, *Preventive War*, *supra* note 15, at 218.

[116] *See* Sections 3.2.1–3.2.2 above.

[117] *See* Chapter 2 above.

movement."[118] This tension weighs heavily against it. Conversely, on the unjustified killing account, aggression is of a normative piece with the rest of international criminal law, and is, moreover, an integral element of the broader human rights movement. This militates powerfully in its favor. Therefore, even if, contrary to the arguments in Sections 3.2.1 and 3.2.2, the traditional account and the unjustified killing account offered equally plausible explanations of the crime, the latter would still be the better normative account.

3.2.4 *Revisiting the History of the Move to a Restrictive* Jus ad Bellum

This focus on the human being is not merely a matter of internal normative logic. It has historical plausibility as part of the regime's purpose. Following the devastation of World War I, human life was the overriding public concern of those who led the intellectual and political movement that ultimately produced the Kellogg–Briand Pact – the key legal hook for the aggression convictions at Nuremberg.[119]

In his 1921 pamphlet laying the foundations for this transition, Salmon Levinson described war as "inhuman" and compared legal toleration of the practice to the toleration of dueling, which had since become "plain murder under our laws."[120] Levinson recognized that the ban would require states to foreswear the sovereign authority to vindicate their rights through the "legal device of violence."[121] Rather than bolstering this argument with a claim that sovereignty would also be augmented by the ban on interstate armed attacks, he insisted that the longstanding maximalist vision of sovereign authority was no longer tenable, given its infliction of "the worst form of violence and crime existing among men."[122] Colonel Raymond Robins, a fellow proponent of the outlawry of war, wrote of the movement as an effort to "declare [war] in international law to be what it is in fact, the supreme enemy of the human race."[123]

Leading political figures also adopted this framing. US President Harding spoke of the move towards a restrictive *jus ad bellum* as the call

[118] Luban, Legal Modernism, *supra* note 31, at 341; *see supra* note 35 and accompanying text.
[119] IMT Judgment, *supra* note 1, at 460–66. [120] Levinson, *supra* note 58, at 14, 16.
[121] *Id.*, at 18. [122] *Id.*, at 23.
[123] Raymond Robins, *Foreword* to Levinson, *supra* note 58, at 10.

"of humanity crying for relief."[124] Former British Prime Minister David Lloyd George reflected in his memoirs on the growing sense in this period that was a "crime against humanity" the "perpetrators and instigators" of which ought to be punished.[125] Secretary of State Frank Kellogg wrote to the French Ambassador in the months before the Pact's conclusion, "From the broad standpoint of humanity and civilization, all war is an assault upon the stability of human society, and should be suppressed in the common interest."[126] Following the Pact, and with the carnage of World War I still fresh in memory, he described it as an "assault on human existence" and noted that the first thought in eliminating war was "the millions of wounded and dead" that result from armed conflict.[127]

The various efforts to ban the use of force reached their first global legal fruition in 1928 in the Kellogg–Briand Pact. Notably, the Pact's preamble emphasized not sovereignty, but states' "solemn duty to promote the welfare of mankind" through the "humane endeavor" of ending war.[128] Picking up on this, Ruti Teitel has described the Pact as a treaty whose focus on humanity forged a "connection ... between the two historical strands of *jus ad bellum* and *jus in bello* (humanitarian law)."[129]

None of this is to say that there would not be sovereignty benefits to banning aggressive war. Nor is it to say that these benefits were unrecognized by those involved in the drafting. But those sovereignty benefits (exchanged for sovereignty sacrifices) were not the focus of the public reasons given for this fundamental legal restructuring. Instead, the focus was on the human wrongs inflicted by those who initiate war without justification. If anything, advocates of the Kellogg–Briand Pact, including

[124] President Warren Harding, Keynote Conference Address (Nov. 12, 1921), *quoted in* LEVINSON, *supra* note 58, at 5.

[125] 1 DAVID LLOYD GEORGE, MEMOIRS OF THE PEACE CONFERENCE 55 (1939).

[126] Letter from Frank B. Kellogg, US Sec'y of State, to Paul Claudel, Ambassador of Fr. (Feb. 27, 1928), *reprinted in* DAVID HUNTER MILLER, THE PEACE PACT OF PARIS: A STUDY OF THE BRIAND–KELLOGG TREATY 174, 176 (1928).

[127] Kellogg, *supra* note 60.

[128] General Treaty for Renunciation of War as an Instrument of National Policy, Aug. 27, 1928, 94 L.N.T.S. 57 preamble.

[129] TEITEL, *supra* note 108, at 27. Presaging this line of thought, Francis Lieber – a key figure in the development of the contemporary *jus in bello* – emphasized that it is the human suffering of war that animates the *jus ad bellum* requirements of justification and necessity. FRANCIS LIEBER, 2 MANUAL OF POLITICAL ETHICS, DESIGNED CHIEFLY FOR THE USE OF COLLEGES AND STUDENTS AT LAW 635 (Boston, Charles C. Little & James Brown 1839).

Kellogg himself, were forced to defend it against the charge that it ceded too much in the way of sovereign authority.[130]

3.2.5 *Criminal Aggression and the Human Dimension at Nuremberg and Tokyo*

This focus on the unjustified infliction of death and human suffering as the normative core of the issue was also palpable at Nuremberg and at Tokyo. Robert Jackson, the lead American prosecutor at the IMT, argued, "what appeals to men of good will and common sense as the crime which comprehends all lesser crimes, is the crime of making unjustifiable war. War necessarily is a calculated series of killings, of destructions of property, of oppressions."[131] In his retrospective on the trials, Jackson's Nuremberg colleague, Whitney Harris, adopted a similar line, reasoning:

> Hitler ordered the killing of men called to the defense of countries which German armies invaded at Hitler's command. Insofar as these invasions were acts of pure aggression, and wholly without legal justification, the resultant killings offended the conscience of mankind just as the slaughter of persons in concentration camps offended universal conscience ... The killing of innocent human beings by order of heads of states is subject to substantially the same moral blame whether it is the killing of civilian populations in connection with war or the killing of troops resisting unlawful aggression ... It is not the fact of initiating and waging aggressive war which reprehends it, but that it is necessarily a course of killings and of brutality which is attained in no other relationship of man or nation.[132]

Nuremberg prosecutor and subsequent University of Chicago law professor Bernard Meltzer, argued that "the Kellogg–Briand Pact and similar agreements are important, not because they directly made aggressive war a crime, but because, by destroying it as a defense, they made the instigators of aggression subject to the universal laws against murder."[133] Hartley Shawcross, the chief British prosecutor at the IMT, brought this

[130] *See, e.g.*, *Hearings on the General Pact for the Renunciation of War, Signed at Paris August 27, 1928 before the S. Comm. on Foreign Relations*, 70th Cong. (1928) (statement of Frank B. Kellogg, US Sec'y of State of the United States).

[131] Robert H. Jackson, *Report of Robert H. Jackson United States Representative to the International Conference on Military Trials*, Dep't of State 51 (1949), www.loc.gov/rr/frd/Military_Law/pdf/jackson-rpt-military-trials.pdf [https://perma.cc/2HDC-TFX9].

[132] WHITNEY R. HARRIS, TYRANNY ON TRIAL 528–29 (1954).

[133] Bernard D. Meltzer, *A Note on Some Aspects of the Nuremberg Debate*, 14 U. CHI. L. REV. 455, 460–61 (1947).

framing into the courtroom, emphasizing in his closing statement that "where a war is illegal . . . there is nothing to justify the killing, and these murders are not to be distinguished from those of any other lawless robber bands."[134]

These were not mere prosecutorial flourishes. The IMT judgment described aggression as "the supreme international crime differing only from other war crimes in that it contains within itself the *accumulated evil* of the whole."[135] Similarly, the NMT described aggression as the "pinnacle of criminality" due to its infliction of "horror, suffering, and loss."[136] The wrong the tribunals recognized in these statements is not the macro violation of sovereignty, but the aggregation of wrongful harms that that macro policy entails.[137] It is the death and destruction internal to aggression that is evil, and it is the accumulation of that evil that warrants criminalizing the war.[138]

The IMTFE was more direct, holding that waging illegal war is the gravest crime because it entails "that death and suffering will be inflicted on countless human beings."[139] Going even further than their IMT counterparts, the prosecutors in Tokyo had supplemented the charge of waging aggressive war with the charge of murder as a crime against the peace, including in the latter the killings of enemy soldiers in the course of an illegal invasion.[140] The Tribunal affirmed the reasoning, declining

[134] Hartley Shawcross, Chief Prosecutor for the UK, Closing Statement at the Nuremberg Trials (July 26, 1946) *in* 19 TRIAL OF THE MAJOR WAR CRIMINALS BEFORE THE INTERNATIONAL MILITARY TRIBUNAL 458 (1948); *see also* Thomas Weigend, *"In General a Principle of Justice:" The Debate on the "Crime against Peace" in the Wake of the Nuremberg Judgment*, 10 J. INT'L CRIM. JUSTICE 41, 50 (2012).

[135] IMT Judgment, *supra* note 1, at 427 (emphasis added); *see also id.*, at 465 (citing favorably the Resolution of the Sixth Pan-American Conference's declaration that a "war of aggression constitutes an international crime against the human species"). Understanding the language on "accumulated evil" in the way suggested here, *see* ADIL AHMAD HAQUE, LAW AND MORALITY AT WAR 3 (2017).

[136] United States v. von Weizsäcker, *in* 14 TRIALS OF WAR CRIMINALS BEFORE THE NUERNBERG MILITARY TRIBUNALS UNDER CONTROL COUNCIL LAW NO. 10, at 1, 342 (1949); *see also id.*, at 318–19, 333 (describing the atrocities and horror inherent to war).

[137] Understanding "accumulated evil" in this way, *see, for example*, DINSTEIN, *supra* note 52, at 128.

[138] *The Crime of Aggression: A Further Informal Discussion Paper*, PREPARATORY COMM'N FOR THE INT'L CRIM. CT., para. 10 (Nov. 13, 2000) (emphasizing the death and destruction that make aggression of global concern), https://documents-dds-ny.un.org/doc/UNDOC/GEN/N00/742/89/PDF/N0074289.pdf [https://perma.cc/VVQ7-47AA].

[139] IMTFE Judgment, *supra* note 1, at 49,769.

[140] *Id.*, at 48,452.

to consider the murder charge only because it was deemed redundant to the charge of waging aggressive war. Specifically, the IMTFE held:

> If, in any case, the finding be that the war was not unlawful then the charge of murder will fall with the charge of waging unlawful war. If, on the other hand, the war, in any particular case, is held to have been unlawful, then *this involves unlawful killings . . . at all places in the theater of war and at all times throughout the period of the war.* No good purpose is to be served, in our view, in dealing with these parts of the offences by way of counts for murder when the whole offence of waging those wars unlawfully is put in issue upon the counts charging the waging of such wars.[141]

More recently, a committee reporting to the ICTY on NATO's aerial campaign against Yugoslavia in 1999 found that "a person convicted of a crime against peace may, potentially, be held criminally responsible for all of the activities causing death, injury or destruction during a conflict."[142] Similarly, British Attorney General Lord Peter Goldsmith warned Prime Minister Tony Blair of the outside possibility that he could be charged with murder for killings by British soldiers in the 2003 invasion of Iraq, should the war be deemed illegal.[143] Meanwhile, Security Council condemnations of aggressions since World War II have expressed concern and indignation not only at the infringement of sovereignty, but at the killing and human suffering entailed.[144]

3.2.6 *A Superior Normative Account*

Taking these five arguments together, an account of aggression that locates its core wrong in unjustified killing better fulfills the criteria of

[141] *Id.*, at 48,452–53 (emphasis added); *see also id.*, at 49,576.

[142] Int'l Crim. Trib.for the Former Yugoslavia, *Final Report to the Prosecutor by the Committee Established to Review the NATO Bombing Campaign against the Federal Republic of Yugoslavia*, United Nations, para. 30 (2000), www.icty.org/x/file/Press/nato061300.pdf [https://perma.cc/LQY6-NBKY].

[143] Memorandum from Peter Goldsmith, Att'y Gen., UK Att'y Gen.'s Office, to Tony Blair, Prime Minister, UK Prime Minister's Office, para. 34 (March 7, 2003) (on file with author).

[144] *See* S.C. Res. 326 pmbl. (Feb. 2, 1973); S.C. Res. 405 pmbl. (Apr. 14, 1977); S.C. Res. 411 pmbl. (June 30, 1977); S.C. Res. 424 pmbl. (Mar. 17, 1978); S.C. Res. 455 pmbl. (Nov. 23, 1979); S.C. Res. 546 pmbl. (Jan. 6, 1984); S.C. Res. 568 pmbl. (June 21, 1985); S.C. Res. 571 pmbl. (Sept. 20, 1985); S.C. Res. 573, para. 4 (Oct. 4, 1985); S.C. Res. 580 pmbl., paras. 1–2 (Dec. 30, 1985); S.C. Res. 611 pmbl. (Apr. 25, 1988). *But see* S.C. Res. 387 (Mar. 31, 1976).

a good normative account of the law than does an approach that focuses instead on the harm to sovereignty.

First, identifying the wrong as the unjustified killing in an aggressive war explains the legal contours of the crime in a way that a focus on sovereignty or even self-determination cannot. The *jus ad bellum* restrains the sovereign capacity to vindicate legal rights using force as much as it protects the sovereign rights to territorial integrity, political independence, and self-determination. Moreover, non-belligerent acts that more severely infringe territorial integrity, political independence, or self-determination than does aggressive war are not criminal. Conversely, other forms of unjustified killing *are* criminalized in some other form. And illegal uses of interstate force that involve no sovereignty violation, or that vindicate territorial integrity or political independence rights without responding to an armed attack, are criminal aggressions. In each of these respects, neither sovereignty nor self-determination can make sense of the *jus ad bellum* and its role in international criminal law. In contrast, a focus on killing and human suffering is illuminating. Were it not criminal, aggressive war would be the key form in which such harms are inflicted on a massive scale without either being justified as a necessary and proportionate response to the threat or infliction of such harms by another, or being criminalized in some other way.

Second, the humanity-based explanation of aggression comports better with the overall purpose of the law in this domain, aligning both with the motivations for the initial outlawry of war and with the overall purposes of international criminal law as a key dimension of the "humanization" of international law. A connection between the killings in aggressive war and the wrong of murder ran through the heart of the prosecutions and convictions at Nuremberg and Tokyo, and has been reiterated in the work of several legal authorities since.

Third, a normative account rooted in humanity coheres with adjacent legal rules: explaining why aggression is the only criminal sovereignty violation and accounting for aggression's fit within the broader legal approach to the unjustified infliction of human suffering. By contrast, as Luban and others emphasize, a crime that privileges sovereignty over humanity would sit extremely uneasily – and possibly in conflict – with the general humanizing posture of international criminal law and the non-criminal status of all other sovereignty violations.[145]

[145] *See supra* notes 32–37, 118 and accompanying text.

Aggression typically involves a sovereignty violation, but it is fundamentally a crime against human beings. It is a "law that has as its purpose protecting the fundamental right to life of millions of people."[146] What makes it special in international criminal law is not that it protects sovereignty, rather than humanity, but that it alone protects the right to life of combatants and proportionate collateral civilians against the wrongful violence of foreign states.

3.3 Two Possible Problem Cases for the Unjustified Killing Account

Before turning to what this normative reconceptualization of the crime entails for soldiers, it is worth addressing an objection that might be thought to arise from two potential problem cases: bloodless invasion (the illegal military taking of territory or usurpation of governmental power without the infliction of casualties) and unauthorized humanitarian intervention (the use of force to prevent atrocity abroad without Security Council authorization).

The objection is this. Both actions are at least plausibly "manifestly illegal" uses of force (and therefore plausibly criminal). Both involve clear infringements of sovereignty. And neither appears to fit the unjustified killing paradigm. Bloodless invasions involve no killing at all, and the killing in a humanitarian intervention is responsive to the illegal human violence and killing of an atrocity crime in much the same way as is the killing in a defensive war *vis-à-vis* the unjustified violence of an armed attack. In that sense, the value of sovereignty appears to better account for the criminality of these actions than does the value of human life.

The objection fails. Even assuming illegality, there is good reason to doubt that either action is criminal. And even assuming criminality, the criminal status of either war would be rooted in the wrongfulness of unjustified killing.

Consider bloodless invasion first. As David Rodin observes, infringing the "territorial integrity or political independence of a state" is "both logically and factually independent of the question of whether the lives of individual citizens within the state are threatened."[147] Russia's use of

[146] Mary Ellen O'Connell & Mirakmal Niyazmatov, *What is Aggression? Comparing the* Jus ad Bellum *and the ICC Statute*, 10 J. Int'l Crim. Justice 189, 192 (2012); *see supra* notes 90, 94 and accompanying text.

[147] Rodin, *supra* note 20, at 132. Rodin's focus is on self-defense, not the crime of aggression. However, his point is to emphasize the significance of bloodless aggression

military and paramilitary force in effecting the 2014 annexation of Crimea entailed a significant violation of Ukrainian territorial integrity, political independence, and arguably self-determination, but it was achieved with minimal casualties.[148] On the orthodox account, the values infringed in such an action are at the crux of aggression's criminal wrongfulness.[149] On the unjustified killing account, they seem not to be. If such actions are indeed criminal, this might be thought to indicate the superiority of the orthodox account in explaining the crime we have.

In fact, the reverse is true. The *criminal* status of an illegal invasion that takes territory or usurps a foreign state's government without spilling a drop of blood is ambiguous and marginal at best. Unlike each of its other invasions, Germany's relatively bloodless annexations of Austria and Bohemia and Moravia were excluded from the criminal indictment before the IMT, which then distinguished them explicitly from wars of aggression in its final judgment.[150] This exclusion is telling. If the core wrong of aggression were its infringement of sovereignty or nullification of a people's self-determination, bloodless aggression would be the paradigmatic form of the crime. Invasions that lack violent military confrontation eviscerate the territorial integrity and political independence of the

in illuminating what is at stake in the legal *jus ad bellum*, and the language he focuses on (territorial integrity and political independence) is anyway common to the bans on the use of force and aggression, not the "armed attack" rule that triggers a right to self-defense. *Cf.* ICC Statute, *supra* note 3, art. 8 *bis* (2); UN Charter, arts. 2(4), 51.

148 For useful overviews of the events in Ukraine and the subsequent reactions, *see* Olivier Corten, *The Russian Intervention in the Ukrainian Crisis: Was Jus Contra Bellum "Confirmed Rather than Weakened"?*, 2 J. Use of Force & Int'l L. 17 (2015); Kristina Daugirdas & Julian Davis Mortenson, *Contemporary Practice of the United States Relating to International Law*, 108 Am. J. Int'l L. 784, 784–815 (2014); Antonello Tancredi, *The Russian Annexation of the Crimea: Questions Relating to the Use of Force*, 1 Questions Int'l L. 5 (2014). On the coercive context in which the Crimean referendum occurred, *see* Office of the UN High Commissioner for Human Rights, Report on the Human Rights Situation in Ukraine, paras. 6, 83–86 (Apr. 15, 2014).

149 Walzer, JUW, *supra* note 4, at 254; *see also id.*, at 53 (describing these as values worth dying for); Luban, *Just War and Human Rights*, *supra* note 31, at 164 (describing aggression's core wrong as "dictatorial interference" by one state in another's affairs and citing Hersch Lauterpacht, International Law and Human Rights 167 (Stevens & Sons 1950). Thus, McMahan observes, a bloodless invasion – what he terms a "lesser aggression" – "is not really lesser according to the traditional theory," for, despite inflicting no immediate physical harm on individuals, it "may be lethal, or severely disabling, in its effect on the *state*." McMahan, *What Rights May Be Defended by Means of War?*, *supra* note 5, at 118 (emphasis added).

150 IMT Judgment, *supra* note 1, at 427. *See also* Definition of Aggression, G.A. Res. 3314 (XXIX), art. 5(2) (Dec. 14, 1974).

victim states with *greater* efficacy than do ordinary wars of aggression, many of which are unsuccessful in unseating the target government or holding territory.[151] The Nazi annexations of Austria and Bohemia and Moravia exemplify this perfectly, so the point would not have been lost on those at Nuremberg.[152]

On the traditional normative account, then, it is difficult to make sense either of the failure to charge those invasions before the IMT, or of their separate normative status in the final judgment. On the account presented here, however, this marginalization makes perfect sense. For, while bloodless invasions are no less harmful to political independence and territorial integrity, they lack the same human violence as aggressive wars involving conflict and casualties.

Of course, although it was the most significant aggression prosecution to date, the IMT's was not the only word on this. The NMT subsequently adopted a broader definition of the crime, which included the invasions of Austria and Bohemia and Moravia.[153] It is in this sense that the Nuremberg legacy on bloodless invasions is ambiguous.

However, the reasoning for the NMT's more expansive approach itself weighs in favor of the unjustified killing account. In explaining the inclusion of these invasions as criminal aggressions, the NMT emphasized the fact that they were achieved against the backdrop of threatened slaughter by an overwhelmingly militarily superior Nazi force.[154] What

[151] *Cf. supra* notes 65–74 and accompanying text (contrasting non-violent violations of territorial integrity with belligerent acts). Compare the decisive impact of Russia's bloodless annexation of Crimea to the far bloodier war in Donbass, the effects of which have been less clear-cut. On the current situation in Donbass, *see, for example*, Office of the UN High Commissioner for Human Rights, Report on the Human Rights Situation in Ukraine, 16 November 2015 to 15 February 2016 (Mar. 3, 2016) [hereinafter OHCHR]. Likewise, were it not for the UN-authorized intervention, Iraq's relatively low-casualty 1990 annexation of Kuwait would have been far more effective than its bloody and ultimately futile aggressive war against Iran in the 1980s. On Iraq's aggression against Iran, *see* Further Report of the Secretary-General, *supra* note 73.

[152] IMT Judgment, *supra* note 1, at 433–436, 573.

[153] *See infra* note 154. Control Council Law No. 10 included both illegal "war" and "invasions of other countries," whereas the IMT Charter focused exclusively on illegal "war." Control Council Law No. 10, *supra* note 1, art. II(1)(a); IMT Charter, *supra* note 113, art. 6(a).

[154] The NMT emphasized the Nazis' use of "overwhelming force" in these actions, noting that Germany perpetrated an "act of war" notwithstanding its "ab[ility] to so overawe the invaded countries" that its invasion was relatively bloodless. Ministries Judgment, *supra* note 136, at 330–31. It emphasized that, in such a situation, the attacked population chooses not to fight for "fear or a sense of the futility of resistance in the face of superior force ... and thus prevents the occurrence of any actual combat." High

made these actions criminal, the tribunal emphasized in the *High Command* case, was "the exerting of violence" by German forces, even though that exertion was met with no resistance and thus the latent killing it entailed was not ultimately consummated.[155]

As Cécile Fabre argues, a key normative link between bloodless invasions and traditional aggressions is that the former involve at their core "individuals posing a lethal threat, either ongoing or imminent, to other individuals."[156] This is what distinguishes both kinds of invasion from the kind of non-belligerent, and non-criminal, sovereignty infringements discussed above.[157] Whereas the latter violate political independence and territorial integrity without exerting violence, the former achieve that end by inflicting latent lethal harm.

This distinction is crucial. If bloodless invasions are criminal (as the NMT suggests they are), the key trait that defines them as such, just as in the ordinary aggression case, is the *means* by which sovereignty is violated, not the fact or degree of the sovereignty violation. The difference between an aggressive military invasion that achieves its sovereignty-infringing end bloodlessly and the illegal foreign manipulation of elections is akin to the interpersonal difference between mugging someone for her wallet with a lethal weapon and pickpocketing the same wallet from her without any physical threat. One inflicts latent violence; the other does not. If aggression is criminal, its criminality as compared to the mere illegality of otherwise similar sovereignty violations would parallel armed mugging's felony status as compared to the misdemeanor status of non-violently stealing the same item.[158]

Command Judgment, *supra* note 40, at 485. Similarly, the IMT held that what made the annexations of Austria and Czechoslovakia condemnable (though not prosecuted) was that they relied on the threatened use of "the armed might of Germany . . . if any resistance was encountered." IMT Judgment, *supra* note 1, at 435. It found that Czech President Emil Hácha submitted only under Göring's explicit threat to "destroy Prague completely from the air" and having been told by the German delegation that their "troops had already received orders to march and that any resistance would be broken with physical force." *Id.*, at 439. This finding was subsequently cited by the NMT. Ministries Judgment, *supra* note 136, at 429. For similar reasoning in Tokyo, *see* IMTFE Judgment, *supra* note 1, at 49,582a–49,583, 49,769.

155 High Command Judgment, *supra* note 40, at 485.

156 Fabre, *supra* note 67, at 99. Fabre is discussing the trigger for self-defense here, but as with Rodin's comment above, the point holds equally well for aggression. *Cf. supra* note 147.

157 *See supra* notes 66, 78, and accompanying text.

158 *Cf.* MODEL PENAL CODE, §§ 222.1, 223.1(2) (AM. LAW INST., Proposed Official Draft 1962).

It remains to be seen what the ICC's approach will be on the question of bloodless invasion. There is, however, both good reason and interpretive space to reject their criminality. To take this position is not to say that those condemning Russia's actions in Crimea as an "aggression" got it wrong.[159] On the contrary, the intervention exemplified several of the acts of aggression listed in Article 3 of the General Assembly's definition – acts that are also included in the identical list in Article 8 *bis* (2) of the Rome Statute.[160]

However, on the question of criminality, Article 8 *bis* (2) is modified by Article 8 *bis* (1), which defines as criminal only those acts of aggression (including explicitly those listed in 8 *bis* (2)) that *also* surpass "character," "gravity," and "scale" thresholds.[161] By the very structure of the provision, not all instances of the listed acts of aggression are criminal.[162] As the official Assembly of States Parties understandings emphasize, "aggression is the most serious and dangerous form of the illegal use of force ... in establishing whether an act of aggression constitutes a manifest violation of the Charter of the United Nations, the three components of character, gravity and scale must be sufficient."[163]

If the analysis in this chapter is right, these thresholds ought to be measured against unjustified human harm. Considered in that light, the latent violence that might underpin the criminality of bloodless invasions is plainly of lesser "seriousness," "danger," and "gravity" and of a different "character" than is consummated violence.[164] Understood in this way, bloodless invasions in the ICC regime (just as at Nuremberg) fall somewhere between clearly non-criminal acts – like illegally, but non-violently manipulating foreign elections – and clearly criminal, high-

159 On the use of the term "aggression" by states condemning Russia's action, see Corten, *supra* note 148, at 29–30; Tancredi, *supra* note 148, at 19.

160 Tancredi, *supra* note 148, at 19–29.

161 *See* ICC Statute, *supra* note 3, art. 8 *bis* (1)–(2).

162 Notably these thresholds are internal to the definition of the crime, unlike the general gravity requirement in the Court's admissibility criteria. ICC Statute, *supra* note 3, art. 17, para. 1(d). *See* also International Criminal Court Assembly of States Parties, Resolution RC/Res.6 (11 June 2010) [hereinafter ICC Aggression Amendments] at annex III, para. 7.

163 *Id.*, at annex III, paras. 6–7.

164 This reflects a general principle that, although the attachment of latent violence to a lower-level legal breach serves as a gravity multiplier, consummated violence is graver still. If an armed mugging is more serious than merely stealing the same item, killing an individual who resists that mugging is more serious a violation still. For more on how latent violence aggravates wrongfulness (as in the difference between armed mugging and merely stealing the same item), *see supra* notes 156–58 and accompanying text.

casualty invasions. This raises the real possibility that even highly effective bloodless invasions are not criminal under article 8 *bis*.

There is an obviously troubling aspect to letting the leaders of a bloodless invasion off the criminal hook. Had their presence been resisted by Ukraine, Russian troops stationed in Crimea would almost certainly have responded with lethal force. That was surely why they were stationed throughout the territory, and it is how Russian forces reacted to resistance in Donbass subsequently.[165] In that sense, the bloodlessness of Crimea was due not to restraint in Moscow, but to supererogatory restraint in Kiev.[166] However, there is nothing unique to aggression here. Persons are standardly judged in morality not on what they would have done had circumstances outside their control been different, but on what they actually did.[167] The criminal law, too, recognizes, however unlikely it may be, that a threat may never have been consummated, and that those who make a threat, even if it succeeds, should not be treated equivalently to those who made and consummated that threat. Moreover, the non-criminality of such actions would be compatible both with the dominant view that Russia engaged in a serious violation of public international law, and with the collective and severe sanctions imposed on Russia in response, including non-recognition of the annexation.[168] It is also possible that the gravity of their latent violence means that such actions ought to be found to be criminal. However, as things stand, their criminality is at the very least open to question.

Seen in this light, bloodless aggression does not provide a counter-example to the humanity-based account of the crime of aggression. On the contrary, in combination with the arguments earlier in this chapter, it

[165] OHCHR, *supra* note 151, para. 28, 37 (on casualties in Donetsk); *id.*, paras. 2, 22 (on Russian involvement).

[166] Although Ukraine's leaders were lauded for their restraint in refraining from using force in Crimea at the Security Council, most would recognize that they had the right to respond militarily to Russia's actions. For statements of the representatives from Luxembourg, the United States, and the United Kingdom praising Ukrainian restraint, *see* UN SCOR, 69th Sess., 7134th mtg. at 8, 19, U.N. Doc. S/PV.7134, at 4–5, 7 (Mar. 13, 2014).

[167] Thomas Nagel, *Moral Luck*, *in* Mortal Questions 24 (1979); Bernard Williams, *Moral Luck*, *in* Moral Luck 20 (1981).

[168] *See* G.A. Res. 68/262, paras. 5–6 (Mar. 27, 2014); Edward Hunter Christie, *Sanctions after Crimea: Have They Worked?*, NATO Rev. Mag., www.nato.int/docu/Review/2015/Russia/sanctions-after-crimea-have-they-worked/EN/index.htm [https://perma.cc/HJ8F-WGD6]; *EU Sanctions against Russia over Ukraine Crisis*, Europa, http://europa.eu/newsroom/highlights/special-coverage/eu_sanctions/index_en.htm [https://perma.cc/NK4T-DPCM].

fills out a context in which that is the only viable account of aggression. First, non-violent but severe infringements of sovereignty are not criminal. Second, large-scale, lethal uses of international force not responsive to armed attacks are criminal, even when they vindicate the core sovereign rights related to territorial integrity, political independence, or self-determination. Third, bloodless invasions that threaten significant human harm are at the margin of criminality – of mixed status at Nuremberg, and of dubious criminal status under the ICC regime. Fourth, when including such invasions in the crime, NMT judges emphasized the latent violence of those actions.

Humanitarian intervention lacking Security Council authorization raises a different set of concerns. Although a small minority of states and other authorities have argued that such interventions can be lawful,[169] the dominant view remains that they are not.[170] Only the latter view raises problems for the account presented here, so the following discussion assumes such actions to be illegal for the sake of argument.

The putative difficulty posed by the presumed illegality of humanitarian intervention is as follows. Article 8 *bis* criminalizes all "manifest

[169] The Dutch, Belgian, and UK governments have articulated this position at various points. Jane Stromseth, *Rethinking Humanitarian Intervention: The Case for Incremental Change*, *in* HUMANITARIAN INTERVENTION: ETHICAL, LEGAL, AND POLITICAL DILEMMAS 232, 239–40 (J. L. Holzgrefe & Robert O. Keohane, eds., 2003); Robin Cook, Sec'y of State for Foreign & Commonwealth Affairs, Speech to the American Bar Association Meeting in London (July 19, 2000), reproduced in *UK Materials on International Law*, 71(2) BRIT. Y.B. INT'L L. 646 (Geoffrey Marston, ed., 2000); *Guidance: Chemical Weapon Use by Syrian Regime, UK Government Legal Position*, PRIME MINISTER'S OFFICE, 10 DOWNING ST. (Aug. 29, 2013), www.gov.uk/government/uploads/system/uploads/attachment_data/file/235098/Chemical-weapon-use-by-Syrian-regime-UK-government-legal-position.pdf [https://perma.cc/VS7X-S3A2]. Shortly after stepping down as US State Department legal adviser, Harold Koh insisted that such interventions are at least arguably lawful. Harold Hongju Koh, *Syria and the Law of Humanitarian Intervention (Part II: International Law and the Way Forward)*, BLOG: JUST SECURITY (Oct. 2, 2013, 9:00 AM), www.justsecurity.org/1506/koh-syria-part2/ [https://perma.cc/SV9P-LT84].

[170] Koh admits "Among international legal commentators, the emerging party line seems to be that President Obama was threatening blatantly illegal military action in Syria . . ." *Id. See also* CHRISTINE GRAY, INTERNATIONAL LAW AND THE USE OF FORCE 47, 51 (3rd edn 2008) (many states have stated that they regard humanitarian intervention to be illegal); Debate Map: Use of Force against Syria, OXFORD PUB. INT'L L (Apr. 29, 2014), http://opil.ouplaw.com/page/debate_map_syria/debate-map-use-of-force-against-syria [https://perma.cc/YPS9-FZT6]. *See also* Tag Archive: Humanitarian Intervention, *Just Security*, www.justsecurity.org/tag/humanitarian-intervention/ (last visited July 1, 2017).

violation[s]" of the UN Charter's rules on the use of force, as defined by their "character, gravity and scale."[171] Efforts during the amendment process to attach an explicit understanding excluding humanitarian intervention from the crime failed.[172] As such, the argument goes, manifestly illegal humanitarian interventions are necessarily criminal.[173] The problem is that genuine and proportionate humanitarian interventions use lethal violence only to defend against criminally wrongful killing and violence.[174] In other words, they lack the wrong of aggression defined above – namely, the infliction of death and violence that is *not* justified by its response to the threat or infliction of the same.[175]

To be clear, humanitarian interventions do involve killing in an illegal action. In other words, they do involve *legally* unjustified killing.[176] However, the lack of legal justification for the killing in such an intervention is derivative of the illegality of the intervention. And the latter is not itself explicable with reference to the deeper wrong of killing without the justification of responding to the threat or infliction of illegal killing or analogous violence. The problem posed by the purported criminality of humanitarian intervention, then, is that the lack of legal justification for killing in a humanitarian intervention seems to reflect a privileging of

[171] ICC Statute, *supra* note 3, art. 8 *bis* (1).

[172] Beth Van Schaack, *The Crime of Aggression and Humanitarian Intervention on Behalf of Women*, 11 INT'L CRIM. L. REV. 477, 482–83 (2011). It is notable also that the preamble to the Rome Statute reaffirms the UN Charter's posture on the use of force and notes in that regard that "nothing in this Statute shall be taken as authorizing any State Party to intervene in … the internal affairs of any State." ICC Statute, *supra* note 3, pmbl., paras. 7–8.

[173] Elaborating the line of interpretation that would include humanitarian interventions as criminal, but predicting that a prosecution on these grounds is unlikely, *see* Sean D. Murphy, *Criminalizing Humanitarian Intervention*, 41 CASE W. RES. J. INT'L L. 341 (2009). Recognizing the possibility of an interpretation that would include humanitarian interventions as criminal, but arguing against it on feminist grounds, *see* Van Schaack, *supra* note 172.

[174] *See, e.g.*, G.A. Res. 60/1, *supra* note 102, para. 139; S.C. Res. 1674, *supra* note 102, para. 4; ICISS REPORT, *supra* note 102, paras. 4.13, 4.19–4.26.

[175] *See supra* notes 83–94 and accompanying text (explaining the basic consistency of this principle across crimes, notwithstanding different thresholds of criminality.). This is what explains why the legal right to use force obtains only when the state responds proportionately to an armed attack, and not when it faces more severe, but non-violent, violations of its territorial integrity or political independence, or of the self-determination of its people. *See supra* notes 66–68, 77–81 and accompanying text.

[176] This, at least, distinguishes them from plainly non-criminal, non-violent sovereignty infringements. Cf. Section 3.2.1 above.

sovereign rights over the value of human life, in line with the orthodox account of the crime.[177]

As with the concern about bloodless invasion, however, the objection fails. First, the best understanding of the (presumed) illegality of humanitarian interventions rests not on protecting sovereignty over human life, but on banning "good" wars so as not to encourage or facilitate "bad" wars. If genuine humanitarian interventions are criminal, it is so as to prevent the unjustified killing of disproportionate or pretextual interventions. Second, there is anyway ample interpretive space, and good reason, to exclude presumptively illegal humanitarian intervention from the crime.

In any domain, there is an inevitable gap between even optimally crafted law and the internal normative foundations of that law.[178] Put another way, there are always hard cases, whose legal status does not reflect their moral status, even when judged against the very moral standards on which the law is premised. This is for the familiar reason that optimal legal rules, unlike the underlying moral principles of right and wrong, must take account of moral hazard, the risks of abuse, the danger of slippery slopes, the collateral impact of rules on broader normative culture, and the "migration" of regulated behaviors out of the intended domain.[179]

[177] This is the root of Luban's charge that the criminalization of aggression has been "a major moral enemy of the human rights movement." *See supra* notes 33–35 and accompanying text. On the sovereignty harms associated with a humanitarian intervention, consider three examples. The Kosovo intervention resulted in the external administration and subsequent secession of the territory. S.C. Res. 1244, para. 10 (June 10, 1999) (establishing the UN Interim Administration Mission in Kosovo (UNMIK), and thus usurping the political authority of Serbia and Montenegro); *International Recognitions of the Republic of Kosovo*, Republic of Kosovo Ministry of Foreign Aff., www.mfa-ks.net/?page=2,224 [https://perma.cc/G8ZF-G6KM] (listing states that have recognized Kosovo's sovereign status). Tanzania's intervention in Uganda resulted in the overthrow of the Ugandan government. Thomas M. Franck, Recourse to Force: State Action against Threats and Armed Attacks 143–44 (2002). India's intervention in East Pakistan precipitated the secession of that territory, which became Bangladesh. *Id.*, at 139–42.

[178] *See* Larry Alexander & Emily Sherwin, The Rule of Rules: Morality, Rules, and the Dilemmas of Law (2001); Arthur Isak Applbaum, Ethics for Adversaries: The Morality of Roles in Public and Professional Life 199 (1999); Larry Alexander, *The Gap*, 14 Harv. J.L. & Pub. Pol'y 695 (1991).

[179] *See, e.g.*, Deborah L. Rhode, *Institutionalizing Ethics*, 44 Case W. Res. L. Rev. 665, 671 (1994); Kim Lane Scheppele, *Hypothetical Torture in the "War on Terrorism,"* 1 J. Nat'l Security L. & Pol'y 285, 307–18 (2005).

On a normative account that has gained particular prominence since NATO's 1999 intervention in Kosovo, and which offers the most coherent explanation of contemporary international law in this area, humanitarian interventions fall precisely into this gap between the law and its own underlying moral posture.[180] Along these lines, an influential independent report on the Kosovo intervention declared NATO's actions to have been "illegal but legitimate."[181] Prominent voices have endorsed this as the appropriate, long-term normative equilibrium for humanitarian intervention.[182] And several of the states that participated in the campaign claimed moral justification, while insisting that the intervention ought not be understood as a legal precedent.[183]

Underpinning this idea is the view that an explicit *ex ante* legal permission for even genuine humanitarian wars would facilitate the waging of both non-humanitarian interventions on a humanitarian pretext and disproportionate interventions that far exceed their humanitarian purpose, and that these twin dangers outweigh the benefit of enabling genuine, proportionate humanitarian interventions.[184] In short, the

180 The account described in this Section is perhaps the most common moral defense of the existing regime. *See* Dino Kritsiotis, *Reappraising Policy Objections to Humanitarian Intervention*, 19 MICH. J. INT'L L. 1005, 1020 (1998); W. Michael Reisman, *Unilateral Action and the Transformations of the World Constitutive Process: The Special Problem of Humanitarian Intervention*, 11 EUR. J. INT'L L. 3, 16 (2000).

181 INDEP. INT'L COMM'N ON KOSOVO, THE KOSOVO REPORT: CONFLICT, INTERNATIONAL RESPONSE, LESSONS LEARNED 4 (2000).

182 THOMAS M. FRANCK, RECOURSE TO FORCE: STATE ACTION AGAINST THREATS AND ARMED ATTACKS 166–89 (2002); OSCAR SCHACHTER, INTERNATIONAL LAW IN THEORY AND PRACTICE 126 (1991). *See also* Anthea Roberts, *Legality vs. Legitimacy: Can Uses of Force be Illegal but Justified?*, *in* HUMAN RIGHTS, INTERVENTION, AND THE USE OF FORCE 179, 212–13 (Philip Alston & Euan MacDonald, eds., 2008) (arguing that the "illegal but justified" frame might "ossify" the law in that posture, obstructing customary reform through shifting practice); Stromseth, *supra* note 169.

183 Stromseth, *supra* note 169, at 239 (on the French and German positions against treating the war as a precedent). These same leaders identified a humanitarian moral imperative to act. *See, e.g.*, DANIEL LEVY & NATAN SZNAIDER, THE HOLOCAUST AND MEMORY IN THE GLOBAL AGE 166 (2006) (noting that the German Chancellor, Foreign Minister, and Defense Minister "all cited the lessons of the Holocaust to justify sending troops to Kosovo"); UN GAOR, 54th Sess., 14th plen. mtg., U.N. Doc. A/54/PV.14 (Sept. 25, 1999); NATO Attack on Kosovo Begins, CNN (March 24, 1999), www.cnn.com/WORLD/europe/9903/24/kosovo.strikes [https://perma.cc/Y2VK-YUJZ] (quoting French President Jacques Chirac's explanation that Serbia's "unacceptable" treatment of Kosovar Albanians had triggered an imperative to act to "contain a tragedy").

184 *See, e.g.*, DINSTEIN, *supra* note 52, at 74; FRANCK, *supra* note 182, at 175–78; GRAY, *supra* note 170, at 52; SCHACHTER, *supra* note 182, at 126; Simon Chesterman, *Hard Cases Make Bad Law: Law, Ethics, and Politics in Humanitarian Intervention*, *in* JUST

aggregate risk of false positives under a permissive regime is thought to outweigh the risk of false negatives under a restrictive regime.

Pretext is a heightened danger here because the *jus ad bellum* is typically evaluated and enforced not by a judicial authority, capable of engaging in fine-grained, case-by-case analysis, but by states acting collectively to sanction and ostracize law-breakers.[185] In that sense, the effective enforcement of the *jus ad bellum* depends on broad consensus in each case. Because the precise threshold for humanitarian intervention is less easily identified than is the armed attack threshold of self-defense, it would be difficult, were genuine humanitarian intervention lawful, for an uncoordinated population of states to engage in such collective enforcement against states that wage illegal war on a humanitarian pretext. Or so the theory goes.

Understanding the illegality of unauthorized humanitarian intervention in this way makes better sense of the contemporary legal structure than does the sovereignty-based account. In particular, it fits with the notion that the Security Council is thought to have a *responsibility* to authorize (and thus render lawful) precisely the same substantive action.[186] The procedural requirement of Council authorization imposes

INTERVENTION 46, 50 (Anthony F. Lang Jr., ed., 2003); Kutz, *supra* note 19, at 230; UK Foreign and Commonwealth Office, Foreign Policy Document No. 148, *reprinted in* 57 BRIT. Y.B. INT'L L. 614, 619 (1986). *But see* Ryan Goodman, *Humanitarian Intervention and Pretexts for War*, 100 AM. J. INT'L L. 107, 107, 110–11, 126–27 (2006) (arguing that having claimed a humanitarian intervention justification is more likely to generate pressure on leaders to limit their uses of force than would claiming self-defense).

185 On the collective enforcement of international law, *see, for example*, Oona Hathaway & Scott J. Shapiro, *Outcasting: Enforcement in Domestic and International Law*, 121 YALE L.J. 252 (2011). *See also infra* note 168 (on the sanctions imposed on Ukraine). On the relevance of disagreement here, consider Hersch Lauterpacht's observation that "the existing imperfections of the law in the matter of determining whether there has occurred a breach of the obligation not to have recourse to aggressive war are themselves part of the law." Hersch Lauterpacht, *The Limits of the Operation of the Law of War*, 30 BRIT. Y.B. INT'L L. 206, 211 (1953).

186 *See supra* note 102 and accompanying text. On the potential impact of even limited Security Council-authorized interventions on the target state's political independence, consider the way in which the narrow aerial intervention in Libya in 2011 led to regime change (whether as a necessary means to (or collateral effect of) its humanitarian aim, or, less charitably, as a deliberate exploitation by the intervening states of the authority granted them by the Council). *See, e.g.*, Mehrdad Payandeh, *The United Nations, Military Intervention, and Regime Change in Libya*, 52 VA. J. INT'L L. 355, 387–91 (2012); Simon Tisdall, *The Consensus on Intervention in Libya Has Shattered*, GUARDIAN (Mar. 23, 2011), www.theguardian.com/commentisfree/2011/mar/23/libya-ceasefire-consensus-russia-china-india [https://perma.cc/PM6P-EP9M].

a political and epistemic check that is likely to block the vast majority of pretextual interventions.[187] Although some genuine humanitarian interventions will be prohibited, the presumption is that this is a defensible tradeoff, especially if the genuine interventions can be excused as legitimate post hoc.[188] This understanding also makes sense of the debate regarding humanitarian intervention's illegality. As a hard case on the law's own normative terms, it is not surprising that different states and commentators have come to different legal views as to its permissibility.[189]

This way of understanding the illegality of humanitarian intervention also clarifies how to account for the criminality of aggression. On this account, humanitarian intervention is illegal (and thus potentially criminal) not because it inflicts the wrong of massive killing without responding defensively to the threat or infliction of the same, but because permitting it would encourage wars that *do* inflict that wrong – that is, pretextual or disproportionate interventions.

This reconciles the illegality (and possible criminality) of humanitarian intervention to the unjustified killing account. However, it also suggests that, even if humanitarian interventions are illegal, the best interpretation of Article 8 *bis* would exclude such wars. The condemnation and punishment inherent in criminal conviction heighten the imperative to narrow the gap between laws and the moral principles that underpin them (especially in a domain focused only on "the most serious

[187] *Cf.* Franck, *supra* note 182, at 102–05 (on the Security Council's "jury" function in checking abuses of preemptive self-defense), 185–87 (on the post fact "jurying" of the UN's political organs in retrospectively excusing a humanitarian intervention).

[188] *See* sources cited in *supra* notes 182–84. Even those who consider the Council to be broken seek to replicate the same function by requiring the endorsement of a diverse coalition or regional organization. *See, e.g.*, ICISS Report, *supra* note 102, paras. 6.28–6.40; Cook, *supra* note 169, at 647 (2000); *see also* Allen Buchanan & Robert O. Keohane, *Precommitment Regimes for Intervention: Supplementing the Security Council*, 25 Ethics & Int'l Aff. 41, 52–55 (2011) (describing the structure of a democratic coalition regime).

[189] *See supra* notes 169–70. Given the recent nature of both the responsibility to protect and the willingness of states to claim the lawfulness of humanitarian intervention, the case for this understanding of the illegality of humanitarian intervention is plainly stronger today than it was in 1998. However, the "benevolent silence" of the international community *vis-à-vis* earlier interventions suggests that it may have been the optimal normative account even at that earlier stage in international law's ongoing evolution. Franck, *supra* note 182, at 154. *See generally id.* ch. 9 (examining the international responses to several humanitarian interventions prior to the development of the responsibility to protect norm).

crimes").[190] International criminal law would lose normative authority if the leader of a genuine humanitarian intervention were convicted of the "supreme international crime" of aggression, despite not inflicting its core "accumulated evil."[191] The justificatory threshold for a regime under which an action is "supremely criminal but legitimate" is significantly higher than is that for a regime under which an action is merely "illegal but legitimate."[192]

Moreover, whereas the *jus ad bellum* is ordinarily enforced collectively by states, international crimes are enforced by a single judicial authority capable of reaching nuanced case-by-case judgments with authoritative effect.[193] In this institutional context, a rule permitting genuine humanitarian interventions would be less likely to encourage large numbers of bad wars than might be the case in the *jus ad bellum* more broadly.[194]

Consider these points together. The justification for criminalizing humanitarian intervention despite it lacking the core wrong is higher than is the threshold for justifying its illegality. And a core aspect of the justification for its illegality is anyway weaker. Combining this with the observation that humanitarian intervention lacks the core criminal wrong, there is good internal reason to exclude humanitarian intervention from the crime. Measuring the "seriousness," "gravity," "character," and "danger" of an illegal use of force by its unjustified infliction of human death and suffering affords plenty of interpretive

[190] On "the gap," *see* Alexander, *supra* note 178, at 696. On the imperative to narrow it, *see id.*, at 698 ("It is difficult to bring ourselves to punish those who have done what we acknowledge was the correct thing to do, even when we understand the consequentialist warrant for punishing them"). On the gravity of international crimes, *see* ICC Statute, *supra* note 3, pmbl., para. 4. *See also* Section 2.1 of Chapter 2, above.

[191] On the notion of aggression as an "accumulated evil" and the "supreme international crime," *see* IMT Judgment, *supra* note 1, at 427.

[192] Claims that a given action could be internationally *criminal*, but legitimate are rare. For a highly controversial position along those lines, *see* H.C.J. 5100/94 Pub. Comm'n against Torture in Isr. v. State of Isr. 53(4) PD 817, para. 40 (1999) (Isr.) (holding that individuals may be criminally liable for engaging in torture, even when doing so is morally required by urgent necessity, and resolving that the best such soldiers can hope for is the post hoc mercy of the prosecutors or the courts).

[193] Under the ICC's system of complementarity, domestic courts have primacy and a final say in the case, unless the relevant domestic actors prove unwilling or unable to investigate and (if appropriate) prosecute perpetrators, at which point the international court takes over. ICC Statute, *supra* note 3, art. 17(1)(a)–(c).

[194] *Cf. supra* notes 185–88 and accompanying text.

room to do that.[195] Pursuant to that reading, genuine humanitarian interventions would fall short of the criminal threshold, even if one considers them to be illegal.[196]

3.4 What This Means for the Soldier

This chapter has debunked a common misconception – that aggression is a normative anomaly in international criminal law, uniquely rooted in a wrong inflicted on the attacked state, rather than in an accumulation of wrongs inflicted on individual human beings. Not only are individuals wronged gravely in an aggressive war, the wrongfulness of their treatment as individuals is at the very crux such wars' criminality. This way of understanding the crime better explains the contours of the crime, comports more closely with the purposes of international criminal law, and better aligns with adjacent areas of international law.

This is significant in thinking about the status of soldiers on either side of an aggressive war. On international law's own terms, the soldiers who fight in an aggressive war are not remotely situated *vis-à-vis* a macro interstate wrong. They inflict the very violence whose wrongfulness is why such wars are criminal. If they are expected to be able to "wash their hands of guilt" from the international legal point of view, there must be some feature of their relationship to their own immediate acts that explains that non-culpability.

Similarly, if those that suffer that violence are not to be granted the status of crime victim, it cannot be because the harms they suffer are ancillary or distant consequences of the crime. On the contrary, those very harms are what makes the crime worthy of condemnation. Here, too, some alternative explanation is needed to account for their exclusion from the class of crime victims. The ensuing chapters explore whether the explanations that might be offered for either position are viable.

195 *Cf. supra* notes 161–64; ICC Statute, *supra* note 3, art. 8 *bis* (1); *see also, e.g.*, Van Schaack, *supra* note 172, at 486 ("[T]he only way for any party to address potentially unlawful but nonetheless legitimate uses of force is with reference to the tripartite factors of character, gravity, and scale . . . The term 'character', as a more qualitative term, is the most elastic of the three factors and might provide an opening"). *But see* Murphy, *supra* note 173, at 362 ("Rather than carve out humanitarian intervention, the purpose of the threshold language . . . seems to be to eliminate minor incidents of armed force from the crime of aggression, such as frontier incidents involving border patrols or coast guards").

196 Harold Hongju Koh & Todd F. Buchwald, *The Crime of Aggression: The United States Perspective*, 109 AM. J. INT'L L. 257, 273 (2015).

PART II

Can International Law's Posture towards Soldiers Be Defended?

4

Military Duress

It is commonly claimed that soldiers participate non-culpably in illegal wars. This claim can take a number of forms. Those forced to fight in a criminal war might be excused by the duress under which they operate. Those unaware of the facts rendering their war illegal might be excused on epistemic grounds. These factors might be thought both to exculpate aggressor soldiers of any *jus ad bellum* responsibility, eliminating any internal basis for a right to refuse, and to close the moral gap between them and those on the other side in a way that complicates victim designation. Alternatively, soldiers might be subject to a special role morality that narrows the scope of wrongdoing for which they can be culpable and of which they can be victims.

In this chapter, the focus is on the first of these ideas. Namely, that home state coercion combines with the mortal threat of combat to force soldiers to fight, rendering them innocent of the criminally wrongful violence they inflict in an aggressive war and perhaps rendering them no less victimized by the crime than the soldiers on the other side.

A common characterization of the relationship between combatants on either side of a war is that they fight in conditions of reciprocal self-defense.[1] As revisionist just war theorists have argued, this is not a tenable frame.[2] At the moral heart of self-defense is the idea that an aggressor forfeits the right to defend herself when her target responds

[1] Paul W. Kahn, *The Paradox of Riskless Warfare*, 22 Phil. & Pub. Pol'y 2, 2–3 (2002); Thomas Nagel, *War and Massacre*, 1 Phil. & Pub. Aff. 123, 138–40 (1972). *See also* G. E. M. Anscombe, *Mr. Truman's Degree*, *in* Ethics, Religion and Politics 67 (Oxford, Basil Blackwell 1981); Anthony Kenny, The Logic of Deterrence 10 (1985); Michael Walzer, Just and Unjust Wars 145, n.* (1977) [hereinafter Walzer, JUW].

[2] David R. Mapel, *Coerced Moral Agents? Individual Responsibility for Military Service*, 6 J. Pol. Phil. 171, 176 (1998); Jeff McMahan, Killing in War 110–15 (2009). *See also* David R. Mapel, *Innocent Attackers and Rights of Self-Defense*, 18 Ethics & Int'l Aff. 81, 84 (2004).

with proportionate and necessary defensive force.[3] This core principle underpins domestic criminal codes across the world and it has been recognized as axiomatic by the ICTY, by the NMT, and in the Rome Statute.[4]

Walzer recognizes this in the ordinary interpersonal setting, but argues that war is different because the soldier does not "choose" the wrongful attack of which he is a part; he is sent forcibly by his state.[5] This coercion, Walzer contends, renders soldiers on both sides subject to a "shared servitude," forced into a context in which they must kill to survive.[6]

Walzer is right that coercion from their home state is morally significant for soldiers in the aggressor force. Even in the era of globally declining conscription, it remains a real part of the soldier's lived experience.[7] Many volunteers sign up without knowing which wars they may be required to fight and without any reason to believe a criminal war is forthcoming. Others sign up under acute economic pressure.[8] States then use the threat of punishment to coerce those troops to deploy and to engage the enemy, regardless of the *jus ad bellum* status of the war.[9]

3 McMahan, *supra* note 2, chs. 1, 4; David Rodin, War and Self-Defense ch. 4 (2002).

4 *See, e.g.*, Kevin Heller & Markus Dubber, The Handbook of Comparative Criminal Law 270–71, 509, 583 (2010); Prosecutor v. Kordić & Čerkez, Case No. IT-95–14/2-T, Trial Judgment, para. 451 (Int.'l Crim. Trib. for the Former Yugoslavia Feb 26, 2001); United States v. von Weizsäcker, *in* 14 Trials of War Criminals before the Nuernberg Military Tribunals under Control Council Law No. 10, at 1329, 334–36, 379 (1949); Rome Statute of the International Criminal Court, U.N. Doc. A/CONF.183/9, 2187 U.N.T.S. 90, art. 31(1) (c) (July 17, 1998) (as amended in 2010 by Doc. C.N.651.2010.TREATIES-8) [hereinafter ICC Statute].

5 Walzer, JUW, *supra* note 1, at 128; *id.*, at 30; Judith Lichtenberg, *How to Judge Soldiers Whose Cause is Unjust*, *in* Just and Unjust Warriors: The Moral and Legal Status of Soldiers 112 (David Rodin & Henry Shue, eds., 2008).

6 Walzer, JUW, *supra* note 1, at 37. He terms them "coerced moral agents." *Id.*, at 306.

7 On declining conscription globally, *see* Joshua C. Hall, *The Worldwide Decline in Conscription: A Victory for Economics?*, Library of Economics & Liberty (Oct. 3, 2001), www.econlib.org/library/Columns/y2011/Hallconscription.html – Table 1.

8 Michael J. Wilson, et al., Youth Attitude Tracking Study 1998: Propensity and Advertising Report tbl. 4.1 (Jan. 17, 2000); Michael Massing, *The Volunteer Army: Who Fights and Why?*, 55 NY Rev. Books 34–36 (Apr. 3, 2008). *See* Andrew Fiala, Public War, Private Conscience: The Ethics of Political Violence 59–60 (2010) (on the phenomenon of the "green card warrior").

9 *See, e.g.*, Uniform Code of Military Justice 10 U.S.C., §§ 885–87, 890, 892, 894, 899–900, 913, 915, arts. 85–87, 90, 92, 94, 99–100, 113, 115 (2006); Mark Osiel, Obeying Orders 85 (1999). On supervision in the field as a method of forcing soldiers to engage the enemy: Lt. Col. Dave Grossman, On Killing 141–48 (rev. edn 2009). S. L. A. Marshall, Men against Fire 82 (University of Oklahoma Press, 2000) (1947).

Social and family pressures supplement this formal coercion,[10] as does the felt need not to abandon beloved comrades.[11]

It is also true that, having deployed under those coercive conditions, soldiers are then faced with their adversary's lethal threat, and will often have to kill to survive. However, the coercive circumstances of the deployment do not transform the latter interaction into one of self-defense. Instead, the essential role of coercion from actors other than those against whom lethal force is used exposes its non-viability as a self-defense claim. At most, the argument underpins a claim of two-way duress – the soldier on the aggressor side is sandwiched between the justified enemy threat on the one side, and the coercive threat from her home government on the other. This situation may force her to inflict wrongful violence in order to survive. But the coercive context would only excuse her from culpability; it could not underpin a justification for the violence she inflicts.[12] In contrast, it does not matter whether the soldier on the other side was coerced by his state to fight, because, from the legal point of view, his fighting is justified to begin with.[13]

Of course, soldiers bear no legal liability for participating in aggression, so they do not need a *legal* excuse. However, precision on the moral underpinnings – and specifically on the distinction between permissibility and non-culpability – matters in fully understanding the law's posture towards soldiers. For one thing, excuses are scalar, not binary, and, unlike justifications, they vary across soldiers perpetrating identical acts on the same side of the same war. Those faced with the death penalty for disobedience may well be fully excused for fighting and killing in

[10] Tim O'Brien, The Things They Carried 20–21, 49–63 (1990) [hereinafter O'Brien, TTTC].

[11] R v. Michael Peter Lyons [2011] EWCA (Crim) 2808, para. 3; Colby v. Min. of Cit. & Immigr. [2008] F.C. 805, para. 7 (Can.); Richard A. Gabriel, *Modernism vs. Pre-Modernism: The Need to Rethink the Basis of Military Organizational Forms*, *in* Military Ethics and Professionalism 55, 71 (James Brown & Michael J. Collins, eds., 1981); Hal Bernton, *Officer at Fort Lewis Calls Iraq War Illegal, Refuses Order to Go*, Seattle Times (June 7, 2006), http://old.seattletimes.com/html/iraq/2003044627_nogo7m.html.

[12] *See, e.g.*, David R. Mapel, *Innocent Attackers and Rights of Self-Defense*, 18 Ethics & Int'l Aff. 81, 84 (2004); McMahan, *supra* note 2, at 116–18; Moshe Halbertal, On Sacrifice 85, 88–89 (2012); 3 Emmerich de Vattel, The Law of Nations, or the Principles of Natural Law, §137 (1758); 3 Hugo Grotius, The Rights of War and Peace 1275–77 (Richard Tuck, ed., Liberty Fund 2005) (1625).

[13] Adil Ahmad Haque, Law and Morality at War 66, 90 (2017) (offering an account of why that killing is justified).

an aggressive war. However, those who face only a minor sanction for refusing would be only partially excused of otherwise identical actions, and those who volunteer freely for a specific criminal war would not be able to avail themselves of the duress excuse at all. This variation poses an obvious difficulty for using duress to explain the general legal posture, which does not adjust for such soldier-specific contexts.

Building on that observation, this chapter spotlights three key problems with the utility of duress as an explanation of the law's posture *vis-à-vis* soldiers on either side of an aggressive war. First, by the standards generally applicable in international criminal law, the level of duress applicable to many soldiers who fight in illegal wars falls far below the threshold required for a full excuse. In isolation, it cannot explain why they are not criminally liable for fighting, let alone why they have no right to refuse. Second, on that latter dimension, the duress argument answers the wrong question: the legally applied coercion that pushes soldiers to fight and kill in an unlawful war is the core normative problem, not its solution. The more severe the soldier's duress, the more profoundly she is wronged by the law's own lights when she is denied the right to disobey. Third, the duress argument does not dispel at all the dissonance of excluding from victim status those subject to the targeted violence of a criminal war. At most, the implication of the duress argument might be thought to imply that some of those soldiers harmed while fighting on the aggressor side should be included as victims *alongside* those harmed fighting against aggression. This idea is explored further below. Here it is sufficient to note that conceptualizing the soldier on the aggressor side in that way risks conflating the concept of being the victim of a specific crime with that of suffering justified defensive harm as a non-culpable perpetrator of that crime.

4.1 Duress and Culpability

As discussed in Chapter 2, the scope of criminal liability, and particularly international criminal liability, is, with rare exceptions, narrower than that of the underlying moral culpability upon which it depends.[14] As such,

[14] On the particularly narrow focus of international criminal law, as compared to domestic criminal law, *see* Kai Ambos, *Command responsibility and Organisationsherrschaft*, *in* SYSTEM CRIMINALITY IN INTERNATIONAL LAW 127, 128–29 n.5 (André Nollkaemper & Harmen van der Wilt, eds., 2009). Applied to criminal liability for aggression, *see* LARRY MAY, AGGRESSION AND CRIMES AGAINST PEACE 248, 266, 268 (2008).

even an excuse sufficient to eliminate criminal liability altogether would not necessarily eliminate entirely the individual's deeper culpability for the criminal wrong in question. And yet, in the context of all other international crimes, duress far greater in severity and imminence than that applicable to many soldiers who fight in aggressive wars fails to excuse them even from criminal liability, much less from the deeper underlying blameworthiness.

To be fully excused from criminal liability at Nuremberg required (on the most lenient version) having a gun to one's head.[15] This threshold has not been lowered since. Indeed, in the first post-Cold War case on this issue, the standard applied was even tougher. During the Srebrenica genocide, Dražen Erdemović, a young soldier in the 10th Sabotage Division of the Bosnian Serb Army (VRS), was told he would be lined up and shot alongside his prospective victims if he did not kill seventy captured Muslim men and boys in the Pilica Farm massacre.[16] Despite this extraordinary duress, the International Criminal Tribunal for the former Yugoslavia (ICTY) sentenced Erdemović to five years' imprisonment, holding that, although the threat he faced warranted a mitigated sentence, it did not render his actions wholly innocent.[17]

In justifying the limited effect of Erdemović's duress, appellate judges McDonald and Vorah quoted Lord Kilbrandon in reasoning: "the decision of the threatened man whose constancy is overborne so that he yields to the threat, is a calculated decision to do what he knows to be wrong, and therefore that of a man with, perhaps to some exceptionally limited extent, a 'guilty mind.'"[18] In this way, international criminal law

[15] United States v. Ohlendorf, 4 Trials of War Criminals before the Nuernberg Military Tribunals under Control Council Law No. 10, at 411, 480–81 (1949); United States v. von Leeb, 11 Trials of War Criminals before the Nuernberg Military Tribunals under Control Council Law No. 10, at 462, 509 (1949) [hereinafter High Command Judgment]; Walzer, JUW, *supra* note 1, at 314 (endorsing this standard). Other cases took a stricter approach more similar to that of the later Int'l Crim. Trib. for the Former Yugoslavia Erdemović case (discussed immediately below). *See, e.g.*, Trial of Max Wielen & 17 Others (Stalag Luft III Case), 11 Law Reports of Trials of War Criminals 31, 49 (1949); *Defence Pleas, in* 15 Law Reports of Trials of War Criminals 153, 173 (1949).

[16] Prosecutor v. Erdemović, Case No. IT-96–22-T*bis* [Second] Sentencing Judgment, paras. 14–15, 17 (Int'l Crim. Trib. for the Former Yugoslavia Mar. 5, 1998) [hereinafter Erdemović Second Trial Sentencing].

[17] *Id.*, at paras. 17, 23.

[18] Prosecutor v. Erdemović, Appeals Judgment, Case No. IT-96–22-A, McDonald, J. & Vorah, J., joint separate opinion), para. 70 (Int'l Crim. Trib. for the Former Yugoslavia Oct. 7, 1997) [hereinafter Erdemović Appeals Judgment]. Lord Kilbrandon had written a

incorporated the longstanding common law perspective on duress in the context of intentional killing.[19]

The untested language of the ICC Statute returns to a standard that seems closer to that articulated at Nuremberg. Duress before the ICC can furnish a full excuse, but only if the crime was perpetrated in response to "a threat of imminent death or of continuing or imminent serious bodily harm," *and* the crime does not involve "a greater harm than the one sought to be avoided."[20] Dissenting in *Erdemović*, Antonio Cassese advanced a similar standard.[21]

The duress imposed on most soldiers with respect to killing in an illegal war falls far below even the lower Nuremberg and ICC threshold. Soldiers in democratic states do not fight in wrongful wars with anything like a gun to their heads. Forty-four of the forty-seven Council of Europe states have ratified a protocol that commits them not to apply the death penalty, even in war.[22] Uniquely among its peers, the United States provides for the formal possibility of that ultimate punishment for deserters, but it has been implemented only once since the Civil War, and has not been used at all for seven decades, despite multiple long wars and many desertions.[23] The penalty actually enforced in most

minority opinion that was subsequently vindicated in R v. Howe [1987] 1 All E.R. 771 (HL). *See id.*, at 777.

19 *See, e.g.*, Matthew Hale, 1 The History of the Pleas of the Crown 50 (1800); William Blackstone, 4 Commentary on the Laws of England 30 (1769); Erdemović Appeals Judgment, *supra* note 18 (McDonald, J. & Vorah, J., dissenting), para. 60. Civil law countries have been more forgiving in that extreme context. *Id.*, at para. 59.

20 ICC Statute, *supra* note 4, art. 31(1)(d).

21 Erdemović Appeals Judgment, *supra* note 18, para. 16 (Cassese, J., dissenting).

22 Protocol No. 13 to the Convention for the Protection of Human Rights and Fundamental Freedoms, concerning the abolition of the death penalty in all circumstances, *opened for signature*, May 3, 2002, C.E.T.S. No. 187 (entered into force July 1, 2003). Russia and Azerbaijan have not signed; Armenia has signed but not ratified. *See* Chart of Signatures and Ratifications as of June 29, 2017, http://conventions.coe.int/Treaty/Commun/ChercheSig.asp?NT=187&CM=&DF=&CL=ENG. Belarus, Kazakhstan, and the Vatican City – uniquely among established European states – are not Council of Europe members. Nor are any of the states whose sovereignty is in dispute (including Kosovo).

23 Uniform Code of Military Justice, 10 U.S.C., § 885(c), art. 85(c) (2006). On executions, *see The US Military Death Penalty*, Death Penalty Information Center, www.deathpenaltyinfo.org/us-military-death-penalty (last visited Aug. 15, 2014). On the frequency of desertion, *see, for example*, *Army Desertion Rate Soaring*, CBS News (Nov. 16, 2007); Sig Christenson, *US Army Desertion Rate at Lowest since Vietnam*, AFP (Nov. 7, 2011); Freedom of Information Act Letter, From: DCDS Pers Secretariat, Ministry of Defence, To: [Redacted], Reference: 20-08-2010-160944-005 (Sept. 13,

democratic states (including the United States) is incarceration for a low single-digit number of years.[24]

Even in a state that does apply the death penalty to deserters, the mere *possibility* of execution back home – itself an anachronism for soldiers in democratic states – plainly falls short of the Nuremberg / ICC test, which requires such "*imminent* physical peril" as to eviscerate the possibility of choice.[25] Of course, in the heat of battle, the lethal threat from the opponent may impair temporarily the soldier's moral capacities such that she does in fact kill at the point of a gun. However, that is just one side of the two-way duress, which lasts for only a short period of time. During the periods outside that situation of immediate threat, if there is not also an imminent lethal threat associated with desertion, the Nuremberg/ICC test is not met. Moreover, a large proportion of soldiers are not in fact under immediate threat from their opponents even in the moment of inflicting death and suffering in war; instead, they are subject to a more nebulous long-term threat from the enemy forces as a whole.[26]

None of this is to deny that many soldiers who fight in illegal wars do so under coercive conditions. Rather, it is to emphasize that the severity of that coercion would not ordinarily underpin a full excuse. By international law's own lights, soldiers ordered to perform wrongful killings or to participate in a massive criminal wrong have a considerably greater duty to resist coercion than that imposed on those required to fight in illegal wars. If soldiers are uniquely innocent in the latter context, it is not due to duress.

2010), www.gov.uk/government/uploads/system/uploads/attachment_data/file/16803/FOI20082010160944005_AWOL_20002010.pdf.

[24] *See, e.g.*, Hinzman v. Minister of Citizenship & Immigration [2007] F.C.A. 171, para. 48 (Can.); Chris Hedges, What Every Person Should Know about War 14–15 (2003). Even following a military crack-down on desertion in the US, sentences remain relatively short. Glass v. Minister of Citizenship & Immigration [2008] F.C. 881, paras. 19, 29 (Can.); Paul von Zielbauer, *Army is Cracking Down on Deserters*, NY Times (9 Apr., 2007), www.nytimes.com/2007/04/09/us/09awol.html. British soldiers who refused to serve in Iraq faced a maximum sentence of ten years, but typically served less than one. R v. Michael Peter Lyons [2011] EWCA (Crim) 2808, paras. 1, 40; *RAF Doctor Jailed over Iraq Refusal*, Guardian (Apr. 13, 2006), www.theguardian.com/uk/2006/apr/13/military.iraq.

[25] High Command Judgment, *supra* note 15, at 509.

[26] *See, e.g.*, Fernando Tesón, *Self-Defense in International Law and Rights of Persons*, 18 Ethics & Int'l Aff. 87, 87 (2004); Daniel Statman, *Targeted Killing*, 5 Theoretical Inquiries L. 179, 181 (2004); Judith Jarvis Thomson, *Self Defense*, 20 Phil. & Pub. Aff. 283, 297 (1991); Walzer, JUW, *supra* note 1, at 138–43.

4.2 Answering the Wrong Question: Moral Perspectives

There is a more fundamental problem with relying on duress to explain the extant legal posture. Even if the soldier's duress were sufficient to warrant not punishing him, this would explain only why soldiers ought not be criminally liable for fighting in illegal wars. To try to make sense of their lack of a *right* to disobey on this basis would be to mistake the explanandum for an explanans. The imposition of that duress by law is precisely the dissonance that needs to be accounted for. The greater the coercive pressure on soldiers to fight, the more severe the denial of their right to refuse, and the more urgent the need to give a compelling normative explanation of that denial and how it coheres with the broader regime.

In the abstract, this seems obvious, but it is worth making it concrete. The leaders and organizations that coerce soldiers to kill in aggressive wars inflict two wrongful harms. The harm done to the ultimate victims is the unjustified violence visited upon them. The harm done to the aggressor state's own soldiers is the moral injury of having participated in the infliction of that primary wrong. As discussed in Chapter 2, this injury has particular legal significance when it is rooted in the law's own underlying moral principles of wrongdoing and culpability. To appreciate fully how that connection works requires examining the multidimensional implications of those underlying principles, specifically with respect to the first-, second-, and third-person moral perspectives.

The third-person perspective is the posture of objective moral analysis. The two questions are: is the action wrongful, and is the actor in question culpable? The criminal law aspires to this third-person perspective. Its purpose is the punishment of culpable wrongdoing above a certain threshold. Chapter 3 established that killing in an aggressive war is wrongful by the law's own lights. Section 4.1 began, and Chapters 5, 6, 7, and 8 continue, the discussion of whether the obedient soldier is culpable by those lights. These evaluations of wrongdoing and culpability are also fundamental to the second- and first-person moral perspectives. However, those perspectives, which are important to the questions at issue here, involve additional normative complexity.

The second-person perspective changes the focus to condemnation. In addition to the objective questions answered from the third-person perspective, this raises a new, interpersonal element: ought I (or ought we) blame the soldier for her action? Wrongfulness and culpability obviously matter here, but so too does the potential blamer's standing to condemn.[27]

When the coercion that the soldier faces is imposed in our names, occurs without our committed and substantive opposition, and is not inflicted on us, whatever standing to blame we might otherwise have had is weakened and probably eliminated.[28] Indeed, when we have been in that privileged and apathetic situation, we probably lack standing to blame *any* soldier who fights obediently, whether or not she is coerced by our state and in our names.

Precisely because that lack of standing is so widespread, it might overwhelm inquiries into culpability and wrongdoing by any commentator who correctly feels the inappropriateness of blaming soldiers for their participation. In other words, what is expressed as an exoneration of soldiers may in fact be an entirely appropriate reluctance to assert standing to condemn for what is wrongful conduct.[29] Rectifying this misdiagnosis should clarify the terms of debate: many of us are right to refrain from blaming soldiers who fight in aggressive wars, but this does not mean that fighting in such a war involves no culpable wrongdoing.

Ultimately, however, the key dimension for the right to disobey is the first-person perspective – the soldier's own moral posture *vis-à-vis* her conduct. Rather than blame, the phenomenon here is that of moral burden. Permissibility and culpability are again foundational. However, as with the second-person perspective, they are not the only important aspects. In this context, standing drops out of the normative picture. Replacing it is the salience of the act to the soldier's understanding of self, its impact on what Scanlon terms her internal "ground relationship."[30]

Whereas others must ask whether they can blame her, and the criminal law must ask whether her culpability rises to the level that warrants punishment, the individual must consider whether she can live comfortably with herself – whether she can endorse an honest self-narrative that incorporates this among her defining acts.[31] The gap between that

[27] *See, e.g.*, G. A. Cohen, *Casting the First Stone: Who Can, and Who Can't, Condemn the Terrorists?*, 58 Royal Inst. Phil. Supp. 113 (2006); Marilyn Friedman, *How to Blame People Responsibly*, 47 J. Value Inquiry 271 (2013); T. M. Scanlon, Moral Dimensions: Permissibility, Meaning, Blame 175–6 (2008).

[28] On the importance of the relationship between blamer and blamed in defining the scope of the former's standing to blame, *see* Scanlon, *supra* note 27, ch. 4 (especially 175–76).

[29] McMahan, *supra* note 2, at 96.

[30] Scanlon, *supra* note 27, at 155

[31] *See, e.g.*, Lynne McFall, *Integrity*, 98 Ethics 5, 7 (1987) (emphasizing that achieving integrity requires honesty to oneself and overcoming the temptation to re-describe acts or

question and the third-person (criminal law) question is recognized in the refugee status of a soldier who flees illegal orders that did not require her to commit a crime and yet would have rendered her reasonably unable to "wash her hands of guilt" for the underlying wrong from the legal point of view.[32]

The gap may be particularly pronounced in the context of duress. Duress mitigates culpability. However, it does not eliminate the actor's intention or the moral choice. Rather, it overwhelms her sufficiently that she makes, in the legal language, "a calculated decision to do what [s]he knows to be wrong."[33] There is no ambiguity regarding which is the right decision; it is just that choosing that path is extraordinarily difficult.

This is crucial, because more important to the individual's internal ground relationship than her precise degree of culpability for the wrongful act is the salience of the wrong in her life. Performing a grave wrong under significant duress may be a relatively low-culpability action. If sufficiently severe, the duress may even warrant a full legal excuse and it may eliminate the standing of many others (especially those connected to the duress) to condemn the perpetrator for the act. But to say that it should therefore be easy for the perpetrator to live with having inflicted that grave wrong would be to misunderstand the first-person perspective. What the soldier seeks in her first-personal moral struggle is a reason to believe she did the *right* thing – the idea that she should not be blamed for doing wrong is likely to ring painfully hollow.[34]

Living with oneself is not simply a process of totting up moral grades and achieving an acceptable average; an individual's life story is punctuated by defining moments and deeds.[35] If that individual is

commitments to make them fit). David Luban calls the strategy of redescription "low road" integrity. On the distinction between this and "high road" integrity (and the significance thereof), *see* David Luban, Legal Ethics and Human Dignity 67–97 (2007). Offering a useful framing in his discussion of self-blame, Scanlon argues that when that internal blame is appropriate, "[o]ne cannot, so to speak, be one's own friend," one experiences "a kind of self-estrangement." Scanlon, *supra* note 27, at 154–55.

[32] *See supra* Section 1.3, of ch. 1. [33] *See supra* note 18.

[34] Nancy Sherman, The Untold War: Inside the Hearts, Minds, and Souls of our Soldiers 92 (2011) (Sherman writes that the US veterans she interviewed, "feel the tremendous weight of their actions . . . they are far more likely to say, 'If only I hadn't' or 'If only I could have,' than 'It's not my fault.'").

[35] On the moral importance of one's connection to specific acts and consequences, *see, for example*, Martha C. Nussbaum, *Luck and Ethics*, *in* Moral Luck 73, 74

even minimally culpable for a grave wrong, the defining significance of that wrong to her conception of self, and the challenge of reconciling herself to it, would ordinarily far exceed its significance as a moral grade and would have little connection to whether others have standing to blame her. A wrongdoer capable of simply washing her hands of guilt or "shrugging off" a severe wrong would thereby exhibit a moral deficiency, even if she were only minimally culpable and even if second-party blame for the initial act would be inappropriate.[36]

The *Erdemović* case exhibits this concept at work in the law. As a young man faced with an immediate and inescapable threat to his life, Dražen Erdemović chose to escape that threat by killing seventy innocents.[37] Although his crime was grave, his culpability was, by any test, mitigated significantly by that extreme duress. Thus, even his reduced sentence of five years was controversially high.[38] Indeed, it can be plausibly argued that he should have been acquitted, as he probably would have been under either the ICC rules or the Nuremberg standard.[39]

However, it would be a mistake to extrapolate from Erdemović's significantly reduced culpability that he ought to be wholly mollified by those mitigating circumstances.[40] Erdemović's first-person moral perspective on the wrong creates for him a different normative engagement with it, even when judged against the standards of wrongfulness and culpability that underpin the criminal law.

In fact, if Erdemović *were* completely mollified by the mitigating circumstances in which he acted, and thereby felt unburdened by his participation in the crime, this would exhibit a callous and condemnable self-satisfaction.[41] Presumably, for precisely this reason, the ICTY found

(Daniel Statman, ed., 1993); Bernard Williams, *Moral Luck*, *in* MORAL LUCK: PHILOSOPHICAL PAPERS 1973–1980, at 20, 29–30 (1981); Susan Wolf, *The Moral of Moral Luck*, 31 PHIL. EXCHANGE 4, 12–18, 20–23 (2001); Margaret Urban Walker, *Moral Luck and the Virtues of Impure Agency*, 22 METAPHILOSOPHY 14, 25 (1991); SCANLON, *supra* note 27, at 126–28.

36 Walker, *supra* note 35, at 18, 21. *See also* Wolf, *supra* note 35, at 7, 9.

37 Erdemović Second Trial Sentencing, *supra* note 16, paras. 14–15.

38 *See* Erdemović Appeals Judgment, *supra* note 18 (Cassese, J., dissenting), at paras. 47–48, 50–51.

39 On the different standards, *see supra* notes 15–21 and accompanying text.

40 *Cf.* Walker, *supra* note 35, at 18–22, 25; discussion in *supra* note 36. I do not mean here to invoke amoral agent regret, but genuine moral burden.

41 *See* Walker, *supra* note 35, at 18–26.

it to be important that Erdemović had struggled greatly with what he did, and held that this weighed in his favor at sentencing.[42]

The burden that Erdemović appropriately bears is not akin to the burden felt by a conscientious driver who, through no fault of her own, hits a child. It is not mere agent regret.[43] Indeed, if Erdemović were to draw an analogy between the two cases, this too would expose a severe lack of moral comprehension. He did not harm his victims accidentally. He intentionally inflicted a profound wrong on them.

Importantly, recognizing this – and recognizing its connection to the posture adopted by the ICTY – does not entail holding that Erdemović deserves a life of inner moral torment. He was put in an awful position and he made a choice that many of us would make, even while recognizing it to be wrongful. But third-person desert is the wrong mode by which to assess his internal relationship. His severe burden is both unfair and entirely appropriate. He suffered cruel moral luck.[44] The nature of the act is such that it cannot but take a central place in his moral understanding of self. The cruelty of his situation is that he is right to struggle to live at ease with himself, despite the fact that most others would have done the same, that he deserves minimal if any punishment, and that very few of us have standing to condemn him.[45]

How the ICTY seems to have thought about Erdemović bears lessons for how we should think (from the legal point of view) about the relevance of duress to the normative position of soldiers coerced into fighting in an aggressive war. Inflicting death or suffering in an illegal war is the core wrong-making feature of the supreme crime. Although duress may mitigate the soldier's culpability for those acts, it does not eliminate it entirely. And, as any war veteran will attest, participating in the violence of any war is one of the central defining experiences in the lives of those who fight it.[46] When the war is wrongful and the

[42] Erdemović Second Trial Sentencing, *supra* note 16, paras. 16(ii) (at 15–16) (finding that Erdemović's post-traumatic stress disorder following Srebrenica "demonstrates how he himself has suffered from being forced to commit the killings against his will" and rejecting the suggestion that he carried no burden).

[43] On the difference between agent regret and moral luck, *see* Williams, *supra* note 41, at 27–31; Scanlon, *supra* note 27, at 148–51 (contrasting "objective stigma" with "genuine cases of moral luck").

[44] *Cf.* Nagel, *supra* note 1, at 33 (on what he calls "luck in circumstances").

[45] *See* Scanlon, *supra* note 27, at 148–51 (arguing that moral luck's truth is in its impact on relationships) and at 154–55 (explaining the individual's internal "ground relationship" with the self). *See also* sources cited in *supra* note 36.

[46] *See supra* Section 1.5 of ch. 1. Sherman, *supra* note 34, at 20.

soldier is even minimally culpable for participating, it is appropriate that the defining chapter will be heavily burdensome, even if the soldier does not deserve punishment and few have standing to blame her for fighting.

Like Erdemović, the soldier in that situation endures indisputably cruel moral luck. As such, despite being normatively appropriate, her burden is also deeply unfair. Few of us have faced that kind of challenge to our moral fortitude. But the unfairness of that burden by the law's own lights is the whole point here. Even if, contrary to the arguments in Section 4.1, the duress imposed on those who fight in illegal wars *were* adequate to shield against criminal liability, it would confuse moral perspectives to hold that this would lift the burden borne by those who participate in illegal wars. Not only does duress fail to alleviate that burden, it is the most important reason why that burden is so unfair; as the severity of the duress rises, so too does the unfairness of the burden imposed on those operating under that duress.

To suggest to Erdemović that he has no complaint against his VRS superiors because the duress they inflicted on him should have wiped the burden from him would be untenable. To suggest that this erasure would have happened (and his basis for complaint would have been overridden) if only the duress had been *more severe* would border on the absurd. Such a position would misunderstand the wrong of being forced to do wrong and would overlook the uniquely first-personal dimension of the refugee law test that an individual fleeing unlawful orders must have been reasonably unable to "wash his hands of guilt" for the underlying legal wrong. Returning to the *jus ad bellum* context, it is entirely coherent for Tim O'Brien to write that he "detested" the coercion imposed by the society that pushed him into Vietnam and "held them personally and individually responsible" for the decision,[47] and yet that he felt the profoundest "self-hatred and self-betrayal" for succumbing to that coercion.[48]

The soldier's duress is real. But that is exactly the problem. The question is how to make normative sense of a regime in which that duress is imposed by law, the action required by it would involve severe culpable wrongdoing by the law's own lights, and yet the soldier is given no lawful escape from it.

[47] O'Brien, TTTC, *supra* note 10, at 49.

[48] Tim O'Brien, *The Vietnam in Me*, NY Times Magazine (Oct. 2, 1994).

4.3 The Tragedy of Deaths on Both Sides

A final way in which duress could be relevant to the issues under review here is that it might be thought to break down the normative distinction between soldiers on either side of the war. If soldiers on both sides are equally coerced into war's hell, as the traditional theory would have it, this weakens the sense in which those on the attacked side can make a unique claim to victim status. On this account, even if soldiers who participate in an aggressive war are insufficiently dissociated from the wrong to escape its moral burden, their coercive deployment might ground a claim to victim status when they are harmed or killed. On this telling, to use Walzer's language, war is a context in which "armies of victims meet."[49]

It is important to be clear about the implications of this line of reasoning. Holding that those harmed while fighting on the aggressor side should be recognized as victims by the law's own lights would not resolve the apparent dissonance of a regime that excludes soldiers on the attacked side from victim status. On the contrary, it would extend the scope of that dissonance to soldiers on both sides, all of whom would be denied victim status by the candidate approaches discussed in Chapter 1.[50]

Nonetheless, the objection deserves attention. At the very least, it would entail that on the issue of eligibility for victim status, soldiers on both sides would stand or fall together. Perhaps that implication would be the premise for a more complex argument for why no soldiers should have victim status.

The objection, however, is mistaken. It is true that those harmed in the course of fighting on the aggressor side are often wronged in that process. They suffer both the wrong of being forced to do wrong by the law's own lights *and* the wrong of being coerced into a situation in which they are the legitimate targets of justified violence. Moreover, the criminalization of aggression is important in rendering the state's coercion in these contexts wrongful. However, there is a qualitative difference between these wrongs and the wrong suffered by those on the other side.

[49] WALZER, JUW, *supra* note 1, at 45.

[50] Arguing that such an expansion to soldiers on both sides *would* be appropriate, *see* Frédéric Mégret, *What is the Specific Evil of Aggression?*, *in* THE CRIME OF AGGRESSION: A COMMENTARY 1398, 1428, 1442–43 (Claus Kreß & Stefan Barriga, eds., 2016); Erin Pobjie, *Victims of the Crime of Aggression*, *in id.* 816, 843–44.

The wrong suffered by troops killed or harmed fighting against an aggressor force inheres in the crime. As argued in Chapter 3, it is because the killing and violence inflicted by an aggressor force is wrongful that the war is criminal. That the aggression involves wrongful violence of that kind is simply what it means for the war to be criminal. It does not matter in this respect whether those killed or harmed fighting against an aggressor side were coerced to fight by their home government.

Although the fact of an illegal war is important to why the aggressor state acts wrongfully by coercing its own soldiers to fight, the wrong done to those soldiers inheres not in the crime itself, but in that wrongful coercion. As such, the fact that the war is criminal does not itself entail that the killing and suffering inflicted on aggressor troops is morally problematic. Those who fight for the known aggressor under no coercion – a category that might include private contractors, those who volunteered for the specific war in question, or those who had the option to refuse – are not wronged by the aggressor state's leaders.

At the same time, when aggressor forces use such un-coerced troops, this ought not be understood to reduce the scope of the criminal wrong.[51] Similarly, a drone-perpetrated aggression in which the aggressor force suffered zero casualties would be no less profound a criminal wrong than a similarly destructive war in which the aggressor suffered significant casualties. In contrast, on the account advanced in Chapter 3, the extent of the criminal wrong *would* be mitigated considerably if the aggressor force were to take territory without inflicting significant loss of life, as in a bloodless invasion.[52]

None of this is to deny either the gravity of the wrong of coercing one's own soldiers into an illegal and unjustified war, or the just claims of those troops and their families for accountability for that wrong.[53] But the tranche of that wrong related to their physical risk is best understood as

[51] Condemning mercenary aggressions, *see* S.C. Res. 405 (Apr. 14, 1977); S.C. Res. 496 (May 28, 1982); ICC Statute, *supra* note 4, art. 8 *bis* (2)(g).

[52] *See* Tom Dannenbaum, *Why Have We Criminalized Aggressive War?*, 126 Yale L.J. 1242, 1304–06 (2017).

[53] Walzer, JUW, *supra* note 1, at 110. *See also* Richard A. Gabriel, To Serve with Honor 160 (1982); Bruce Kent, Letter to the editor, *Why Did our Sons Die? An Inquiry into the Iraq War is Essential*, Guardian (Mar. 25, 2009), www.theguardian.com/politics/2009/mar/25/iraq-war-enquiry; *Tony Blair has "Blood on his Hands", says Father of Killed Soldier*, Telegraph (Oct. 10, 2009), www.telegraph.co.uk/news/worldnews/middleeast/iraq/6286081/Tony-Blair-has-blood-on-his-hands-says-father-of-killed-soldier.html; Dante Zappala, *It's Official: My Brother Died in Vain*, LA Times (Jan. 14, 2005), at B11.

a domestic abuse of coercive power, not as an international infliction of unjustified killing. It is a likely consequence of, but not the reason for, the criminalization of aggression. It is an abuse external to the crime.

To be clear, it would be entirely appropriate for the physical harm suffered by soldiers to be addressed separately from the prosecution of aggression. Exemplifying this, consider, for example, the decision to reserve for the families of British soldiers and civilians killed in Iraq one third of the seats for Tony Blair's testimony before the Chilcot Inquiry.[54] In that domestic forum for the analysis of the government's decision-making, they were thought particularly deserving of an accounting. But recognizing the value in that kind of recognition of the abuse of coercive power does not mean identifying them as victims of the crime of aggression.

[54] *Seats Ballot for Tony Blair's Grilling on Iraq War*, BBC News (Jan. 5, 2010), http://news.bbc.co.uk/1/hi/uk_politics/8441040.stm.

5

Shedding Certain Blood for Uncertain Reasons[1]

Of course, duress is not the only factor mitigating the aggressor soldier's culpability. A second dimension is epistemic. This spotlights a real difference between the situation of many soldiers involved in a typical war of aggression and the situation of soldiers involved in a typical war crime. Few in Dražen Erdemović's position would be uncertain about the wrongfulness of what he was asked to do. There is no context in which killing defenseless civilians is not criminal. In contrast, the very killing that makes aggression a crime would be completely lawful when perpetrated by the other side, and soldiers often lack sufficient information to be certain whether they are on the aggressor side or not. States engaged in armed conflict tend to assert public justifications rooted in relatively uncontroversial legal doctrines.[2] Rather than one side openly violating the law, each presents facts that fit its narrative of legality.[3] Soldiers often lack access to the information that would allow them to evaluate these claims.

There are exceptions.[4] As discussed above, when the UN Security Council authorizes one side, the necessary implication is that the other is engaged in a manifestly illegal use of force, which, if sufficiently grave,

[1] Tim O'Brien, The Things They Carried 44, 49 (1990) (writing of the American war in Vietnam, "[c]ertain blood was being shed for uncertain reasons" because the population at home was too apathetic to understand a context that "was all too damned complicated").

[2] Christine Gray, International Law and the Use of Force 10–12, 114–15, 118–19, 121, 169–70 (3rd edn 2008); Thomas M. Franck, *The Power of Legitimacy and the Legitimacy of Power: International Law in an Age of Power Disequilibrium*, 100 Am. J. Int'l L. 88, 96–97 (2006). Lauterpacht predicted this pattern early in the UN Charter era. Hersch Lauterpacht, *The Limits of the Operation of the Law of War*, 30 Brit. Y.B. Int'l L. 206, 220 (1953).

[3] Christine Gray, *supra* note 2, at 115–16.

[4] Arguing that many soldiers know or ought to know their wars to be wrongful, *see* Adil Ahmad Haque, Law and Morality at War 3 (2017).

would constitute a criminal aggression.[5] Leaks of classified information also have the capacity to expose criminality in going to war. Moreover, the current rise of populist nationalism may cause at least some leaders to feel less constrained by the language of international law and to engage in aggressions that are more brazen.[6]

However, the fact remains that many aggressor soldiers are likely to be less than certain about the criminality of their wars. And this uncertainty might be thought to explain why they ought not bear any liability for participating in such wars, why they ought to have no difficulty "washing their hands of guilt" when they do participate, and perhaps why they are no less the victims of aggression than are their opponents.

5.1 Invincible Ignorance and the Fog of Criminal War

The thrust of this line of argument follows in a rich tradition. From "fathers of international law" like Francisco de Vitoria and Hugo Grotius to contemporary theorists such as David Estlund, Christopher Kutz, and David Luban, many thinkers have argued that as long as there is doubt as to the war's *jus ad bellum* status, those who fight obediently are morally "invincible" in their ignorance.[7] Given the scarcity of wars whose criminality is patently clear to the lower-level participants, this "invincible ignorance" theory amounts to a friendly amendment to the orthodox

[5] A notable recent case was the multilateral action against Libya. S.C. Res. 1973 (Mar. 17, 2011). For older cases, *see, for example*, Christine Gray, *supra* note 2, ch. 8. On findings of aggression, *see especially id.* 256–58.

[6] Antonello Tancredi, *The Russian Annexation of the Crimea: Questions Relating to the Use of Force*, 1 Questions Int'l L. 5, 7–8 (2014) (Putin eventually admitted that "the Russian servicemen did back the Crimean self-defense forces" and made "a substantial, if not *the decisive*, contribution to enabling the people of Crimea to express their will").

[7] Francisco de Vitoria, *On the Law of War*, *in* Political Writings 295, 308, 317, 327 (Anthony Pagden & Jeremy Lawrance, eds., 1991) (1539); 1 Hugo Grotius, The Rights of War and Peace 337–37 (Richard Tuck, ed., Liberty Fund 2005) (1625) (on the general duty to disobey orders contrary to the law of nature); *id.* vol. 2, at 1167, 1177 (applying this to war); *id.*, at 1130 (on the invincible ignorance excuse); David Estlund, *On Following Orders in an Unjust War*, 15 J. Pol. Phil. 213, 229–30 (2007) (Estlund's argument requires that "the political and institutional process producing the commands is duly looking after the question whether the war is just," in which case, obedience is appropriate as long as the war falls within an acceptable "range of error" and is not manifestly unjust); Christopher Kutz, *The Difference Uniforms Make: Collective Violence in Criminal Law and War*, 33 Phil. & Pub. Aff. 148, 173–74 (2005) [hereinafter Kutz, *Uniforms*]; David Luban, *Knowing When Not to Fight*, *in* Oxford Handbook of the Ethics of War (Helen Frowe & Seth Lazar, eds.) (forthcoming) [hereinafter Luban, *Knowing When*].

normative account.[8] Soldierly ignorance on the *jus ad bellum* dimension is, on this view, a "parametric" feature of war, rather than a contingent fact.[9] Thus, Dill and Shue argue that soldiers are so "unavoidably ignorant" of the *jus ad bellum* status of their wars, that their deliberation and responsibility ought to be attached exclusively to the *jus in bello*.[10]

The invincible ignorance theory is largely consistent with prevailing standards of international criminal responsibility in the context of obedience and aggression. The obedient perpetrator of an international crime is only held responsible when the command was manifestly unlawful.[11] The same is true in many domestic military codes.[12] Even in the absence of superior orders, liability for aggression attaches only to those who know of the facts rendering the war criminal and only to manifestly unlawful wars.[13]

On the one hand, this might be thought to suggest a coherence between the normative posture of international criminal law and the exclusion of soldiers from criminal liability from aggression, given that the latter are generally not certain of their wars' illegality. On the other

[8] Indeed, orthodox theorists often reference soldiers' epistemic constraints. MICHAEL WALZER, JUST AND UNJUST WARS 35, 39, 289 (1977) [hereinafter WALZER, JUW]; Avishai Margalit & Michael Walzer, *Israel: Civilians and Combatants*, 56 NY REV. BOOKS (May 14, 2009); *see also* LARRY MAY, AGGRESSION AND CRIMES AGAINST PEACE 242–46 (2008); Dan Zupan, *A Presumption of the Moral Equality of Combatants: A Citizen-Soldier's Perspective*, *in* JUST AND UNJUST WARRIORS: THE MORAL AND LEGAL STATUS OF SOLDIERS 214, 217–18 (David Rodin & Henry Shue, eds., 2008).

[9] Luban, *Knowing When*, *supra* note 7, at n. 7 (citing Seth Lazar and Laura Valentini, "Proxy Battles in the Ethics of War (2014) manuscript).

[10] Janina Dill & Henry Shue, *Limiting the Killing in War: Military Necessity and the St. Petersburg Assumption*, 26 ETHICS & INT'L AFF. 311, 325 (2012).

[11] United States v. Ohlendorf, 4 TRIALS OF WAR CRIMINALS BEFORE THE NUERNBERG MILITARY TRIBUNALS UNDER CONTROL COUNCIL LAW NO. 10, at 470–73 (1949); Rome Statute of the International Criminal Court, U.N. Doc. A/CONF.183/9, 2187 U.N.T.S. 90, art. 33(1) (c) (July 17, 1998) (as amended in 2010 by Doc. C.N.651.2010.TREATIES-8), [hereinafter ICC Statute]. *See also* United States v. von Leeb, 11 TRIALS OF WAR CRIMINALS BEFORE THE NUERNBERG MILITARY TRIBUNALS UNDER CONTROL COUNCIL LAW NO. 10, at 462, 512 (1949) (the test is whether a subordinate of "normal intelligence" would recognize the order's illegality).

[12] *See* Mark J. Osiel, *Obeying Orders: Atrocity, Military Discipline, and the Law of War*, 86 CAL. L. REV. 939, 951–52 (1998). The Israeli test is famously that the orders must "wave like a black flag." Chief Military Prosecutor v. Malinki (Mil. Ct. Appeal, 1959), 2 PALESTINE Y.B. INT'L L. 69, 109–10 (1985) [Kfar Qassem case]; Attorney Gen. of the Gov't of Isr. v. Eichmann, 36 I. L. R. 275, 277 (Sup. Ct. 1962).

[13] ICC Statute, *supra* note 11, art. 8 *bis* (1). *See also* Elements of Crimes, INT'L CRIM. CT. 30, art. 8 (*bis*), element 4 (2013), www.icc-cpi.int/resource-library/Documents/ElementsOf CrimesEng.pdf [http://perma.cc/8VEX-6XJF].

hand, precisely because soldiers who obey without that certainty would anyway fail the *mens rea* requirements of international criminal law, the fact that *jus ad bellum* uncertainty is widespread among lower-level troops cannot explain why the Nuremberg and ICC standards exclude from criminal liability even the few to whom the criminality of the war *is* clear. If uncertainty is involved in the explanation for soldiers' blanket exclusion from criminal liability for aggression, it can only be as one part of a more complicated argument. Such an argument is discussed in Chapters 7–8.

The more immediately important point is that a criminal law *duty* to disobey is not all that is at stake. Just as in the duress analysis, there is no reason to believe that the scope of the soldier's criminal responsibility should be coterminous with the broader culpability that would underpin a *right* to disobey. Here, again, the gap between the two is uncontroversial when applied to the *jus in bello*.

In the United States, the *jus in bello* right to disobey covers any orders that can be shown to have been unlawful, even if they were not patently so.[14] Some states go even further, extending the right to disobey to orders that the soldier reasonably believes to be illegal, even if they are in fact lawful orders.[15] Canadian and English refugee courts have held that the key determinant of the right to asylum for disobedient soldiers is whether, had the applicant obeyed, he "would not [have been] able to wash his hands of guilt" for, or "might [have been] associated with," the legal wrong, even though not criminally liable for it.[16]

If "guilt" by the law's own lights can be broader than criminal responsibility, then the mere fact that certainty is required to trigger criminal

[14] United States v. New, 55 M.J. 95, 100 (C.A.A.F. 2001) (permitting soldiers to challenge the legality of orders that are not patently illegal, though placing the evidentiary burden on the disobedient soldier in the case of orders that are illegal, but not patently so); US Dep't of Def., Manual for Courts-Martial United States, para. 14(c)(2)(a)(i), at iv–19 (2008).

[15] Mark Osiel, Obeying Orders 242 (1999). In Germany, this has been extended to the *jus ad bellum* context. *See infra* Section 10.3 of Chapter 10. In some states, the *duty* to disobey is (at least in theory) applicable whenever it is unreasonable to believe the order to be illegal (even if it is not manifestly illegal). *See* Osiel, *supra*, at 75–76. Osiel advocates expanding both the right and the duty in the *jus in bello* realm in that direction. *Id.* chs. 1, 15–22.

[16] Zolfagharkhani v. Minister of Employment & Immigration) [1993] 3 F.C. 540 (Can.). *See also* Key v. Minister of Citizenship & Immigration [2008] F.C. 838, paras. 23, 29 (Can.) [hereinafter *Key* Federal Court Judgment]; Krotov v. Sec'y of State for the Home Dep't [2004] EWCA (Civ.) 69, para. 117 (Eng.).

liability for following orders does not entail straightforwardly that obedience is non-culpable up to that point of certainty. The first task, then, is to determine what the normative significance of uncertainty *is* in the *jus ad bellum* context. That task is discharged here in two parts. This chapter rejects the viability of a cosmopolitan story of invincible ignorance. The following chapter considers the interaction between uncertainty and the soldier's associative and political relationships to his state and its people, finding in them a stronger, but ultimately unpersuasive basis for the extant legal postures on disobedience and victim status.

Separating the analysis in this way takes seriously the notion of international law's humanization and aggression's place in it.[17] The unifying principle of various humanization trends in international law is the cosmopolitan idea that basic standards of human treatment are of sufficient importance to warrant global attention and regulation. Within this limited scope, individual human beings are understood to be objects of global normative concern in and of themselves.[18] The most important of these rules (including the ban on aggression) are generally considered to be *jus cogens* and *erga omnes* norms – obligations around which states cannot contract and that are owed to the world community. If aggression's criminality is rooted ultimately in the wrong of unjustified killing and human violence, it makes sense to examine the soldier's *jus ad bellum* uncertainty through this cosmopolitan lens before considering the extent to which his particular political and associative relationships might change the normative story.

5.2 A Spectrum of Uncertainty

The invincible ignorance account is typically framed in starkly binary terms. The soldier is either certain that the war is wrongful, or is not. Terms like "ignorance," "error," and "doubt" are conflated to reflect a common standard: if the soldier has even the smallest of doubts that the war is wrongful, he is deemed non-culpable.[19] This binary frame is misleading. Individuals' evidence-based certitude regarding a given claim (such as the claim that

[17] *See* Chapter 2 and Section 3.2.3 of Chapter 3 above.

[18] Ruti Teitel, Humanity's Law 4–5 (2011) (focusing in this respect on international human rights law, international criminal law, and international humanitarian law).

[19] Grotius, *supra* note 7, at 1130; Vitoria, *supra* note 7, at 308; Estlund, *supra* note 7, at 229–30; Lene Bomann-Larsen, *License to Kill? The Question of Just v. Unjust Combatants*, 3 J. Mil. Ethics 142, 155 (2004).

his war is lawful) can be anywhere on a spectrum of probability from 0 (knowing that it is not true) to 100 (knowing that it is true).[20]

For invincible ignorance theorists the only relevant distinction is whether a soldier is certain that his war is illegal (0) or not certain that it is illegal (1–100). They accept the culpability of fighting at 0, but hold that such certitude never realistically obtains and that soldiers with epistemic postures of ≥ 1 are not in any way culpable for killing and inflicting suffering in a wrongful war.

Other thresholds of normative significance, however, are obscured by this. For example, one might think that it would only be reasonable to believe that the war is lawful when that has a probability higher than 50.[21] This is the threshold used by the US National Security Agency to define a "reasonable belief" that an individual satisfies the legal criteria for being surveilled.[22] Another threshold would be whether there is a "substantial likelihood" that the war is lawful; a third would be whether there is a "substantial likelihood" that it is *un*lawful.[23]

Wherever precisely these thresholds are on the epistemic spectrum, they are plainly much higher than 1. In other words, soldiers typically classified as "invincibly ignorant" include those who fight and kill in situations in which it is plainly unreasonable to believe that that killing is not perpetrated in the context of an aggressive war, as well as those for whom there is no substantial likelihood that the war is lawful. The key question, then, is whether, from the legal point of view, soldiers in *those* positions get it wrong when they find themselves unable to "wash their hands of guilt" for the human violence they inflict.

5.3 The Normative Vincibility of Ignorance

The notion that uncertainty can do the work of hand-washing here is difficult to maintain. Intentionally killing while having strong reasons to

[20] *Cf.* JEFF MCMAHAN, KILLING IN WAR 138 (2009).

[21] *Cf.* Niko Kolodny, *How Does Coherence Matter?*, 107 PROC. ARISTOTELIAN SOC'Y 229, 233 (2007).

[22] Ed Pilkington, *Washington Post Releases Four New Slides from NSA's Prism Presentation*, GUARDIAN (June 30, 2013), www.theguardian.com/world/2013/jun/30/washington-post-new-slides-prism. *See also NSA Slides Explain the PRISM Data-Collection Program*, WASHINGTON POST (last updated July 10, 2013), www.washingtonpost.com/wp-srv/special/politics/prism-collection-documents/?hpid=z1.

[23] *Cf.* Prosecutor v. Blaškić, Case No. IT-95-14-A, Appeals Judgment, para. 42 (Int'l Crim. Trib. for the Former Yugoslavia July 29, 2004).

believe that doing so is wrongful is ordinarily a profoundly culpable act, *even if* one has lingering, or even substantial, doubts as to that wrongfulness. The basic moral rule is: "don't know, don't kill."[24]

This principle is reflected throughout the law. To avoid a murder conviction for an intentional homicide, it is not enough to say that one did not know that the justificatory conditions for killing did not obtain. In many states, one must have *reasonably believed* that the justificatory conditions *did* obtain.[25] States that are more lenient excuse perpetrators that have genuine, subjective beliefs that the conditions obtain, but even in those states, merely doubting that the conditions did not obtain is plainly inadequate.[26] Whether international human rights law requires states to criminalize intentional killing that fails the first (reasonable belief) test or second (genuine subjective belief) test is a matter of dispute, but it is clear that a state's right to life obligations require criminal prosecution when the perpetrator merely doubted that the justificatory conditions did not obtain.[27]

There are, of course, important differences between the interpersonal context and that of interstate uses of force. The most morally consequential is the lack of an overarching sovereign in the latter. On a Hobbesian

[24] Alexander A. Guerrero, *Don't Know, Don't Kill: Moral Ignorance, Culpability, and Caution*, 136 PHIL. STUD. 59 (2007) (arguing against killing when one does not know if the target has moral status (such as a fetus or an animal), but asserting that the same thesis would apply to factual uncertainty as to whether accepted justificatory conditions for killing obtain). On the relevance of this to the soldier in an unjust war, *see* MCMAHAN, *supra* note 19, at 138.

[25] *See, e.g.*, People v. Goetz, New York Court of Appeals, 68 N.Y.2d 96, 497 N.E.2d 41 (1986); Fiona Leverick, *Unreasonable Mistake in Self-Defence*, 13 EDINBURGH L. REV. 100 (2009); Caroline Forell, *What's Reasonable? Self-Defense and Mistake in Criminal and Tort Law*, 14 LEWIS & CLARK L. REV. 1401, 1403 (2010); Francisco Muñoz Conde, *Putative Self-Defense: A Borderline Case between Justification and Excuse*, 11 NEW CRIM. L. REV. 590, 603–08 (2008); GEORGE P. FLETCHER, BASIC CONCEPTS IN CRIMINAL LAW 162 (1998).

[26] *See* R v. Gladstone Williams [1987] 3 All E.R. 411, 415 (Lord Lane, CJ); Criminal Justice and Immigration Act 2008 c.4, § 76, paras. 4–6. *See also* Stanley Yeo, *Commonwealth and International Perspectives on Self-Defence, Duress, and Necessity*, 19 CURRENT ISSUES IN CRIM. JUSTICE 345, 351 (2008). In Germany, an honest but unreasonable belief that the conditions for self-defense obtain can protect the accused from conviction for intentional murder, but may be convicted of a lesser, negligence offense. MARKUS DUBBER & TATJANA HÖRNLE, CRIMINAL LAW: A COMPARATIVE APPROACH 414 (2014).

[27] *See, e.g.*, Da Silva v. United Kingdom, App. No. 5878/08 Eur. Ct. H. R., paras. 245–52 (Mar. 30, 2016); McCann v. United Kingdom, App. No. 18984/91 Eur. Ct. H. R., para. 200 (Sept. 27, 1995). Compare FIONA LEVERICK, KILLING IN SELF-DEFENCE, ch. 10 (2006).

account, precisely that reality undermines the viability of any normative restrictions on the aggressive use of force.[28] Contemporary international law, however, rejects that position. Starting from the premise that normative order can be imposed – whether through institutions of mutual benefit, multilateral outcasting, domestic (or transnational) enforcement, or otherwise – it articulates narrow *jus ad bellum* rights, with epistemic limits not unlike those applicable in domestic criminal law.

Towards the tail end of the long and brutal war between Iran and Iraq in the 1980s, several US-flagged commercial ships and American naval vessels were hit by mines and a torpedo while navigating international waters in the Persian Gulf.[29] Claiming the right of self-defense, the United States responded by attacking Iranian oil platforms and other targets.[30] Iran brought suit before the ICJ.

One of the key questions before the court was whether the American vessels had been attacked by Iran (a necessary precondition of the former's right to use force in self-defense against the latter). Iran claimed the mines that hit US ships were not Iranian, and that the torpedo had been fired from elsewhere.[31] The preponderance of the evidence clearly favored the United States on this issue, but things were not entirely clear-cut – Iraq had also been laying mines in the Gulf and there was not total certainty as to the source of the torpedo.[32]

Despite accepting that the evidence was "highly suggestive" of Iranian responsibility, the ICJ found that the United States did not act in lawful self-defense, holding that only "conclusive" evidence that the justificatory conditions obtained would have rendered a use of force lawful.[33] Even moderate uncertainty as to the source of the attack mandated military inaction.

This presumption against the use of force in conditions of uncertainty permeates the *jus ad bellum*. It is the most plausible reason why anticipatory defensive force is currently permitted, on most accounts, only in

[28] On the impact the sovereign makes on the duty to be conservative in one's use of force, *see* Thomas Hobbes, Leviathan 74–78, 136–45 (1651) (Edwin Curley, ed., Hackett 1994); *see also* Stephen C. Neff, War and the Law of Nations 127 (2005); Henry Shue, *Laws of War, Morality, and International Politics*, 26 Leiden J. Int'l L. 271, 273–74 (2013).

[29] Oil Platforms (Iran v. US), Judgment, 2003 I.C.J. 161 (Nov. 6), paras. 23–26, 52, 69 [hereinafter Oil Platforms Judgment].

[30] *Id.*, at paras. 25–26, 46–48, 65–68.

[31] *Id.*, at paras. 54–55, 70.

[32] *Id.*, at paras. 58–61, 71–72.

[33] *Id.*, at para. 71.

the clearest cases of inescapably imminent attack.[34] That this should be the case is hardly obvious. Preventing wrongful violence is the very justificatory basis for using force in self-defense.[35] Even in response to a devastating armed attack, a belligerent reaction is lawful only if necessary to prevent ongoing and future attacks.[36] Punitive or retaliatory uses of force are unambiguously illegal.[37]

In principle, then, it is *preferable*, by international law's own normative lights, that defensive force be used in advance of an attack, rather than when an attack is ongoing. But the uncertainty that a prospective wrongful attack will actually occur militates strongly against allowing the preemptive use of force in any but the clearest and most narrowly defined cases.[38] The underlying moral concern is precisely that such action involves killing and the infliction of human suffering when the justificatory basis may not actually be present.[39] The danger of inflicting wrongful harm due to an erroneous prediction of future attack outweighs the possibility that the prediction is correct and the

[34] Christine Gray, *supra* note 2, at 160–65, 203–27; David Harris, Cases & Materials on International Law 931–33 (6th edn 2004); UN High-Level Panel on Threats, Challenges & Change, *A More Secure World: Our Shared Responsibility*, paras. 188–92, U.N. Doc. A/59/565 (2004). For a controversially broader approach, *see* Attorney General of the United Kingdom, Speech at the International Institute for Strategic Studies (Jan. 11, 2017), www.gov.uk/government/speeches/attorney-generals-speech-at-the-international-institute-for-strategic-studies. However, even this position requires "a reasonable and objective basis for concluding that an armed attack is imminent."

[35] *See, e.g.*, Neff, War and the Law of Nations, *supra* note 28, at 97; Derek Bowett, *Reprisals Involving Recourse to Armed Force*, 66 Am. J. Int'l L. 1, 2–3 (1972) (noting that the key distinction between self-defense (which is lawful) and forcible reprisals (which are not) is that the former is preventive, whereas the latter are punitive).

[36] *See infra* note 92.

[37] Declaration on Principles of International Law Concerning Friendly Relations and Co-operation among States in Accordance with the Charter of the United Nations 180 (Oct. 24, 1970); Bowett, *supra* note 35, at 1, 7 (on the Security Council's consistent finding that forcible reprisals are illegal). *Cf.* Section 3.2.1 in Chapter 3, above.

[38] W. Michael Reisman & Andrea Armstrong, *The Past and Future of the Claim of Preemptive Self-Defense*, 100 Am. J. Int'l L. 525, 526 (2006); Miriam Sapiro, *Preempting Prevention: Lessons Learned*, 37 N.Y.U. J. Int'l L. & Pol. 357, 367 (2005); UN High-Level Panel on Threats, Challenges & Change, *supra* note 34, paras. 188–92. *See also* Jeff McMahan, *Preventive War and the Killing of the Innocent*, *in* The Ethics of War 169, 173 (Richard Sorabji & David Rodin, eds., 2006).

[39] McMahan, *supra* note 38, at 185; David Luban, *Just War and Human Rights*, *in* International Ethics 195, 218 (Charles R. Beitz et al., eds., 1985) (hereinafter Luban, JWHR); Walzer, JUW, *supra* note 8, at 80; Samuel Pufendorf, On the Law of Nature and Nations 1296 (C.H. Oldfather & W.A. Oldfather trans., 1934).

force justified. Similar reasons limit the scope of permissible anticipatory humanitarian intervention.[40]

Precisely the worry about waging war without adequate confidence that the justificatory conditions for doing so obtain was at the heart of the legal and moral objections to using force against Iraq in 2003. Many, including the most senior British government lawyers, worried that the American-led invasion of Iraq in 2003 was an unlawful, even criminal, war.[41] But few objectors claimed that Iraq was *clearly* innocent of the kind of wrong that would justify a forceful response – whether that was preparing an attack (or supporting the preparation of terrorist attacks) and thus triggering a right of anticipatory self-defense, or whether it was violating the conditions of the UN's 1991 ceasefire (by developing weapons of mass destruction) and thus reviving the initial authorization to use force provided in Security Council Resolution 678 of 1990.[42]

40 Int'l Comm'n on Intervention & State Sovereignty, The Responsibility to Protect (2001) [hereinafter ICISS Report], paras. 4.18, 4.21; Walzer, JUW, *supra* note 8, at 86.

41 Michael Wood [Foreign & Commonwealth Office Legal Adviser] to the Foreign Secretary's Private Secretary, *Iraq: Legal Basis for Use of Force* (Jan. 24, 2003), www.iraqinquiry.org.uk/media/226676/2003-01-24-minute-wood-to-ps-fco-iraq-legal-basis-for-use-of-force-with-manuscript-comment-mcdonald-to-wood-28-january.pdf; Elizabeth Wilmshurst, *Resignation Letter* (Mar. 2003), http://news.bbc.co.uk/2/hi/uk_news/politics/4377605.stm (describing war without a further Security Council resolution as criminal). Lord Peter Goldsmith to Prime Minister Tony Blair, *DRAFT – Iraq: Interpretation of Resolution 1441* (Jan. 14, 2003) [hereinafter Goldsmith to Blair, 14 January] (describing war without a further Security Council resolution as illegal). Lord Peter Goldsmith to Prime Minister Tony Blair, *Memo: Iraq: Resolution 1441*, paras. 27–28 (Mar. 7, 2003) [hereinafter Goldsmith to Blair – 7 March] (reversing course and holding that war without a further resolution could be lawful, although recognizing (legal, rather than factual) uncertainty on that front).

42 The preemption argument, though the focus of much public discussion, was not the primary legal justification put forward. The core argument was instead that the American-led coalition could invade Iraq in 2003 pursuant to a revival of the authorization to use force provided by Security Council Resolution 678 (1990), due to Iraq's fundamental breach of the conditions of the ceasefire, as stipulated in Resolution 687 (1991) and reiterated in Resolution 1441 (2002). *See* Permanent Representative of the United Kingdom of Great Britain and Northern Ireland to the United Nations, Letter dated Mar. 20, 2003 from the Permanent Representative of the United Kingdom of Great Britain and Northern Ireland to the United Nations addressed to the President of the S.C., U.N. Doc. S/2003/350 (20 March, 2003); Permanent Representative of the United Kingdom of Great Britain and Northern Ireland to the United Nations, Letter dated Mar. 20, 2003 from the Permanent Representative of the United Kingdom of Great Britain and Northern Ireland to the United Nations addressed to the President of the S.C., U.N. Doc. S/2003/351 (20 March, 2003); Permanent Representative of Australia to the United Nations, Letter dated Mar. 20, 2003 from the Permanent Representative of Australia to

Indeed, on the latter point, the Security Council itself had made quite clear in Resolution 1441 (2002) that the grounds for using force were potentially present.[43]

Instead, opponents of the war emphasized the dubiousness of the information underpinning the *jus ad bellum* claims of the coalition partners. The pre-emptive self-defense argument was disputed primarily by pointing to the flimsiness of the intelligence linking the Iraqi regime to any imminent attack or to terrorist groups planning any such attack.[44] The argument that Iraq was in fundamental breach of the Security Council's 1991 ceasefire conditions was disputed on several grounds, but the core of at least two of these was epistemic.[45] First, it was argued that the work of the inspectors, rather than questionable intelligence, should guide determinations of fundamental breach, and that no war was warranted without a "smoking gun."[46] Second, it was argued that it was for the Security Council (and not individual states) to determine whether

the United Nations addressed to the President of the S.C., U.N. Doc. S/2003/352 (20 March, 2003); UK Foreign and Commonwealth Office, *Legal Basis for the Use of Force* (Mar. 17, 2003), www.iraqinquiry.org.uk/media/243926/2003-03-17-letter-straw-to-anderson-iraq-legal-position-concerning-the-use-of-force-attaching-pq-and-paper.pdf; Attorney-General of Australia, *Memorandum of Advice on the Use of Force against Iraq* (Mar. 18, 2003).

43 S.C. Res. 1441, paras. 1–2, 12, 13 (Nov. 8, 2002).

44 Christine Gray, *supra* note 2, at 216–20; Dominic McGoldrick, From "9–11" to the "Iraq War 2003" 67–76 (2004); *id.*, at 78; Haroon Siddique, *Iraq Inquiry: Saddam Posed Very Limited Threat to UK, Ex-MI5 Chief Says*, Guardian (July 20, 2010), www.theguardian.com/uk/2010/jul/20/iraq-inquiry-saddam-mi5-chief; Christopher Marquis, *Powell Admits No Hard Proof in Linking Iraq to Al Qaeda*, NY Times (Jan. 9, 2004), at A10; *45-Minute Claim: "Uncharacteristically Poor"*, BBC News (July 14, 2004), http://news.bbc.co.uk/1/hi/uk_politics/3893641.stm.

45 The non-epistemic arguments included a general objection to Security Council authorization revival, particularly after a delay of 12 years, and the argument that the plain text of Resolution 1441 required a new authorization prior to the use of force. On the plain text argument: Goldsmith to Blair 14 January, *supra* note 41, paras. 4–11; Nigel D. White, *Submission to the Iraq Inquiry in Response to the Invitation to International Lawyers* (June 2, 2010). On general objections to revival: Christine Gray, *supra* note 2, at 361–62; Melinda Janki, *Submission to the Iraq Inquiry: The Legality of the Grounds for the Use of Force against Iraq in 2003*, www.iraqinquiry.org.uk/media/184805/submission-international-law-janki-2010-09-12.pdf.

46 Christine Gray, *supra* note 2, at 363; Sia Spiliopoulou Åkermark, *Storms, Foxes, and Nebulous Legal Arguments: Twelve Years of Force against Iraq, 1991–2003*, 54 Int'l & Comp. L. Q. 221, 224 (2005); George Jones, *Blix Charges Blair and Bush with "Dramatising" the Threat of WMD*, Telegraph (Feb. 9, 2004), www.telegraph.co.uk/news/world news/middleeast/iraq/1453854/Blix-charges-Blair-and-Bush-with-dramatising-the-threat-of-WMD.html; *We Need More Time, UN Inspectors Say*, Chicago Trib. (Jan. 14, 2003).

such fundamental breach had occurred.[47] A leading reason (though not the only reason) for the latter position was the Security Council's check on purely political motives for war, such that only clearly justified wars tend to pass the threshold for authorization.[48]

Relying on these lines of argument, many of even the most vehement claims that the invasion of Iraq was unambiguously illegal were rooted in the assessment that the grounds for attacking were too uncertain, and that more information was needed to warrant using force. Attacking without that information amounted to inflicting death and human suffering while uncertain as to whether the justificatory conditions for doing so obtained. And doing *that* was clearly illegal.

More recently, the importance of establishing that force is actually (and not just possibly) responsive to illegal human violence found support in British and American positions on the potential military intervention against the government of Syria in 2013. US President Barack Obama admitted that there were questions as to whether international law would support an intervention in Syria "without a UN mandate *and without clear evidence that can be presented.*"[49] On a political level, the lack of certainty regarding the *jus-ad-bellum*-relevant facts also played a key role in the Conservative-led coalition government's historic failure to

[47] *See, e.g.*, Severin Carrell and Robert Verkaik, *War on Iraq was Illegal, Say Top Lawyers*, INDEPENDENT (May 25, 2003), www.independent.co.uk/news/uk/crime/war-on-iraq-was-illegal-say-top-lawyers-106099.html; MCGOLDRICK, *supra* note 44, at 77–84; CHRISTINE GRAY, *supra* note 2, at 362–65.

[48] THOMAS M. FRANCK, RECOURSE TO FORCE 187 (2002); Franck, *supra* note 2, at 102–05; Thomas M. Franck, *Reflections on Force and Evidence*, 100 AM. SOC'Y INT'L L. PROC. 51, 53 (2006); UN High-Level Panel on Threats, Challenges & Change, *supra* note 34, paras. 188–91; Allen S. Weiner, *The Use of Force and Contemporary Security Threats: Old Medicine for New Ills?*, 59 STAN. L. REV. 415, 428 (2006). Needless to say, political reasons *not* to wage war may very well prove decisive. *See, e.g.*, Robert O. Keohane, *Global Governance and Legitimacy*, 18 REV. INT'L POL. ECONOMY 99, 104–05 (2011); Evan Osnos, *What Does China See in Syria?*, NEW YORKER (Feb. 28, 2012), www.newyorker.com/news/evan-osnos/what-does-china-see-in-syria; Esmira Jafarova, *Solving the Syrian Knot: Dynamics within the UN Security Council and Challenges to its Effectiveness*, 13 CONNECTIONS: Q.J. 25 (2014). The claim is only that the political antipathies among the permanent five veto-wielding states prevent politically motivated wars from being *authorized*. On the other hand, raising concern about the Security Council's epistemic quality, *see* Matthew C. Waxman, *The Use of Force against States that Might Have Weapons of Mass Destruction*, 31 MICH. J. INT'L L. 1, 35–36 (2009); Therese O'Donnell, *Naming and Shaming: The Sorry Tale of Security Council Resolution 1530 (2004)*, 17 EUR. J. INT'L L. 945 (2007).

[49] *Barack Obama on the Lead with Jake Tapper*, CNN (aired Aug. 23, 2013, 16:30 ET).

get preliminary parliamentary authorization for British participation in such an operation in 2013.[50]

The basic principle that it is wrongful to inflict death and human suffering without a high level of confidence that the justificatory conditions for doing so obtain also underpins key rules of the *jus in bello*.[51] Article 50(1) of Additional Protocol I provides, "In case of doubt whether a person is a civilian, that person shall be considered to be a civilian."[52] In other words, persons of doubtful status (persons who *might* be combatants) are not legitimate objects of attack.[53]

Controversially, the United States has taken the position that this rule on doubt is not a requirement of customary international law.[54] However, a US Military investigation subsequent to the articulation of that position held that the actors involved in the 2015 airstrikes on a Médecins Sans Frontières center had violated the law of armed conflict because there should have been "doubt in their mind" that the target was a legitimate military objective, and any belief on their part that it was a military objective would have been "unreasonable."[55]

In connecting this to criminal liability, the 1987 Commentary to Additional Protocol I emphasizes both that criminal liability attaches to the "reckless" soldier who, "without being certain of a particular result [such as the killing of civilians], accepts the possibility of its happening," *and* that, for the purposes of the war crime of attacking civilians, the

[50] Rowena Mason, *Syria: Coalition MPs Defy Cameron and Clegg's Call for Military Action*, GUARDIAN (Aug. 29, 2013), www.theguardian.com/world/2013/aug/30/syria-debate-coalition-mps-defy-government (citing MPs David Davis, Cheryl Gillan, Richard Ottaway and others on the ambiguities in the intelligence presented to Parliament).

[51] *See, e.g.*, NILS MELZER (ICRC), INTERPRETIVE GUIDANCE ON THE NOTION OF DIRECT PARTICIPATION IN HOSTILITIES UNDER INTERNATIONAL HUMANITARIAN LAW 74–76 (2009); Prosecutor v. Tadić, Case No. IT-94-1-I, Decision on Defence Motion for Interlocutory Appeal on Jurisdiction, para. 100 (Int'l Crim. Trib. for the Former Yugoslavia Oct. 2, 1995), www.icty.org/x/cases/tadic/acdec/en/51002.htm. [http://perma.cc/4C98-SP5E].

[52] Protocol (I) Additional to the Geneva Conventions of 12 August 1949, and Relating to the Protection of Victims of International Armed Conflicts, art. 50(1) (1977) [hereinafter AP I].

[53] *Id.*, art. 51.

[54] DEP'T OF DEF., LAW OF WAR MANUAL, §5.4.3.2 (2015), http://archive.defense.gov/pubs/Lawof-War-Manual-June-2015.pdf [https://perma.cc/5SYE-ESMC].

[55] Investigation Report of the Airstrike on the Médecins Sans Frontières I Doctors without Borders Trauma Center in Kunduz, Afghanistan on Oct. 3, 2015, paras. 59–62 (updated Apr. 28, 2016), www3.centcom.mil/foia_rr/FOIA_RR.asp?Path=/5%20USC%20552%28a%29%282%29%28D%29Records&Folder=1.%20Airstrike%20on%20the%20MSF%20Trauma%20Center%20in%20Kunduz%20Afghanistan%20-%203%20Oct%202015.

Article 50(1) rule on doubt is the applicable standard for determining whether an individual has civilian status.[56] The US has interpreted international law more restrictively, requiring the knowing targeting of civilians for criminal liability.[57] The former is closer to the standard adopted by the International Criminal Tribunal for the former Yugoslavia.[58] The latter is closer to the Rome Statute approach.[59] Notably, in one instance, an ICTY Trial Chamber reasoned, "A person shall not be made the object of attack when it is not reasonable to believe, in the circumstances of the person contemplating the attack, including the information available to the latter, that the potential target is a combatant."[60]

Even if the higher epistemic threshold advocated by the United States and enshrined in the Rome Statute is correct, it is worth emphasizing again that international criminality attaches only at a high level of guilt. As the Additional Protocol Commentary notes, a lower standard of "culpable negligence" may not be internationally criminal, but *does* involve culpable wrongdoing from the perspective of international law, and ought to be "punishable at least by disciplinary sanctions."[61] It is

[56] Commentary of 1987, to the Geneva Conventions of 12 August 1949, and relating to the Protection of Victims of International Armed Conflicts (Protocol I) of 8 June 1977, paras. 3474–75 (Yves Sandoz, Christophe Swinarski, & Bruno Zimmermann, eds., 1987) [hereinafter Commentary to AP I].

[57] US Department of Defense Press Briefing by Army General Joseph Votel, commander, US Central Command (Apr. 29, 2016), www.defense.gov/News/Transcripts/Transcript-View/Article/746686/department-of-defense-press-briefing-by-army-general-joseph-votel-commander-us/.

[58] Prosecutor v. Perišić, Case No. IT-04–81-T, Trial Judgment, paras. 112, 558, 593 (Int'l Crim. Trib. for the Former Yugoslavia Sept. 6, 2011), www.icty.org/x/cases/perisic/tjug/en/110906_judgement.pdf; Prosecutor v. Blaškić, Case No. IT-95–14-A, Appeals Judgment, para. 42 (Int'l Crim. Trib. for the Former Yugoslavia July 29, 2004), www.icty.org/x/cases/blaskic/acjug/en/bla-aj040729e.pdf. *See also*, Prosecutor v. Galić, Case No. IT-98–29-A, Appeals Judgment, para. 140 (Int'l Crim. Trib. for the Former Yugoslavia Nov. 30, 2006), www.icty.org/x/cases/galic/acjug/en/gal-acjud061130.pdf; Prosecutor v. Strugar, Case No. IT-01–42-A, Appeals Judgment, para 270 (Int'l Crim. Trib. for the Former Yugoslavia July 17, 2008), www.icty.org/x/cases/strugar/acjug/en/080717.pdf.

[59] ICC Statute, *supra* note 11, art. 30(2); Prosecutor v. Bemba, ICC-01/05–01/08, Decision on the Confirmation of Charges, para. 369 (June 15, 2009), www.icc-cpi.int/CourtRecords/CR2009_04528.PDF. Criticizing the ICC approach, *see* Haque, *supra* note 4, at 249.

[60] Prosecutor v. Galić, Case No. IT-98–29-T, Trial Judgment, para. 50 (Int'l Crim. Trib. for the Former Yugoslavia Dec. 5, 2003), www.icty.org/x/cases/galic/tjug/en/gal-tj031205e.pdf.

[61] Commentary to AP I, *supra* note 56, at para. 3474.

notable in this respect that, despite refraining from criminal punishment, the United States did impose disciplinary sanctions on those involved in the Kunduz attack.[62]

In addition to the rule on doubt, Additional Protocol I also provides those who plan or decide upon an attack must "do everything feasible to verify" that the objects of attack are legitimate military targets and must cancel any attack if it becomes apparent that the target is not legitimate.[63] The permission to attack civilians who participate directly in hostilities only "for such time" as they are participating has also been interpreted as a prohibition on dubious killings, given the heightened possibility of mistaken identity when targets are not uniformed combatants.[64]

Arguments in favor of even tighter *jus in bello* restrictions on dubious killing have started to gain traction in the realm of targeted killings. The United States claims to apply a "near certainty" standard to its targeted strikes and the Israeli Supreme Court has emphasized that the "burden of proof on the attacking army is heavy."[65] Officially, both states have adopted a "capture if possible" rule for such programs.[66] In the context of military prosecutions, Osiel has argued that "evidence of unreasonableness

[62] US Department of Defense Press Briefing, *supra* note 57.

[63] AP I, *supra* note 52, arts. 57(2)(a)(iii), 57(2)(b).

[64] *Id.*, art. 51(3). *See, e.g.*, Kristen Eichensehr, *Comment: On Target? The Israeli Supreme Court and the Expansion of Targeted Killings*, 116 Yale L.J. 1873, 1877–79 (2007). *Cf.* Monica Hakimi, *A Functional Approach to Targeting and Detention*, 110 Mich. L. Rev. 1365, 1396, 1402–03 (2012); Melzer, *supra* note 51, at 76; Matthew Waxman, *Detention as Targeting: Standards of Certainty and Detention of Suspected Terrorists*, 108 Colum. L. Rev. 1365, 1382–83 (2008); Chris Downes, *"Targeted Killings" in an Age of Terror: The Legality of the Yemen Strike*, 9 J. Conflict & Security L. 277, 285 (2004); Michael Scharf, *In the Cross Hairs of a Scary Idea*, Washington Post (Apr. 25, 2004), at B1, www.washingtonpost.com/archive/opinions/2004/04/25/in-the-cross-hairs-of-a-scary-idea/f5a2c93a-26b3-479b-bc5e-cb6d6b736c3d/?utm_term=.d32af71d4b53.

[65] Barack Obama, The Future of our Fight against Terrorism, National Defense University (May 23, 2013); Procedures for Approving Direct Action against Terrorist Targets Located Outside the United States and Areas of Active Hostilities, paras. 1.C(8), 1.E(1–2) (May 22, 2013), www.justice.gov/oip/foia-library/procedures_for_approving_direct_action_against_terrorist_targets/download; H.C.J. 769/02 Public Committee against Torture in Isr. v. State of Isr., para. 40 (2006) (Isr.) [hereinafter *PCATI Targeted Killings* Case]. Arguing for a broader application of tighter epistemic standards in armed conflict, *see* Adil Ahmad Haque, *Killing in the Fog of War*, 86 Southern Cal. L. Rev. 63 (2012) and Adil Ahmad Haque, Law and Morality at War ch. 5 (2017). For tighter epistemic standards for obedient soldiers, *see* Osiel, *supra* note 15.

[66] Obama, The Future of our Fight, *supra* note 65; Procedures for Approving Direct Action, *supra* note 65, at § 1.C(8); *PCATI Targeted Killings* Case, *supra* note 65, at paras. 40, 60.

supports a mental state of knowing or intentional wrongdoing. It thereby permits conviction for murder, rather than manslaughter."[67]

In short, a strong presumption *against* excusing dubious killing is manifest in domestic criminal law, in the *jus ad bellum*, and in the *jus in bello*. Merely having doubts that such harming is wrongful cannot warrant inflicting the harm. On the contrary, even having significant doubts at the other end of the spectrum (doubts that the harming is permissible) militates against action. The precise point at which deliberately inflicting severe human suffering is excusable on epistemic grounds varies, and the standard for international criminal liability is appropriately set at a high level of culpability, but across domains there is a consistent normative principle: spilling certain blood for uncertain reasons is condemnable and legally prohibited. If this principle does not apply to obedient soldiers or the crime of aggression, that requires an explanation that is not merely epistemic. Ignorance is not invincible.

5.4 Why Uncertainty Mandates Restraint

Underpinning this judgment appears to be a second moral principle, also reflected in the relevant domains of international law – the distinction between killing and letting die.[68] At the most basic level, defensive force is justified because it saves lives from unjustified attack. Refraining from using defensive force thus entails failing to save those lives. In a basic interpersonal context, if one is completely uncertain (50 on the spectrum from 0–100) whether the justificatory conditions for defensive lethal force obtain and one life is at stake on either side, the possibility that killing the targeted individual would rightly save a life is equal to the possibility that doing so would wrongly take a life. Killing or refraining from killing in this context would be equally likely to result in a wrongful death.

A strict act consequentialist may be indifferent between these two options, but that is not a normative posture enshrined in law. On the contrary, across a broad range of domains, the law reflects a judgment that it would be worse to kill than to refrain from killing under such conditions of uncertainty. This reflects a widely shared moral intuition.

67 *See also* Mark Osiel, Obeying Orders 82–83 (1999).

68 *See* McMahan, *supra* note 19, at 141–43. On the other hand, *see* Haque, *supra* note 4, at 117–28 (arguing that the reason not to kill without a reasonable belief that doing so is justified is about more than just the difference between killing and letting die).

Suppose one were to stumble upon a plainly fatal fight between two strangers, not knowing who is the aggressor and able to intervene only by shooting one of them fatally. Few would dispute that one ought not shoot either. And, while one would be vulnerable to criminal sanction were one to shoot one of the fighters, one would face no reprimand whatsoever were one to fail to shoot.[69] This is so even though there is a 50 percent chance that by failing to do so one would fail to save a person from death by unjustified attack, and a 50 percent chance that by shooting one would save a life from a wrongful killing.

At the root of this assessment is the judgment that intentionally killing is an act of greater moral gravity than is intentionally refraining from action that would save a life.[70] So-called "Good Samaritan" laws that punish those who fail to engage in rescue are narrower, underpin lesser offenses, and come with weaker penalties than do proscriptions on *acts* that would result in an analogous harm.[71]

Here, too, the interpersonal principle extends to the international context. International law clearly holds using force wrongfully to be worse than failing to use force when doing so is justified. States are never legally required to go to use force in their international relations. Third states are legally (and on most accounts, morally) permitted to remain neutral with respect to a war in which one side is a clear aggressor.[72] Even the attacked state has no obligation to wage a defensive war.[73]

[69] *See supra* notes 24–27.

[70] *See, e.g.*, MICHAEL S. MOORE, ACT AND CRIME: THE PHILOSOPHY OF ACTION AND ITS IMPLICATIONS FOR CRIMINAL LAW 54–59 (1993).

[71] *See, e.g.*, Gabriel D. M. Ciociola, *Misprison of Felony and its Progeny*, 41 BRANDEIS L.J. 697, 735–38 (2003); Edward A. Tomlinson, *The French Experience with a Duty to Rescue*, 20 N.Y. L. SCH. J. INT'L & COMP. L. 451 (2000). *See also* MOSHE HALBERTAL, ON SACRIFICE 65–66 (2012) ("The mainstream view in Jewish law is that a person may be obligated to risk or give up his life so as not to kill an innocent person, but may not be expected to give up his life to save another").

[72] Hague Convention (V) Respecting the Rights and Duties of Neutral Powers and Persons in Case of War on Land, Oct. 18, 1907, 36 Stat. 2310; Hague Convention (XIII) Concerning the Rights and Duties of Neutral Powers in Naval War, Oct. 18, 1907), 36 Stat. 3415; LASSA OPPENHEIM, INTERNATIONAL LAW, § 293 (Hersch Lauterpacht, ed., 8th edn 1952). On the history of neutrality, *see generally* STEPHEN C. NEFF, THE RIGHTS AND DUTIES OF NEUTRALS: A GENERAL HISTORY (2000); Hersch Lauterpacht, *Neutrality and Collective Security*, *in* INTERNATIONAL LAW 613 (Sir Elihu Lauterpacht, ed., 2004). *See also* WALZER, JUW, *supra* note 8, at 233–38; NEFF, WAR AND THE LAW OF NATIONS, *supra* note 28, at 151.

[73] YORAM DINSTEIN, WAR, AGGRESSION, AND SELF-DEFENCE 190–91 (5th edn 2012). Article 51 of the UN Charter provides only for a state's "right" to act in self-defense, not its duty. UN Charter, art. 51. *See also* WALZER, JUW, *supra* note 8, at 69–73. *But see* Legal Consequences of the Construction of a Wall in the Occupied Palestinian Territory,

Similarly, participating in Security Council-authorized actions is optional under current law.[74]

Mass atrocities may call out more powerfully for an affirmative duty to wage war – as per the emergent doctrine of the responsibility to protect[75] – and the government controlling a territory *does* have a legal obligation to use force internally when necessary to protect its people from killings and other security violations.[76] However, there is no such duty on any external state to intervene abroad to stop atrocity. At most, such a transnational responsibility to protect is thought to apply only to the "international community," through the Security Council.[77] Although academics are starting to think about ways in which international failures to uphold the responsibility to protect might be legally actionable,[78] these arguments

Advisory Opinion, 2004 I.C.J. 136, 195 (July 9) (Israel "has the right, and indeed the duty, to respond in order to protect the life of its citizens") [hereinafter *Wall* Opinion].

74 *See, e.g.*, DANESH SAROOSHI, THE UNITED NATIONS AND THE DEVELOPMENT OF COLLECTIVE SECURITY 149–53 (1999) (there is no obligation to contribute, but there may be a duty not to withdraw once a state has contributed).

75 The most notable official documents in this regard are: ICISS REPORT, *supra* note 40, paras. 6.13–6.28; S.C. Res. 1674 (Apr. 28, 2006); World Summit Outcome, G.A. Res. 60/1, para. 138 (Sept. 16, 2005); UN Secretary-General, *Implementing the Responsibility to Protect* 8–9, U.N. Doc. A/63/677 (Jan. 12, 2009); Draft Articles on Responsibility of States for Internationally Wrongful Acts with Commentaries, Rep. of the Int'l Law Comm'n on the Work of its Fifty-Third Session, U.N. Doc. A/56/10, arts. 40–41 (2001) [hereinafter Articles on State Responsibility with commentaries].

76 S.C. Res. 1973, preamble (Mar. 17, 2011); UN Secretary-General, *Implementing the Responsibility to Protect*, *supra* note 75, at 8–9; S.C. Res. 1674 (Apr. 28, 2006), para. 4; World Summit Outcome, G.A. Res. 60/1, para. 138 (Sept. 16, 2005); UN High-Level Panel on Threats, Challenges & Change, *supra* note 34, paras. 29–30; ICISS REPORT, *supra* note 40, paras. 1.35, 2.14–2.15, 2.30–2.32. On due diligence requirements in human rights law and humanitarian law, *see, for example*, ALISTAIR MOWBRAY, THE DEVELOPMENT OF POSITIVE OBLIGATIONS UNDER THE EUROPEAN CONVENTION ON HUMAN RIGHTS BY THE EUROPEAN COURT OF HUMAN RIGHTS (2004); Velasquez Rodriguez Case [v. Honduras], Judgment, Inter-Am. Ct. H.R. (ser. C) No. 4, para. 166 (July 29, 1988); Human Rights Comm'n, General Comment 31: The Nature of the General Legal Obligation Imposed on States Parties to the Covenant, paras. 8, 10, U.N. Doc. CCPR/C/21/Rev.1 /Add.13 (May 26, 2004); Armed Activities on the Territory of the Congo (Dem. Rep. Congo v. Uganda), Judgment, 2005 I.C.J. 168 (Dec. 19), paras. 178–80, 219–29, 248–50 [hereinafter Armed Activities Judgment]; Hague Convention (XIII) Concerning the Rights and Duties of Neutral Powers in Naval War (Oct. 18, 1907), 36 Stat. 3415 Hague Convention (IV) Respecting the Laws and Customs of War on Land and its annex: Regulations concerning the Laws and Customs of War on Land, art. 43 (Oct. 18, 1907), 36 Stat. 2277 (hereinafter Hague Regulations IV of 1907).

77 ICISS REPORT, *supra* note 40, at 17–18, 47–55.

78 *See, e.g.*, RESPONSIBILITY TO PROTECT: FROM PRINCIPLE TO PRACTICE (Julia Hoffman & André Nollkaemper, eds., 2012).

remain speculative, and courts have not taken any preventive responsibilities in this respect to include the use of military force.[79]

Moreover, while it may be appropriate in certain cases to condemn leaders who have the means to intervene to stop atrocity and fail to do so, this moral blame does not approach the depth of censure we reserve for leaders who wage criminally aggressive wars.[80] No one advocates holding leaders who veto, or fail to order, humanitarian intervention criminally liable for that failure, even in the most blatant cases. The most virulent critics of Bill Clinton have never called for him to be formally sanctioned in any way for the failure to intervene in Rwanda.[81] Critics of George W. Bush, Dick Cheney, Tony Blair, and other leaders of the Iraq invasion, on the other hand, call regularly for their criminal accountability.[82] This cannot be boiled down to lives lost and total aggregate destruction. Instead, it seems to reflect a moral judgment about the deep difference between the two types of failure.

At both the interpersonal and the international levels, the strong presumption against inflicting human suffering and death when uncertain as to whether the justificatory conditions obtain is rooted in the normative principle that inflicting suffering and death wrongfully is more profound an offense than is failing to use force when needed to protect against the infliction of wrongful suffering.

[79] Application of the Convention on the Prevention and Punishment of the Crime of Genocide (Bosn. & Herz. v. Serb. & Mont,) 2007 I.C.J. Rep. 43 (Feb. 26), para. 438 [hereinafter Bosnian Genocide Judgment]; Gerechtshof's-Gravenhage, July 5, 2011, LJN: BR 5388, para. 6.22 (Nuhanović v. Netherlands).

[80] Condemning the failure to intervene, *see, for example*, SAMANTHA POWER, A PROBLEM FROM HELL: AMERICA AND THE AGE OF GENOCIDE (2002).

[81] There have been efforts to prosecute the Dutch commanders at Potocari who failed to protect those killed at Srebrenica. *Former commander of Dutchbat troops in Srebrenica, Thom Karremans, may be prosecuted*, RADIO NETHERLANDS WORLDWIDE (May 10, 2012). However, these have focused on the role of the Dutch battalion in evicting Bosnian Muslims within their compound, not in their failure to intervene. For more on the situation, *see* Tom Dannenbaum, *Killings at Srebrenica, Effective Control, and the Power to Prevent Unlawful Conduct*, 61 INT'L & COMP. L. Q. 713 (2012). Ultimately, even this prosecution was dropped. *Dutch Peacekeeper Not Prosecuted for Srebrenica*, Associated Press (Mar. 7, 2013).

[82] Mark Littman, *A Supreme International Crime*, GUARDIAN (Mar. 10, 2003), www.theguardian.com/politics/2003/mar/10/iraq.world; *War with Iraq Could be Illegal*, BBC NEWS (Mar. 6, 2003), http://news.bbc.co.uk/1/hi/uk/2826331.stm; Philippe Sands, *Realm of the Possible*, GUARDIAN (Jan. 8, 2007), www.theguardian.com/commentisfree/2007/jan/08/post881.

5.5 The Structure of the *Jus ad Bellum*

Recognizing this poses a severe challenge to the utility of invincible ignorance in explaining the extant legal framework. It is true that few soldiers are likely to be absolutely certain that their war is criminal. But, by the same token, few are likely to be absolutely certain that their war is lawful. And, crucially, the structure of the *jus ad bellum* is such that a significant proportion of the remaining majority on at least one side are likely to be in a position in which it would be unreasonable to believe their war to be lawful.

This is a straightforward implication of the *jus ad bellum*'s basic structure.[83] Under international law, it is impossible for opposing sides in an international armed conflict to pursue lawful causes against one another.[84] The *jus ad bellum* allows for unilateral (or extra-UN multilateral) uses of force only in response to an unlawful use of force by another state or group of states.[85] Even when armed conflict arises out of a series of border skirmishes, as was the case in the turn-of-millennium conflict between Ethiopia and Eritrea, the rule is that one side must have violated the *jus ad bellum* by taking the final illegal step that shifted the face-off from a chain of skirmishes to full-on armed conflict.[86] The Security Council has a broader authority to mandate the proactive use of force, but, conversely, there is no unilateral or multilateral right to use force against a Council-authorized operation.[87]

Moreover, in contrast to the non-mutuality of lawful cause, it *is* possible for both sides of an international war to prosecute *un*lawful causes against one another.[88] Examples include two states warring over foreign territory and control of a foreign population;[89] a third state intervening unilaterally against the aggressor in a bilateral armed conflict over the

[83] McMahan, *supra* note 19, at 143–44. [84] Dinstein, *supra* note 73, at 189–90.

[85] Art. 2(4) prohibits the use of force. The two exceptions to this are art. 51, which provides states a right to act unilaterally in self-defense and ch. VII, which provides for the permissibility of UN-authorized actions. UN Charter, arts. 2(4), 39, 42, 51, 53. On self-defense, *see also* United States v. Ernst von Weizsäcker, *in* 14 Trials of War Criminals before the Nuernberg Military Tribunals under Control Council Law No. 10, at 1, 329 (1949).

[86] *See, e.g.*, Partial Award: *Jus ad Bellum* – Ethiopia's Claims 1–8 (Eri. v. Eth.), 16 R.I.A.A., paras. 11–12, 16 (Eri.–Eth. Claims Comm'n 2005).

[87] *See* Section 3.2.2 in Chapter 3, above.

[88] Margalit & Walzer, *supra* note 8 ("both sides may be wrong, and often are").

[89] S.C. Res. 1304, paras. 3–4 (June 16, 2000).

objection of the defensive state;[90] and a military fighting against an illegal humanitarian intervention to protect the perpetrators and thus facilitate an atrocity crime.[91] Even a war prosecuting a lawful cause will itself be lawful only if it is also necessary and proportionate.[92] Overall, then, knowing nothing about a given state's use of force against another state, the proper starting presumption is that it violates the *jus ad bellum*.

If that is correct, if Chapter 3's identification of unjustified death and human suffering as the criminal wrong of aggression holds, and if inflicting such harms when uncertain as to whether the justificatory conditions for doing so obtain is culpable, then the natural question is whether the invincible ignorance account is viable at all. Certainly, if soldiers justifiably and correctly appraise those wars as illegal and possibly criminal, it is difficult to argue that they ought to be able to wash their hands of guilt for participating and killing in those wars.

5.6 Deference

The obvious response here, of course, is to invoke the principle of justified deference.[93] The invincible ignorance account does not insist that

90 Military and Paramilitary Activities in and against Nicaragua (Nicar. v. US), Judgment, 1986 I.C.J. 14 (June 27), paras. 196–98 (hereinafter Nicaragua Judgment).

91 This would arguably include the wars fought between Pakistan and India (1971), Uganda and Tanzania (1979), and Kampuchea and Vietnam (1978), although India, Tanzania, and Vietnam all asserted (fairly implausible) self-defense claims in addition to the humanitarian grounds for war. *See* Christine Gray, *supra* note 2, at 33–35. On the development of the law post-Kosovo, *see id.*, at 39–55 and *infra* Section 10.4; ICISS Report, *supra* note 40; S.C. Res. 1674, para. 4 (Apr. 28, 2006); World Summit Outcome, G.A. Res. 60/1, U.N. Doc. A/60/L.1, at 138 (Sept. 16, 2005); UN Secretary General, *Implementing the Responsibility to Protect*, *supra* note 75; S.C. Res. 1973, preamble (Mar. 17, 2011). *See also* Carsten Stahn, *Responsibility to Protect: Political Rhetoric or Emerging Legal Norm*?, 101 Am. J. Int'l L. 99, 118 (2007); Humanitarian Intervention: Ethical, Legal, and Political Dilemmas chs. 1–2, 5–7 (J. L. Holzgrefe & Robert O. Keohane, eds., 2003).

92 Both criteria were articulated in the seminal Anglo-American diplomatic correspondence following the *Caroline* incident in 1837 (widely considered to be expressive of customary international law), and both have been affirmed repeatedly by the ICJ in its jurisprudence on the *jus ad bellum*. Letter from Daniel Webster, Sec'y of State, US Dep't of State, to Henry S. Fox, British Minister to the United States (Apr. 24, 1841), http://avalon.law.yale.edu/19th_century/br-1842d.asp [http://perma.cc/AS9B-AN9H]; Nicaragua Judgment, *supra* note 90, paras. 176, 194; Oil Platforms Judgment, *supra* note 29, paras. 43, 51, 73–74.

93 On the essential role of deference in epistemic life, *see* Gilbert Harman, *Reasoning and Evidence One Does Not Possess*, 5 Midwest Studies in Phil. 163, 170 (1980).

ignorance itself exculpates. Instead, it holds that the non-culpability of the soldier is a function of ignorance combined with trusting deference to the judgment of those with far greater relevant knowledge, namely his leaders. Vitoria distinguishes the wise men in the policy-making class, who are not to support a war that is even "*perhaps* unjust," from those beneath them, who are to trust the former's judgment unless the war is *patently* wrongful.[94] Contemporary advocates of invincible ignorance eschew the notion of a hierarchy of wisdom but reach a similar result by emphasizing leaders' institutional advantages in accessing the relevant facts.[95]

On that contemporary view, the superiority of state leaders' epistemic position over that of their soldiers is guaranteed by three factors. First, obtaining raw information relevant to *jus ad bellum* determinations – particularly information on foreign military maneuvering and intent – demands sophisticated intelligence methods. If such methods are to be durably effective, and if the information is to be actionable, much of that intelligence must remain classified.[96]

Second, putting aside access to the raw information – and it is worth noting that much classified information is available to relatively low-level operatives in at least some states – leaders receive analysis of that information from multiple agencies, providing them with a more sophisticated assessment than would be available to someone with access to the information, but not the broader analytic apparatus.[97]

Finally, leaders typically have an intimate understanding of the diplomatic history and context underlying the conflict, including the various interactions that occur out of the public eye. They are better placed to know who started what, where, and with what immediate effects than does any individual soldier.[98] They know what has been tried and what is

[94] VITORIA, *supra* note 7, at 306–08, 327 (doubt as to the grounds for war militates inaction for both the Prince and his advisors); *id.*, at 308, 313 (doubt exculpates soldiers).

[95] Zupan, *Presumption*, *supra* note 8, at 218; Luban, *Knowing When*, *supra* note 7. On Estlund's position on this, *see* Section 6.4 of Chapter 6, below.

[96] *See, e.g.*, DANIEL H. JOYNER, INTERNATIONAL LAW AND THE PROLIFERATION OF WEAPONS OF MASS DESTRUCTION 292 (2009); Michael N. Schmitt, *Counter-Terrorism and the Use of Force in International Law*, 2002 ISR. Y.B. HUM. RTS 53, 113 (2002); Ruth Wedgwood, *Unilateral Action in the UN System*, 11 EUR. J. INT'L L. 349, 359 (2000).

[97] *See* MARK M. LOWENTHAL, INTELLIGENCE: FROM SECRETS TO POLICY (4th edn 2009) chs. 3–6.

[98] Consider, for example, the wars between Iran and Iraq (1980–88) and Ethiopia and Eritrea (1998–2000).

simply infeasible – an important factor in light of the *jus ad bellum*'s requirement that non-violent alternatives have been exhausted.[99]

Together, these factors produce a significant informational asymmetry between the soldier and his leaders. Speaking to Henry Kissinger prior to the latter's receipt of his Secretary of State security clearance, Daniel Ellsberg referred to "whole libraries of hidden information," and warned,

> You will feel like a fool for having studied, written, talked about these subjects, criticized and analyzed decisions made by presidents for years without having known of the existence of all this information, which presidents and others had and you didn't, and which must have influenced their decisions in ways you couldn't even guess.[100]

In short, for invincible ignorance theorists, even if it is unreasonable for the soldier to believe the war to be lawful based on the information available *directly* to him, the most defensible epistemic course would be defer to the *jus ad bellum* assertions of his state's leaders.[101]

The problem with this argument is that when deference runs the risk of facilitating the infliction of wrongful harm, there is a deep normative imperative to interrogate with skepticism the claims of the better informed.[102] Even if effective interrogation is impossible, the mere fact of epistemic asymmetry is not an adequate moral basis for deference. Much depends on what the individual "knows or should know at the outset about the organization, its work, and her role in it."[103] Most fundamentally, in addition to its greater access to information, the epistemic authority must also be presumptively honest and reliable.

[99] *See supra* note 92.

[100] DANIEL ELLSBERG, SECRETS: A MEMOIR OF VIETNAM AND THE PENTAGON PAPERS (2002). Ellsberg went on to emphasize the converse danger – that access to intelligence blinds the decision-maker to the limits of her own knowledge. *See infra* note 117–24.

[101] Judith Lichtenberg, *How to Judge Soldiers Whose Cause is Unjust*, *in* JUST AND UNJUST WARRIORS, *supra* note 8, at 112, 123–24; Margalit & Walzer, *supra* note 8; Shue, *Laws of War, Morality, and International Politics*, *supra* note 28, at 274–75.

[102] On the importance of the stakes in determining one's epistemic responsibilities, *see* David Luban, Alan Strudler, & David Wasserman, *Moral Responsibility in an Age of Bureaucracy*, 90 MICH. L. REV. 2348, 2382–83 (1992); Guerrero, *supra* note 24, at 69; Keith DeRose, *Contextualism and Knowledge Attributions*, 52 PHIL. & PHENOMENOLOGICAL RESEARCH 913, 914–15 (1992); LORRAINE CODE, EPISTEMIC RESPONSIBILITY 72–83 (1987).

[103] Luban, Strudler, & Wasserman, *supra* note 102, at 2389.

Invincible ignorance theorists often simply presume without argument that the latter two criteria hold. Lt. Col. Kenneth Wenker, for example, argues,

> One of the reasons that individuals can obey so readily is that they have *good grounds for trusting in their superiors and in the political and legal system within which the armed forces operate* . . . [I]f the individual cannot trust his or her superiors and the system within which they function, the best moral decision may well be to disobey.[104]

However, these grounds for trust cannot merely be asserted. Features of the legal and political system that might warrant such deference must be articulated and explained.[105]

Although there can be little doubt that decision-makers in any given state are epistemically advantaged relative to their troops, three factors undermine the soldier's grounds for presuming the reliability and honesty of his state's official position on the *jus ad bellum* status of a war: the inevitability of countervailing epistemic authorities, the interestedness of the soldier's leaders, and a global history of state mendacity and mistakes on *jus ad bellum* facts.[106]

Typically, states on both sides of a conflict assert a *jus ad bellum* claim in terms that make the case for war appear unimpeachable, asserting facts that support its claim robustly under an uncontroversial interpretation of the law.[107] This pattern often applies even in transnational conflicts between a state and a non-state actor, in which the "host" state may dispute key facts claimed by the warring state.[108]

[104] Lt. Col. Kenneth H. Wenker, *Morality and Military Obedience*, Air Univ. Rev. 82 (1981).

[105] For ways in which the grounds for deference might be improved, *see* Chapter 10 below.

[106] *Cf.* McMahan, *supra* note 19, at 137–54.

[107] *See supra* notes 2, 3; Nicaragua Judgment, *supra* note 90, para. 57; John J. Mearsheimer, Why Leaders Lie: The Truth about Lying in International Politics 81 (2011); Peter A. French, War and Moral Dissonance 300–02 (2011).

[108] *See, e.g.*, Charles Homans, Joshua Keating, & David Kenner, *Osama bin Who? A Decade of Denials and Downplaying from Pakistani Leaders*, Foreign Pol'y (May 2, 2011), http://foreignpolicy.com/2011/05/02/osama-bin-who-2/; Arif Rafiq, *The bin Laden Aftermath: Pakistan Caught in a Web of Lies*, Foreign Pol'y (May 2, 2011), http://foreignpolicy.com/2011/05/02/the-bin-laden-aftermath-pakistan-caught-in-a-web-of-lies/; Farhan Bokhari, James Blitz, & Steve Negus, *Pakistan Claims al-Qaeda Command Destroyed*, Fin. Times (July 25, 2005), www.ft.com/content/95c6b4c6-fd3b-11d9-b224-00000e2511c8.

This is a severe problem for the deference model. The enemy and third states have the same epistemic advantage over the soldier as does his own state. The soldier ought to know that at least one of the belligerent states' public *jus ad bellum* assessments is necessarily wrong, whether due to mendacity or misperception.[109] And there is no universally applicable *epistemic* reason for the soldier to favor the determination of his own state over that of the others (political and associative reasons for such deference are explored in the next chapter).

If anything, purely epistemic reasons actually militate *against* the soldier deferring to his own state. The legal status of his state's acts and the criminal liability of its leaders are directly at stake. Any belligerent leader is thus an interested party, whose statements are guaranteed to affirm the legality of her state's actions, irrespective of whether its position is defensible on the facts.[110] On a purely epistemic analysis, justified deference applies not to the soldier's own state or its leaders, but to the preponderance of neutral states and international organizations (in the rare scenarios in which they make public declarations of this sort).[111] Even in that form of deference there is reason to proceed with epistemic caution, particularly if the soldier's own state is economically or politically powerful, or if the enemy is politically unpopular.[112]

[109] *See supra* notes 84–92 and accompanying text. On misperception, *see* ROBERT JERVIS, PERCEPTION AND MISPERCEPTION IN INTERNATIONAL POLITICS (1976); Ellsberg, *supra* note 96; Waxman, *supra* note 48, at 15; JOSEPH CIRINCIONE ET AL., WMD IN IRAQ: EVIDENCE AND IMPLICATIONS 61 (2004).

[110] Luban, JWHR, *supra* note 39, at 208 ("States [are] seldom to be trusted. They are, by and large, composed of men and women enamored of the exercise of power, men and women whose interests are consequently at least slightly at variance with those of the rest of us").

[111] Consider, for example, some of the official statements of non-participants in the Iraq War. EUR. PARL. RESOLUTION ON THE SITUATION IN IRAQ, P5_TA(2003) 0032 (Jan. 30, 2003) ("a pre-emptive strike would not be in accordance with international law and the UN Charter and would lead to a deeper crisis involving other countries in the region"); *Arab States Line Up behind Iraq*, BBC NEWS (Mar. 25, 2003), http://news.bbc.co.uk/2/hi/middle_east/2882851.stm (Arab League (minus Kuwait) called the invasion "a violation of the United Nations Charter"); Ewen MacAskill & Julian Borger, *Iraq War was Illegal and Breached UN Charter, says Annan*, GUARDIAN (Sept. 16, 2004), www.theguardian.com/world/2004/sep/16/iraq.iraq (quoting the UN Secretary General stating: "it was not in conformity with the UN Charter. From our point of view and from the charter point of view it was illegal"); *Chirac Damns War as Illegal without UN Stamp*, ABC NEWS [Austl.] (Mar. 22, 2003), www.abc.net.au/news/2003-03-22/chirac-damns-war-as-illegal-without-un-stamp/1821210.

[112] *See, e.g.*, Randall Newnham, *"Coalition of the Bribed and Bullied?" US Economic Linkages and the Iraq War Coalition*, 9 INT'L STUD. PERSP. 183 (2008); David Armstrong, *US Pays*

These observations are, of course, abstracted from any particular war. The specifics of the states involved in a given conflict and of what is publicly known about the conflict itself may provide the soldier epistemic reasons to defer to his state over its opponent.[113] However, if one of the belligerent states were more reliable in this way, the epistemic grounds for deferring to that state's claims regarding the war in question would apply equally to soldiers on both sides of the conflict, undermining the basis for home-state deference among soldiers on the other side.

Compounding these structural reasons against the soldier deferring to his own state is the historical record. Throughout the UN Charter era, belligerent states, including liberal democracies, have, in their public *jus ad bellum* claims, engaged in distortions, misrepresentations, misleading omissions, exaggerations, translations of hypotheses into facts, and outright lies.[114] As Mearsheimer observes of the 2003 invasion of Iraq,

> Saddam told the truth about his WMD capabilities before the 2003 Iraq war, while senior figures in the Bush administration lied about what they knew regarding those weapons. They also lied about some other important matters. This behavior by the two sides might seem surprising, maybe even shocking, to some readers. One might think that at the very least it is a highly unusual case. But that conclusion would be wrong.[115]

He goes on to claim that leaders' propensities to lie to their own people are particularly strong in "democracies like the United States" and argues that leaders of liberal states are prone to lying in order to "disguise their illiberal actions with idealistic rhetoric."[116]

Back Nations that Supported the War, S.F. CHRONICLE, May 11, 2003; Geneive Abdo, *US Offers Incentives for Backing on Iraq*, BOSTON GLOBE (Feb. 13, 2003).

113 Chapter 10 outlines some methods of alleviating the soldier's burden by improving the public reasons for trusting her state's *ad bellum* assessments.

114 *See generally*, ERIC ALTERMAN, WHEN PRESIDENTS LIE: A HISTORY OF OFFICIAL DECEPTION AND ITS CONSEQUENCES (2004); JOHN QUIGLEY, THE RUSES FOR WAR: AMERICAN INTERVENTIONISM SINCE WORLD WAR II (2nd edn 2007); MEARSHEIMER, *supra* note 107; ICISS REPORT, *supra* note 40, para. 4.28; David D. Kirkpatrick, *After Disclosures by WikiLeaks, Al Jazeera Replaces its Top News Director*, NY TIMES (Sept. 21, 2011), A12, www.nytimes.com/2011/09/21/world/middleeast/after-disclosures-by-wikileaks-al-jazeera-replaces-its-top-news-director.html.

115 MEARSHEIMER, *supra* note 107, at 5.

116 *Id.*, at 13, 23. Perversely, one of the stimulants for such lying is the "powerful norm of transparency in democracies, which means that leaders are expected to provide serious answers." *Id.*, at 70. Mearsheimer also notes the strong inclination of both democracies and autocracies to lie in order to assert the conformity of their actions to international law. *Id.*, at 81. On democratic leaders lying to their publics to justify fighting wars of choice in foreign lands, *see id.*, at 102.

Sometimes, this will involve straightforward mendacity at the highest levels. But there are other routes to distorted and untruthful claims on the part of state leaders. Key information can be exaggerated, painted in a misleading light, or simply excised as the intelligence ascends the chain of command. Colin Powell writes of his infamous presentation in advance of the 2003 invasion of Iraq,

> It was the most vivid presentation of the intelligence information that we had ... When I presented it to the UN, I had every assurance from the intelligence community that the information I had was correct ... Some [members of the CIA] say that they tried to get it up to the top levels of the CIA, that those sources should not be used.[117]

George Ball, an Undersecretary of State at the time of the equally infamous information failures surrounding the Gulf of Tonkin incident in 1964, explains:

> You don't look at the cables, you don't look at the underlying documents. If [the Secretary of Defense] tells you that the evidence is that there was an attack, then that is the basis for the discussion, that's the underlying assumption ... presumably, it's been vetted with the experts.[118]

In fact, the discussions in which Ball was involved were informed by information generated by a process significantly messier, and less subject to expert vetting, than he presumed.[119]

The danger in such situations is not necessarily deliberate deception by those in leadership positions, it is instead the erosion of nuance, caveat, and doubt in a way that distorts both their decision-making and whatever information is made public.[120] A particularly pernicious form of this

[117] Colin Powell, It Worked for Me (2012).

[118] *Quoted in* Robert Scheer, *Vietnam A Decade Later - Cables, Accounts Declassified*, LA Times (Apr. 29, 1985), A1, http://articles.latimes.com/1985-04-29/news/mn-12824_1_north-vietnam.

[119] "McNamara asked Sharp, 'There isn't any possibility there was no attack, is there?' Sharp replied, 'Yes, I would say there is a slight possibility.' McNamara then said, 'We obviously don't want to do it (attack North Vietnam) until we are damned sure what happened,' and asked Sharp, 'How do we reconcile all this?'

"When the admiral suggested that the order to retaliate be postponed 'until we have a definite indication that this happened,' McNamara instructed him to leave the 'execute order in force.' McNamara informed Johnson and McGeorge Bundy about the doubts, but Bundy said he depended on McNamara's evaluation of the data." *Id.*

[120] This was the more benign interpretation of some of the intelligence failures leading up to the 2003 invasion of Iraq. *See, e.g.*, Rt. Hon the Lord Butler of Brockwell et al., Review of Intelligence on Weapons of Mass Destruction Report of a

cycle occurs when senior government leaders' desire for a certain outcome drives the objectives of those involved in intelligence collection and analysis, who write affirming reports, which are accepted by the leaders without adequate skepticism, precisely because they confirm existing biases.[121] The result is an institutional lie, a falsehood that does not involve bald-faced, individual mendacity, but that is created collectively by a combination of preferences and incentives.

This kind of cycle of falsehood may have been particularly prevalent in the build-up to the 2003 invasion of Iraq. Whether or not there was deliberate fabrication, it is clear that claimed "facts" turned out to be wrong.[122] Among the most notorious was the British Government's claim that intelligence revealed Iraq's capacity to hit Britain in 45 minutes.[123] This experience later loomed large in the UK Parliament's rejection of a preliminary authorization of the use of force against Syria in August 2013.[124]

Committee of Privy Councillors HC 898, at 53, paras. 427–59 (July 14, 2004) [hereinafter Butler Report]. *See also id.*, paras. 330, 332, 460–69 (on the lack of appropriate caveats and doubts in the public dossier on Iraq's weapons programs); The Report of the Iraq Inquiry HC 264, § 4.3 (July 6, 2016), *available at* www.iraqinquiry.org.uk/the-report/ [hereinafter Chilcot Report] (on the false conveyance of certainty regarding Iraq's weapons programs, capabilities, and intent, and the failure to consider alternative hypotheses). *See also* Robert Jervis, *Reports, Politics, and Intelligence Failures: The Case of Iraq*, 29 J. Strategic Stud. 3, 14–18, 20–21 (2006).

121 *See* Jervis, *supra* note 120, at 22–27. The force of confirmation bias is one interpretation of British Prime Minister Tony Blair's defense of a 2003 British report on Iraq as "solid" and "accurate," even though "large sections" had been lifted from magazines and academic journals as old as 1997. Sarah Lyall, *Britain Admits that Much of its Report on Iraq Came from Magazines*, NY Times (Feb. 8, 2003), A9, www.nytimes.com/2003/02/08/world/threats-responses-intelligence-assessment-britain-admits-that-much-its-report.html.

122 *Iraqi Weapons of Mass Destruction Programs, Hearing before the S. Armed Service Comm'n*, 108th Cong. (2004) (statement of David Kay, former top US weapons inspector: "we were all wrong"), http://edition.cnn.com/2004/US/01/28/kay.transcript/ (last visited Aug.15, 2014); Comm'n on the Intelligence Capabilities of the US Regarding Weapons of Mass Destruction, Unclassified Version of the Report of the Commission on the Intelligence Capabilities of the United States Regarding Weapons of Mass Destruction ch. 1 (Mar. 31, 2005) (hereinafter WMD Commission Report); Chilcot Report, *supra* note 120, § 4; Waxman, *supra* note 48, at 63; Cirincione et al., *supra* note 109, at 61; Walter H. Pincus, *Report Details Errors before War*, Washington Post (Sept. 9, 2006), A26, www.washingtonpost.com/wp-dyn/content/article/2006/09/08/AR2006090801719.html.

123 Butler Report, *supra* note 120, para. 449; Chilcot Report, *supra* note 120, § 4.4, paras. 627–30, 637–39.

124 Mason, *supra* note 50 (MPs referenced "past dossiers" and being "duped" in the Iraq build-up as reasons for voting against authorizing military action against Syria).

Soldiers whose states either have no history of fighting wars under false pretexts or have robust internal checks against waging wrongful wars have stronger grounds to defer to their governments than do soldiers in other states.[125] However, neither of those characteristics describes states that wage war frequently, and when states with such robust checks do go to war, there is especially strong reason for the soldiers on the other side to be wary of their own state's claims.

Overall, the zero-sum structure of the *jus ad bellum*, the fact of disagreeing epistemic authorities, the interestedness of the soldier's state, and the history of deception and mistake all militate strongly against any epistemic basis for the soldier to defer to his state's *jus ad bellum* claims, despite its superior access to the pertinent facts.

5.7 The Implications of the Vincibility of Ignorance

At the crux of the invincible ignorance account is the idea that the soldier's uncertainty as to the *jus ad bellum* status of their wars dissociates those soldiers morally from the wrongful killings they perpetrate in an illegal war.[126] The arguments above call this account into question as a cogent normative account of the extant regime.

First, terms like "uncertainty" and "ignorance" mask enormous diversity. Sometimes a soldier's war will be clearly lawful. About as often, it will be clearly illegal. In most cases, as the invincible ignorance theorist correctly insists, it will be at least somewhat uncertain to those with his level of epistemic access. To be sure, within this category of uncertain wars, it is sometimes reasonable for the soldier to believe his war to be permissible, but, at least as often, the only objectively reasonable posture is for him to believe it to be unlawful.[127] In a final category, it may be that the only reasonable epistemic posture is to withhold

[125] Germany has judicial review on *jus ad bellum* grounds, has an operative criminal prohibition on aggression, and has had a robust political aversion to militarism since 1945. *See* Section 10.3 in Chapter 10 below. The British Parliament's initial wariness regarding intervention in Syria arguably enhanced its status as a body worthy of deference. *See supra* note 50.

[126] *See supra* notes 7–8 and accompanying text. Zupan, *supra* note 8, at 214.

[127] This balance is rooted in the structural asymmetry that means that fighting against a lawful use of force is illegal, but fighting against an illegal use of force could be either lawful or unlawful. *See supra* notes 84–92 and accompanying text. Those who try to disobey on *jus ad bellum* grounds and are refused permission to do so are ultimately making the claim that the evidence available to them points strongly in favor of the view that their wars are illegal.

judgment.[128] Crucially, all of this holds *even once warranted epistemic deference to the soldier's state is accounted for.*

As argued above, the fact that many soldiers in an aggressive war are likely to be uncertain about their war's illegality does not itself show why the few that are better informed on that front should not be held criminally liable for their participation. The explanation for their exclusion from criminal liability is provided in Chapters 8 and 9; the point here is that it requires more than the fact of widespread uncertainty.

More importantly here, even if we focus on those who are not certain of the illegality of their war, the arguments above indicate that, although this does reduce their culpability (below the criminal threshold in many cases), it is not enough to demand that they "wash their hands of guilt" when they fight. Domestic criminal law, the *jus ad bellum*, and the *jus in bello* all rely on the basic moral judgment that it is culpable to inflict violence, death, and human suffering without robust reason to believe that the justificatory conditions for such actions obtain. Merely *not knowing for sure that those conditions do not obtain* is ordinarily inadequate. And yet, most soldiers are in that latter category.

In the majority of cases, if soldiers can dissociate themselves from the wrongfulness of the death and suffering they inflict in an illegal war, it will not be on purely epistemic grounds.[129] The denial of their right to disobey cannot rest on the fact of widespread uncertainty.

On the issue of victim status, there is a direct parallel here between the duress argument and the epistemic argument. One might argue that soldiers who reasonably but incorrectly believe their war to be lawful due to potent state propaganda and mendacity are no less victims of the war than soldiers harmed fighting against them. Both fight in good faith and both suffer harms and even death as a result. Conversely, those who fight against aggression, but lack the information to provide strong reasons for believing in the lawfulness of their cause, might be considered no less culpable than those on the other side with a similar epistemic posture. As such, they might be thought ineligible for victim status.

There is an important truth here. Combatants are at the mercy of luck. Some fight in criminal wars despite good reasons to believe their wars to

[128] *Cf.* Kolodny, *supra* note 21, at 234–35, n.14. On similar grounds, despite the dissimilar context, in his dissent from the Nicaragua judgment, Judge Stephen Schwebel argued that in the face of profound uncertainty as to the key facts, the only appropriate decision for the Court was to withhold judgment altogether. Nicaragua Judgment, *supra* note 90, paras. 69, 71 (Schwebel, J., dissenting).

[129] On the issue of criminal liability, *see* Chapter 7 below.

be lawful. Others fight in lawful wars without sufficient grounds for believing those wars to be lawful. The latter act more culpably than the former, and yet only the former perpetrate criminally wrongful killings. Similarly, only the latter suffer a criminal wrong.

However, as in the context of duress, the unfairness in that distribution of luck ought not be rectified through a distortion of victim status at the ICC. Just like the soldier who fights in an illegal war under duress, the soldier who fights unknowingly in such a war due to his state's mendacity and manipulation of information has a valid moral claim against his home state. A plausible case can be made that that claim should also have status in law. The soldier suffers the wrong of being misled into placing himself in a situation in which he is the legitimate target of defensive violence and in which he unwittingly inflicts criminally wrongful harm. Whether killed, harmed, or morally burdened by this situation, his suffering is tragic and he is wronged by his state.

However, the wrong inflicted on him is the wrong of being exploited through lies, and thereby exposed to extraordinary risk. That wrong, grave as it is, is distinct from the criminal infliction of violence on those fighting against aggression, or caught in the crossfire. In the absence of the aggressor soldier's state's mendacity – which, like duress, does not inhere in the crime – he would not be wronged.[130] Whatever claim he has against the state is not a claim that should be channeled through the ICC.

The soldier fighting against aggression with good, but mistaken reasons to believe his war to be *un*lawful (perhaps even believing it to be so) is also an uncomfortable case. Such an actor would be mistaken to find vindication for his posture in an ICC judgment against the enemy leaders. For those reasons, there are practical reasons, addressed in Chapter 8, to be concerned about the inclusion of such persons in the class of victims – particularly to the extent such inclusion might advance nationalist myth-making. However, the mere fact of an individual's guilty mind is not ordinarily sufficient to preclude his standing as a victim when he has suffered a grave legal wrong himself. Moreover, investigating the mental state of each soldier injured or killed fighting against aggression would be infeasible in almost any imaginable case. Ultimately, since victim participation and reparation in an aggression prosecution at the ICC would likely need to be collective, the discomfort of such examples may not have great import in practice.

130 *See* Section 4.3 of Chapter 4 above.

6

Legal Spheres and Hierarchies of Obligation

There is something potentially grating about the cosmopolitan perspective adopted in the previous chapter. Fundamental to the soldier's normative experience of war is the special relationships she shares with her state and her political community. Recognizing the normative force of those relationships may change how we think about the implications of uncertainty. Specifically, one might argue that the state's sovereign authority and the soldier's attached political obligation explain why *her* state, rather than any other, is the appropriate authority to which to defer. On this view, rather than deferring on epistemic grounds to an informed authority, soldiers defer on political grounds to a sovereign authority. Relatedly, one might argue that soldiers' special duties to protect their co-citizens, their common life, and their domestic institutions (including the principle of civilian control) together preclude refusing to fight, at least in wars that are not patently illegal. One might even argue that when soldiers die fighting against aggression, theirs is a sacrifice to their state and its community – a sacrifice that it is within that community's right to demand – and not a harm that they suffer individually as victims of the aggressor force.

There are elements of truth in some of these arguments, at least in dubious wars. However, neither the political nor the associative obligations they identify can displace the fundamental cosmopolitan obligations implicit in the criminalization of aggression. At best, they spotlight a normative impasse. They cannot make sense of international law's dissonant treatment of soldiers.

6.1 Political Deference and International Crime

The political account is at the heart of the way many people think about war. Describing its strongest form, Walzer writes that once the soldier's political community has made its collective decision to engage in armed conflict, fighting "becomes a legal obligation and a patriotic duty."[1] On his account, although soldiers have an obligation to oppose any patently wrongful war in their capacity as citizens contributing to public deliberation about whether to fight, they have a firm political duty to obey, once the decision has been made.[2] At that point, "they fight as members of the political community," irrespective of the justice or legality of their cause.[3] Similarly, Kahn argues that it is because soldiers "act in politically compelled roles" that it makes sense to describe soldiers on both sides as engaged in "reciprocal self-defense."[4]

On this view, once the sovereign decision has been made, the soldier becomes, for *jus ad bellum* purposes, an instrument of the state.[5] Unlike in the case of *jus in bello* violations, the soldier on this view loses agency; the killings she inflicts in an aggressive war are not hers, but those of her state and its leader.[6]

This unwavering patriotic commitment to obey the sovereign on the *jus ad bellum* is, for many, the *Grundnorm* of the military institutional ethic.[7] Outsiders laud it as a noble virtue.[8] It often underpins the notion that citizens ought to "support the troops" even while protesting a wrongful war.[9] It is a vision of virtue captured (satirically) by W.H. Auden in *The Unknown Citizen*:

1 Michael Walzer, Just and Unjust Wars 28 (1977) [hereinafter Walzer, JUW]. *See also id.*, at 27, 30, 39, 127.

2 *Id.*, at 299–301. 3 *Id.*, at 299–300, n.*.

4 Paul W. Kahn, *The Paradox of Riskless Warfare*, 22 Phil. & Pub. Pol'y 2, 2–3 (2002).

5 Walzer often emphasizes the normative significance of the fact that the soldier does not choose his war. *See, e.g.*, Walzer, JUW, *supra* note 1, at 28, 39.

6 Describing the *jus-in-bello*-compliant killings in war as the acts of the leaders, and explicitly *not* the acts of the soldiers who actually pull the trigger or drop the bombs (in contrast to their descriptions of *jus in bello* violations), *see, for example*, Michael Walzer, *Kosovo* (1999), *in* Arguing about War 99, 101 (2004); Michael Walzer, *Emergency Ethics* (1988) *in* Arguing about War 33, 45 (2004); Daniel S. Zupan, War, Morality, and Autonomy: An Investigation into Just War Theory, 127 (2003).

7 Gen. Douglas MacArthur, Duty, Honor, Country, Speech to the Corps of Cadets at the US Military Academy at West Point, NY (May 12, 1962); James H. Toner, True Faith and Allegiance: The Burden of Military Ethics 132 (1995).

8 Oliver Wendell Holmes, Jr., The Soldier's Faith, Memorial Day Address to Graduating Class of Harvard University (May 30, 1895), *in* The Essential Holmes: Selections from the Letters, Speeches, Judicial Opinions, and Other Writings of Oliver Wendell Holmes, Jr. 87, 89 (Richard Posner, ed., 1992); Samuel P. Huntington, The Soldier and the State: The Theory and Politics of Civil–Military Relations, 465–66 (1964).

9 Phillip Jensen, *Apocalypse Again and Again*, 47 Christianity Today, May 2003, at 34.

> [I]n the modern sense of an old-fashioned word, he was a saint,
> For in everything he did he served the Greater Community . . .
> When there was peace, he was for peace: when there was war, he went.[10]

Notwithstanding its popularity, this notion of soldiering cannot explain international law's posture on aggression. The IMT rejected explicitly the submission by the defense counsel that "where the act in question is an act of state, those who carry it out are not personally responsible," holding it to be "the very essence of the [Tribunal's] Charter" that the individual can and indeed *must* extend her normative horizon beyond the state and disobey the latter when it "moves outside its competence under international law."[11] The position was clear: the global cosmopolitan duties of international criminal law "transcend the national obligations of obedience," even when the latter obligations come from the highest levels of the defendant's government in the form of validly enacted and constitutionally compliant domestic laws.[12]

In line with that core tenet of international criminal law, when perpetrators of crimes other than aggression describe their wrongs in the terminology of patriotic obedience to the sovereign command, that framing is rejected as a mischaracterization.[13] Simply invoking patriotic

[10] W.H. Auden, *The Unknown Citizen*, *in* COLLECTED POEMS 252, 252 (Vintage, 1991).

[11] United States v. Göring, Judgment, *in* 22 TRIAL OF THE MAJOR WAR CRIMINALS BEFORE THE INTERNATIONAL MILITARY TRIBUNAL 411, 446 (1948) [hereinafter IMT Judgment]. *See supra* Section 1.2 of Chapter 1.

[12] IMT Judgment, *supra* note 11, at 446. *See also* Charter of the International Military Tribunal, art. 8, Aug. 8, 1945, 59 Stat. 1544, 82 U.N.T.S. 279 [hereinafter IMT Charter]; United States v. von Leeb et al., *in* TRIALS OF WAR CRIMINALS BEFORE THE NUERNBERG MILITARY TRIBUNALS UNDER CONTROL COUNCIL LAW NO. 10, at 462, 508 (1949) [hereinafter High Command Judgment]; United States v. Alstötter, *in* 3 TRIALS OF WAR CRIMINALS BEFORE THE NUERNBERG MILITARY TRIBUNALS UNDER CONTROL COUNCIL LAW NO. 10, at 954, 1084–87 (1951) [hereinafter Justice Judgment]; W. Michael Reisman, *The Quest for World Order and Human Dignity in the Twenty-First Century*, 351 RECUEIL DES COURS 368 (2012); TELFORD TAYLOR, NUREMBERG AND VIETNAM: AN AMERICAN TRAGEDY 16 (1970). For a contrasting view of the moral duty to disobey, *see* Michael Walzer, *Two Kinds of Military Responsibility* (1980), *in* ARGUING ABOUT WAR 23, 27 (2004) (for whom the duty is "best understood as an appeal up the chain of command over a superior officer to the superiors of that superior officer" and thus a vindication of domestic law and authority).

[13] Many perpetrators of *jus in bello* crimes try to frame them in precisely these terms. *Trial Transcript of the Morning Session*, United States v. Göring et al. (Aug. 31, 1946), *in* 22 TRIAL OF THE MAJOR WAR CRIMINALS BEFORE THE INTERNATIONAL MILITARY TRIBUNAL 366, 368, 373, 381, 385 (1948) [hereinafter IMT Trial Transcript of Aug. 31]. *See also* JEFF MCMAHAN, KILLING IN WAR 129 (2009); Bob Greene, *Life after Wartime*, NY TIMES (Nov. 12, 2007); Richard Goldstein and Paul W. Tibbets Jr., *Pilot*

or political obligation cannot explain why aggression should be any different, at least in the case of patently criminal wars. Whether such an argument could combine with *jus ad bellum* uncertainty to better address the issue is addressed in Section 6.4 below.

6.2 Associative Ties and the Responsibility to Protect

A different way of grounding the soldier's blanket duty to fight for her state would be to emphasize her special duty to protect both those with whom she shares a common political life and the institutions that sustain that life.[14] Depending on one's theory of political obligation, this associative duty might actually be what underpins the obligation to obey the sovereign.[15] The question is whether focusing on protection as the normatively central element can help to identify what, if anything, makes aggression unique.

Consider again the situation in which a third party can only intervene effectively in a fatal fight between two people by killing one of them. As discussed above, the elevated gravity of killing as compared to letting die would ordinarily demand restraint unless the intervener is reasonably certain which one is the aggressor. When one of the parties is the potential intervener's brother, however, things look different. The love for her brother might be thought to *demand* that she kill his adversary, *even if* she lacks strong reason to believe that her brother is the innocent party. Killing may be worse than letting die, but there is something different about letting *him* die. The special duty to protect her brother conflicts with the impartial duty not to kill the stranger.[16] Refraining

of Enola Gay Dies at 92, NY Times (Nov. 2, 2007); Mark A. Drumbl, Atrocity, Punishment, and International Law 2 (2007).

[14] *See* Seth Lazar, *Liberal Defence of (Some) Duties to Compatriots*, 27 J. Applied Phil. 246, 247 (2010) (defining associative duties as "duties grounded in a particular relationship that we share with the beneficiary of the duties"). Emphasizing its distinction from the political obligation argument, Walzer suggests that this kind of associative imperative can actually place a moral demand on persons to *refuse* to fight when they have countervailing associative duties stronger than their associative duties to the political community in which they happen to live. Michael Walzer, Obligations: Essays on Disobedience, War, and Citizenship 14–23 (1970).

[15] Grounding political obligation in protective duties, *see* Christopher Heath Wellman, *Doing One's Fair Share*, *in* Is There a Duty to Obey the Law? 30, 33 (Christopher Heath Wellman & A. John Simmons, 2005).

[16] Seth Lazar, *Do Associative Duties Really Not Matter?*, 17 J. Pol. Phil. 90, 90 (2009) (on the conflict between associative and general duties); Seth Lazar, *Associative Duties and the Ethics of Killing in War*, J. Prac. Ethics (2013), www.jpe.ox.ac.uk/papers/associative-duties-and-the-ethics-of-killing-in-war/.

from killing the stranger would be objectively justified, but that path might be thought of as betraying her brother, violating the demands of familial love.[17]

The associative bonds between those who share common domestic political institutions and a common civic life are thinner and harder to identify than are the bonds of love between siblings. To the extent they exist, they may be thought to arise from the mutual cooperation and collaboration of social and political action and from the collective agreement to stand together as a community (even if that agreement is tacit or imagined).[18] More controversially, some argue that the strength of such connections is augmented by a shared national identity.[19] Lazar instead focuses on the much narrower and deeper bonds between loved ones, arguing that they underpin a statewide duty because, "in most political communities, most people will share most of their special relationships with other people who are resident in the same territory."[20]

Each of these proposed justifications for strong associative duties rests on contestable premises, but contesting them is not necessary here. Even if they hold, there is inevitably great variance across states (and indeed persons) in the strength of each of the proposed normative foundations and the degree to which its reach overlaps with the boundaries of the state. As such, the presence and strength of the duties generated would seem to vary significantly from state to state and person to person.[21] Nonetheless, the associative claim is that at least some of the bonds

[17] Bernard Williams has argued against objective morality by emphasizing the strain it places on these kinds of personal obligations. Bernard Williams, *Integrity*, *in* UTILITARIANISM: FOR AND AGAINST 108 (J. J. C. Smart & Bernard Williams, eds., 1973). Lazar suggests that refusing to accept any special associative duties would be "repellent." Lazar, *supra* note 16, at 96.

[18] At the very heart of the idea of a social contract is the principle that members commit to protect one another from threats, external and internal, through unifying their decisions and acting in concert. The seminal articulation of this, is, of course, THOMAS HOBBES, LEVIATHAN 106 [ch. 17] (Edwin Curley, ed., Hackett 1994) (1651).

[19] DAVID MILLER, CITIZENSHIP AND NATIONAL IDENTITY 27, 49, 83 (2000); DAVID MILLER, ON NATIONALITY (1997); YAEL TAMIR, LIBERAL NATIONALISM (1993). Rawls emphasizes the normative significance of "common sympathies" as one of the grounds for his focus on "peoples" rather than states. JOHN RAWLS, THE LAW OF PEOPLES (1999) 23–24. *See also* MARGARET LEVI, CONSENT, DISSENT, AND PATRIOTISM ch. 6 (1997). RONALD BEINER, LIBERALISM, NATIONALISM, CITIZENSHIP: ESSAYS ON THE PROBLEM OF POLITICAL COMMUNITY (2003).

[20] Lazar, *Associative Duties and the Ethics of Killing in War*, *supra* note 16.

[21] Recognizing variance, *see*, *for example*, Lazar, *supra* note 14, at 253–54; JOHN RAWLS, THE LAW OF PEOPLES 23–24, 91 (1999).

among members of a state are sufficiently common, deep, and far-reaching to underpin a general duty to protect one's own state, its people, and its institutions.[22] For Lazar, this is possible because protecting the state is the only effective way of protecting loved ones, so obedience to the state is justified by the latter, deeper associative duty, regardless of the thinness of the associative bonds between co-citizens generally.[23]

Like the notion of an overriding patriotic obligation, this line of normative thought regarding a special duty to protect one's own community plays a prominent role in the self-conception of the military,[24] in leading accounts of the soldier's role,[25] and in the idea that we should "support the troops," even when they are waging a wrongful war.[26] More significantly for the discussion here, elements of associative priority are reflected in international law.

Multiple *jus in bello* principles spotlight a normative presumption that the soldier is tied to her community in a way that warrants special concern for its survival and the survival of its people.[27] First, humanitarian law makes special accommodation for the *levée en masse*. To gain the privileges of belligerency under Geneva Convention III,[28] combatants

[22] Walzer writes of the soldier's "moral investment in the state," WALZER, JUW, *supra* note 1, at 39. Vitoria argued: "A prince neither can nor ought always to explain the reasons for war to his subjects; if subjects were unable to fight until they understood the justice of the war, the safety of the commonwealth would be gravely endangered." Francisco de Vitoria, *On the Law of War* (1539), *in* POLITICAL WRITINGS 295, 311 (Anthony Pagden & Jeremy Lawrance, eds., 1991), *cited* (with a different translation) *in* WALZER, JUW, *supra* note 1, at 39.

[23] *See* Lazar, *Associative Duties and the Ethics of Killing in War*, *supra* note 16.

[24] BRIGADIER GEN. AVI BENAYAHU, ISRAEL DEFENSE FORCES, A SPECIAL SURVEY: THE IDF'S SOCIAL COMMITMENT (January 2010); MacArthur, *supra* note 7.

[25] H.C.J. 7622/02 Zonstein v. Judge Advocate General, para. 16 (2002) (Isr.). *See also* Cheyney Ryan, *Democratic Duty and the Moral Dilemmas of Soldiers*, 122 ETHICS 10 (2011).

[26] Jensen, *supra* note 9; Ryan, *supra* note 25, at 19.

[27] In each case, the rules apply regardless of the *jus ad bellum* status of the war, emphasizing the fact that it is the associative pull of the state, not the justice or legality of its action that accords it special favor. Notably, one of the architects of The Hague conferences in 1899 and 1907, Russian representative Friedrich Martens, praised at the 1899 conference "the heroic sacrifices which nations might be ready to make in their defence" and insisted, "It is not our province to set limits to patriotism." *Minutes of the Second Subcommission, Second Commission, Conference of 1899, Eleventh Meeting*, 20 June 1899, *in* THE PROCEEDINGS OF THE HAGUE PEACE CONFERENCES: THE CONFERENCE OF 1899, at 547 (John Scott, ed., 1920).

[28] Privileges that include, most notably, immunity from prosecution for *jus-in-bello*-compliant participation in hostilities. *See infra* Chapter 7.

must (among other things) wear fixed distinctive signs recognizable at a distance and subject themselves to organized command.[29] However, recognizing a people's associative imperative to protect its common life and the independence of its political community, these requirements are dropped in the case of "inhabitants of a non-occupied territory, who on the approach of the enemy spontaneously take up arms to resist the invading forces, without having had time to form themselves into regular armed units."[30] The importance of enabling last-ditch associative protection in such cases overrides the imperative to maintain the uniform and organization requirements despite the latter's role in buttressing the core *jus in bello* principle of distinction.

Second, although a soldier may be forced by her own state to participate in a criminal war, she may never be forced to fight against her state, even when it is engaged in a gravely aggressive war. Compelling a prisoner of war, an inhabitant of occupied territory, or a national of the enemy "to serve in the forces of the hostile Power" is a war crime.[31] Indeed, inhabitants of occupied territory may not even be subjected to "pressure or propaganda" to enlist in the occupying forces.[32] It is a war crime to compel persons to participate in a war against their country of

[29] Geneva Convention (III) Relative to the Treatment of Prisoners of War, art. 4(A)(2) (1949) [hereinafter GC III]. Additional Protocol I reduced the force of this requirement. Protocol (I) Additional to the Geneva Conventions of 12 August 1949, and Relating to the Protection of Victims of International Armed Conflicts 44 (1977) [hereinafter AP I].

[30] GC III, *supra* note 29, art. 4(A)(6). *See also* FRANCIS LIEBER, GENERAL ORDER NO. 100: INSTRUCTIONS FOR THE GOVERNMENT OF ARMIES OF THE UNITED STATES IN THE FIELD 18, art. 51 (1863); Hague Convention (IV) Respecting the Laws and Customs of War on Land and its Annex: Regulations Concerning the Laws and Customs of War on Land, art. 2 (Oct. 18, 1907), 36 Stat. 2277 [hereinafter hereinafter Hague IV]; Project of an International Declaration Concerning the Laws and Customs of War, art. 10 (Aug. 17, 1874).

[31] GC III, *supra* note 29, art. 130; Geneva Convention (IV) Relative to the Protection of Civilian Persons in Time of War, art. 147 (Aug. 12, 1949) [hereinafter GC IV); Rome Statute of the International Criminal Court, U.N. Doc. A/CONF.183/9, 2187 U.N.T.S. 90, art. 8(2)(a)(v) (July 17, 1998) (as amended in 2010 by Doc. C.N.651.2010.TREATIES-8) [hereinafter ICC Statute]; United States v. Ernst von Weizsäcker, *in* 14 TRIALS OF WAR CRIMINALS BEFORE THE NUERNBERG MILITARY TRIBUNALS UNDER CONTROL COUNCIL LAW NO. 10, at 1, 549, 551 (1949) [hereinafter Ministries Judgment].

[32] GC IV, *supra* note 31, art. 51. *See also* Hague IV, *supra* note 30, art. 52 (inhabitants of occupied territory shall not be subject to requisitions and in kind services that would involve them "in the obligation of taking part in military operations against their own country"); H.C.J. 3799/02 Adalah v. GOC Central Command, paras. 22–25 (2005) (Isr.) (prohibiting the use of a local resident in the occupied territory to "relay an 'early warning' to a wanted person in a place besieged by the army, against his will").

nationality, even if they were in the service of the compelling state before the war.[33]

Third, Additional Protocol I to the Geneva Conventions denies combatant privileges to mercenaries,[34] who are defined in part by being "neither a national of a party to the conflict nor a resident of territory controlled by a Party to the conflict."[35] In other words, this provision allows individuals to fight for their country in ways that would lose them the privileges of belligerency if done on behalf of any other state.

Beyond these specific *jus in bello* rules, self-determination is widely considered a foundational principle of contemporary international law as a whole.[36] Additional Protocol I counts wars of self-determination as international armed conflicts, thereby granting those fighting for self-determination the possibility of privileged belligerency and a range of more robust protections than would otherwise apply.[37] This manifests international recognition of the value of enabling peoples with a shared sense of identity and purpose to construct and protect a common political and social life. Arguably, implicit in this is an acceptance of the special value that individuals place on their people and their community.[38]

33 Hague IV, *supra* note 30, art. 23(h); ICC Statute, *supra* note 31.

34 AP I, *supra* note 29, art. 47.

35 *Id.* art. 47(2)(d). *See also* Council of Ministers of the Org. of African Unity Res. 817, O.A.U. Doc. CM/817, Annex I Rev. 3, Convention for the Elimination of Mercenarism in Africa, art. 1(d) (July 3, 1977); G.A. Res. 44/34, International Convention against the Recruitment, Use, Financing, and Training of Mercenaries, art. 1(1)(c) (Dec. 4, 1989).

36 The right is enshrined in the UN Charter, the ICCPR, and the ICESCR. UN Charter, art. 1(2); G.A. Res. 2200A(XXI), International Covenant on Civil and Political Rights, art. 1 (1966) (hereinafter ICCPR); G.A. Res. 2200A(XXI), International Covenant on Economic, Social and Cultural Rights, art. 1 (1966) (hereinafter ICESCR). The I.C.J. held it to be an "essential" principle in the East Timor judgment. Case Concerning East Timor (Portugal v. Austl.) [1995] I.C.J. Rep. 90 (June 30), para. 29, in which it also declared the principle an obligation owed *erga omnes*. *Id.* The I.L.C. has termed it *jus cogens* and *erga omnes*. Draft Articles on Responsibility of States for Internationally Wrongful Acts with Commentaries, Rep. of the Int'l Law Comm'n on the Work of its Fifty-Third Session, U.N. Doc. A/56/10, at 85, 112–14, 120 (2001) [hereinafter Articles on State Responsibility with commentaries]. *See also*, ANTONIO CASSESE, SELF-DETERMINATION OF PEOPLES: A LEGAL REAPPRAISAL 133–40 (1998); especially *id.*, at 136–37, nn. 67–72; G.A. Res. 1514(XV), Declaration on the Granting of Independence to Colonial Countries and Peoples (Dec. 14, 1960).

37 AP I, *supra* note 29, art. 1(4).

38 It should be noted here that this is not the only, nor necessarily the most plausible, justificatory basis for self-determination. Other accounts focus more on self-determination as a form of collective of individual rights. Arguably, that sits better with

The associative theme running through these various provisions and principles was also present at Nuremberg. The *I.G. Farben* tribunal considered it excessive to insist that the German citizen not certain of his war's criminality must "lay aside his patriotism, the loyalty to his homeland and the defence of his own fireside" in order to avoid criminal liability.[39] Similarly, in acquitting Ernst von Weizsäcker of crimes against peace for his failure to warn the USSR of Germany's pending aggression, the *Ministries* Tribunal held,

> [T]he revelation of the actual situation to the Russian Ambassador, even if it remained secret, would not cause Hitler to change his plans but would necessarily entail death and suffering to thousands of German youth ... The prosecution insists, however, that there is criminality in his assertion that he did not desire the defeat of his own country. The answer is: Who does? ... [T]he time has not yet arrived when any man would view with satisfaction the ruin of his own people and the loss of its young manhood. To apply any other standard of conduct is to set up a test that has never yet been suggested as proper, and which, assuredly, we are not prepared to accept as either wise or good. We are not to be understood as holding that one who knows that a war of aggression has been initiated is to be relieved from criminal responsibility if he thereafter wages it, or if, with knowledge of its pendency, he does not exercise such powers and functions as he possesses to prevent its taking place. But we are firmly convinced that the failure to advise a prospective enemy of the coming aggression in order that he may make military preparations which would be fatal to those who in good faith respond to the call of military duty does not constitute a crime.[40]

The tribunal's refusal in the penultimate sentence to exculpate those who knowingly wage an illegal war after it has begun is significant, but the passage is nonetheless laced with affirmation of an associative priority of protection towards one's own people and state.

In each of these respects, the importance of associative duties is recognized and reflected in international law. For reasons explained

the location of self-determination in international human rights documents that are otherwise focused primarily on individual rights. For a useful overview of different approaches to understanding the normative substance of self-determination, *see, for example*, Allen Buchanan, *Theories of Secession*, 26 PHIL. & PUB. AFF. 31 (1997).

39 United States v. Krauch et al., Military Tribunal VI, *in* 8 TRIALS OF WAR CRIMINALS BEFORE THE NUERNBERG MILITARY TRIBUNALS UNDER CONTROL COUNCIL LAW NO. 10, at 1126 (1949) [hereinafter I.G. Farben Judgment]. *See also id.*, at 1125–126; Ministries Judgment, *supra* note 31, at 321–22.

40 *See* Ministries Judgment, *supra* note 31, at 382–83, *see also id.*, at 378.

immediately below, the power of associative duties cannot ground the innocence of soldiers' participation in patently criminal wars. The more complicated and interesting question is whether associative duties can do that work when the *jus ad bellum* status of the war is not manifestly obvious from the soldier's point of view. That question is addressed in Section 6.4.

6.3 The Myth of an Aggressive Moment

The view that associative duties can exonerate participation in even patently criminal wars might be termed the "aggressive moment" conception of the *jus ad bellum*.[41] On this account, once the fighting begins, it immediately ceases to matter which side is in the wrong – what is of overriding importance is that losing would bring catastrophic consequences for the defeated state. The empirical assumption underpinning this account is that if a state waging a criminal war were beset by mass disobedience, this would invite a forceful response by its adversary, leading to some combination of: the collapse of the aggressor's institutions, the subjugation of its people, the destruction of their common life, and a loss of life for the aggressor's citizens beyond what could be expected if its criminal action had been successful. The claim is that when these are the stakes, the soldier, driven by an associative duty to protect, fights non-culpably even when she *knows* the war to be criminal.[42]

International law's recognition of the value of associative bonds notwithstanding, this argument is untenable as an explanation of the existing

[41] This is linked to the view that once the war has started, the *jus ad bellum* has no ongoing application; only the *jus in bello* remains. Philip Alston (Special Rapporteur on extrajudicial, summary or arbitrary executions), *Report of the Special Rapporteur on Extrajudicial, Summary or Arbitrary Executions, Addendum: Study on Targeted Killings*, U.N. Doc. A/HRC/14/24/Add.6, para. 43 (May 28, 2010) (citing Christopher Greenwood, *The Relationship between Jus ad Bellum and Jus in Bello*, 9 REV. INT'L STUD. 221, 222–23 (1983)). *Cf.* Ethiopia's Damages Claims (Eri. v. Eth.), 26 R.I.A.A., paras. 289–305 (Eri.–Eth. Claims Comm'n 2009) (limiting Eritrea's *jus ad bellum* liability to the consequences of the initial attack, not the entire war). *But note id.*, at para. 312; Eri.–Eth. Cl. Comm'n, Decision Number 7: Guidance Regarding Jus ad Bellum Liability, paras. 5, 23, 32 (July 27, 2007) (emphasizing that the limited scope of liability was due in part to a finding that this was not a war of aggression, but a lesser *jus ad bellum* violation).

[42] WHITNEY R. HARRIS, TYRANNY ON TRIAL: THE EVIDENCE AT NUREMBERG 531 (1954). Often, this view is implied without being directly connected to the *jus ad bellum*. Thus, for example, without relying on the assumption that the war is lawful or just, it is often emphasized within the military that the survival of the state is at stake in winning. *See, e.g.*, MacArthur, *supra* note 7.

legal approach to participation in wrongful war. It stands on a false empirical premise, it is morally implausible, and it is inconsistent with the post-Nuremberg regime.

First, the premise is often false. In many contemporary wars, hostilities occur far from the homeland of at least one of the parties. This is particularly common both for major military powers like the United States, France, and Britain, which are highly militarily active in areas far removed from their own borders, and also (by definition) for a significant proportion of the partners in any broad coalition action.[43]

This empirical reality matters. In cases in which the state in breach of the *jus ad bellum* is fighting far from its homeland, the collapse of its action would not *itself* trigger a direct and immediate danger to its people or its common life.[44] There would be no danger of a wave of enemy troops breaking through its disintegrated front lines and sweeping through its territory. At most, military breakdown would create a danger of failing in the aggressive action. But associative bonds do not (and cannot plausibly) demand success in inflicting a criminal wrong independent of the instrumental value of that in protecting those with whom one shares those bonds. At most, the associative duties argument indicates that performing that protective function might override the duty not to inflict such a wrong. Where the protective function is absent, the argument breaks down.

Of course, a failed distant aggression could inspire reprisals, either through similarly distant conventional attack, or through terrorist or cyber-attacks. However, such a response would be retaliatory, rather than opportunistic; it is not generated by the opportunity created by the aggressor's crumbling front line. It could even be that a *successful* aggression is more likely to provoke such reactions, and thus more likely to cause harm to the soldier's home state.[45]

The aggressive moment argument might be thought to be stronger in territorial wars between neighbors. In those scenarios, it is more plausible

[43] Recent military actions by one or more of France, Britain, or the United States include operations in Afghanistan, Bosnia, Cambodia, CAR, Chad, Grenada, Iraq, Kosovo, Kuwait, Nicaragua, Laos, Libya, Mali, Pakistan, Panama, Sierra Leone, Somalia, Syria, Vietnam, and Yemen, among others.

[44] In addition to the discussion in this chapter, *see also* Chapter 9, below.

[45] This may be particularly the case in the context of transnational terrorism. Suicide terrorism, in particular, is likely to be motivated by foreign aggression against or occupation of the actors' perceived homeland. *See generally* Robert A. Pape, Dying to Win (2005).

to worry that the aggressor's disintegrated front line would invite the defensive state to push across the border and inflict substantial harm. However, even in that scenario, such an outcome is unlikely.

Many of the most obviously aggressive wars are likely to involve significant power asymmetries. In these cases, the relative weakness of the defensive state excludes any serious risk to the stronger power. No soldier in the Russian aggression against Finland in 1939, the Nazi German aggressions against states like Austria, Czechoslovakia, or Denmark in the same period, Iraq in its aggression against Kuwait in 1990, or Russia in its ongoing aggression against Ukraine could claim credibly to fear that the collapse of his state's military action in any of those cases would have invited the defensive state to sweep back through the aggressor, killing its people, or destroying their common political and social life.[46]

There are, of course, wars between neighbors in which the strength of the defensive state is such that a collapse of the aggressor's military action would render the latter vulnerable to a powerful foe. Wars between the United States and Japan, Britain and Nazi Germany, Israel and Egypt, Ethiopia and Eritrea, Iran and Iraq, the former Yugoslav states, or India and Pakistan might be thought to fall into this category. These might be considered wars implicating national survival for both sides, regardless of which one was the aggressor.[47] Even in such cases, however, the aggressive moment argument depends on the assumption that the defensive state would actually exploit a collapse in the aggressor's military action to inflict disproportionate and defensively unnecessary killing, destruction, or annexation.

Such an unlawful response is possible, but in most contemporary cases there is good reason to doubt that it would occur.[48] Even when the

[46] For a useful history of the war between Russia and Finland, *see* ROBERT EDWARDS, THE WINTER WAR: RUSSIA'S INVASION OF FINLAND, 1939–1940 (2008). On Iraq's invasion of Kuwait, *see, for example*, JUDITH MILLER & LAURIE MYLROIE, SADDAM HUSSEIN AND THE CRISIS IN THE GULF, at ch. 11 (1990); UN Secretary General, *The United Nations and the Iraq-Kuwait Conflict 1990*–1996, paras. 14–25, U.N. Doc. DPI/1770 (1996). On the military disparity between Nazi Germany on the one hand and Czechoslovakia, Austria, and Denmark on the other, *see* Ministries Judgment, *supra* note 31, at 330, 334.

[47] A number of Israeli soldiers engaged in the Six Day War with Egypt in 1967 described having a genuine fear for national survival. *See, e.g.*, AVRAM SHAPIRA, ED., THE SEVENTH DAY: SOLDIERS TALK ABOUT THE SIX-DAY WAR 22, 26, 27, 137–39, 146, 165, 181 (1970). And yet, the conflict resulted in a sweeping victory for Israel, including the military occupation of a large swathe of Egypt (the Sinai peninsula). *See infra* note 48.

[48] Israel's occupation of the Sinai is an example of a scenario in which Egyptian collapse invited a sweeping occupation. For the perspective of the former head of military intelligence for the IDF on the collapse, *see* Yesoshafat Harkabi, *Basic Factors in the Arab Collapse during the Six Day War*, 11 ORBIS 677 (1967). *See also* George W. Gawrych,

formal military has disintegrated, waging war in enemy territory is extremely costly, as are military occupation and annexation.[49] Moreover, a disproportionate or unnecessary response in the face of the aggressor's military breakdown is likely to be condemned internationally, losing the defensive state what goodwill it would have gained from suffering the initial aggression.[50] Any form of annexation is particularly likely to meet with severe condemnation, and quite possibly non-recognition, and is thus increasingly rare.[51]

Unless the defensive state is already globally ostracized, or unless the gains reaped from such an action are likely to be particularly profound, an opportunistic war, occupation, or annexation may well impose greater costs on a defensive state than it would reap in benefits. Any occupation would trigger international pressure on the occupying state to act humanely and rebuild what it has destroyed.[52] Russia's recent annexation

The Egyptian Military Defeat of 1967, 26 J. CONTEMP. HIST. 277, 280 (1991). However, even this sweeping victory led only to a partial occupation (of the Sinai peninsula, not Egypt as a whole) – an occupation that was itself temporary. A Framework for Peace in the Middle East Agreed at Camp David, 17 I.L.M. 1466 (Sept. 17, 1978).

49 Two recent examples of the high costs of military occupation in the face of hostile forces are the American-led operations in Afghanistan and Iraq. Even though Saddam's forces and the Taliban collapsed quickly, the ensuing decade of occupation in the two states has been extremely costly for the allied forces, and has achieved limited success. Pew Research Center, *More Now See Failure than Success in Iraq, Afghanistan* (Jan. 30, 2014), www.people-press.org/files/legacy-pdf/1-30-14%20Iraq%20and%20Afghanistan%20Release.pdf; WARS IN PEACE: BRITISH MILITARY OPERATIONS SINCE 1991 (Malcolm Chalmers & Michael Clarke, eds., 2014); David Held & Kristian Coates Ulrichsen, *Wars of Decline: Afghanistan, Iraq, and Libya*, OPEN DEMOCRACY (Dec. 12, 2011), www.opendemocracy.net/david-held-kristian-coates-ulrichsen/wars-of-decline-afghanistan-iraq-and-libya.

50 Expressing a common refrain, Lionel Barber writes, "President George W. Bush's response to the assault on the Twin Towers and the Pentagon was to launch two wars of choice against Afghanistan and Iraq, a pugnacious unilateralism at the expense of alliances and international law, and a near evangelical promotion of liberal democracy in the Middle East. His administration's hard-edged policies fractured alliances in Europe and triggered a sharp fall in America's standing abroad." Lionel Barber, *The End of US Hegemony: Legacy of 9/11*, FIN. TIMES (5 Sept., 2011), www.ft.com/content/f6acf1a6-d54d-11e0-bd7e-00144feab49a.

51 On the ways that perpetrators are denied the benefits of international cooperation in response to international law-breaking, *see, for example*, Oona Hathaway & Scott J. Shapiro, *Outcasting: Enforcement in Domestic and International Law*, 121 YALE L.J. 252 (2011).

52 Articulating the basis for the obligation to rebuild, *see, for example*, NOAH FELDMAN, WHAT WE OWE IRAQ: WAR AND THE ETHICS OF NATION BUILDING (2004); Jean Bethke Elshtain, *The Ethics of Fleeing: What America Still Owes Iraq*, WORLD AFF. (Spring, 2008), www.worldaffairsjournal.org/article/ethics-fleeing-what-america-still-owes-iraq;

of Crimea and its broader engagement in eastern Ukraine is the exception that proves the rule, although that, too, has been costly.[53]

Even if the factual assumption on which the aggressive moment argument depends were more commonly accurate, the second and more fundamental problem with it as a normative account of the extant legal framework is its moral implausibility. It purports to render non-culpable the wrongful infliction of death and human suffering on the grounds that the victims of that wrong, if not defeated, might overreact to the wrongful attack on them by inflicting disproportionate death and suffering on the soldier's own society and its people.

Obviously, if such a disproportionate response were to occur, it would be appropriate to react with force against it.[54] However, the fact that it may be extremely difficult to do that once one's initial aggression has broken down through mass disobedience is insufficient to warrant pursuing a criminal war (and all of the wrongful killing and destruction it entails) to its final conclusion so as to preempt the mere *possibility* of such an unlawful response, particularly when that possibility is (per the first point) remote.

International law is generally intolerant of the infliction of criminal harm in order to protect against the possibility of other wrongdoing. In a rare and highly controversial deviation from that rule, the ICJ in its *Nuclear Weapons* advisory opinion seemed to open the door to breaching the *jus in bello* in order to protect against a certain, imminent, and unlawful existential threat.[55] But even that standard – itself among the

Gary Bass, *Jus Post Bellum*, 32 PHIL. & PUB. AFF. 384, 406–08 (2004); *The Iraq War: Why They Should Stay*, ECONOMIST, Sept. 15, 2007.

53 On some of the long-term costs to Russia associated with its policies *vis-à-vis* Ukraine, *see, for example*, Robert Coalson, *The Costs of Russia's Ukraine Victory*, RADIO FREE EUROPE, May 22, 2014; Justyna Pawlak & Eric Beech, *EU and US Announce New Sanctions on Russia over Ukraine*, REUTERS, July 30, 2014, www.reuters.com/article/us-ukraine-crisis-east-idUSKBN0FY0OX20140730; Vladislav Inozemtsev, *Russian Expansion into Eastern Ukraine Could Cost Putin Dearly*, WASHINGTON POST (Mar. 13, 2014), www.washingtonpost.com/opinions/russian-expansion-into-eastern-ukraine-could-cost-putin-dearly/2014/03/13/bd7d4972-a952-11e3-8d62-419db477a0e6_story.html?utm_term=.106e7133edea; Jonathan Wilson, *Crimean Cup Teams Could Cost Russia the Right to Host 2018 World Cup*, GUARDIAN (Aug. 19, 2014), www.theguardian.com/football/blog/2014/aug/19/2018-world-cup-russian-cup-crimean-teams.

54 HUGO GROTIUS, 3 THE RIGHTS OF WAR AND PEACE 1182–83 [bk 2, ch. 26] (1625) (Richard Tuck, ed., Liberty Fund 2005); MCMAHAN, *supra* note 13, at 15; Jeff McMahan, *The Ethics of Killing in War*, 114 ETHICS 693, 712–14 (July 2004).

55 *Nuclear Weapons. Advisory Opinion on the Legality of Nuclear Weapons*, 1996 I.C.J. Rep. 226 (July 8), paras. 95–97 [hereinafter *Nuclear Weapons Advisory Opinion*]. Walzer

most heavily criticized of the ICJ's positions – would clearly rule out participating in criminal war as a way of protecting against a *possible* counter-aggression by the enemy state.[56] In almost any conceivable case, the potential counter-aggression would be insufficiently severe, imminent, or certain.[57] Moreover, the claimed wrong against which the soldier would be protecting would be provoked by the very criminal action in which she engages.

Finally, as indicated in the earlier quotation from the *Ministries* judgment, the aggressive moment account is contradicted directly by the scope of the crime of aggression, which includes not just planning, preparing, or initiating a wrongful war, but also waging or executing it.[58] The case law leaves no doubt that the crime of waging or executing such a war extends beyond the war's initiation.[59] Karl Dönitz and

took a similar (and also highly controversial) line in his discussion of Germany's invasion of neutral Belgium in 1914 (which he condemns) and Britain's use of terror bombing in response to the threat of Nazi takeover (for which he has some sympathy during the period of genuine emergency, but which he still deems morally tainting (if a lesser evil). WALZER, JUW, *supra* note 1, at 241, 251–63. Whether the supreme emergency argument is persuasive, what Walzer gets right is that it certainly does *not* hold unless the survival imperative is real and powerful. It is not enough that the state might lose the war. The prospect of such defeat must be proximate and the consequences of the loss must be severe. Even under those conditions, the perpetrator of the wrongful killings will bear a moral burden.

56 Criticizing the holding: Wil Verwey, *The International Court of Justice and the Legality of Nuclear Weapons: Some Observations*, *in* INTERNATIONAL LAW: THEORY AND PRACTICE (ESSAYS IN HONOUR OF ERIC SUY) 751, 760 (Karel Wellens, ed., 1998); Luigi Condorelli, *Nuclear Weapons: A Weighty Matter for the International Court of Justice: Jura Non Novit Curia?*, 37 INT'L REV. RED CROSS 9, 19 (1997) (describing the holding as "extraordinarily incomplete, defective and disquieting"); CHRISTOPHER GREENWOOD, JUS AD BELLUM AND JUS IN BELLO IN THE NUCLEAR WEAPONS ADVISORY OPINION, INTERNATIONAL LAW, THE INTERNATIONAL COURT OF JUSTICE AND NUCLEAR WEAPONS 247 (Laurence Boisson de Chazournes & Philippe Sands, eds., 1999).

57 There is a parallel here with what is wrong with preventive war. Walzer comments: "there is a great difference . . . between killing and being killed by soldiers who can plausibly be described as the present instruments of an aggressive intention and killing and being killed by soldiers who may or may not represent a distant danger to our country. In the first case, we confront an army recognizably hostile, ready for war, fixed in a posture of attack. In the second, the hostility is prospective and imaginary, and it will always be a charge against us that we have made war upon soldiers who were themselves engaged in entirely legitimate (non-threatening) activities." WALZER, JUW, *supra* note 1, at 80.

58 IMT Charter, *supra* note 12, art. 6(a); ICC Statute, *supra* note 31, art. 8 *bis* (1); Elements of Crimes, INT'L CRIM. CT. 30 (2013), www.icc-cpi.int/resource-library/Documents/ElementsOfCrimesEng.pdf [http://perma.cc/8VEX-6XJF].

59 United States v. Araki et al., Judgment of 12 November 1948, *in* 20 THE TOKYO WAR CRIMES TRIAL 48,413, 49,786–88; 49,798; 49,808; 49,812; 49,833–34; 49,841; 49,851.

Mamoru Shigemitsu were convicted of crimes against peace even though each rose to the leadership level necessary for criminal responsibility only after the conflict had become existential for both sides.[60] As those and other cases exemplify, criminal liability was triggered not just by participating in the aggressors' wrongful advance, but also by continuing to wage the criminal war in retreat and with the imminent prospect of total defeat and enemy occupation.[61]

In short, by international law's own lights, if associative sympathies weigh in favor of inflicting wrongful death and suffering in a patently criminal war in order to guard against the vulnerability of one's own state, those associative sympathies pressure the soldier to do the wrong thing.[62] Love for one's brother may demand that one kill his adversary even when it is plainly the brother who is the aggressor and the adversary who is acting in legitimate self-defense, but in that case love demands that one do wrong; such killing is murder.[63]

6.4 Revising the Invincible Ignorance Account

Neither political obligation nor associative duty can make sense of the law's posture on participation in patently criminal wars. They cannot explain why soldiers are not criminally liable for such participation, and they cannot explain why soldiers in that position are denied the right to refuse to participate.

One might, however, argue that both political obligation and associative duty complicate the normative stakes in a context of uncertainty as to the war's legality, potentially opening the door to a revision of the

(R. John Pritchard & Sonia Magbanua Zaide, eds., 1981) [hereinafter IMTFE Judgment]; High Command Judgment, *supra* note 12, at 486, 490–91; IMT Judgment, *supra* note 11, at 577; Ministries Judgment, *supra* note 31, at 399, 417.

60 IMT Judgment, *supra* note 11, at 556–57; IMTFE Judgment, *supra* note 59, at 49,831–32. *See also* High Command Judgment, *supra* note 12, at 488, 490; IMT Judgment, *supra* note 11, at 467; IMTFE Judgment, *supra* note 59, at 48,421–48,423. As Telford Taylor observed in response to Schlesinger's comments on Vietnam (*see supra* note 41): "the reasons why we are in Vietnam are part of 'the situation that exists' and the question – what those reasons are – is both a moral and a practical issue of great moment." TAYLOR, *supra* note 12, at 183

61 IMTFE Judgment, *supra* note 59, at 49,786–87, 49,798, 49,808, 49,812, 49,833–34, 49,851, 49,841.

62 Notably, in elaborating the leadership requirement, the High Command Judgment held that the "great mass of soldiers and field officers" were used by the leadership to "carry out an international crime." High Command Judgment, *supra* note 12, at 489.

63 *See* examples discussed in *supra* notes 15–17 and accompanying text.

invincible ignorance theory that could better withstand the cosmopolitan rebuttal in Chapter 5. This would leave an explanatory gap in the case of wars that are patently criminal from the soldier's perspective, but, given the rarity of such wars, it would make sense of the vast majority of cases.

Giving voice to this softer version of a political obligation argument, Walzer contends that as long as the state's professed reasons for war are "only doubted" soldiers' "law-abidingness, their fear, their patriotism [and] their moral investment in the state" all favor fighting.[64] On this view, even if uncertainty does not warrant *epistemic* deference to any particular sovereign, it does justify the soldier's *political* deference to *her* sovereign.[65]

At various junctures, the Nuremberg judges evinced a degree of sympathy for this view. The tendency of subjects to believe their leader was termed "natural";[66] the power of propaganda was acknowledged;[67] the "necessity" of serving one's government in a time of war was recognized;[68] and it was deemed untenable to require that a soldier become a "traitor to his country" when having only "vague knowledge" of the relevant facts.[69] The *Ministries* Tribunal made a similar point in associative terms:

> Obviously, no man may be condemned for fighting in what he believes is the defence of his native land, even though his belief be mistaken. Nor can he be expected to undertake an independent investigation to determine whether or not the cause for which he fights is the result of an aggressive act of his own Government.[70]

In part, these dicta evince a commitment to applying a high *mens rea* standard in the context of international criminal law combined with a recognition that patriotic and associative biases are sufficiently distorting of judgment to cause widespread mistaken belief in the war's

[64] Walzer, JUW, *supra* note 1, at 39. It is not precisely clear what Walzer's own view on this is, although he seems at times to endorse the political duty to fight obediently even in an illegal war. *See supra* notes 1–6.

[65] Vitoria, too, argues that when the war is only dubious, soldiers "may lawfully go to war trusting the judgment of their *superiors*." Vitoria, *supra* note 22, at 308 [emphasis added]. *See also* Dan Zupan, *A Presumption of the Moral Equality of Combatants: A Citizen-Soldier's Perspective*, *in* Just and Unjust Warriors: The Moral and Legal Status of Soldiers 214, 217–18 (David Rodin & Henry Shue, eds., 2008).

[66] I.G. Farben Judgment, *supra* note 39, at 1107

[67] Ministries Judgment, *supra* note 31, at 321–22.

[68] I.G. Farben Judgment, *supra* note 39, at 1125–26.

[69] *Id.*, at 1126.

[70] Ministries Judgment, *supra* note 31, at 337

lawfulness.[71] Accepting such bias as natural would further reduce the population of soldiers for whom a given war is manifestly criminal, although there is no reason to believe it would eliminate that category completely. Similarly, it would, at most, change the proportion of soldiers whose culpability is insufficient for criminal liability, but whom the law cannot expect to "wash their hands of the guilt."[72] The categorically different treatment of aggression from other international crimes requires something different; it requires a categorical explanation.

An alternative understanding of the Nuremberg dicta along those lines would be that whenever the *jus ad bellum* status of the war is not patently clear from the perspective of a subordinate soldier, associative or political duties simply displace whatever normative link the soldier has to the *jus ad bellum*. Consider what this would mean in the political obligation and associative duty forms respectively. The first of these runs into several difficulties.

As discussed in the previous chapter, the *jus in bello* right to disobey includes orders that are unlawful, but not patently so; indeed, in some states this extends to orders that the soldier reasonably believes to be illegal, even if they are in fact lawful.[73] In those cases, too, there is a combination of political obligation and a lack of total certainty regarding the criminality of the conduct, but the law recognizes that performing the wrongful act is burdensome and leaves at least some space for a soldier to disobey. The different treatment of the *jus ad bellum* case must be explained on grounds other than the combination of political duty and uncertainty.

But put that inconsistency to one side. Is the normative structure of the proposed displacement morally plausible? The criminal wrong of aggression is the wrongful killing it entails. What is it about political obligation that can displace the basic duty not to engage in such wrongdoing? David Estlund offers an answer that focuses on the importance of upholding just institutions.[74] To make the argument, he analogizes the role of the soldier to that of the domestic jailer.[75] For Estlund, if the process for

71 On patriotic bias: JONATHAN GLOVER, CAUSING DEATH AND SAVING LIVES 253 (1977); George Orwell, *Notes on Nationalism* [originally in POLEMIC, No. 1, October, 1945], *in* ORWELL AND POLITICS: ANIMAL FARM IN THE CONTEXT OF ESSAYS, REVIEWS AND LETTERS SELECTED FROM THE COMPLETE WORKS OF GEORGE ORWELL 355, 363 (Peter Davison, ed., 2001).

72 *See* Section 1.4 of Chapter 1 above.

73 *See* Section 1.4 of Chapter 1 above.

74 David Estlund, *On Following Orders in an Unjust War*, 15 J. POL. PHIL. 213 (2007)

75 *Id.*, at 216–20 (2007)

determining the relevant facts is reasonably just (in the jailer's case, this requires that the prisoner received a "fair trial"), any error regarding those facts can be categorized as an "honest mistake."[76] As long as the outcome of such a process falls within a "range of error" whereby the required action would be just if the facts were as stipulated and the holding is at least "close to a reasonable conclusion based on the appropriate materials," the state agent is required to execute the command.[77] Thus, even the jailer with strong reasons to believe that his prisoner's conviction is erroneous has an unequivocal obligation to fulfill the judgment, unless it is patently wrongful.[78] In such contexts, Estlund contends, we should "make ourselves available for the pursuit of certain collectively authorized purposes."[79]

In the absence of political obligation, the jailer would plainly be culpable for imprisoning an individual without adequate reason to believe him to be guilty (even once epistemic deference to the state is factored in). But *political* deference (and therefore obedience) is appropriate because it is essential to the functioning of a broadly justified political authority, because any error regarding the justification for the detention in question is an "honest mistake," and because the decision in question is not patently wrongful.

Although not directly related to obedience itself, something like this idea seems to be imminent in several of the domains of international law focused on human protection and human values. The European Court of Human Rights and other similar bodies use tools like the "margin of appreciation" and related doctrines to affirm the primacy of domestic authority in resolving normative ambiguity and in applying or adapting rules to their own concrete situations.[80] Similarly, the ICC grants domestic courts primacy in prosecuting international crimes via the principle of complementarity, deferring to domestic judgments unless they are not

[76] *Id.*, at 221. [77] *Id.*, at 230.

[78] *Id.*, at 216–18. Estlund allows for an exception to this rule in cases of first-hand knowledge, such as if the jailer actually witnessed the crime and thus *knows* the convict to be innocent. *Id.*, at 218.

[79] *Id.*, at 228–29.

[80] *See, e.g.*, Jeroen Schokkenbroek, *The Basis, Nature and Application of the Margin-of-Appreciation Doctrine in the Case-Law of the European Court of Human Rights*, 19 Hum. Rts. L.J. 30 (1998); Eyal Benvenisti, *Margin of Appreciation, Consensus, and Universal Standards*, 31 N.Y.U. J. Int'l L. & Pol. 843 (1998–99); Howard Charles Yourow, The Margin of Appreciation Doctrine in the Dynamics of European Human Rights Jurisprudence (1995).

genuine, independent, and impartial.[81] Under each regime, it is only when the domestic structure clearly fails to uphold international norms in its internal affairs that international institutions step in and apply international law directly. There are pragmatic reasons for this deference, particularly regarding limited international capacity, but there are also normative reasons rooted in precisely the value of collective political authorship that underpins Estlund's argument. That value is itself connected to the fundamental international law principle of self-determination.

The question is whether it makes sense to view the soldier's duty to obey her state's order to fight in a wrongful war through this same prism. Estlund insists that it does. He argues: "when the political and institutional process producing the commands is duly looking after the question whether the war is just, the soldier would be wrong to substitute his own private verdict and thwart the state's will."[82] Under such conditions, he insists, we ought to conclude that "even though the victim is wronged by the unjustly warring side, the soldier on that side is nevertheless morally obligated (and so morally permitted) to follow all normally binding orders – those that would be binding at least if the war were just."[83]

However, there are essential differences between the case of the soldier and the jailer, and these differences call into question the straightforward transposition of the reasoning applicable in the latter case to the former. For one thing, many *jus ad bellum* decisions fail the "honest mistake" standard; that is, after all, why skepticism regarding the state's *jus ad bellum* assertions is warranted.[84] More fundamentally, the political duty applicable to the soldier does not extend to those that suffer at her hands. This is crucial.

Both the jailer *and* the prisoner are politically obligated to accept the state's processes, decisions, and actions.[85] Because they participate in, and benefit from, the same political system under the same political authority, the legitimacy of that authority's decisions in overriding independent normative frameworks applies equally to both actors. Both have

[81] ICC Statute, *supra* note 31, preamble, arts. 1, 17. *See generally* The International Criminal Court and Complementarity: From Theory to Practice (Carsten Stahn & Mohamed M. El Zeidy, eds., 2011).

[82] Estlund, *supra* note 74, at 213. [83] *Id.*, at 215.

[84] *See supra* Section 5.6 of Chapter 5.

[85] This may not always hold, as noted below, and where the line is drawn in this regard depends to a certain extent on which theory of political obligation one adopts. But this issue need not divert attention here. The case of international war falls clearly on one side of that line.

a duty to facilitate and enable their shared society's "collectively authorized purposes," and (in theory at least), both benefit from its effective pursuit of those purposes. As such, when the conviction is wrongful (but an honest and reasonable mistake), it is plausible to hold that the prisoner would have a claim against the state to rectify the wrong, but he would have no claim against the jailer.

However, the plausibility of this view breaks down quickly once it is extended to actors that do not share a source of political obligation. Irrespective of which theory of political obligation one adopts, the targets (and collateral victims) of the soldier's action in an international armed conflict have no political obligation to *her* state – i.e. the state against which they are fighting. They have no voice in the actions of the enemy state;[86] they have no claim to have their interests taken into account by that government, and that government does not take their interests into account in any systematic way;[87] they do not benefit from its institutions;[88] they have no protections against being wronged by those institutions; they have not consented, tacitly or expressly, to its authority;[89] and it is difficult to see how they could have a general duty to uphold enemy institutions as a matter of justice.[90] By definition, they are not part of the collective that engages in self-determination through that authority; the very premise of the political obligation account is that enemy soldiers are subject to competing political authorities.

Given this context, a soldier's political obligation to fight (unlike the jailer's political obligation to enforce court judgments) lacks any normative force or meaning for those she harms or kills. It cannot straightforwardly redefine her normative relationship with those persons or reformulate the basic cosmopolitan obligation not to kill or harm them

86 *See* Jean-Jacques Rousseau, *Of the Social Contract*, *in* THE SOCIAL CONTRACT AND OTHER LATER POLITICAL WRITINGS 39, 53–54 [bk. 1, ch. 8] (Victor Gourevitch, trans. & ed., 1997); *id.*, at 122–25 [bk IV, ch. 2].

87 *See* A. D. M. Walker, *Political Obligation and the Argument from Gratitude*, 17 PHIL. & PUB. AFF. 191 (1988).

88 *See* Plato, *Crito* (G. M. A. Grube, transl.), *in* THE COMPLETE WORKS OF PLATO 37, at 50a (John M. Cooper, ed., Hackett 1997); H. L. A. Hart, *Are There Any Natural Rights?*, 64 PHIL. REV. 175, 185 (1955).

89 *See* HOBBES, *supra* note 18, at 106–17, 136–45 (chs. 17–18, 21); John Locke, *The Second Treatise: An Essay Concerning the True Original, Extent, and End of Civil Government* (1690), *in* TWO TREATISES OF GOVERNMENT AND A LETTER CONCERNING TOLERATION 100, §§ 95–122 (ch. 8) (Ian Shapiro, ed., 2003); HARRY BERAN, THE CONSENT THEORY OF POLITICAL OBLIGATION (1987); PETER STEINBERGER, THE IDEA OF THE STATE 218 (2004).

90 JOHN RAWLS, A THEORY OF JUSTICE 98–100 (1971).

without justification, because the political authority does not serve for both as a mutual normative authority for the regulation of those aspects of their relationship governed by domestic law.

This is not necessarily to say that the soldier's political obligation to fight is void. The point is simply that that political obligation cannot subsume, displace, or otherwise resolve the more fundamental normative imperatives regarding the infliction of human suffering under conditions of uncertainty. If such displacement is ever possible, it rests on the mutual applicability of the displacing authority. Instead, the political obligation exists alongside the more fundamental (and in this case countervailing) normative duty.

At most, the force of political obligation in this context may be something more like that articulated by Christopher Kutz. He argues that the soldier who fights for a minimally just state in a wrongful war has "an essentially political permission to do violence" pursuant to his "participatory obligation" to do his part in a collective project to which he has and is committed.[91] Kutz argues that this undermines any basis for punishing soldiers who act pursuant to that political permission, unless the war is "clearly criminal" or "grossly unjust."[92] However, while affirming that political obligation and permission, Kutz also recognizes that the soldier fighting in such a war still "wrongs those he kills, and bears a share of responsibility for their deaths."[93] Indeed, Kutz accepts that such a soldier "may have acted badly, in moral terms, insofar as he took part in collective violence on grounds he knew or had reason to know were morally dubious, and the deaths he caused should sit uneasily on his conscience."[94] Ultimately, however, this moral burden is the price of doing his political duty, and Kutz is sympathetic to the decision to discharge that duty, notwithstanding the culpability that accompanies it.

The notion that a political duty and permission can endure in the face of competing moral duties of this kind is controversial.[95] But even if it can, international law on this issue claims the very normative ground that Kutz acknowledges is not displaced by political duties.[96] The prohibition

[91] Christopher Kutz, *The Collective Work of Citizenship*, 8 Legal Theory 471 (2002); Kutz, *Uniforms*, *supra* note 407, at 156, 173, 176. *Cf.* Rousseau, *supra* note 86, at 46–47 [bk. 1, ch. 4].

[92] *Id.*, at 173–74. [93] *Id.* [94] *Id.*, at 179. [95] McMahan, *supra* note 13, at 81–82.

[96] *See supra* Chapter 2, and particularly Section 2.1.

on aggression's status as a *jus cogens* norm identifies it as a rare norm that stands above even the core sovereign authority to consent to international law.[97]

What this means for international law's posture towards soldiers who fight in wars of aggression is addressed in Section 6.5, below. Before turning to that question, consider whether the associative duties discussed above can do more than political obligation arguments to strengthen the invincible ignorance account.

Seen through an associative lens, failing to fight in a war of uncertain *jus ad bellum* status does not simply mean avoiding potentially wrongful killing and destruction at the risk of failing to protect against wrongful killing and destruction. It means the soldier avoiding potentially wrongful killing and destruction at the risk of failing to protect *her people* and *her state* from that fate.[98] As Luban puts it, "Innocent lives are at stake in either direction," but the soldier that refuses to fight under such conditions "risks exposing *those she is sworn to defend* to mortal danger."[99]

As explored in the discussion of associative duties above, an immediate problem with this line of argument is that it is not universally applicable. It hinges completely on the bond between the soldier and *her* community and so applies only in cases in which there is a facially plausible claim that soldiers' disobedience would actually invite or facilitate a wrongful attack on *that* political community or its people. Where that community is not implicated, there is no basis for shifting the normative priority from not killing to not letting die. And, as discussed above, in many

[97] Military and Paramilitary Activities in and against Nicaragua (Nicar. v. US), Judgment, 1986 I.C.J. 14 (June 27), para. 205; RESTATEMENT (THIRD) OF FOREIGN RELATIONS LAW OF THE UNITED STATES, § 702 cmts. d-i, § 102 cmt. k (Am. Law Inst. 1987). The Inter-American Commission on Human Rights describes *jus cogens* as "superior order of legal norms, which the laws of man or nations may not contravene" due to their role in protecting "public morality." Domingues v. United States, Inter-Am. C.H.R. No. 62/02, at para. 49 (2003). *See also* Reisman, *The Quest for World Order*, *supra* note 12, at 380.

[98] Note that this is a fundamentally different dilemma from that suggested in the aggressive moment account, which required endorsing the wrongful infliction of death and human suffering on the grounds that the victims of that wrong, if not defeated, might overreact to the wrongful attack on them by inflicting disproportionate death and suffering on the soldier's own society and its people.

[99] David Luban, *Knowing When Not to Fight*, *in* OXFORD HANDBOOK OF THE ETHICS OF WAR (Helen Frowe & Seth Lazar, eds.) (forthcoming) [hereinafter Luban, *Knowing When*].

contemporary armed conflicts the soldier's own community is not at immediate risk.

This is the case whenever the conflict is remote from one of the warring parties. It will often be the case for many partners in a broad coalition action. And even in the case of neighbors, it is true when there is a significant power imbalance between the parties.[100] In some of these cases, the soldier's state may not even claim that it is at threat, focusing instead on arguments of collective self-defense, military intervention to suppress an insurgency with host state consent, or humanitarian intervention.

To be concrete, a collapse of NATO's 1999 intervention in the FRY would not plausibly have led to a significant loss of life in the participating states, much less to the destruction of their political institutions or to the subjugation of their people.[101] It would have been similarly implausible to argue that the collapse of the French interventions in Chad, the Central African Republic, or Rwanda would have led to the fall of Paris, or that the disintegration of the British intervention in Sierra Leone would have led to the subjugation of the United Kingdom to Freetown.[102]

[100] *See supra* note 43.

[101] Nor was this ever suggested in the submissions of any of the defendants in the suits brought by the then Federal Republic of Yugoslavia against ten NATO participants. Case Concerning the Legality of Use of Force (Yugoslavia v. US) [1999] I.C.J. Rep. 916 (June 2); (Yugoslavia v. Spain) [1999] I.C.J. Rep. 761 (June 2); (Serb. & Montenegro v. UK) [2004] I.C.J. Rep. 1307 (Dec. 15); (Serb. & Montnegro v. Port.) [2004] I.C.J. Rep. 1160 (Dec. 15); (Serb. & Montenegro v. Neth.) [2004] I.C.J. Rep. 1011 (Dec. 15); (Serb. & Montenegro v. It.) [2004] I.C.J. Rep. 865 (Dec. 15); (Serb. & Montenegro v. Ger.) [2004] I.C.J. Rep. 720 (Dec. 15); (Serb. & Montenegro v. Fr.) [2004] I.C.J. Rep. 575 (Dec. 15); (Serb. & Montenegro v. Can.) [2004] I.C.J. Rep. 429 (Dec. 15); (Serb. & Montenegro v. Belg.), [2004] I.C.J. Rep. 279 (Dec. 15). The same could be said of the contributors to the NATO intervention in Libya in 2011, although that action was authorized by the UN Security Council, and was thus plainly lawful, rather than of dubious *jus ad bellum* status (at least in its initial form – there were later arguments that the mission exceeded the Council's authorization). S.C. Res. 1973 (Mar. 17, 2011). The lack of such downside in the Libya case was stated explicitly by State Department Legal Adviser Harold Koh in his memorandum and testimony articulating why American participation in that action did not violate domestic law. In short, there was no real risk to the United States if things were not to go as planned. *US Dep't of State on Libya and War Powers before the Senate Foreign Relations Committee*, 112th Cong. 8 (2011) (testimony by Legal Adviser Harold Hongju Koh), www.law.uh.edu/faculty/eberman/NSL/HaroldKohTestimony-Libya-and-War-Powers-June-28-2011.pdf.

[102] For discussions of these conflicts, *see, for example*, ANDREW M. DORMAN, BLAIR'S SUCCESSFUL WAR: BRITISH MILITARY INTERVENTION IN SIERRA LEONE (2009); PETER BAXTER, FRANCE IN CENTRAFRIQUE: FROM BOKASSA AND OPERATION BARRACUDA TO THE DAYS OF EUFOR (2011).

Italy, Spain, the United Kingdom, or Poland would have suffered no significant vulnerabilities had the invasion of Iraq in 2003 collapsed.[103] This is almost certainly true of the United States, too, although it did at least make two (weak) claims to self-defense (preemptive self-defense against Iraqi nuclear attack and reactive self-defense against Iraq for its alleged role in the terrorist attacks of September 11, 2001).[104] US drone attacks in Pakistan on anti-government insurgents identified by Islamabad (rather than targets identified as threats to the United States) are also difficult to account for in associative terms.[105]

None of this is to deny the good reasons to participate in wars of collective self-defense, suppressions of foreign insurgencies, or humanitarian interventions. If the requisite elements of the *jus ad bellum* obtain, such actions are permissible and potentially valuable. But there are no special *associative* reasons for fighting such wars. Thus, if there is *not* good reason to believe that the *jus ad bellum* elements obtain, the analysis of Chapter 5 applies, and there is no intervening associative duty to complicate that calculation. The fact that a given foreign intervention or war of collective self-defense might advance the soldier's state's broader strategic interests does not change this, as those are, by definition, not themselves just or lawful causes for inflicting human violence.

Wars of collective self-defense are more complex. States in robust military alliances may depend on one another for protection and defense.[106] Soldiers in such states may have associative reasons for

[103] To be clear, the question here is whether *once the invasion had started*, ceasing to fight would itself have provided the Iraqi forces with an opportunity to strike at core national and human interests in those European states, *not* whether ceasing to fight would undermine the initial belligerent objective of the coalition partners. The purported worry is that breakdown would *invite* a response against the homeland.

[104] *See, e.g.*, Dino Kritsiosis, *Arguments of Mass Confusion*, 15 Eur. J. Int'l L. 233, 246–51, 255–59 (2004).

[105] On US participation in actions against insurgents that pose a threat to the regimes in Islamabad or Kabul (as opposed to the US homeland), and who are selected as targets by the Pakistani government, *see, for example*, Bob Woodward & Greg Miller, *Pakistan's Involvement in Deadly Drone Campaign Revealed*, Independent (Oct. 24, 2013), www.independent.co.uk/news/world/asia/pakistan-s-involvement-in-deadly-drone-campaign-revealed-government-officials-played-direct-role-in-8902432.html; Jane Mayer, *The Predator War*, New Yorker (Oct. 26, 2009), www.newyorker.com/magazine/2009/10/26/the-predator-war.

[106] Consider for example NATO [The North Atlantic Treaty, 63 Stat. 2241, 34 U.N.T.S. 243 (4 April 1949), art. 4], the EU [Treaty on European Union (Consolidated Version, 2012), Title V, ch. 2, § 2, arts. 42–46]; ECOWAS [Revised Treaty of the Economic Community of West African States (24 July 1993), art. 58]; the CSTO (Collective Security Treaty

protecting those other alliance member states when doubtful as to whether they are the defensive states under the *jus ad bellum* even if there is no immediate threat to their own state. Arguably, for example, a French soldier would have associative reasons for fighting in defense of a European Union state because of the strength of trans-European associative bonds.[107] However, such an associative argument would apply plausibly only to particularly deeply rooted alliances. Moreover, it would apply only if an alliance member were under threat, not if the alliance were engaged in an action unrelated to the immediate defense of one of its members (as in NATO's war in Kosovo).

All of this is to say that even the combined epistemic-associative argument is simply not applicable in a significant range of cases. Even in the remaining wars, it is important to be clear about how associative duties might affect the overall picture. If they are to be considered in the same normative register as universal duties, the most that associative duties can plausibly do is to heighten the normative significance of letting a particular person or group die or letting a particular set of institutions fail. This may narrow (and perhaps even eliminate) the difference between killing and letting die, but to sustain the invincible ignorance view, the associative duties would need to perform a far more radical (and significantly less plausible) rebalancing than that.

Uncertain as to the *jus ad bellum* status of her war, the soldier is faced with the risk of killing and destroying wrongfully, on the one hand, and the risk of failing to protect against wrongful killing and destruction, on the other. Participating in war is not merely a way of protecting her people, their institutions, and their collective life; it is a way of protecting them by killing others and destroying the institutions and common life of others, potentially undermining that other people's capacity for self-determination. Whatever their force, associative duties to compatriots cannot obscure this latter point, and the soldier's strengthened duty to

Organization) of central Asia [Collective Security Treaty (15 May, 1992)]; the Arab League [Arab League Treaty of Joint Defence (1955) 49 AM. J. INT'L L. SUPP. (1955); SEATO [South East Asia Collective Defense Treaty, 209 U.N.T.S. 20 (1954)]; and the AU [African Union Non-Aggression and Common Defence Pact (2005)], among others.

107 In the aftermath of Brexit and, indeed, the credible candidacy of Marine Le Pen in France itself, these bonds are in greater doubt than they have been for some time. Nonetheless, there are arguably some genuine associative bonds among EU citizens. *See, e.g.*, Standard Eurobarometer 85, European Citizenship: Report (May 2016) [Survey carried out by TNS Opinion & Social at the request of the European Commission, Directorate-General for Communication].

protect her society cannot weaken the duty not to inflict wrongful harms on other societies.[108] To hold that associative duties could override the latter whenever there is *any* doubt that the war is wrongful would require an extraordinary and implausible normative prioritization of those with whom the soldier shares associative ties.

More plausibly, associative duties can make a difference at the epistemic margins (when the soldier's epistemic posture is relatively close to 50). As the soldier's position on the epistemic spectrum lowers, the effect of any associative duties weakens because the risk that her state is the wronged party (and that her protective duty obtains) lessens. Simultaneously, the risk that her participation would involve wrongful killing and destruction heightens, strengthening the imperative to refrain from action.

Recognizing this puts a significant proportion of even dubious wars out of explanatory reach for the epistemic-associative account. Although military actions such as the US wars in Vietnam and in Iraq were not patently illegal to most troops, there were very good reasons to hold them to be illegal based on the information that was publicly available. If either could be classified as a war to which associative duties would apply at all (itself a highly questionable claim, given their distance from the US homeland), it is difficult to argue that those duties would be sufficient to nullify a disobedient soldier's claim that fighting would render him unable to wash his hands of guilt.

6.5 Conflicting Obligations and the Right to Do the Right Thing

An alternative way of thinking about associative duties is that they simply sound in a normative register different from that of universal moral duties, just as do the political duties articulated by Kutz.[109] This creates the possibility of inherently opposed, and yet coexisting, normative obligations. The question is how international law is to address that conflict.

[108] *Cf.* Thomas Pogge, *Cosmopolitanism: A Defence*, 5 CRITICAL REV. INT'L SOCIAL & POL. PHIL. 86, 90–91 (2002) ("special relationships can increase what we owe to our associates . . . but they cannot decrease what we owe to everyone else").

[109] Lazar, *supra* note 16, at 100 (arguing of the clash between serious associative duties and universal imperatives that "it seems plausible to assert that these tradeoffs would be genuine quandaries" that cannot be resolved with reference to a common normative framework).

In his essay on "dirty hands," Walzer insists that genuine normative imperatives can clash in a way that leaves no clean resolution, but provides for certain core commitments to be "*overridden*, a painful process which forces a man to weigh the wrong he is willing to do in order to do right, and which leaves pain behind, and should do so, even after the decision has been made."[110] At most, killing and destroying on associative or political grounds in a war of significantly uncertain *jus ad bellum* status ought to be understood in this way.

There is a plausibility to that position. In the interpersonal example described in Section 6.1, the observer's love for her brother does not dispel the moral obligation not to kill his opponent without good reason to believe the latter to be the aggressor. Similarly, the associative duty to her brother is not dispelled by that moral obligation. Instead, she faces a tragic choice. Unless the evidence suggests fairly strongly that her brother is the wrongful aggressor, she might be thought deficient as a sibling if she were to let him die. However, unless she reasonably believes the opponent to be the aggressor, she would surely wrong the opponent by killing him. Her duties conflict, and either choice would leave her bearing a substantial normative remainder. She cannot live up to the duties of love and morality simultaneously.

A soldier ordered to fight in a seemingly illegal war in which the security of her state and its people appears to be at stake may be faced with a similar kind of moral tragedy.[111] Doing right by her community is likely to be burdensome insofar as it requires killing when there is good reason to believe that the justificatory conditions for doing so do not obtain. Doing right by humanity is likely to be burdensome insofar as it requires treating her community without the strong priority her association with it might be thought to demand

In this scenario, which (to reiterate) does not arise in many armed conflicts, it would surely be extraordinarily harsh to punish the soldier for fighting, just as the Nuremberg *dicta* quoted above suggest. Equally, however, the killing remains wrongful, and one cannot argue from the

[110] Michael Walzer, *Political Action: The Problem of Dirty Hands*, 2 PHIL. & PUB. AFF. 160, 173–74 (1973).

[111] Along related lines, Sartre uses the example of a soldier forced to choose between caring for his dying mother or fighting in a just war for the liberation of his nation to highlight this form of normative dilemma. JEAN-PAUL SARTRE, EXISTENTIALISM AND HUMANISM 35–38 (1946) (Philip Mairet, trans., Methuen, 1973).

international legal point of view that a soldier who refuses to fight in such a war is wrong to insist that she cannot be expected to "wash her hands of guilt" if she fights. On the contrary, from that point of view, she is right to assert that she cannot.

Despite international law's apparent sympathy for the normative significance of associative duties, it is noteworthy that states – whose protective duties are more fundamental than are those of their citizens[112] – do *not* have a legal right to act when significantly uncertain as to whether the justificatory conditions for doing so obtain,[113] do *not* have any legal responsibility to wage defensive wars,[114] and have a moral responsibility to wage defensive war that is clearly weaker than their duty not to engage in aggression.[115]

The denial of any right or protection for the soldier who refuses to fight is particularly dissonant given that the duty not to engage in wrongful killing is universal, whereas the soldier's associative responsibility, on any plausible account, varies with the strength of the associative ties within the state in question, the justice of the state, the connection of the particular individual to the state, and so on.[116] By refusing to kill in a wrongful war, the soldier expresses a determination that in her case, the associative duty is insufficient to override the universal duty not to kill when it is not reasonable to believe that the justificatory conditions obtain.

Since the strength of the associative duty is specific to the soldier and her community, it is difficult to hold from the international point of view that the soldier *must* prioritize her associative duty over the cosmopolitan duty not to kill innocents (or not to kill when uncertain as to whether the justificatory conditions obtain). In fact, a core objective of refugee law is to protect those who face punishment in their home state due to their

[112] Protection being a core *raison d'être* of the state, and a duty recognized in the developing legal doctrine of the responsibility to protect (*supra* Section 6.3).

[113] *See* Section 5.3 of Chapter 5 above. [114] *See* Section 5.4 of Chapter 5 above.

[115] On legal recognition of the principle that governments have a moral duty to protect their people from outside attack, *see, for example*, Velasquez Rodriguez Case [v. Honduras], Judgment, Inter-Am. Ct. H.R. (ser. C) No. 4, para. 154 (July 29, 1988); Legal Consequences of the Construction of a Wall in the Occupied Palestinian Territory, Advisory Opinion, 2004 I.C.J. 136, 195 (July 9); Michael Walzer, *Inspectors Yes, War No* (September 2002), *in* ARGUING ABOUT WAR 143, 146 (2004).

[116] *Cf.* Walzer's argument that associative duties may actually require some citizens to stand against their own state if they maintain associative bonds stronger than that of co-nationality with groups fundamentally opposed to the action in question. *See supra* note 14.

political detachment from it.[117] Needless to say, this protection does not extend to all political dissidents, but paragraph 171 of the UNHCR Handbook takes precisely the view that those who are punished by their state *for refusing to perpetrate its international wrongs* thereby suffer *political* persecution. It may make sense for international law to refrain from punishing participation in dubious wars on the grounds that soldiers may reasonably be torn between associative duties and universal duties. But it cannot on those grounds deny protection to those who deliberately break away from associative and political bonds in an effort to vindicate core universal values. International law cannot expect such a soldier to fight and "wash her hands of guilt."

6.6 Civilian Control of the Military

A final argument worth considering here focuses on the importance of maintaining civilian control over the military. The central demand of civilian control is that, while members of the military may (and sometimes should) give contrary advice in private, once their civilian leaders have made a decision, the military must execute that decision unflinchingly.[118] Strict adherence to that norm is thought to guard against the risk of a *coup d'ètat* or similar threats to rights-protecting, good governance.[119]

To a certain extent, this argument runs into problems already discussed in this chapter. The value of civilian control is contingent on the existence of constitutional, democratic, and rights-respecting institutions – elements that do not obtain in all states.[120] And, as with all of

[117] Convention Relating to the Status of Refugees, July 28, 1951, 189 U.N.T.S. 150 (as amended by the Protocol of 1967, 66 U.N.T.S 267), art. 1(A)(2).

[118] Samuel Huntington, perhaps the most prominent advocate of this position, argues on these grounds that loyalty and obedience must be considered the "highest military virtues," HUNTINGTON, *supra* note 8, at 73–74. *See also* Parker v. Levy, 417 US 733, 751 (1974).

[119] Luban, *Knowing When*, *supra* note 99; MARK OSIEL, OBEYING ORDERS 86–87 (1999).

[120] OSIEL, *supra* note 119, at 87–88. In other contexts, the military can provide a useful check against rights-abusing civilian regimes. Ozan O. Varol, *The Military as the Guardian of Constitutional Democracy*, 50 COLUM. J. TRANSNAT'L L. 547 (2013) (arguing that certain militaries have played a democracy-promoting role in the initial phases of a transition from autocracy to constitutional democracy, focusing in particular on military political interventions in Turkey and Portugal in 1960 and 1974, respectively, which toppled authoritarian civilian regimes and established democratic regimes in their place). On Turkey, *see, for example*, David Capezza, *Turkey's Military Is a Catalyst for*

the arguments in this chapter, its demand that soldiers inflict wrongful violence on outsiders in order to maintain those internal institutions is difficult to reconcile with the core values of international criminal law. It does, however, have important points of traction. Limiting tyranny and promoting liberal democratic institutions is an important universal value, as is recognized in numerous human rights instruments.[121] The democratic peace literature indicates that it also contributes to global stability and human security beyond the borders of the state in question.[122] As such, David Luban argues that to ignore or dismiss the value of civilian control in thinking about *jus ad bellum* disobedience would be a "mistake of monumental proportions."[123]

However, civilian control is not ultimately a compelling basis for international law's posture towards soldiers. Asserting the right *not* to participate in a criminal military action against an external actor is qualitatively different from asserting the right to *take action* not authorized by the civilian leadership, let alone engaging in a coup.[124]

Defenders of the civilian control account might reject that distinction, arguing obedience to civilian demands has to be unconditional in order to render the military "politically sterile and neutral" in the way that durable and effective civilian control requires.[125] On this view, once the door is open to questioning decisions, military neutrality and sterility is undermined, and the most important bulwark against military tyranny is removed. Passive refusal to perform a demanded act risks being the first step towards enabling an active coup.

International law, however, directly rejects such a system. Most obviously, refusal to participate in war crimes is *required* of all members of the military, even when the commands to perpetrate those crimes come from civilian decision-makers acting pursuant to democratically passed

Reform, MIDDLE EAST Q. 13, 13 (Summer, 2009); WILLIAM HALE, TURKISH POLITICS AND THE MILITARY (1994).

121 *See, e.g.*, in multiple articles of the ICCPR. ICCPR, *supra* note 36, arts. 1, 21, 22.

122 On the theoretical foundations, Immanuel Kant, *Perpetual Peace: A Philosophical Sketch*, *in* KANT: POLITICAL WRITINGS 93 (Hans Reiss, ed., H. B. Nisbet trans., 1991); MICHAEL DOYLE, LIBERAL PEACE: SELECTED ESSAYS (2011).

123 Luban, *Knowing When*, *supra* note 99.

124 Although by permission, rather than right, it is notable that generals in many states are permitted to resign without sanction to avoid participating in a war to which they fundamentally object. RICHARD A. GABRIEL, TO SERVE WITH HONOR: A TREATISE ON MILITARY ETHICS AND THE WAY OF THE SOLDIER 188, 200 (1982).

125 HUNTINGTON, *supra* note 8, at 84.

legislation.[126] But the tension between international criminal law and civilian control extends also to the crime of aggression.

Concern about empowering the military and encouraging institutional overreach applies most plausibly to high-ranking members of the military, and especially to the top brass.[127] Military leaders are the individuals whose contrary views, if publicized, would pose the greatest threat to the civilian government.[128] They are the members of the military whose opinions on the *jus ad bellum* status of a war would be most likely to be accepted by the public as sophisticated, informed, untainted by fear or self-preservation, and backed by access to the highest security intelligence. It is their dissent that would most embarrass the political authorities. It is they who could most effectively give voice to the position of the military in any institutional confrontation with the civilian commander-in-chief. It is they, ultimately, who could execute a coup.

And yet, under the extant legal regime, these members of the top brass are the only persons in the entire military system that have the *duty* to disobey orders to violate the *jus ad bellum.* Obedient generals like Chief of the Oberkommando der Wehrmacht, Field Marshal Wilhelm Keitel, were convicted of the *jus ad bellum* crime at Nuremberg.[129] Under the ICC regime, those criminally liable for aggression are those who "exercise control over or . . . direct the political *or* military action" of the state.[130] For the italicized "or" to have meaning, there must be a category of persons whose criminal liability hinges on their control over the state's military action, but who lack control over its political action. Those who most clearly fit that description are none other than the military top brass in a state in which political and military control are separated. These are also the only members of the military with clear eligibility for international legal protection if they face domestic punishment for refusing to participate in such a war.[131]

[126] Luban, *Knowing When*, *supra* note 99. [127] Osiel, *supra* note 119, at 87

[128] Even when rejecting an off-duty second-lieutenant's right to engage in dissenting speech against the American war in Vietnam, the Court of Military appeals explained the decision not in terms of the threat posed by that individual's dissent, but with reference to a slippery slope leading to a military "man on a white horse" challenging civilian control of the military. United States v. Howe, 17 U.S.C.M.A. 165, 175, 37 C.M.R. 429, 439 (1967).

[129] *See supra* notes 60 and accompanying text. Compare the acquittal of those immediately below in the High Command Judgment, *supra* note 12.

[130] ICC Statute, *supra* note 31, art. 8 *bis* (1) [emphasis added].

[131] On the shielding of top leaders from being forced to obey, *see* Section 1.3 of Chapter 1 and Section 11.1 of Chapter 11.

In short, the very individuals whose disobedience poses the greatest threat to civilian control are the individuals the extant regime *requires* to disobey on *jus ad bellum* grounds. Moreover, the ultimate aspiration of international criminal law with respect to such military leaders is not that they resign when ordered to prosecute a criminal war, although that would save them from liability, but that they use their "control over" the military to prevent the wrong from happening.

This regime provides a far stronger pretext for military intervention in domestic politics or even military usurpation of domestic control than would protections for lower-level soldiers against being forced to fight in wrongful wars. No coherent defense of international law's failure to provide the latter protections can be rooted in the claim that this is necessary to preserve civilian control.

6.7 Political Obligation, Associative Duties, and Reparations

The associative and political arguments discussed in this chapter have been focused on whether the soldier who fights in an aggressive war is culpable, rather than on whether the violence she inflicts in an aggressive war is wrongful. As such, these arguments have had little to say about the question of victim status at the ICC. Even if, contrary to the positions presented above, political or associative duties *were* sufficient to "wipe ... the crime" of aggression "out of" the soldiers who participate, that radical exculpation would not entail that the people they kill and maim are not wronged by the infliction of those harms.[132]

One might, however, think that at least one dimension of political authority is relevant to the latter question. Domestic law tends to shield states from suit by their own troops for combat-related harms.[133] One way of understanding this (and its roots in sovereign immunity) is that a core element of the sovereign's prerogative is the authority to make

[132] The quote is that of a soldier responding to a query: William Shakespeare, King Henry the Fifth, Act 4, Scene 1 (1599), in The Complete Works of William Shakespeare 485, 505 (Wordsworth Library Collection, 2007)

[133] Feres v. United States, 340 U.S. 135 (1950); Federal Torts Claims Act, 28 U.S.C.A., § 2680(j)–(k); Smith (No. 2) v. Ministry of Defence [2013] U.K.S.C. 41, para. 157 (Lord Carnwarth, dissenting) ("We have not been referred to any authority in the higher courts, in this country or any comparable jurisdiction, in which the state has been held liable for injuries sustained by its own soldiers in the course of active hostilities").

operational decisions in armed conflict freely and without special regard for the lives or safety of its troops – the authority, in short, to sacrifice its soldiers in war.[134] That supreme authority might be justified in contemporary terms with reference to its utility as a foundation of effective fighting.[135] Those who hold this view recognize the state's sovereign responsibility to take care of its wounded soldiers and bereaved military families.[136] What they object to is the notion that the soldier or her family has standing to bring claims against the government in the realm of war fighting.

If this posture is right, it might be thought to entail a reason not to identify combatants killed or harmed fighting against aggression as victims at the ICC. An objection along these lines might worry that such identification would artificially individualize the soldier's relationship to war's violence, and that this would undermine the notion of a collective under supreme sovereign authority, competent to sacrifice any specific members of that collective without owing them an accounting. On this view, recognizing that those soldiers suffer a grave legal wrong when they are killed may underpin not just their claims against the wrongdoer, but also a possible claim against their own state or its leaders for putting them at grave risk of suffering that wrong. In short, if their deaths and injuries in fighting aggression are seen as individual wrongs, this might be thought to diminish the principle that, in combat, they are part of a collective in which individual rights are essentially suspended.

There are, of course, already efforts to use human rights law to question the state's blanket authority to sacrifice its troops in war. A recent Supreme Court case in the United Kingdom held that under European human rights law, not all "deaths or injuries in combat that result from the conduct of operations by the armed forces" are shielded

[134] *See, e.g.*, 340 U.S. 135, at 141–42, 146 (on the unique relationship between soldier and state, given the latter's military duty and the former's supreme authority in this realm). ("course of military duty").

[135] *See, e.g.*, Smith v. Ministry of Defense, *supra* note 133 (Lord Hope), para. 37; Richard Ekins, Jonathan Morgan, & Tom Tugendhat, *Clearing the Fog of Law*, Policy Exchange 23–26 (2015), policyexchange.org.uk/wp-content/uploads/2016/09/clearing-the-fog-of-law.pdf.

[136] On state compensation: 340 U.S. 135, at 145; Ekins, Morgan, and Tugendhat, *supra* note 135, at 39–41; Ben Farmer, *MoD to Pay More Compensation for Wounded and Killed Troops*, Telegraph (Dec. 1 2016), www.telegraph.co.uk/news/2016/12/01/mod-pay-compensation-wounded-killed-troops-tries-cut-legal-claims/.

from human rights review *vis-à-vis* the troops' home state.[137] Having taken that position, the Court was careful to state that most operational decisions ought to remain non-justiciable.[138] Nonetheless, it took the first step in articulating an international law limit on the state's prerogative to sacrifice its troops, potentially laying the foundation for a broader curtailment of that purportedly fundamental sovereign authority. Were the notion of human rights review of the state's sacrifice of its own troops to develop further, this would dampen somewhat the force of the sovereign prerogative argument for limiting recognition of soldiers as the crime victims of aggression, at least insofar as that argument can provide an account of the law.

But even if such a development does not occur, the more fundamental response to this sovereignty argument is that there is no reason that the law cannot affirm both the sovereign prerogative to sacrifice its own troops in war and the position that soldiers killed by an aggressor force are criminally wronged by the latter and eligible for reparation. Recognizing soldiers as among the core crime victims of aggression does not entail any question about their state's authority to demand that they make themselves vulnerable to that crime, nor their duty to do so in order to protect others and further the war effort.

Indeed, militaries have long fought wars in which their soldiers face a high risk of being criminally wronged as individuals in the course of hostilities, and in which the operational decisions of the soldiers' state may heighten that risk. Members of an enemy force that fails systematically to comply with the conditions of the privileges of belligerency (including all non-state actors not attached to a state that is party to the conflict), can be prosecuted for murder when they kill troops on the other side.[139] Soldiers can also be the primary victims of various international war crimes, such as the use of illegal weapons, perfidy, or crimes against prisoners of war.[140] Any state that sends its troops to fight against an unprivileged adversary, a non-state adversary, or an adversary that routinely engages in the above-mentioned war crimes thereby demands that its troops expose themselves to a high risk of being criminally wronged. Such individuals or their families would plainly have victim status in an ICC prosecution for any of those crimes, and have been

137 Smith v. Ministry of Defence, *supra* note 135, para. 58.
138 *Id.*, at paras. 37, 58, 76.
139 *See* Chapter 7, below, on the privileges of belligerency.
140 *See* ICC Statute, *supra* note 31, arts. 8(2)(a), 8(2)(b)(vi, vii, x–xii, xv, xvii–xxii), 8(2)(c), 8(2)(e)(vi, ix–xi) .

recognized as victims by the UNCC.[141] More generally, there is a growing recognition that such persons suffer individual violations generating a right to remedy.[142] This is entirely compatible with affirming the authority of their sovereign to make operational decisions that expose them to a very high risk of being wronged in those ways.

141 Eligibility for Compensation of Members of the Allied Coalition Armed Forces, UNCC Governing Council 1, U.N. Doc. S/AC.26/1992/11, at p. 1 (June 26, 1992); Recommendations Made by the Panel of Commissioners Concerning Individual Claims for Serious Personal Injury or Death (Category "B" Claims) 14, U.N. Doc. S/AC.26/1994/1 (May 26, 1994); Report and Recommendations Made by the Panel of Commissioners Concerning Part One of the Second Instalment of Claims for Serious Personal Injury or Death (Category "B" Claims) 11–12, U.N. Doc. S/AC.26/1994/4 (Dec. 1994).

142 Basic Principles and Guidelines on the Right to a Remedy and Reparation for Victims of Gross Violations of International Human Rights Law and Serious Violations of International Humanitarian Law, G.A. Res. 60/147, at paras. 8–11, (Dec. 16, 2005); International Law Association, *Declaration of International Law Principles on Reparation for Victims of Armed Conflict (Substantive Issues)*, Report of the Seventy-Fourth Conference held in The Hague 30, arts. 3–4, 6 (15–19 August 2010); Lisbeth Zegveld, *Remedies for Victims of International Humanitarian Law*, 85 Int'l Rev. Red Cross 497 (2003).

7

Understanding the Warrior's Code

The key difficulties with both associative and political obligation arguments are tied fundamentally to their particularism. It is not just that these arguments do not apply to all soldiers in all aggressive wars, although that is true. Nor is the problem simply that aggression tends to destroy and undermine in the attacked state the very political and associative connections that the obedient soldier hopes to uphold in his own state, although that too is true. The deeper problem is that the particular duties a soldier has to his co-citizens and his political community cannot simply override or displace the basic duty not to inflict wrongful violence. Holding the killing and human violence in a criminal war to be gravely wrongful, international law can recognize that soldiers might appropriately feel torn by their political and associative duties, and this may provide part of the reason not to punish those who fight. But the law cannot insist on those grounds that soldiers who refuse to fight deserve no protection from domestic prosecution because they ought to have been able to "wash their hands of guilt" while inflicting the very killing and maiming that makes aggression a crime. Nor can it say to those fighting against aggression that their state's political authority to demand their sacrifice means that they do not suffer personally a profound and criminal wrong when they are harmed or killed.

Departing from the particularism of the previous chapter, the next two chapters seek to make sense of the peculiar relationship between the soldier and the criminal wrong of aggression using a different lens – that of a soldier's role morality rooted in the protection of global values. This chapter focuses on the idea of a "warrior's code" designed to uphold the *jus in bello* and facilitate peace; Chapter 8 focuses on the importance of military institutional functioning to global security. Both lines of argument bear more fruit in providing a coherent normative account of the existing regime than have the arguments discussed thus far. However, neither can fully dispel the dissonance identified in Chapter 1. That failure has interpretive and institutional implications.

The idea of a "warrior's code" trades on the notion that war is a normatively distinct space in which soldiers are governed by a morality separate from that applicable in ordinary life.[1] That separate morality is rooted purportedly in the conventions and customs of war and the moral value they provide in the context of armed conflict.

At the substantive heart of any such code (and the laws of war to which it attaches) is the application of the same rules of belligerent conduct to soldiers on either side of a war, irrespective of which side is the aggressor. If comprehensively definitive of the soldier's moral framework, from the legal point of view, this code might seem to override the notions that soldiers on the aggressor side do wrong when they perpetrate ordinary acts of belligerent violence and that soldiers on the other side suffer wrongs when harmed in those conditions. The arguments that follow explain why there is value in a certain symmetry between belligerents and why it can help to explain soldiers' protection from criminal liability for aggression, but also why it does not wholly define the parameters of the soldier's normative space from the legal point of view.

7.1 The War Convention and Mitigating the Hell of War

The term "warrior's code" is used here not to invoke chivalric codes of honor, but to identify the role morality that might arguably be tied to current legal rules of fighting.[2] This line of reasoning starts from the premise that war happens and that when it does, law and morality must adjust to that reality so as to minimize war's horror, even if that means adjusting what might otherwise appear to be bedrock principles of human interaction.

On this view, once war is underway, the *jus ad bellum* has already failed to restrain the aggressor, and the presumption ought to be that

[1] *Cf.* Walzer's dismissal of revisionist just war theory as providing "a careful and precise account of what individual responsibility in war would be like if war were a peacetime activity." Michael Walzer, *Response to McMahan's Paper*, 34 PHILOSOPHIA 43, 43 (2006).

[2] On the genealogical links between chivalric war-fighting and the contemporary laws of war, *see* Theodor Meron, *International Humanitarian Law from Agincourt to Rome*, 75 INT'L L. STUD. SER. US NAVAL WAR COL. 301 (2000); G. I. A. D. Draper, *The Interaction of Christianity and Chivalry in the Historical Development of the Law of War*, 5 INT'L REV. RED CROSS 7 (1965); GEOFFREY BEST, HUMANITY IN WARFARE 60 (1980); MICHAEL WALZER, JUST AND UNJUST WARS 16, 35 (1977) [hereinafter WALZER, JUW]; TELFORD TAYLOR, NUREMBERG AND VIETNAM: AN AMERICAN TRAGEDY 20 (1970).

that party will fight as if the *jus ad bellum* were on its side.[3] Its persistence in that respect might be because it is mistaken about the *jus ad bellum* status of its actions, because it wants to maintain the public appearance of *jus ad bellum* compliance, or simply because, if there were any disparity in the *jus in bello* rules applicable to the aggressor and its opponent, the aggressor would inevitably adopt the more permissive regime and assert whatever factual or other claims would be necessary to justify doing so.

As Janina Dill and Henry Shue put it, "[A]gents to whom rules for the conduct of war are addressed have a prior commitment to the pursuit of military success, having already decided to resort to war."[4] Any *jus in bello* rule that bans pursuit of that success or otherwise fails to take seriously the parametric nature of the parties' commitment to it is not responsive to the context it seeks to regulate.

This premise paves the way for a framework of generally agreed standards of conduct in war, defined by two objectives. First, "alleviating as much as possible the calamities of war" by requiring humane restraint on both sides, limiting righteous excesses, and precluding the adjustment of what is permissible based on the perceived justice or lawfulness of one's own cause.[5] Second, providing the foundations for the *post bellum*

[3] Janina Dill & Henry Shue, *Limiting the Killing in War: Military Necessity and the St. Petersburg Assumption*, 26 Ethics & Int'l Aff. 311, 319 (2012). *See also* Adil Ahmad Haque, Law and Morality at War 3 (2017).

[4] Dill & Shue, *supra* note 3, at 324.

[5] The quoted text is famously articulated in the preamble to the earliest international *jus in bello* treaty, the St. Petersburg Declaration. St. Petersburg Declaration Renouncing the Use, in Time of War, of Explosive Projectiles under 400 Grammes Weight preamble, Dec. 11, 1868, *reprinted in* 1 Am. J. Int'l L. (Supp. 1907). The objective of making war as humane as possible given its nature is fundamental for many thinkers and is the putative objective of much legal regulation. Henry Shue, *Do We Need a "Morality of War"?*, *in* Just and Unjust Warriors: The Moral and Legal Status of Soldiers 87, 87 (David Rodin & Henry Shue, eds., 2008); Hersch Lauterpacht, *The Limits of the Operation of the Law of War*, 30 Brit. Y.B Int'l L. 206 (1953); Walzer, JUW, *supra* note 2, at 33, 129–37; Paul Christopher, The Ethics of War and Peace 163 (1994); Tamar Meisels, *Combatants – Lawful and Unlawful*, 26 Law & Philosophy 31, 45 (2007); James Turner Johnson, Just War Tradition and the Restraint of War (1981). One of the leaders in this movement was Henri Dunant, who demanded in his poignant *Memory of Solferino*, "[I]s it not a matter of urgency, since unhappily we cannot always avoid wars, to press forward in a human and truly civilized spirit the attempt to prevent, or at least to alleviate, the horrors of war?" Henri Dunant, A Memory of Solferino (1862) (International Committee of the Red Cross, 1959). One year after that plea, Dunant formed the International Committee of the Red Cross (hereinafter ICRC), which has since played a central role in the legal codification of key *jus in bello* norms. 1 Jean-Marie Henckaerts & Louise Doswald-Beck, Customary International Humanitarian Law XXV (2005).

project of a lasting peace by leaving populations on either side capable of overcoming belligerent antipathies.[6]

Fundamental to this regime serving its purpose is its strict independence from the *jus ad bellum*. Once the bullets are flying, the guiding principle is that "the remaining moral achievement available [to the regime regulating hostilities] is to limit all killing as much as possible."[7] To rely at this point on the *jus ad bellum* to inform the rules of conduct would be to rely on a regime that at least the aggressor has already rejected, ignored, or determined (incorrectly) to be in its favor. Either both sides would simply adopt the less restrictive standards, asserting *jus ad bellum* authority,[8] or overt aggressors (rare as they are) would have no reason to comply with the *jus in bello*, since all of their acts would anyway be unlawful under the *jus ad bellum*.[9]

Two key pillars of the *jus in bello* (applicable equally to both sides) are considered essential to the regime's performance in guarding against those dangers and minimizing the horrors of war. The first is the provision of core principles of belligerent conduct that allow both sides to fight. Namely, the principles of distinction, precautions, and proportionality, whereby combatants may not target civilians, must minimize collateral and other harm to civilians in various ways, and must refrain from an attack altogether if the collateral civilian costs are disproportionate to the military gain.[10] The second is the prisoner of war (POW)

[6] WALZER, JUW, *supra* note 2, at 132–33, 335; Michael Walzer, *Terrorism and Just War*, *in* THINKING POLITICALLY 264, 266 (2007); JOHN RAWLS, THE LAW OF PEOPLES 94, 96 (1999); Gary Bass, *Jus Post Bellum*, 32 PHIL. & PUB. AFF. 384, 398 (2004).

[7] Dill & Shue, *supra* note 3, at 319.

[8] Meisels, *supra* note 5, at 41; Hersch Lauterpacht, *The Limits of the Operation of the Law of War*, 30 BRIT. Y.B. INT'L L. 206, 220 (1953); YORAM DINSTEIN, WAR, AGGRESSION, AND SELF-DEFENCE 169 (5th edn, 2012); Robert D. Sloane, *The Cost of Conflation: Preserving the Dualism of Jus ad Bellum and Jus in Bello in the Contemporary Law of War*, 34 YALE J. INT'L L. 47, 74 (2009); Avishai Margalit & Michael Walzer, *Israel: Civilians and Combatants*, N.Y. REV. BOOKS, May 14, 2009, at 21; DAVID A. WELCH, JUSTICE AND THE GENESIS OF WAR 217–18 (1993); Henry Shue, *Laws of War, Morality, and International Politics*, 26 LEIDEN J. INT'L L. 271, 280–88 (2013).

[9] Hersch Lauterpacht, *The Limits of the Operation of the Law of War*, 30 BRIT. Y.B. INT'L L. 206, 212 (1953); YORAM DINSTEIN, WAR, AGGRESSION, AND SELF-DEFENCE 169 (5th edn 2012).

[10] On distinction, *see* HENCKAERTS & DOSWALD-BECK, *supra* note 5, at Rules 1–24; Protocol (I) Additional to the Geneva Conventions of 12 August 1949, and Relating to the Protection of Victims of International Armed Conflicts 48 (1977) [hereinafter AP I]. On proportionality, *see id.*, arts. 51(5)(b), 85(3)(b); HENCKAERTS & DOSWALD-BECK, *supra* note 5, at Rule 14; Rome Statute of the International Criminal Court, U.N. Doc. A/CONF.183/9, 2187 U.N.T.S. 90, art. 8(2)(b)(iv) (July 17, 1998) (as amended in 2010 by

convention, whereby parties to the conflict agree to grant benevolent quarter to surrendering enemy troops and to afford them immunity for any acts of war not proscribed by the *jus in bello*.[11]

The *jus ad bellum* has no impact on these rules. Unlike civilians or persons *hors de combat*, soldiers fighting against aggression have no *jus in bello* protection against being targeted. Meanwhile, attacks targeting civilians, or affecting them disproportionately, are banned equally for both sides. And aggressor soldiers gain the privilege of immunity for all acts compliant with the *jus in bello*, facing no greater *in bello* restriction on their conduct than do their adversaries.[12]

This separation and independence of the *ad bellum* and *in bello* regimes is fundamental. The premise that each side is committed to fighting is thought to mean that any *jus in bello* permission

> will invariably be invoked by both those who are morally and legally justified in a resort to force *and those who are not* . . . [T]his cannot be changed by changing the content of the laws, because the fact of appeal to the laws of conduct by both sides is not a result of some peculiarity of the law's content.[13]

If the rules governing the conduct of hostilities were to prohibit aggressor forces from killing combatants, it would be both "redundant of" the *jus ad bellum* and, more significantly, ineffective in furthering "the morally valuable alternative of limiting the harm done by all sides in all the wars that are in fact fought."[14] The rampant violation of such an unworkable rule might even undermine the authority of the *jus in bello* as a whole.

Doc. C.N.651.2010.TREATIES-8) [hereinafter ICC Statute]. Different theorists advance different understandings of how best to conceptualize the notion of proportionate harm, but the notion that collateral damage is to be minimized is relatively uncontroversial. WALZER, JUW, *supra* note 2, at 127–33, 152–57; Thomas Hurka, *Proportionality in the Morality of War*, 33 PHIL. & PUBL. AFF. 34, 46 (2005).

11 *See* Convention (III) relative to the Treatment of Prisoners of War. Geneva (1949) [hereinafter GC III], AP I, *supra* note 10, arts. 43–45.

12 AP I, *supra* note 10, art. 43(2); GC III, *supra* note 11, arts. 4, 82–88; Inter-American Commission on Human Rights, *Report on Terrorism and Human Rights*, para. 68 OEA/Ser.L/-V/II.116 Doc.5 rev.1 corr. (22 Oct. 2002). *See also* Waldemar A. Solf & Edward R. Cummings, *A Survey of Penal Sanctions under Protocol I to the Geneva Conventions of August 12, 1949*, 9 CASE W. RES. J. INT'L L. 205, 212 (1977) (privileged belligerents are "immune from criminal prosecution for those warlike acts which do not violate the laws and customs of war but which might otherwise be common crimes under municipal law").

13 Shue, *supra* note 8, at 280–81 [emphasis added]. *See also* sources cited in *supra*, note 8.

14 Dill & Shue, *supra* note 3, at 324. *See also id.*, at 323.

On the other hand, the protection of civilians on both sides is potentially effective, it is claimed, both because it is clear in its application and because it does not deny either the capacity to pursue successfully its commitment to fight.[15] As such, it provides "a morally thin, but honest, workable, and – most important – definitive limit on killing in war."[16] Quite apart from protecting against blanket non-compliance, the application of these limits on civilian killing to both sides is thought to help guard against the *jus ad bellum* becoming a tool of unrestrained normative empowerment that would open the door to crusade-like wars.[17] It prohibits the worst form of unjustified killing.[18]

The provision of immunity to privileged belligerents for all acts that do not violate the *jus in bello* is thought essential to making these rules work. Any effort to punish those who engage in *jus-in-bello*-compliant killings or destruction in violation of the *jus ad bellum* would either be invoked by those (incorrectly) assuming their side to be fighting a lawful cause, or would eviscerate the incentive of those committed to fighting on the aggressor side to comply with the *jus in bello* or to surrender.[19] In contrast, granting blanket immunity to POWs who comply with the *jus in bello* is thought to incentivize compliance with that regime and to ensure that those fighting a lawful war are not wrongfully punished by an opponent incorrectly asserting its own *jus ad bellum* authority.

To be sure, one might question the empirical validity of a number of these claims. It is not obvious that granting immunity for the *jus ad bellum* violations is in fact essential to deterring *jus in bello* violations; the two regimes could be applied cumulatively, as they are in the case of

15 Dill & Shue, *supra* note 3, at 321; Gabriella Blum, *The Laws of War and the "Lesser Evil,"* 35 YALE J. INT'L L. 1, 50–51 (2010).

16 Shue, *Laws of war, Morality, and International Politics*, *supra* note 8, at 330. Blum suggests this concern with rules that lack bright lines is overplayed in the context of a humanitarian necessity exception (Blum, *supra* note 15, at 51–53), but she is less sanguine about the viability of a *jus ad bellum* derived rule of conduct. Gabriella Blum, *The Dispensable Lives of Soldiers*, 2 J. LEGAL ANALYSIS 69, 133–34 (2010).

17 WALZER, JUW, *supra* note 2, at 114; Sloane, *supra* note 8, at 76; Anthony Coates, *Is the Independent Application of* Jus in Bello *the Way to Limit War?*, *in* JUST AND UNJUST WARRIORS, *supra* note 5, at 176, 181. Expressing skepticism of the idea that the *jus in bello* can restrain this, *id.*, at 184.

18 HAQUE, *supra* note 3, ch. 3.

19 *Supra* notes 8–9. WALZER, JUW, *supra* note 2, at 151 (on the surrender convention); JEFF MCMAHAN, KILLING IN WAR 190–91 (2009); Jeff McMahan, *The Morality of War and the Law of War*, *in* JUST AND UNJUST WARRIORS, *supra* note 5, at 19, 29.

leaders and states.[20] Furthermore, the notion that the line between civilians and combatants is "definite" or "clear" (and therefore more viable than any rule tied to the *jus ad bellum*) seems something of an anachronism in an age of guerilla forces, terrorist cells, and the emphasis on fighting against "civilians directly participating in hostilities."[21] However, for the purposes of argument, the discussion that follows accepts these widely held empirical assumptions.

7.2 The Normative Force of Convention

The central idea of a warrior's code is that in light of this context and the widespread agreement around the core rules of the *jus in bello* regime, soldiering should be understood as governed by a special role morality, defined by those rules. The most straightforward aspect of this claim is that adhering to these widely accepted, conventional rules of combat becomes obligatory even if a moral assessment independent of the convention might allow expanded permissions due to the justice of the cause.[22]

For example, one might think that soldiers have a moral duty to wear a "fixed sign" discernible at a distance. Legally, this is a condition of the privileges of belligerency.[23] The notion of a warrior's code is that this creates a deeper moral duty, even when the soldier is fighting on the right

[20] *See infra* notes 46–47 and accompanying text. *See, e.g.*, Christopher Kutz, *The Difference Uniforms Make: Collective Violence in Criminal Law and War*, 33 Phil. & Pub. Aff. 167–68 (2005) [hereinafter Kutz, *Uniforms*].

[21] *See, e.g.*, Nils Melzer, Interpretive Guidance on the Notion of Direct Participation in Hostilities under International Humanitarian Law (Geneva: ICRC, 2009).

[22] Walzer, JUW, *supra* note 2, at 47; 132, 228–31; Thomas Nagel, *War and Massacre*, 1 Phil. & Pub. Aff. 123, 125 (1972); George I. Mavrodes, *Conventions and the Morality of War*, 4 Phil. & Pub. Aff. 117 (1975); Margalit & Walzer, *supra* note 8; Jonathan Glover, Causing Death and Saving Lives 78 (1977).

[23] GC III, *supra* note 11, art. 4(2); Knut Dörmann, *The Legal Situation of Unlawful/Unprivileged Combatants*, 85 Int'l Rev. Red Cross 45, 70–71 (2003); *Ex parte* Quirin et al. 317 U.S. 1 (1942); Osman bin Haji Mohamed Ali v. Public Prosecutor [1969] 1 AC 430 (PC); Richard Baxter, *So-Called "Unprivileged Belligerency": Spies, Guerrillas and Saboteurs*, 28 Brit. Y.B. Int'l L. 325 (1951). Additional Protocol I controversially (*see, for example*, Geoffrey Robertson, Crimes against Humanity, at 183 (1999)) extended this looser requirement to "situations in armed conflicts where, owing to the nature of the hostilities an armed combatant cannot" wear a fixed distinctive sign. However, it was further provided that this was "not intended to change the generally accepted practice of States with respect to the wearing of the uniform by combatants." AP I, *supra* note 10, art. 44(3, 6).

side. Indeed, such a soldier may be thought to commit a grave wrong if he uses his lack of uniform to kill enemy combatants by relying on the trust they place in his apparent civilian status, even though they (as aggressor forces) are liable to be killed and he (as someone fighting against aggression) is not.[24]

In short, what might have been permissible morally (fighting without a uniform) becomes wrongful due to the normative force of the conventional practice. Or so the argument goes.[25] This might be the best way of understanding international law's criminalization of perfidy, irrespective of the *jus ad bellum*, and its removal of POW immunity for those that fight without a uniform.

Although mutual adherence is important to the convention's normative weight, its advocates argue that even if the enemy in a given conflict or context breaches the rules, the code retains force due to the importance of protecting all civilians and preserving the relevant rule's status among soldiers and militaries more generally.[26] In short, assuming the empirical assertions obtain, it is plausible to argue that the benefits of upholding the core objectives of peace and humanity provide a powerful duty not to exceed the bounds of the warrior's code even when external moral factors may pull in another direction.

None of this, however, establishes (from the legal point of view), the position that soldiers have a code-derived *permission* to kill one another irrespective of the *jus ad bellum* status of their wars. To take that position would require holding that the warrior's code not only creates obligations that would not exist absent the widely accepted rules and practices of war, but that it provides an *exhaustive* normative framework of soldierly conduct in war, from the legal point of view. On that view, what the *jus in bello* does not prohibit is therefore wholly permissible for soldiers in war.

Two aspects of that more expansive idea are worth considering here. The first is the notion that soldiers killed by an aggressor force in conformity with the *jus in bello* are not wronged, because their role morality defines not just what they may and may not do, but also what may or may not be done to them. The second is the argument that soldiers do

24 ICC Statute, *supra* note 10, art. 8(2)(b)(xi).

25 Although recognizing the value of the war convention, McMahan argues that there may be contexts in which the value of the convention is outweighed by more pressing moral imperatives. Jeff McMahan, *Killing in War: A Reply to Walzer*, 34 PHILOSOPHIA 47 (2006). *See also* GLOVER, *supra* note 22, at 279. *But see* WALZER, JUW, *supra* note 2, at 151.

26 Margalit & Walzer, *supra* note 8.

no wrong when they fight for an aggressor force, because they act in conformity with all of the requirements of the *jus in bello* and the warrior's code that it defines.

7.3 The Warrior's Code and Combatant Reparations[27]

The idea that the warrior's code dictates that soldiers that suffer *jus-in-bello*-compliant killings and violence ought not be considered victims of the crime of aggression can be framed in different ways. One approach is to argue that soldiers participate consensually in a rule-governed activity in which the rules dictate that their killing is permissible, even for a bad cause. On this view, they are not wronged at all. An alternative approach is to argue that if the law were to recognize soldiers as the victims of the crime of aggression, this would undermine *jus in bello* conventions and practices. On this view, they may be wronged, but the law cannot recognize that wrong. Neither approach is convincing.

The consent argument proceeds as follows. Having joined the military and donned a uniform in the context of war, soldiers have entered a rule-governed practice of conflict in which they are permitted to harm others pursuant to the rules, but in which they thereby also consent to being legitimate targets pursuant to those same rules.[28] The soldier on this view might be analogized to a boxer, whose own participation in a rule-governed activity involving mutual efforts to harm is thought to involve the authorization of rule-governed attacks by his opponent in exchange for his own permission to engage in rule-governed attacks on said opponent.[29]

[27] The latter part of this section overlaps with an argument provided in Tom Dannenbaum, *The Criminalization of Aggression and Soldiers' Rights*, EUR. J. INT'L L. (forthcoming).

[28] Thomas Hurka, *Liability and Just Cause*, 20 ETHICS & INT'L AFF. 199 (2007). *See also* WALZER, JUW, *supra* note 2, at 128, 135, 145; MICHAEL IGNATIEFF, VIRTUAL WAR: KOSOVO AND BEYOND 161 (2000); BARRIE PASKINS & MICHAEL DOCKRILL, THE ETHICS OF WAR 224–25 (1979); Yitzhak Benbaji, *The Moral Power of Soldiers to Undertake the Duty of Obedience*, 122 ETHICS 43 (2011). Zupan, though rejecting the notion of rights forfeiture, nonetheless argues that even a soldier fighting a defensive war is a legitimate target because "has adopted a maxim whereby he deliberately intends to harm me" and he has the option of withdrawing from the contest, through surrender or desertion. DANIEL S. ZUPAN, WAR, MORALITY, AND AUTONOMY: AN INVESTIGATION INTO JUST WAR THEORY, 48, 100 n.22 (2003). On the notion that donning the uniform means accepting target status, *see, for example*, GEORGE P. FLETCHER, ROMANTICS AT WAR 107–08 (2002).

[29] *See, e.g.*, Hurka, *supra* note 28, at 210.

The analogy does not hold. The plausibility of the boxing example rests on background presumptions of mutually free consent and the fact that death is neither the aim of the reciprocal attacks, nor a likely outcome. This is crucial to how we understand its relevance to the law's posture on soldiering.

The right to life is widely held to be morally and legally inalienable, with very narrow (and highly controversial) exceptions. The only case of consent-based killing given any significant recognition in the law is euthanasia, which is permitted by only a small number of legal regimes and only under strict conditions. The limited number and scope of those laws reveals a baseline principle, common across societies: if the victim's consent ever gets the killer off the hook, it is only in extreme circumstances (like terminal illness), when the consent is informed, explicit, unequivocal, free from coercion, and freely revocable.[30]

None of these conditions obtains in the case of a soldier on the receiving end of a wrongful aggression. Most importantly, such a soldier faces two cumulative and severely coercive choices that undermine the freedom, and therefore authority, of any putative consent to being attacked. His first choice is to fight or to stand by while an aggressor force inflicts wrongful violence on innocent people (often including people with whom he shares deep associative bonds), and often to the end of overriding wrongfully the politics of a state and its people (in many cases, his own).[31] If he is unwilling to stand by, the soldier's second choice is to fight within the *jus in bello* rules (including by wearing a uniform) or to wrong innocents on the other side, endanger civilians on

[30] *See, e.g.*, Death with Dignity Act (Oregon), OR. REV. STAT., §§ 127.800–897 (1997); Death with Dignity Act (Washington), WASH. REV. CODE, § 70.245.010–904 (2009); Baxter v. Montana, 224 P.3d 1211, 1215 (Mont. 2009); Carter v. Canada, paras. 38, 1243 (2012), B.C.S.C. 886 (Can. B.C.); JOHN GRIFFITHS ET AL., EUTHANASIA AND LAW IN EUROPE 82 (2008); S. A. Hurst and A. Mauron, *Assisted Suicide and Euthanasia in Switzerland: Allowing a Role for Non-Physicians*, 326 BMJ 271(Feb. 1, 2003). www.bmj.com/content/326/7383/271. For a philosophical analysis, *see* Joel Feinberg, *Voluntary Euthanasia and the Inalienable Right to Life*, 7 PHIL. & PUB. AFF. 93 (1978). On consent as a defense to wrongful harm, *see, for example*, MARKUS DUBBER & TATJANA HÖRNLE, CRIMINAL LAW: A COMPARATIVE APPROACH 457–73 (2014).

[31] As Walzer notes, in a war of self-defense, it is "terribly important to win." WALZER, JUW, *supra* note 2, at 72. *Id.*, at 31. To adopt the boxing analogy used by Thomas Hurka in his consent-based account, if a mafia boss were to hold an individual's family hostage and to threaten their execution unless that individual engages in and wins a boxing match with a mafia henchman, the individual's decision to fight could hardly be deemed sufficient to waive her right.

his own side (by rendering them indistinguishable from him), undermine the *jus in bello* in the long run, and risk worse treatment for himself if captured (having lost POW privileges).[32] Under these conditions, the notion that fighting, wearing a uniform, and taking advantage of the *jus in bello* rules entails consenting to being killed by an aggressor force is neither morally credible, nor compatible with the law's normative underpinnings.

One might insist that the key point about the boxing analogy is the exchange – the consent to attack in exchange for the permission to attack. But those responding to aggression need no special *in bello* authorization to use force in response. Moreover, even if such an exchange of permissions were in play here, the whole point of the crime of aggression is that international law prohibits at least the leaders of an aggressor force from inflicting that violence. Therefore, any exchange-based consent here would at most be consent to the conduct of *soldiers* on the other side (a matter picked up again in the next section), not consent to the attack itself, which is also attributable to the state leaders.

More plausibly, Dill and Shue argue, "the best available rules for conduct in war explicitly depart from moral prescriptions regarding individual rights."[33] On their account, combatants fighting against an aggressor force are wronged when they are attacked, and they have a right not to be subject to such attack, but the *jus in bello* cannot protect that right effectively.[34] The latter regime focuses instead on those rights it can protect successfully, including most notably civilian rights.[35] This, it is argued, is the best we can do once war is underway.[36] To aim for full rights protection would, in practice, mean failing to protect any rights at all in armed conflict.[37]

On this account, the *jus in bello* creates important prohibitions and refrains from regulating beyond its capacity for efficacy, but does not thereby authorize what it does not prohibit. This understanding fits with an account on which the crime of aggression exists to fill a gap left by the

[32] On the "fixed and distinctive sign" condition of privileged belligerency, *see* GC III, *supra* note 11, art. 4(A)(2). Diluting it somewhat, *see* AP I, *supra* note 10, art. 44. On the point about drawing fire away from one's own civilians, *see, for example*, McMahan, Killing in War, *supra* note 19, at 55. It is, of course, the primary criticism of guerilla fighters that they fail to do precisely that. *See* Walzer, JUW, *supra* note 2, at 179–80, 183–84, 192.

[33] Dill & Shue, *supra* note 3, at 312. [34] *Id.*, at 322–23. [35] *Id.*, at 329.

[36] *Id.*, at 325. [37] *Id.*, at 324.

jus in bello in the criminalization of wrongful killing. It explains why the gap exists, but rejects the view that *in bello* non-regulation entails the latter regime's deeper endorsement of that killing.

These arguments notwithstanding, some soldiers taken by the idea of a warrior's code may reject the notion that they are the victims of the crime of aggression. For these men and women, the older concept of a chivalric code of honor or some other warrior's ethic may better capture how they think about war and the sacrifices they make in it. On that view, it might be considered a slight, both to them and perhaps to their adversaries to classify their martial sacrifice as part of a criminal wrong in which they are the victims. As such, individuals in these positions may reject that status at the ICC.

Putting the term "victim" to one side, the notion that soldiers are criminally wronged when killed or harmed in war does not ordinarily change the sense of honor in fighting those wars. Soldiers are already in this situation in wars against unprivileged belligerents and wars against forces committing widespread war crimes, without any clear indication that this weakens their sense of martial honor. Indeed, those who survive war crimes are often lauded as heroes who *exemplify* the military ethos.[38]

Nonetheless, some soldiers may feel a warrior's respect for those on the other side that comply with the *jus in bello*, and, like a boxer, may reject the notion that they are wronged by such adversaries when killed or harmed by them. However, it is doubtful that that sentiment of solidarity and understanding would extend to the leader of the aggressor force, so it is far less likely that many would reject the notion that they were criminally wronged by him. He, of course, is the individual who would be in the dock for any victim participation and who would be liable for any reparations at the ICC.

That said, it is possible that even those that recognize that they were criminally wronged may not want to be classed as victims at the ICC simply for having suffered the ordinary harms of war. This possibility raises a genuine challenge for the victim participation and reparations

[38] This at least was the widely held view in response to then candidate Donald Trump's claim that Senator John McCain, who was captured and tortured during the Vietnam War, was not a war hero. *See, e.g.*, John Hubbell, *Sorry Trump: The Story of John McCain the War Hero*, NEWSWEEK, July 20, 2015, www.newsweek.com/sorry-trump-story-john-mccain-war-hero-355617.

apparatus. However, it is not one that is unique to aggression. Across a range of crimes involving large numbers of victims, there will inevitably be deep and meaningful divisions among those criminally wronged about whether reparations should be provided, in what form, and with what engagement on their side.[39] Responding in a productive and respectful way to such divisions across victim constituencies requires careful institutional design, including ensuring that those wronged have some ownership over the reparative process, and the option to opt out entirely.[40] Approaches along those lines are discussed further in Chapter 11. The point for the moment is that such challenges do not change the reality of who is wronged by the crime.

A separate challenge to the identification of soldiers as victims would assert not that the *jus in bello* eliminates the wrongfulness of the death and violence inflicted on soldiers by an aggressor force, but rather that recognizing that wrongfulness explicitly in legal process would lead to the *jus ad bellum* undermining or swallowing the *jus in bello*. The Ethiopia–Eritrea Claims Commission gave something like this rationale for its exclusion of *jus-in-bello*-compliant combatant deaths and harms from its *jus ad bellum* reparations awards.[41] This message was muddied somewhat by the inclusion of *jus-in-bello*-compliant harm to *civilians*

[39] *See, e.g.*, BRANDON HAMBER, TRANSFORMING SOCIETIES AFTER POLITICAL VIOLENCE: TRUTH, RECONCILIATION, AND MENTAL HEALTH 108–09 (2009); José María Guembe, *Economic Reparations for Grave Human Rights Violations: The Argentinean Experience*, *in* THE HANDBOOK OF REPARATIONS 21, 24–25 (Pablo de Greiff, ed., 2006); Ariel Colonomos & Andrea Armstrong, *German Reparations to the Jews after World War II: A Turning Point in the History of Reparations*, *in id.* 390, 393, 396–97; Brandon Hamber, Narrowing the Micro and Macro, *in id.* 560, 568; Victor Espinoza Cuevas, María Luisa Ortiz Rojas, and Paz Rojas Baeza, *Truth Commissions: An Uncertain Path*? 37–38 (2002); MARTHA MINOW, BETWEEN VENGEANCE AND FORGIVENESS 93 (1998).

[40] *See, e.g.*, HAMBER, *supra* note 39, 108–14 (2009); Prosecutor v. Lubanga, International Center for Transitional Justice: Public submission on reparations issues, ICC-01/04-01/06, paras. 43–44 (May 10, 2012), www.ictj.org/sites/default/files/ICTJ-DRC-Reparations-Submission-ICC-Full-2012-English.pdf.

[41] Ethiopia's Damages Claims (Eri. v. Eth.), 26 R.I.A.A., para. 316 (Eri.–Eth. Claims Comm'n 2009) [hereinafter EECC: *Ethiopia's Award*]. The Commission also reasoned that combatant killings were excluded by the treaty governing its work. *Id.*, at para. 338. However, the referenced treaty text arguably precluded the ruling on *ad bellum* liability altogether, so a strict interpretation of the treaty can only go so far in explaining the failure to include combatant deaths and harms. *Cf.* Christine Gray, *The Eritrea/Ethiopia Claims Commission Oversteps its Boundaries: A Partial Award?*, 17 EUR. J. INT'L L. 699, 704–08 (2006). Agreement between the Government of the Federal Democratic Republic of Ethiopia and the Government of the State of Eritrea of December 12, 2000, art. 5(1).

in the final award.[42] Nonetheless, the notion has sufficient support to warrant consideration.[43]

The nature of the harm to the *jus in bello* could take different forms. On one view, its capacity to incentivize compliance would be diluted. Alternatively, one might think it would be undermined more fundamentally as an independent regime with its own normative authority. Consider these in turn.

The difficulty with arguing for the exclusion of combatants from *jus ad bellum* reparations on the first of these grounds at the ICC is that the *scope* of *jus ad bellum* reparations is only at issue in cases in which a leader (or state) has been found criminally (or otherwise) responsible for aggression and liable for repairing the victims.[44] It is difficult to imagine that merely *adding* civil liability for the deaths of enemy soldiers would distort leaders' (or states') incentives to comply with the *jus in bello* if the necessarily prior prospect of criminal (or state) liability for that very aggression were not already enough to do so.[45]

To be clear, as discussed further below, the importance of sharpening *jus in bello* incentives for soldiers is an important part of the reason they should not be held criminally liable for aggression. However, the ICC's own posture presumes that leaders are in a position in which a cumulative regime of *jus ad bellum* and *jus in bello* obligations can be effective.[46]

[42] EECC: *Ethiopia's Award*, *supra* note 41, at paras. 321–49, 388, 426–27. Thus Vaios Koutroulis argues that the commission's approach "unequivocally confirms both the parallel application of and the separation between jus ad bellum and jus in bello." Vaios Koutroulis, *And Yet It Exists: In Defence of the "Equality of Belligerents" Principle*, 26 LEIDEN J. INT'L L. 449, 468 (2013).

[43] Veijo Heiskanen and Nicolas Leroux, *Applicable Law:* Jus ad Bellum, Jus in Bello *and the Legacy of the UN Compensation Commission*, *in* WAR REPARATIONS AND THE UN COMPENSATION COMMISSION 51 (T. Feighery, C. Gibson, & T. Rajah, eds., 2015); Luisa Castagnetti, *The Damages Awards of the Ethiopia-Eritrea Claims Commission: War Damages and Reparations for Violations of the Jus ad Bellum*, 19 ITAL. Y.B. INT'L L. ONLINE 279, 293–94 (2009). *See also* WALZER, JUW, *supra* note 2, at 37–39; Shue, *Do We Need a "Morality of War"?*, *supra* note 5, 87, at 89. Paulus objects to the criminalization of aggression itself on these grounds. Andreas Paulus, *Second Thoughts on the Crime of Aggression*, 20 EUR. J. INT'L L. 1117, 1126 (2009).

[44] ICC Statute, *supra* note 10, art. 75(2).

[45] *Cf.* Paulus, *supra* note 43, at 1126 (objecting to the criminalization of aggression itself on these grounds).

[46] Applying the *jus ad bellum* and *jus in bello* cumulatively: H. of Lords H. of Commons Joint Comm'n on Human Rights, The Government's Policy on the Use of Drones for Targeted Killing, Second Report of Session 2015–16, HL Paper 141 HC 574, para. 3.40, 3.12, 3.13, 3.16, 3.40 (May 10, 2016) (UK), https://publications.parliament.uk/pa/jt201516/jtselect/jtrights/574/574.pdf. *See also* Christopher Greenwood, *The Relationship between Jus Ad Bellum and*

And there are good reasons for that. In most cases, the likelihood of a conclusive *jus in bello* ruling (and thus the expected reparative cost of violation) is higher than is that of a *jus ad bellum* ruling. In any event, violating the *jus in bello* would entail additional, steeper criminal and reparative costs on top of *jus ad bellum* liabilities. And since subordinates have a duty to disobey only orders requiring that they violate the *jus in bello*, issuing such orders would risk triggering disobedience and undermining the war effort.[47]

The deeper worry might be that treating combatant killings as part of aggression's criminal wrong would entail the *jus ad bellum* swallowing the *jus in bello*, in violation of the regimes' independence from one another.[48] This, however, is a mistake. The true independence of these regimes means recognizing that the two bodies of law prohibit and condemn *different* wrongs.[49] As Adil Haque puts it, they share a "division of moral labor."[50] The fact that one regime does not prohibit an action cannot preclude the prohibition of that action by the other. Such preclusion would render the latter regime subservient to the former in precisely the way that the principle of independence denies.[51] It is uncontroversial that *jus in bello* violations can be prosecuted and otherwise sanctioned as illegal, even when perpetrated in the service of a lawful cause. The converse is also true; *jus ad bellum* reparations must apply even (perhaps especially) to "acts or practices which in themselves comply with the rules of the law of war."[52] Recognizing that soldiers killed or harmed

Jus In Bello, 9 Rev. Int'l Studs. 221, 226, 230–32 (1983); Frédéric Mégret, *Should Rebels Be Amnestied?*, *in* Jus Post Bellum: Mapping the Normative Foundations 519, 536 (Carsten Stahn, Jennifer S. Easterday, & Jens Iverson, eds., 2014).

47 Erin Pobjie, *Victims of the Crime of Aggression*, *in* The Crime of Aggression: A Commentary 816, 841 (Claus Kreß & Stefan Barriga, eds., 2016); Claus Kreß, "Time for Decision: Some Thoughts on the Immediate Future of the Crime of Aggression", 20 Eur. J. Int'l L. 1129, 1134 (2009).

48 Walzer, JUW, *supra* note 2, at 38, 128.

49 Mégret, "What is the Specific Evil of Aggression?", in Kreß and Barriga, *supra* note 47, 1398, 1435, 1445. *See also* David Rodin's distinction between the "symmetry thesis" and the "independence thesis." *Supra* note 69.

50 Haque, *supra* note 3, at 3. *See also id.*, at 31.

51 *Id.*, at 34; Kreß, *supra* note 47, at 1135. Note in this respect, the disappointment of Ethiopia in the EECC's relatively small *jus ad bellum* award as compared to its *jus in bello* awards. Michael J. Matheson, *Eritrea–Ethiopia Claims Commission: Damage Awards*, 13 ASIL Insights (Sept. 4, 2009) www.asil.org/insights/volume/13/issue/13/eritrea-ethiopia-claims-commission-damage-awards.

52 Armed Activities on the Territory of the Congo (Dem. Rep. Congo v. Uganda), Judgment, 2005 I.C.J. 168 (Dec. 1), Declaration of Judge Ad Hoc Verhoeven, § 5. *See also* UN

fighting against aggression are victims of the *jus ad bellum* crime in no way diminishes the additional *jus in bello* criminality of targeting civilians in any war (aggressive or not).

7.4 The Warrior's Code and Immunity vs. Non-Culpability

The next question, then, is whether the warrior's code can make a difference to the culpability of soldiers on the aggressor side. Whereas the earlier discussion recognized that the value of a warrior's code is such that it could create and impose otherwise inapplicable legal and moral requirements on soldiers fighting against an aggressor force, the question here is whether compliance with the warriors' code would be *sufficient* to act morally, according to the normative foundations of international law.

One might think that that is precisely the normative position of international law here. After all, soldiers bear no legal liability for violations of the *jus ad bellum*. The POW convention grants them blanket immunity for all acts of war that comply with the *jus in bello* – including killing enemy soldiers in an aggressive war.[53] As discussed in Section 7.5, below, this immunity is defensible and is part of why criminal liability for aggression is limited to a small cohort of state leaders.

However, interpreting this immunity to exculpate such killing would misunderstand the function and normative authority of the war convention and would mistake immunity for either permission or non-culpability.[54] The reasons for forgoing punishment do not eliminate the underlying duty not to participate, and cannot make any difference to the moral burden borne by those who fight in a criminal war.[55] As Dill

Environment Programme, Conclusions by the Working Group of Experts on Liability and Compensation for Environmental Damage Arising from Military Activities, U.N. Doc. UNEP/Env.Law/3/Inf.1 (Oct. 15, 1996), *in* Liability and Compensation for Environmental Damage, Nairobi 119, 119–20 (Aleksandr Timoshenko, ed., 1998).

[53] *See supra* note 12.

[54] HAQUE, *supra* note 3, at 23–26. Confusion on this point is not helped by legal language suggesting that combatants are "entitled" to attack the enemy, or that they have a "right" to do so, rather than that they are protected from punishment for doing so. *See, e.g.*, AP I, *supra* note 10, arts. 43(2), 44(2); Claude Pilloud et al., COMMENTARY ON THE ADDITIONAL PROTOCOLS OF 8 JUNE 1977 TO THE GENEVA CONVENTIONS OF 12 AUGUST 1949, at 515 (1987).

[55] Shue rightly emphasizes the "crucial distinction ... between the moral justification for neutral laws of the conduct of war themselves and the moral justification for those who abide by those laws. Those who abide by morally justified laws of the conduct of war are not themselves fully morally justified unless they have also complied with the principles

and Shue put it, the rules governing the conduct of hostilities "need not be in the business of blessing what they do not prohibit."[56] This is also important to understanding the force (if any) of the purported consensual exchange between combatants on either side, whereby soldiers on either side might be thought to consent to being attacked in exchange for the permission to attack. The most plausible version of this exchange is as an exchange of agent-specific immunities, or protections from legal sanction for engaging in such attacks, not the kind of deeper permission that fails for the reasons noted above.[57]

The distinction between protection from prosecution or litigation and full absolution by the law's own lights is precisely the distinction between criminal liability and the question of whether an individual can reasonably be expected to "wash his hands of guilt."[58] It is at the crux of immunity. Affirming Germany's immunity in foreign courts for war crimes committed in those other states in World War II, the International Court of Justice described the shielded actions "as displaying a complete disregard for the 'elementary considerations of humanity.'"[59]

On the point at hand, the preamble to Additional Protocol I states explicitly that its symmetrical application to both parties to the conflict is *not* to be understood as in any way "legitimizing or authorizing" violations of the *jus ad bellum*.[60] Its function is to mitigate the calamity in situations in which the *jus ad bellum* has been violated, not to override or redefine the *jus ad bellum* prohibitions.

for the resort to war." Shue, *Laws of war, Morality, and International Politics*, *supra* note 8, at 284.

56 Dill & Shue, *supra* note 3, at 319. *See also supra* notes 33–37 and accompanying text; Haque, *supra* note 3, at 15, 195.

57 *See supra* notes 28–33.

58 *See supra* Section 1.3 of Chapter 1.

59 Jurisdictional Immunities of the State (Germany v. Italy; Greece Intervening) Judgment, 2012 I.C.J. Reports 99 52 (Feb. 3). *See also* Al-Adsani v. UK, App. No. 35763/97, Eur. Ct. H.R., paras. 48, 59, 61 (Nov. 21, 2001); *id.* (Zupancic, J., concurring) (the imperative to condemn and punish "the disgrace of torture" is constrained by "practical considerations"); Case Concerning the Arrest Warrant of 11 April 2000 (Dem. Rep. Congo v. Belg.), Judgment [2002] I.C.J. Rep. 3 (Feb. 14), para. 60.

60 The preamble provides that the provisions of the Protocol (and the provisions of the four Geneva Conventions of 1949) apply "without any adverse distinction based on the nature or origin of the armed conflict or on the causes espoused by or attributed to the Parties to the conflict" but specifies that "nothing in the Protocol or in the Geneva Conventions of 12 August 1949 can be construed as legitimizing or authorizing any act of aggression or any other use of force inconsistent with the Charter of the United Nations." AP I, *supra* note 10, preamble.

As discussed above, the value of achieving that end may create role morality obligations for soldiers not to go beyond what the *jus in bello* permits, even when the normative force of that prohibition is derivative of the conventional status of the practice. However, accepting this does not mean accepting that soldiers may fight non-culpably in criminal wars. Soldiers are under no warrior's code duty to fight in such wars. Moreover, adhering to the fundamental duty *not* to participate in wrongful violence and killing would not in any way undermine or impede the efficacy of the *jus in bello* or the warrior's code in realizing its core value.[61] On the contrary, when soldiers refuse to fight in wrongful wars, they cause less harm to civilians, they do nothing to harm the POW convention, and they avoid contributing to the bad blood that makes peace negotiations difficult. If anything, they complement and further the core objectives of the warrior's code.

As such, it is misleading when commentators depict an "antagonism" between the two regimes.[62] It is not that the *in bello* regime *authorizes* killings in violation of the *jus ad bellum.* Rather, "by not prohibiting some wrongful killing [the former regime] can effectively prohibit even greater evils – namely, unlimited (including much wrongful) killing."[63] Embracing this conclusion in their defense of the *jus in bello*, Dill and Shue observe, "Limiting the further harms and wrongs issuing from activity that ought not to be occurring at all is a morally distasteful, yet morally vital, enterprise at the heart of the laws for the conduct of war."[64]

The role ethicist defending the non-culpability of participation in wrongful wars must adopt an implausibly harder line, insisting instead that the soldier's obligations with respect to war are defined exclusively by the warrior's code.[65] Walzer seems to adopt such a position when he

[61] On this point, *see, for example*, Jeff McMahan, *The Ethics of Killing in War*, 114 ETHICS 693, 703 (July 2004).

[62] MICHAEL BOTHE, KARL JOSEF PARTSCH, & WALDEMAR A. SOLF, NEW RULES FOR VICTIMS OF ARMED CONFLICTS: COMMENTARY ON THE TWO 1977 PROTOCOLS ADDITIONAL TO THE GENEVA CONVENTIONS OF 1949, at 32 (1982).

[63] Dill & Shue, *supra* note 3, at 319

[64] *Id.*, at 325. The result is that "[m]any of the killings that will not be prohibited [by the war convention] will be morally wrong" precisely because they violate the *jus ad bellum.* Dill & Shue, *supra* note 3, at 319.

[65] Along these lines, in earlier work, Shue argued that "where the laws of war are morally justified, there is no function to be performed by a competing "morality of war" consisting of alternative rules. We do not need a "morality of war" if we can get a morally justified set of laws of war." Shue, *supra* note 5, at 89. In more recent work, Shue takes a more nuanced view. *See infra* notes 72–73, 75 and accompanying text.

argues, "It would be very odd to praise [Erwin] Rommel for not killing prisoners unless we simultaneously refused to blame him for Hitler's aggressive wars. For otherwise, he is simply a criminal, and all the fighting he does is murder or attempted murder."[66] This parallels the worry that recognizing soldiers as victims of aggression would allow the *jus ad bellum* to swallow the *jus in bello*.

Here, too, that worry is misplaced. *Ad bellum* immunity may be justified, but joint assessment of the *jus ad bellum* and *jus in bello* is entirely morally comprehensible. All blameworthy acts are not equally bad and we are fully capable of supplementing one form of moral condemnation or burden with another without losing the distinctions. It is for that reason that we surely understand morally (no less than legally) what it meant for the IMT to condemn and punish Nazi leaders for culpably orchestrating both Germany's wars of aggression and the *jus in bello* atrocities perpetrated therein.[67] The two kinds of wrong can be distinguished, criticized in different tones and for different reasons, and prosecuted as different crimes.[68] Their normative independence from one another is why this parallel structure of evaluation is viable, not an obstacle to it.[69] Walzer's claim, of course, is that it is difficult to explain why we might *praise* Rommel for not killing prisoners if he is blameworthy for the overall operation. Even that is far from obvious.[70] But it also begs the question. Why should we praise Rommel in the first place?

[66] WALZER, JUW, *supra* note 2, at 38.

[67] *See generally Judgment*, *in* 22 TRIAL OF THE MAJOR WAR CRIMINALS BEFORE THE INTERNATIONAL MILITARY TRIBUNAL 411 (1948); International Military Tribunal for the Far East, Judgment of 12 November 1948, *in* 20 THE TOKYO WAR CRIMES TRIAL (R. John Pritchard & Sonia Magbanua Zaide, eds., 1981).

[68] Shue is right to argue that there is something peculiarly "cruel" about methods such as torture or attacks on the defenseless that render them worthy of special moral condemnation, but this does not mean we cannot criticize unjust attacks on those with some hope of defending themselves. *See* Henry Shue, *Torture*, 7 PHIL. & PUB. AFF. 124, 129–30 (1978).

[69] *See* David Rodin, *Two Emerging Issues of Jus Post Bellum: War Termination and the Liability of Soldiers for Crimes of Aggression*, *in* JUS POST BELLUM 53, 68–76 (Carsten Stahn & Jann K. Kleffner, eds., 2008); David Rodin, *The Moral Inequality of Soldiers: Why* Jus in Bello *Asymmetry is Half Right*, *in* JUST AND UNJUST WARRIORS, *supra* note 5, at 44.

[70] Praise is not inconceivable. We are capable, for example, of respecting (and maybe even praising) the decision of a hostage taker to accept significant risks to his mission so as to provide good medical treatment to one of his captives. And we can do so even as we blame him for the overall operation, including the ongoing detention of the hostage.

For the soldier's adherence to the warrior's code to dissociate him morally from the wrongfulness of killing in a manifestly criminal war, there would need to be a duty rooted in that code of sufficient normative heft to override the presumptive moral duty not to fight in such a war.[71] There is no such code-based duty. One can defend and uphold the independence and internal symmetry of the *jus in bello*, while holding that combatants adhering perfectly to its rules of conduct are nevertheless "[a]bsolutely not" justified in fighting in an aggressive war.[72]

In sum, the following five conclusions are wholly compatible with and supportive of the *jus in bello* and the warrior's code attached thereto.

> (1) Killing even combatants in an unlawful war is wrong from the legal point of view and the soldier has a *prima facie* moral duty not to do it from that perspective unless there is a code-based duty of sufficient normative heft to override that external moral duty.
>
> (2) Deliberately killing civilians in any war (lawful or unlawful) is wrong from the legal point of view, due in part (though not exclusively) to its breach of the warrior's code and the moral values on which it is based (including the values of humanity and peace). From that perspective, the soldier has a moral duty not to do it regardless of the *jus ad bellum* status of his war.[73]
>
> (3) Accepting (1) does not entail denying (2). Soldiers and leaders engaged in a lawful war are subject to the requirements of the *jus in bello*.[74]

[71] Lawyers often rely on a professional code to justify behavior that advances an immoral cause, or to justify actions *vis-à-vis* their adversaries that would be considered wrongful harms were it not for the intervening standards of the code. However, if we are to accept these arguments, it would not be solely on the grounds that the code does not proscribe such action, but also on the grounds that it *requires* that kind of action (under the code-based duty of "zealous advocacy," for example). If there is no professional duty to engage in what would otherwise be wrongful action, the fact that it would not breach the professional code would not, itself, be sufficient to justify the lawyer's participation in that action. This is true even if the code might grant the lawyer legal immunities for the wrongdoing.

[72] Shue, *Laws of War, Morality, and International Politics*, *supra* note 8, at 283–84. *See also* Dill & Shue, *supra* note 3, at 318.

[73] Shue, *Laws of War, Morality, and International Politics*, *supra* note 8, at 279; Dill & Shue, *supra* note 3, at 325–26.

[74] Apart from the pull of the war convention itself, Anthony Coates argues persuasively that the *jus ad bellum* requirement of right intention creates an imperative to fight humanely and with the objective of peace. Coates, *supra* note 17, at 191. *See also* WALZER, JUW, *supra* note 2, at 121.

(4) Accepting (1) does not mean that the soldier does not perform additional (and perhaps more serious) wrongs when he deliberately kills civilians or soldiers *hors de combat* in a criminal war.[75] Indeed, a leader can be held criminally liable simultaneously for violations of the *jus in bello* and for waging an aggressive war.

(5) Accepting (1) does not entail rejecting immunity for soldiers who kill combatants in the course of prosecuting a wrongful war. Nothing about the application of such an immunity here affects the wrongful nature of the killings or the culpability of those who perpetrate them.

7.5 A *Jus ad Bellum* Crime of Appropriately Narrow Scope

The final question regarding the warrior's code is whether the value of furthering the *jus in bello* can in fact provide a sufficient reason for soldiers' absolute protection from criminal liability for aggression. As foregrounded above, the immunity of privileged belligerents from prosecution for *jus ad bellum* crimes helps to further the *jus in bello* in several ways. It can sharpen the incentives of combatants to comply with the latter code even while fighting a wrongful war, to distinguish themselves from civilians, and to surrender rather than fighting to the death. It can also help to pave the way for peace by resolving the fate of detained enemy combatants and protecting against mass punishments on both sides.

Alone, however, these reasons are not sufficient to provide an internal normative account of soldiers' blanket *jus ad bellum* immunity. The first applies equally to leaders, in whose case it is clear (from the legal point of view) that the *jus ad bellum* and *jus in bello* can be applied cumulatively.[76] The remaining reasons apply more specifically to lower-level soldiers, but they explain mainly why soldiers should be shielded from *jus ad bellum* punishment by the enemy, not why they should be shielded from such punishment in other contexts (such as in the courts of their home state, a neutral state, or an international court).

To be clear, the value of sharpening *jus in bello* incentives is certainly an important factor in the best account of soldiers' non-liability for aggression. However, that account must draw on additional factors to

[75] Stated another way, "a combatant who is in violation of the principles of resort can still comply with the rules of conduct." Shue, *Laws of War, Morality, and International Politics*, *supra* note 8, at 284.

[76] *Cf. supra* notes 46–47 and accompanying text.

explain why soldiers, unlike leaders, warrant absolute protection in this realm. Two such factors stand out: the generally low level of *jus ad bellum* culpability among troops, and the importance of functioning military institutions. Given these conditions, a plausible case can be made that cumulative application is unlikely to provide great value. In that context, sharpening *jus in bello* incentives through guaranteeing soldiers' non-liability for the crime of aggression is the best the law can do.

To rely on soldiers' generally low level of culpability for aggression at this juncture may seem in tension with some of the arguments above. After all, a core claim throughout this book has been that a coherent account of international law in this domain must recognize the normative burden of participation in wrongful wars. Underpinning that burden is the fact of culpable participation in wrongdoing. The implication of this is that some proportion of soldiers *is* culpable to some degree when they participate in aggressive wars.

However, adopting this position does not entail holding either that such soldiers are in the majority or that the culpability of such participation exceeds the high threshold necessary to warrant international criminal sanction. The latter point is particularly significant here. International criminal punishment is properly restricted to the most culpable perpetrators of the gravest wrongs.[77] Even those soldiers who fight culpably in an aggressive war are unlikely to surpass that threshold, for precisely the reasons canvassed in Chapters 4–6.[78] Many of those soldiers fight under some level of state coercion. Most are likely uncertain as to the *jus ad bellum* status of their war. And, even when the illegality of a war is relatively clear, a large proportion are likely to feel bound by domestic political obligations, or the associative duty to protect their society, their co-nationals, and their political institutions.

For the reasons elaborated in the previous chapters, to recognize this context is not to hold that the killing and violence in an aggressive war is not wrongful. Nor do these factors justify or fully excuse participation in a wrongful war. However, in combination, they arguably provide a partial excuse that mitigates considerably the blameworthiness of many soldiers, dragging it below the high threshold of international criminality.[79] Most

[77] LARRY MAY, AGGRESSION AND CRIMES AGAINST PEACE 248 (2008); ICC Statute, *supra* note 10, preamble & art. 17(1)(d).

[78] On a related point, *see* MCMAHAN, *supra* note 19, at 110–15.

[79] Kutz accepts that a soldier fighting in a dubious war "may have acted badly, in moral terms, insofar as he took part in collective violence on grounds he knew or had reason to

fundamentally, in most cases, soldiers will lack the knowledge required for criminal liability for aggression.[80]

In short, a significant proportion of soldiers are not innocent when they kill in wrongful wars, but most are not *sufficiently* culpable to warrant criminal sanction. The suffering that these men and women already experience in the course of fighting such a war and the moral and psychological burden they are likely to bear in its aftermath is more than many deserve for their roles in the wrongdoing.[81]

Of course, not all soldiers are quite so easily excused. Some participate zealously, with a full understanding of the aggressive objective and with the aim of advancing that end and killing as many enemy combatants as possible in the process. In theory, members of this latter group may deserve criminal punishment for fighting. However, the logistics of determining which individual participants fall into this class of heightened culpability in any given war would overwhelm any criminal justice system.[82] Those logistics would get even more complicated if equally culpable civilians who engage in zealous, active, and voluntary support for an

know were morally dubious, and the deaths he caused should sit uneasily on his conscience. The question of whether it is legitimate . . . to punish him, however, is far more difficult." Kutz, *Uniforms*, *supra* note 20.

80 Elements of Crimes, Int'l Crim. Ct. 30 (2013), www.icc-cpi.int/resource-library/Documents/ElementsOfCrimesEng.pdf [http://perma.cc/8VEX-6XJF]. May argues particularly strongly for the importance of purposive intent in justifying criminal punishment for aggression, despite recognizing that we may properly attach moral culpability at a much lower level. Larry May, Aggression and Crimes against Peace chs. 7, 8, 12 (2008). On the comparison between criminal liability and moral culpability on this point *see, for example, id.*, at 266, 268. As noted above, the *mens rea* requirement was important at Nuremberg, which required *actual subjective knowledge* of the aggressive purpose of the war (*see, for example*, United States v. von Weizsäcker et al., *in* 14 Trials of War Criminals before the Nuernberg Military Tribunals under Control Council Law No. 10, at 1, 337 (1949); United States v. von Leeb et al., *in* 11 Trials of War Criminals before the Nuernberg Military Tribunals under Control Council Law No. 10, at 462, 488 (1949) [hereinafter High Command Judgment].

81 *See* Section 1.5 of Chapter 1 and Section 4.2 of Chapter 4 above.

82 *See, e.g.*, Ernst J. Cohn, *The Problem of War Crimes Today*, Transactions Grotius Soc'y 125, 144 (1941); McMahan, *supra* note 19, at 191; David R. Mapel, *Innocent Attackers and Rights of Self-Defense*, 18 Ethics & Int'l Aff. 81, 83 (2004); David R. Mapel, *Coerced Moral Agents? Individual Responsibility for Military Service*, 6 J. Pol. Phil. 171, 186 (1998); Lene Bomann-Larsen, *License to Kill? The Question of Just v. Unjust Combatants*, 3 J. Mil. Ethics 142, 155 (2004); McMahan, *The Ethics of Killing in War*, *supra* note 61, at 730–31; Judith Lichtenberg, *How to Judge Soldiers Whose Cause is Unjust*, *in* Just and Unjust Warriors, *supra* note 5, at 112, 125.

aggressive war were to be included, too.[83] The prospect of any wide-ranging prosecution along these lines could also undermine the possibility of a negotiated end to hostilities, and weigh down the peaceful recovery of the aggressor state.[84]

These kinds of concern were emphasized repeatedly at Nuremberg, where the judges worried that eliminating the leadership requirement would trigger the impossible task of finding "a logical place to draw the line between the guilty and the innocent among the great mass of German people,"[85] and would necessarily entail holding criminally responsible "the private soldier on the battlefield, the farmer who increased his production of foodstuffs to sustain the armed forces or the housewife who conserved fats for the making of munitions."[86]

In taking this view, the post-war tribunals did not identify non-leaders as morally innocent under the normative principles guiding the legal regime. Instead, they found that the leadership element provided a workable and clear line dividing the criminal from the merely morally culpable and avoiding the counter-productive outcome of "mass punishments."[87] It was a way of avoiding an infeasible and dangerous expansion of criminal liability.

The final factor underpinning soldiers' blanket *jus ad bellum* immunity is that expanding criminal liability for aggression to lower-level troops would undermine the functioning of military institutions in lawful wars, with deleterious consequences for global human security. That argument connects to a broader argument against the right to disobey and is elaborated in full in the next chapter.

[83] GLOVER, *supra* note 22, at 274; Mavrodes, *supra* note 22, at 118, 121–24; Rosa Ehrenreich Brooks, *War Everywhere: Rights, National Security Law, and the Law of Armed Conflict in the Age of Terror*, 153 UNIV. PENN. L. REV. 676, 730 (2004). *See also* WALZER, JUW, *supra* note 2, at 299–303; Michael Green, *War, Innocence, and Theories of Sovereignty*, 18 SOC. THEORY & PRAC. 39, 43 (1992). *Cf.* Section 2.5 *supra.*

[84] The obvious historical lesson in the latter regard can be seen in the effects of the Allies' imposition of crippling reparations on Germany in the aftermath of World War I under the Treaty of Versailles.

[85] United States v. Krauch, Military Tribunal VI, in 8 TRIALS OF WAR CRIMINALS BEFORE THE NUERNBERG MILITARY TRIBUNALS UNDER CONTROL COUNCIL LAW NO. 10, at 1126 (1949) [hereinafter I.G. Farben Judgment]; The High Command Judgment also noted the "great mass of the soldiers and officers [who are used to] carry out" the crime of aggression. High Command Judgment, *supra* note 80, at 462, 489.

[86] I.G. Farben Judgment, *supra* note 85, at 1125.

[87] *Id.*, at 1124–25. *See also* High Command Judgment, *supra* note 80, at 486; Woermann – Order and Memorandum of the Tribunal & Separate Memorandum of Presiding Judge Christianson, *in* 14 TRIALS OF WAR CRIMINALS BEFORE THE NUERNBERG MILITARY TRIBUNALS UNDER CONTROL COUNCIL LAW NO. 10, at 965, 966 (1949).

In sum, most soldiers are insufficiently culpable to warrant criminal sanction for participating in aggression; the logistics of identifying the few who are would be overwhelming; and, as elaborated below, an expansion of criminal liability in this direction could undermine global human security. In this context, providing blanket *jus ad bellum* immunity is a justified mechanism for sharpening *jus in bello* incentives and thus improving the efficacy of the latter regime.

8

Global Norms, Domestic Institutions, and the Military Role

The argument thus far has established the following. By international law's own lights, soldiers kill and inflict suffering wrongfully when they participate in illegal wars. Conversely, soldiers suffer a criminal wrong when harmed or killed fighting against aggression. Those basic judgments are at the crux of the criminalization of waging such wars. Aggression fills a normative gap, providing criminal law protection against what would be an otherwise anomalously non-criminal violation of the right to life.

Together, the utility of *ad bellum* immunity in sharpening *in bello* incentives and the ordinarily low (and frequently null) level of soldierly culpability on the *ad bellum* dimension due to factors like ignorance, duress, and associative bonds go a long way towards establishing why it makes sense that soldiers cannot be held criminally liable for inflicting the wrongful violence of an aggressive war. However, on any coherent internal normative account of the extant regime, these are neither grounds for aggressor soldiers' normative dissociation from those wrongs, nor grounds for failing to recognize that aggression is criminalized primarily to condemn and protect against the wrongful violence inflicted on combatants and civilians.

From the international legal point of view, then, it seems that soldiers who struggle to reconcile themselves to having fought in illegal wars get it right, even though having done otherwise would have met with unchecked domestic criminal sanction. Soldiers killed or harmed by an aggressor force have the strongest presumptive claim to victim status at the ICC.

This chapter considers a final factor in making sense of this combination of positions – military institutional necessity as a foundation of global human security. In addition to serving as a third reason that combines with low culpability and *jus in bello* sharpening to justify soldiers' blanket protection from *ad bellum* criminal liability, this necessity argument also goes further than any of the accounts discussed above to make sense of the criminal punishment of those that refuse to fight in aggressive wars. The chapter closes with a shorter consideration of whether global human security might weigh against including combatants as victims in ICC aggression proceedings.

8.1 Obedience and Military Functioning

For any complex organization to operate effectively, central decisions must be followed with some degree of predictability. The state, and all of the value it brings, depends fundamentally on the presumption that each actor in the chain of command performs her task irrespective of personal agreement and without individual evaluation.[1] In the absence of this presumption, there would be no rule of law.[2]

This need for predictable internal compliance is heightened in the military. The pressures on all actors in war are extreme, the threat of disobedience is particularly acute, and the dangers it poses are especially grave.[3] Thus, the US Supreme Court has long held that the military "constitutes a specialized community"[4] in which individual rights "must perforce be conditioned to meet certain overriding demands of discipline and duty."[5]

1 *See, e.g.*, Robert M. Cover, *Violence and the Word*, 95 YALE L.J. 1601, 1618–19 (1986); W. Michael Reisman, *The Quest for World Order and Human Dignity in the Twenty-First Century*, 351 RECUEIL DES COURS 368, 374 (2012).

2 Cover, *supra* note 1, at 1618.

3 *See, e.g.*, SAMUEL P. HUNTINGTON, THE SOLDIER AND THE STATE: THE THEORY AND POLITICS OF CIVIL–MILITARY RELATIONS 73 (1964); JAMES H. TONER, TRUE FAITH AND ALLEGIANCE: THE BURDEN OF MILITARY ETHICS 56 (1995); RICHARD A. GABRIEL, TO SERVE WITH HONOR: A TREATISE ON MILITARY ETHICS AND THE WAY OF THE SOLDIER 161 (1982); Martha Minow, *Living up to Rules: Holding Soldiers Responsible for Abusive Conduct and the Dilemma of the Superior Orders Defence*, 52 MCGILL L.J. 1, 5 (2007); William George Eckhardt, *My Lai: An American Tragedy*, 68 UMKC L. REV. 671, 693 (2000); Gary D. Solis, *Obedience of Orders and the Law of War: Judicial Application in American Forums*, 15 AM. U. INT'L L. REV. 481, 483 (1999); Robert G. Gard, *The Military and American Society*, FOREIGN AFF., July 1971, at 699; Malham Wakin, *The Ethics of Leadership II*, WAR, MORALITY, & THE MILITARY PROFESSION 200, 204, 208 (1986); Lt. Col. Kenneth H. Wenker, *Morality and Military Obedience*, AIR UNIV. REV. 82 (1981).

4 Orloff v. Willoughby, 345 U.S. 83, 94 (1953).

5 Burns v. Wilson, 346 U.S. 137, 140 (1953); Gard, *supra* note 3 ("Military organization is hierarchical, not egalitarian, and is oriented to the group rather than to the individual; it stresses discipline and obedience, not freedom of expression; it depends on confidence and trust, not *caveat emptor*. It requires immediate decision and prompt action, not thorough analysis and extensive debate; it relies on training, simplification and predictable behavior, not education, sophistication and empiricism. It offers austerity, not material comforts").

This idea of a separate and specialized community is central to the military's self-understanding. From the moment of enlistment, militaries aim to instill a pervasive obedience and uniformity; individual values, dissent, and diversity are suppressed.[6] Unquestioning, immediate, and anti-deliberative obedience is prized above all else.[7] In short, militaries have traditionally aimed to be what Erving Goffman calls "total institutions."[8] Swift and severe punishment is considered essential to prevent institutional collapse.[9]

Of course, from the international legal point of view, institutional collapse is not always a bad thing. Part of the legacy of Nuremberg is precisely the idea that when they are ordered to break the law, soldiers have both a right and a duty to refuse to do so.[10] Military breakdown in that scenario is not only an acceptable cost of disobedience, it is surely one of the core *objectives* of the law.[11]

Just as the operational collapse of a military unit engaged in war crimes or crimes against humanity is a goal of international criminal law, it is equally clear that the collapse of a military fighting an *illegal* war is also highly desirable from the international legal point of view.[12] The

[6] This is obvious from the first moments of basic training. *See, e.g.*, CHRIS HEDGES, WHAT EVERY PERSON SHOULD KNOW ABOUT WAR 12 (2003).

[7] *In re* Grimley, 137 U.S. 147, 153 (1890); Lloyd Matthews, *Resignation in Protest*, 40 ARMY, No. 1, Jan. 1990, at 12; Eckhardt, *supra* note 1, at 693; MICHAEL WALZER, JUST AND UNJUST WARS 289 (1977) [hereinafter WALZER, JUW]; BERNARD BRODIE, WAR AND POLITICS 492 (1973); Richard Wasserstrom, *Roles and Morality*, *in* THE GOOD LAWYER 25, 31 (David Luban, ed., 1983); Wenker, *supra* note 3.

[8] ERVING GOFFMAN, ASYLUMS (1961).

[9] Parker v. Levy, 417 U.S. 733, 763 (1974) (Blackmun, J., concurring); FRANCIS LIEBER, 2 MANUAL OF POLITICAL ETHICS 667 (rev. 2nd edn 1881).

[10] *See* Section 1.2 of Chapter 1 above.

[11] This, one would think, is part of how we understand the broad liability for even low-level participation in criminal systems like concentration camps. UN War Crimes Comm'n, *Dachau Concentration Camp Case*, 11 LAW REP. OF TRIALS OF WAR CRIMINALS 14 (1947); Jack Ewing & Alan Cowell, *Demjanjuk Convicted for Role in Nazi Death Camp*, NY TIMES (May 13, 2011), at A4. *See also* Prosecutor v. Tadić, Case No. IT-94-1-A, Appeals Judgment, para. 191 (Int'l Crim. Trib. for the Former Yugoslavia July 15, 1999); Trial of Gustav Alfred Jepsen and others, PROCEEDINGS OF A WAR CRIMES TRIAL, held at Lüneburg, Germany (Judgment of Aug. 24, 1946), at 241; Trial of Feurstein and others, PROCEEDINGS OF A WAR CRIMES TRIAL, held at Hamburg, Germany (Judgment of Aug. 25, 1948), at 7–8; Rome Statute of the International Criminal Court, U.N. Doc. A/CONF.183/9, 2187 U.N.T.S. 90, art. 7(1)(d) (July 17, 1998) (as amended in 2010 by Doc. C.N.651.2010.TREATIES-8) [hereinafter ICC Statute].

[12] *Cf.* JEFF MCMAHAN, KILLING IN WAR 99–100 (2009). Those who argue for refusal often do so precisely *because* if generalized it would render the aggressor state unable to perform the wrongful action. *See, e.g.*, PETER A. FRENCH, WAR AND MORAL

sanctions imposed on Iraq in order (in part) to nullify its threat to international peace and security following its illegal aggression against Kuwait decimated its military capacity, and had profound collateral consequences for the Iraqi population.[13] The Security Council-authorized operations in Libya in 2011, and the authorized military action against Iraq twenty years earlier, sought to prevent and turn back illegal military actions through killing large numbers of Iraqi and Libyan soldiers and destroying the military equipment and infrastructure of the two states, all the while inflicting collateral civilian damage on the respective civilian populations.[14] Debates about whether the scope of the Libya action exceeded its mandate notwithstanding, these profoundly destructive actions were not just permitted by international law, they were its very enforcement.[15]

In other words, while its value to the government waging the war is obvious, the preservation of the military organization of a state fighting an illegal war counts for nothing from the international legal point of view.[16] International law encourages and depends on decimating precisely such military organizations through violence and the infliction of massive societal pain. It cannot recoil simultaneously from the prospect of analogous, non-violent military collapse by mass protected

DISSONANCE 314 (2011). It should also be noted that forcing soldiers to fight in a war they consider wrongful can undermine military efficacy in a number of ways. *See, e.g.*, LEONARD M. HAMMER, THE INTERNATIONAL HUMAN RIGHT TO FREEDOM OF CONSCIENCE 215 (2001).

[13] The latter effect, in particular, played an important role in motivating the move to "smarter," more targeted sanctions in future cases. But in all such scenarios, the impact of sanctions in deteriorating military functioning is *supposed* to be significant. That's the whole point. On the military impact of the Iraq sanctions, *see, for example*, ANTHONY H. CORDESMAN, IRAQI WAR FIGHTING CAPABILITIES: A DYNAMIC NET ASSESSMENT 7–8 (2002), http://csis.org/files/media/csis/pubs/iraq_dynamic%5B1%5D.pdf. For the former UH Humanitarian Coordinator for Iraq's strong criticisms of the humanitarian impact of the Iraq sanctions, *see, for example*, HANS-CHRISTOF VON SPONECK, A DIFFERENT KIND OF WAR: THE UN SANCTIONS REGIME IN IRAQ (2006). On the move to targeted sanctions (and some of its problems), *see, for example*, MIKAEL ERIKSSON, TARGETING PEACE: UNDERSTANDING UN AND EU TARGETED SANCTIONS (2011). On the significance of Iraq in motivating the move to targeted sanctions, *see id.*, at 20–22.

[14] S.C. Res. 678 (Nov. 29, 1990); S.C. Res. 1973 (Mar. 17, 2011).

[15] On the Libya debate, *see, for example*, Mehrdad Payandeh, *The United Nations, Military Intervention, and Regime Change in Libya*, 52 VA. J. INT'L L. 355 (2012).

[16] As discussed in Section 2.1 of Chapter 2 above, it may well be that the existing regime is explained by states' interest in ensuring their capacities to fight in illegal wars, but that does not provide a compelling defense of the extant regime as a coherent *normative* order.

disobedience. If such an organizational implosion were to occur as a result of a regime of legal protection for those who disobey, it would be difficult to imagine a more humane way for illegal war to be prevented and international rule of law affirmed.

The reason not to protect soldiers who disobey orders to fight in illegal wars cannot, therefore, be that their state's military action would collapse in that particular instance. Instead, the worry must be that there is no way of protecting disobedience in illegal wars without undermining obedience and military functioning in lawful wars.[17] This is not an unfamiliar concern. Precisely this objection was leveled against the right (and indeed duty) of soldiers to disobey orders to violate the *jus in bello*. The worry in that case was that provision for disobedience in that narrow case would eviscerate the commander's authority and cause widespread disobedience of lawful and necessary orders.[18] In the trials at Leipzig after World War I, the superior orders defense was highly effective in enabling defendants to escape conviction or receive heavily reduced sentences.[19]

In the *jus in bello* context, the post-Nuremberg legal regime has sought a balance that cabins the right to disobey sufficiently to preclude the migration of widespread disobedience (and organizational breakdown) from illegal acts to lawful acts. Soldiers under this regime have a duty to disobey patently illegal orders and have a broader right to disobey illegal orders more generally, but they may be punished for disobeying lawful orders, typically even if it was reasonable to question those orders' legality.[20]

For the institutional necessity account to make sense of the very different rules regarding the *jus ad bellum*, the argument would have to establish that there is something fundamentally different about that context, such that any protection for those who refuse to fight in illegal

[17] Along similar lines, *see* Cheyney Ryan, *Democratic Duty and the Moral Dilemmas of Soldiers*, 122 ETHICS 10, 24 (2011); United States v. Lusk, 21 M.J. 695, 700 (A.C.M.R. 1985).

[18] Eminent voices predicted incorrectly that enforcing a duty to disobey orders contrary to the *jus in bello* would undermine military functioning. Prior to the end of World War II, Hans Kelsen and Clyde Eagleton opposed punishment for obedient soldiers on these grounds. Hans Kelsen, *Collective and Individual Responsibility in International Law with Particular Regard to the Punishment of War Criminals*, 31 CAL. L. REV. 530, 556 (1943). *See also* Clyde Eagleton, *Punishment of War Criminals by the United Nations*, 37 AM. J. INT'L L. 495, 497 (1943).

[19] GARY JONATHAN BASS, STAY THE HAND OF VENGEANCE 80–81 (1999).

[20] *See* Sections 1.2 and 1.3 of Chapter 1 above.

wars would inevitably undermine the state's capacity to engage in lawful military action.

8.2 The Question of Interpretive Authority

One way in which the *jus ad bellum* is sometimes distinguished from the *jus in bello* in this respect is on the claimed ground that there is no institution with the authority and credibility to determine a war's legality.[21] This echoes the traditional reason for segregating substantive *ad bellum* questions to the domain of natural law and restricting positive international law to a combination of procedural rules for "war in due form" and a more substantive *jus in bello*.[22]

That, however, is no longer the regime we have. The question at hand is whether, in the international order *as transformed* by the Kellogg–Briand Pact, the UN Charter, the Nuremberg trials, and ultimately the Kampala Amendments, it is coherent to hold that soldiers may be denied protection against being forced to fight in criminal wars.

Plainly, the answer cannot hinge on the indeterminacy of the *jus ad bellum* or the lack of authoritative interpretive bodies.[23] The contemporary international legal framework is committed to precisely the opposite position.[24] The ICJ, the Security Council, and the ICC are variously given the final word on state responsibility for violating the *jus ad bellum*,[25] the

[21] *See, e.g.*, Hersch Lauterpacht, *The Limits of the Operation of the Law of War*, 30 Brit. Y.B. Int'l L. 206, 211, 220–21 (1953); Gabriella Blum, *The Laws of War and the "Lesser Evil,"* 35 Yale J. Int'l L. 1, 9 (2010); Gabriella Blum, *The Dispensable Lives of Soldiers*, 2 J. Legal Analysis 69, 133–34 (2010); Telford Taylor, Nuremberg and Vietnam: An American Tragedy 184 (1970).

[22] For Grotius, the lack of a common and accepted legal authority to determine the dispute is a definitive feature of war. 1 Hugo Grotius, The Rights of War and Peace 133 [bk. I, ch. 1, § 1] (Richard Tuck, ed., Liberty Fund 2005) (1625). On the early positivist preference for formal requirements – war in due form, rather than a substantive *jus ad bellum* doctrine, *see, for example*, Stephen C. Neff, War and the Law of Nations 99–111 (2005).

[23] Christopher Kutz, *The Difference Uniforms Make: Collective Violence in Criminal Law and War*, 33 Phil. & Pub. Aff. 148, 168 (2005) [hereinafter Kutz, *Uniforms*].

[24] *See, e.g.*, R v. Jones [2006] UKHL 16 (Lord Bingham of Cornhill), para. 19.

[25] The ICJ has issued clear *jus ad bellum* determinations in three cases and made significant *jus-ad-bellum*-relevant findings in two further cases. Military and Paramilitary Activities in and against Nicaragua (Nicar. v. US), Judgment, 1986 I.C.J. Rep. 14 (June 27) (the bulk of the judgment, although not all of it, is *jus-ad-bellum* relevant); Oil Platforms (Islamic Rep. Iran v. US), 2003 I.C.J. Rep. 161 (Nov. 6), paras. 43–78; Armed Activities on the Territory of the Congo (Dem. Rep. Congo v. Uganda), 2005 I.C.J. Rep. 168 (Dec. 19), paras. 92–165 [hereinafter *Armed Activities* Judgment]. *See also*,

authorization of a state to use force,[26] and individual criminal liability.[27] If a domestic or human rights court were to protect disobedience based on the *jus ad bellum* rulings of one of those institutions, this could not be objectionable on indeterminacy grounds from the international legal point of view.

In the absence of a decision from one of those internationally authorized bodies, things would be more complicated. Domestic courts in many states lack the authority or competence to rule on the *jus ad bellum*.[28] But even here, arguments of institutional incompetence or indeterminacy can only go so far. Waging an aggressive war is a domestic crime in more than thirty-five states, and this number is expected to grow as states ratify the ICC's aggression amendments.[29] The fact that even the longer-standing provisions of this kind have been dormant since their promulgation should not be mistaken for evidence of their nullity. Consider, by way of comparison, the prolific use of the Alien Tort Claims Act in the

Corfu Channel Case (UK v. Alb.), Judgment, 1949 I.C.J. Rep. 4, 32–35 (Apr. 9); Legal Consequences of Construction of Wall in Occupied Palestinian Territory, Advisory Opinion, 2004 I.C.J. 136, 195 (July 9), paras. 138–42. In addition to ICJ competence on this issue, Ethiopia and Eritrea accepted a binding arbitration decision on the issue. Partial Award: *Jus Ad Bellum* – Ethiopia's Claims 1–8 (Eri. v. Eth.), 16 R.I.A.A. 457, 464–67 (Eri.–Eth. Claims Comm'n 2005) (holding Eritrea responsible for violating the *jus ad bellum* in the 1998–2000 border war); Final Award: Ethiopia's Damages Claim (Eri. v. Eth.), paras. 306–17, Part XII(B) (Eri.–Eth. Claims Comm'n 2009) (determining Eritrea's financial liability for violations of the *jus ad bellum*).

26 Under article 39 of the UN Charter, the Security Council may base such actions on a prior determination of the existence of a "threat to the peace, breach of the peace, or act of aggression." UN Charter, arts. 39, 41, 42, 53. On Council activity in this regard, *see* S.C. Res. 82 (1950); S.C. Res. 217 (1965); S.C. Res. 678 (1990); S.C. Res. 836 (1994); S.C. Res. 958 (1994); S.C. Res. 940 (1994); S.C. Res. 1973 (2011). Christine Gray, International Law and the Use of Force chs. 7–8 (3rd edn 2008). *See also* UN Security Council, *Sanctions Committees*, www.un.org/sc/committees (last visited Aug. 8, 2013). On the illegality of fighting against UN forces, *see* Section 3.2.2 of Chapter 3 above.

27 As discussed in Chapter 6, it would be particularly absurd to take such a position in the case of a Security Council decision, given that the latter can trigger the use of violence against the very military institution that would be under threat by disobedience.

28 This is referenced briefly in in Section 1.3 of Chapter 1 above.

29 *See* The Global Campaign for Ratification and Implementation of the Kampala Amendments on the Crime of Aggression ["GCRIKACA"], *Implementation Documents*, http://crimeofaggression.info/resourcessearch/implementation-documents (last visited June 1, 2017).

United States since 1980 after two centuries of inactivity previously.[30] Even when a domestic statute does not incorporate the crime of aggression, common law might do so in those states in which it applies.[31]

There is, however, a key difference between the competence of such domestic courts to exercise jurisdiction over the crime of aggression and their competence in exercising jurisdiction over disobedience claims rooted in the *jus ad bellum*. Any domestic criminal case would almost certainly occur after the war, thus avoiding the danger of judicial interference in the executive's capacity to fight the war in the moment. If such a court were to err in its legal interpretation, this would have profound consequences for the individual defendant, but that defendant would have the right of appeal and there would be no time pressure on the case. In contrast, if a court were to rule erroneously in favor of a soldier's right to disobey in the early stages of a conflict, this could cause military chaos and mass disobedience – a danger not entirely obviated by the prospect of appeal. Given the immediate, irreversible, and grave consequences of any judicial error, the question of competence is more fraught in the disobedience scenario.

Even that distinction, however, is not fundamental. As examined further in Chapters 9 and 10, there are ways of protecting disobedience retrospectively, after the war. Under such a system, the risk of domestic judicial error

[30] Alien Tort Claims Act of 1789, 28 U.S.C. , § 1350; PETER HENNER, HUMAN RIGHTS AND THE ALIEN TORT STATUTE (2009); Katherine Gallagher, *Civil Litigation and Transnational Business: An Alien Tort Statute Primer*, 8 J. INT'L CRIM. JUSTICE 745 (2010); Lawfare, *Lawfare Archive: Alien Tort Statute: Litigation*, www.lawfareblog.com/category/alien-tort-statute/alien-tort-statute-litigation. This particular cascade of litigation has been limited in significant ways (especially with respect to abuses abroad by foreign entities) by the *Kiobel* decision, but the statute will continue to be an important basis for litigation. Kiobel v. Royal Dutch Petroleum Co., 133 S.Ct. 1659 (2013). On aggression: German courts and public prosecutors have been among the most active, addressing the issue on multiple occasions and not always ruling in favor of the government. *See* Section 10.2 in Chapter 10 below. Arguing against domestic jurisdiction, *see, for example*, YORAM DINSTEIN, WAR, AGGRESSION, AND SELF-DEFENCE 155 (5th edn 2012); Anthony A. D'Amato, Harvey L. Gould, and Larry D. Woods, *War Crimes and Vietnam: The "Nuremberg Defense" and the Military Service Resister*, 57 CAL. L. REV. 1055 (1969).

[31] UK Attorney General Lord Goldsmith wrote to Prime Minister Tony Blair in advance of the Iraq invasion that the crime of aggression may be part of UK courts' common law jurisdiction. Memorandum from Lord Peter Goldsmith to Prime Minister Tony Blair, Iraq: Resolution 1441, para. 34 (Mar. 7, 2003) [hereinafter Goldsmith to Blair – 7 March]. This position was later rejected, *obiter dictum*, by the House of Lords. R v. Jones [2006] UKHL 16 (Lord Bingham of Cornhill), para. 23. The High Court of England and Wales has since held that there is no prospect of the Supreme Court departing from the position that there is no crime of aggression in the common law. R (AL Rabbat) v. Westminster Magistrates' Court and others [2017] EWHC 1969.

would be no more (and possibly less) concerning in the disobedience context than in the context of the criminal punishment of a state leader.

In short, the necessity account cannot rest on an objection to the competence of courts or other bodies (domestic or international) to rule on the *jus ad bellum*. It is a competence that many already have. The heart of the necessity argument must focus instead on the risks of *soldiers* making the initial determination not to fight, even if that decision would ultimately be subject to competent judicial review.

8.3 Military Functioning and Soldiers Making Evaluative Decisions

That, after all, is the standard scenario. At the moment of disobedience, the soldier needs to make her own judgment on the *jus ad bellum* status of her war. That imperative is obviated only on the very rare occasion that the Security Council or another international authority has already made the relevant determination.

The need for the soldier to evaluate, of course, is not unique to the *jus ad bellum*. A soldier ordered to attack a particular target must also determine for herself in that moment whether doing so would violate the *jus in bello*. The legal standard is stated in advance, but its application to her situation requires individual judgment. And yet, in that context, she has not just the right, but also the duty to disobey illegal orders.

The necessity account must explain how *in bello* and *ad bellum* disobedience would raise qualitatively different institutional challenges in this respect. The distinction cannot rest on the typically divergent epistemic posture of the soldier in the two scenarios. It is true that limiting the duty to disobey to orders that *manifestly* violate the *jus in bello* is supposed to make her recognition of the need to disobey quasi-automatic, thus minimizing the need for deliberation.[32] However, the same quasi-automaticity could apply also in the rare case of a patently aggressive

[32] Mark Osiel, Obeying Orders 115 (1999); *id.*, at 137–39; Ronald A. Anderson, Wharton's Criminal Law and Procedure, § 118, at 258 (1957). Moshe Halbertal, *The Goldstone Illusion: What the UN Report Gets Wrong about Gaza – and War*, New Republic (Nov. 6, 2009) ("moral considerations have to be an essential part of military training. If there is no time for moral reflection in battle, then moral reflection must be accomplished before battle, and drilled into the soldiers who will have to answer for their actions after battle"). On bright line rules, *see* W. Hays Parks, *Part IX of the ICRC "Direct Participation in Hostilities" Study: No Mandate, No Expertise, and Legally Incorrect*, 42 NYU J. Int'l Law & Politics 769, 810 (2010).

war.[33] Moreover, even that standard does not eliminate the need for deliberation. An American soldier ordered to waterboard a detainee in 2002 would have needed to consider whether waterboarding was *manifestly* illegal, even if she was highly confident that it was in fact illegal.[34]

Of course, assuming her judgment on the latter point to have been correct, such a soldier would have had a legally cognizable *right* to disobey under international law, whether or not the order rose to the level of triggering a *duty* to disobey.[35] But this raises a further question: why would *protecting* soldiers who refuse to fight in aggressive wars that are not patently illegal from their perspective involve an institutional challenge different from that posed by protecting disobedience to orders that violate the *jus in bello*, but that are also not patently illegal?

The answer is not that the distributions of soldiers' epistemic postures on the *ad bellum* and *in bello* questions look very different. Regardless of proportion, each regime has clear cases and each has ambiguous cases. Instead, the key is a divergence in what protected disobedience entails, individually and institutionally in the two realms.

Individually, a right to protection in the two domains would have very different implications. If *jus ad bellum* disobedience were protected and a soldier were to disobey correctly on those grounds, she would ordinarily gain the right to exit armed conflict altogether.[36] In contrast, a soldier who

[33] Among the most obvious marginal *jus in bello* cases is that of illegal interrogation. *See infra* note 34.

[34] It had, after all, been authorized within the administration. Memorandum from Jay S. Bybee, Assistant Attorney General, Office of Legal Counsel, to John Rizzo, Acting General Counsel, Central Intelligence Agency, Interrogation of al Qaeda Operative (Aug. 1, 2002) [hereinafter Bybee, Interrogation of al Qaeda Operative]. *Cf.* Daniel Kanstroom, *On "Waterboarding": Legal Interpretation and the Continuing Struggle for Human Rights*, 32 B.C. INT'L & COMP. L. REV. 203, 216 (2009); Evan Wallach, *Drop by Drop: Forgetting the History of Water Torture in US Courts*, 45 COLUM. J. TRANSNAT'L L. 468, 472 (2007).

[35] *See* Sections 1.2–1.3 of Chapter 1 above.

[36] The exception to this would be if his state were fighting multiple independent wars simultaneously. This is most likely for a major power. Notably, at least some soldiers who refused to fight in the United States' war in Iraq from 2003 onwards indicated a full willingness to fight in Afghanistan (indeed, some already had). *See, e.g.*, MATTHEW GUTMANN & CATHERINE LUTZ, BREAKING RANKS: IRAQ VETERANS SPEAK OUT AGAINST THE WAR 54 (2010); James Dao, *War and Conscience: Expanding the Definition of Conscientious Objection*, NY TIMES BLOG: AT WAR – NOTES FROM THE FRONT LINES (Nov. 10, 2010), http://atwar.blogs.nytimes.com/2010/11/10/war-and-conscience-expanding-the-definition-of-conscientious-objection; Nancy Sherman, *Big Think Interview* (Apr. 23, 2012), http://bigthink.com/videos/big-think-interview-with-nancy-sherman.

disobeys correctly on *jus in bello* grounds has a right not to be forced to perform the specific act in question, but may be forced to continue to fight in the war.[37] Three factors explain why this means that disobedience protection on *jus ad bellum* grounds would pose a graver threat to *lawful* military functioning than does disobedience protection on *jus in bello* grounds.

The first goes to judgment. War is hell.[38] For many soldiers on both sides, exit cannot come soon enough. If escape without penalty or dishonor were a possibility, motivated cognitive bias might cause such soldiers to believe that the conditions necessary for that exit obtain, despite a lack of significant supporting evidence, or even perhaps in the face of objectively superior countervailing evidence.[39]

Therefore, permitting disobedience on *jus ad bellum* grounds may carry the risk of influencing soldiers overwhelmed by war's hell to refuse to fight in *lawful* wars, their judgment distorted by the desperate hope to extricate themselves honorably and without punishment.[40] That tendency towards a mistaken belief in a lawful war's illegality could be exacerbated by cynicism born of exposure to the massive human waste of even "good" wars.[41]

To be sure, there are strong countervailing forces. Soldiers fighting a wrongful war may fall prey to the common moral delusion that their extreme self-sacrifice entails the honor and righteousness of their action.[42] In that sense, the hell of war could actually strengthen participating

[37] Although there are cases of protected *jus in bello* disobedience that do involve protecting the soldier's total exit from armed conflict, these are rare and involve considerable hurdles beyond simply refusing and stating a legal claim. For example, soldiers who seek refugee status to avoid following orders that violate the *jus in bello* do thereby escape the conflict altogether, but they must somehow get to a potential asylum state, they are vindicated only if they would not have found protection in their domestic courts, and, even if successful, they take on all the considerable burdens of being a refugee.

[38] For Walzer, this phrase, made famous by General William Tecumseh Sherman, is the starting point for moral thinking about war. WALZER, JUW, *supra* note 7, at 26–30.

[39] PETER L. STROMBERG ET AL., THE TEACHING OF ETHICS IN THE MILITARY 30 (1982) (on the necessity of obedience for those "working under outrageously adverse conditions or risking their lives"); OSIEL, *supra* note 32, at 65; ALAN DONAGAN, THE THEORY OF MORALITY 207 (1977) ("nearly everybody's judgment is disturbed by the anticipation of calamity").

[40] *See generally* Rasyid Sanitioso, Ziva Kunda, & Geoffrey T. Fong, *Motivated Recruitment of Autobiographical Memories*, 59 J. PERSONALITY & SOCIAL PSYCHOLOGY 229, 229 (1990).

[41] *See, e.g.*, CHRISTIAN G. APPY, WORKING CLASS WAR: AMERICAN COMBAT SOLDIERS AND VIETNAM 8 (1993).

[42] MOSHE HALBERTAL, ON SACRIFICE 68, 77–78, 89–90 (2012).

soldiers' belief in the virtue of fighting. Alternatively, or additionally, having followed their initial orders to deploy, soldiers may develop a strong cognitive bias in favor of affirming that initial decision.[43] Others may be motivated to believe their leaders because they take their own success to depend on that of their state,[44] or simply because their patriotism demands trust in their government.[45] And, supplementing all of this is the ordinary predilection to obey an authority even in the absence of coercion, and even when the demanded action appears plainly wrongful.[46]

The net effect of these competing factors will vary across individual combatants. If disobedience on *jus ad bellum* grounds were permitted, it may well be that most soldiers would still have an aggregate bias towards participating in lawful and even unlawful wars. However, a plausible case can be made that a non-negligible number of soldiers offered the prospect of legally protected escape from war and jaded by its horrors might be biased towards believing that the conditions of that protection obtain, even in the absence of adequate evidence for that position. The perceived nobility of patriotic sacrifice notwithstanding, when soldiers flee battle, they do the natural thing.[47]

The second mechanism by which protected *jus ad bellum* disobedience could undermine military functioning in lawful wars is through creating decision paralysis in battle. In addition to motivating exit, the hellish features of war – profound fear for oneself and one's comrades, on the one hand, and the moral anguish of inflicting violence, on the other – can create panic among those involved, making it difficult to act effectively.[48]

[43] Leon Fesstinger, A Theory of Cognitive Dissonance 128–34 (1957) (after making a decision individuals tend to suppress or manipulate information that casts doubt on that decision).

[44] *Cf.* Steven L. Neuberg & Susan T. Fiske, *Motivational Influences on Impression Formation: Outcome Dependency, Accuracy-Driven Attention, and Individuating Processes*, 53 J. Pers. & Soc. Psychol. 431 (1987).

[45] *See* Chapter 6 above. *See also* McMahan, *supra* note 12, at 119–21.

[46] Stanley Milgram, Obedience to Authority: An Experimental View (1974). *See also* David Luban, Legal Ethics and Human Dignity 240–53 (2007) [hereinafter Luban, LEHD].

[47] As Ryan observes, they do it even in wars widely deemed just and worth fighting. Ryan, *Democratic Duty*, *supra* note 17, at 35.

[48] Osiel, *supra* note 32, at 64–65; Henry Shue, *Laws of War, Morality, and International Politics*, 26 Leiden J. Intl L. 271, 275 (2013). On paralyzing fear, *see, for example*, Maj. Gregory A. Daddis, *Understanding Fear's Effect on Unit Effectiveness*, 84 Military Rev. 22 (2004). On the difficulty of killing, *see* Lt. Col. Dave Grossman, On Killing, at XXXV, 4–29, 74, 88, 92, 252 (rev. edn 2009); David Hardan, ed., The Moral and Existential Dilemmas of the Israeli Soldier 35, 41 (1985); SLA Marshall, Men

The standard institutional prophylactic against that danger is a system of mechanistic obedience.[49] From the first days of training, even insignificant forms of insubordination are punished so as to drill anti-deliberative and automatic compliance.[50] Introducing complex normative evaluation into the practice of soldiering in war might be thought to weaken that mechanism, creating the conditions for decision paralysis, and risking military breakdown.[51]

As noted above, this danger arises also with respect to the right and duty to disobey commands that violate the *jus in bello*.[52] However, empowering soldiers to disobey on *jus ad bellum* grounds could pose even greater challenges to institutional functioning. The *jus ad bellum* status of a war affects the normative status of every act within the war and is open to at least some questions in the vast majority of wars. Consequently, the prospect of protected *jus ad bellum* disobedience is likely to raise the specter of choice in a more insidious way, potentially doing more than does protected *in bello* disobedience to undermine the automaticity that enables effective, coordinated action in the chaos of conflict.

AGAINST FIRE 79 (1947) (2000). Adding to this problem is the general clouding of judgment in battle. CARL VON CLAUSEWITZ, 2 ON WAR 180 (1832) (Michael Howard & Peter Pare, eds. & trans., 1976).

49 On automaticity overcoming fear and mental paralysis, *see, for example*, TR FEHRENBACH, THIS KIND OF WAR 246 (1963); J. GLENN GRAY, THE WARRIORS: REFLECTIONS ON MEN IN BATTLE 102 (1959). *See also* GROSSMAN, *supra* note 48, at 143; MARSHALL, *supra* note 48, at 82; Daddis, *supra* note 48, at 24–26. But *see* JOHN KEEGAN, THE FACE OF BATTLE 324 (1976) (the mechanics of modern battle actually compel the soldier to fight, rather than paralyzing him); OSIEL, *supra* note 32, at 171, 211–21, 227, 275 (arguing that the threat of penal sanction does not contribute to efficacy in war – soldiers empowered to take initiative, small group loyalties, and training are all more important than the threat of punishment).

50 *See supra* note 18 and accompanying text. MORRIS JANOWITZ, THE PROFESSIONAL SOLDIER 39 (1960). On total institutions, *see, for example*, GOFFMAN, *supra* note 8. On stifling deliberation, *see supra* notes 1–9. *See also* CHRIS HEDGES, WHAT EVERY PERSON SHOULD KNOW ABOUT WAR 12 (2003) (on the breaking down of individuality and the emphasis on conformity and obedience in military training).

51 *See, e.g.*, Halbertal, *The Goldstone Illusion*, *supra* note 32 (noting that soldiers respond to his advocacy of the ethical code of conduct by asking: "Do you want to say that, before I open fire, I have to go through all these moral dilemmas and calculations? It will be completely paralyzing. Nobody can fight a war in such a straitjacket!"); W. Hays Parks, *Part IX of the ICRC "Direct Participation in Hostilities" Study: No Mandate, No Expertise, and Legally Incorrect*, 42 INT'L LAW & POLITICS 769, 810 (2010); Eckhardt, *supra* note 1, at 693.

52 *See supra* note 18.

Nonetheless, the dangers of judgment distortion and choice paralysis alone would affect only a portion of soldiers in any given conflict. Strong countervailing biases push in the opposite direction, and the threat of punishment for those who refuse to fight in a lawful war would be a deterrent.[53] As such, these factors would be unlikely to cripple a force fighting a lawful war. However, their initial impact is likely to be amplified by the third and most significant mechanism: the breakdown of unit cohesion.

There is good reason to believe that the most important factor in the typical soldier's will to fight is not fear of punishment, patriotism, belief in the war's cause, or adherence to the martial virtues of courage and sacrifice, but a sense of obligation towards beloved comrades.[54] At the heart of that obligation is a reciprocal commitment to stand together and never to leave a brother or sister behind.[55] If disobedience on *jus ad bellum* grounds were permitted (or, indeed, required) a small proportion of disobedient soldiers could shatter the cohesion underpinning that norm, causing disillusionment among those that deploy (or remain), and undermining the will of the latter to keep fighting, potentially initiating a disobedience cascade.[56]

When disobedience is warranted, the prospect of this kind of cascade is highly desirable. It is one reason for requiring disobedience to *jus in bello* crimes even among those perpetrators whose refusal would have no

[53] Indeed both of those factors are important in minimizing mistaken *jus in bello* disobedience to lawful orders.

[54] Grossman, *supra* note 48, at 149–55; US Army Field Manual 6–22.5, Combat Stress (June 23, 2000), at §§ 2–5; J. Glenn Gray, *supra* note 49, at 91; Tim O'Brien, The Things they Carried 16 (1990) [hereinafter O'Brien, TTTC]; Osiel, *supra* note 32, at 212–21; John Keegan & Richard Holmes, Soldiers: A History of Men in Battle 52–53, 265, 273 (1985). *See generally* Ben Shalit, The Psychology of Conflict and Combat (1988).

[55] Despite dissenting from the majority in *Parker* v. *Levy*, Justice Stewart accepted, "The internal loyalty and mutual reliance indispensable to the ultimate effectiveness of any military organization can exist only among people who can be counted on to do their duty." Parker v. Levy, 417 US 733, 788 (1974) (Stewart, J., dissenting). *See also* Nate Rawlings, *The Warrior Ethos: Why We Leave No One Behind*, Time, May 17, 2012.

[56] Osiel, *supra* note 32, at 224–30 (on disobedience contagion, good and bad); R v. Michael Peter Lyons [2011] EWCA (Crim) 2808, para. 39; Gabriel, *supra* note 3, at 60–61; Daddis, *supra* note 48, at 26–27; Hammer, *supra* note 12, at 212 (noting the operational burden arising from conflicts between soldiers on this issue). *But see* Andrew Fiala, Public War, Private Conscience: The Ethics of Political Violence 151, 154 (2010) (arguing that allowing selective conscientious objection would improve unit cohesion, which is disrupted significantly by the presence of soldiers opposed to the war).

impact on the outcome. As Milgram and others have observed, the exemplary refusal of one can provide "the cognitive and motivational conditions" that empower others to overcome the deep urge to obey authority even in the context of clear wrongdoing.[57]

However, if it is correct to worry that *jus ad bellum* disobedience protection would lead to misguided disobedience or choice paralysis for a non-negligible proportion of soldiers, the picture may not be so sanguine. The danger is that that initial wave of disobedience would trigger disobedience cascades in *lawful* wars. With their former brothers and sisters shielded from sanction for leaving them behind (at least until the former's *jus ad bellum* judgment is rejected as mistaken by the relevant authority), the concern is that those who remain will wonder what they are fighting for. Their fraternal bond would be broken, its normative implication nullified. This would only be exacerbated if a court were to rule mistakenly in favor of a disobedient soldier by finding a lawful war to be illegal.

The prospect and application of swift and certain punishment and ostracism for those who refuse is thought by its advocates to prevent the initial wave of mistaken disobedience and choice paralysis and to deter potential second movers and thus stifle the momentum of any such cascade.[58] Within the unit, those who disobey can be dismissed as outlaws, perhaps even augmenting the unity among those who remain.[59]

In sum, the institutional necessity account holds that requiring or even protecting disobedience on *jus ad bellum* grounds would instigate misguided disobedience among those jaded by the stupidity of conflict and desperate to escape war's hell, paralyze others with the prospect of choice in battle, and, most fundamentally, shatter unit cohesion and trigger disobedience cascades. The result would be a heightened risk of military breakdown in lawful wars. If that is right (and it can be assumed so for the sake of argument here), it raises two further questions. What does

[57] Herbert C. Kelman & V. Lee Hamilton, Crimes of Obedience: Toward a Social Psychology of Authority and Responsibility 160 (1989); Milgram, *supra* note 46, at 119.

[58] United States ex rel. Toth v. Quarles, 350 U.S. 11, 22 (1955); Letter from Abraham Lincoln to New York Democrats (June 12, 1863), *in* The Political Thought of Abraham Lincoln (Richard Current, ed., 1967); Keegan & Holmes, *supra* note 54, at 55. *See also* Osiel, *supra* note 32, at 51–52 (virtually all militaries provide for urgent summary discipline in the field).

[59] O'Brien, TTTC, *supra* note 54, at 20–21.

this mean for the legal protection of disobedience? And, what does it mean for whether the soldier ought to refuse to fight from the legal point of view?

8.4 International Law, Global Human Security, and Military Competence

Some might object that an international rule on disobedience that would weaken states' capacity to mobilize for lawful wars while more severely weakening their capacity to wage unlawful wars would be a good thing.[60] In a world of generally law-abiding states or an effective global government, it probably would be. The use of force would decline, and the success of illegal force would likely decline further.

However, those conditions do not obtain. There is no global sovereign, and, although various factors (including international institutions, trade, and normative internalization) bolster compliance with international law,[61] self-help and deterrence remain essential to upholding the strict legal protection against aggressive force.[62] Perhaps uniquely among legal regimes, international law depends fundamentally on the strength of its primary subjects (states) for the advance of one of its core ends (peace and global human security).[63]

A consequence of this is that a *jus ad bellum* disobedience rule that would undermine compliant states' capacities in the crucial areas of defensive force and deterrence could actually facilitate aggression by states willing to obstruct the application of any disobedience protections to their own troops and keen to exploit compliant states' military weakness. Conversely, empowering states to force their soldiers to fight in all wars (including criminally aggressive wars) may be an essential part of preserving states' capacities to respond to aggression effectively and to

[60] Advocates of selective conscientious objection have sometimes asserted that it would reduce wrongful violence. McMahan, *supra* note 12, at 97–101.

[61] On the factors contributing to compliance, *see* Section 2.1 of Chapter 1, above.

[62] Yitzhak Benbaji, *The Moral Power of Soldiers to Undertake the Duty of Obedience*, 122 Ethics 43, 43–47 (2011). *See also* Lauterpacht, *supra* note 21, at 211 (arguing that the "fundamental deficiency in the legal sanction of the prohibition of illegal recourse to force . . . sets a limit to the operation of legal logic in relation to the consequences of the illegality of the war").

[63] Reisman, *The Quest for World Order*, *supra* note 1, at 374. *See also* Oona Hathaway & Scott J. Shapiro, *Outcasting: Enforcement in Domestic and International Law*, 121 Yale L.J. 252, 302, 305 (2011); Lauterpacht, *supra* note 21, at 211–12.

deter it before it happens.[64] Paradoxically, failing to protect soldiers from being forced to fight in illegal wars may lead to fewer illegal wars.[65]

If the empirical premises hold, the institutional necessity account provides a normative defense of the extant regime's treatment of soldiers that is rooted in the very moral foundations of international law. Soldiers may be forced by law to kill in criminal wars because that structure is necessary to strengthen the prohibition of precisely those wars and limit their incidence.

8.5 The Enduring Culpability of Obedient Participation in Illegal Wars

The necessity account offered above is not without flaws. The chapters that follow spotlight its weaknesses and show why it cannot provide a comprehensive defense of international law's failure to protect soldiers when they refuse to fight in criminal wars. But even if it were to obtain without caveat, the necessity account would not wash soldiers' hands of guilt from the legal point of view when they kill and maim in criminal wars. Instead, it would explain why international law cannot protect them from criminal punishment when they do right by the law's own lights – an equilibrium in which soldiers are left to suffer punishment or to bear the normative remainder created by international law's weakness. Or so I argue in what follows.

Against this unsettling assessment, one might contend that "a direct implication of the right of states to have obedient armies" (as a necessary foundation of global human security) is that soldiers have a "moral right

[64] Benbaji, *supra* note 62, at 59 (arguing that for the global security system "to be morally optimal states must be able to expect their soldiers to obey their commands"). Complicating the deterrence claim here, it is worth noting that deterrence is not necessarily achieved with the same means that would be useful in actually fighting a war. *See, e.g.*, Glenn H. Snyder, *Deterrence and Defense*, *in* The Use of Force: Military Power and International Politics 25 (Robert J. Art & Kenneth N. Waltz, eds., 3rd edn 1988). Nonetheless, for most states, an effective military is a key aspect of deterrence.

[65] This position has a long history. Thomas Hobbes, Leviathan 78 (1651) (Edwin Curley, ed., Hackett 1994). The role of deterrence in preserving stability remains an important principle in international security studies (for influential work in international strategy on the challenges of effective deterrence and coercion, *see* Thomas C. Schelling, Arms and Influence (1966)), although it is also recognized that states' efforts to achieve deterrent ends can have perversely destabilizing effects by provoking militarism in other threatened states (the realists' classic security dilemma).

to undertake the duty of obedience."[66] On such an argument, the normative grounds for preserving military institutional functioning restructure the normative framework within which the members of those institutions act. If anyone outside the military were to kill or inflict violence in an aggressive war, he would engage in culpable wrongdoing from the legal point of view, for all of the reasons canvassed in the previous chapters. However, the soldier's commitment to obey and the importance of that commitment and its fulfillment to institutional functioning mean that her moral framework is exhausted by a combination of institutional obedience and compliance with the *jus in bello*.

This notion of a separate and narrow soldier's morality defined principally by obedience is a familiar one.[67] In contrast to the associative and political obligation arguments discussed previously, this version is rooted in the cosmopolitan value of global human security. The point, as Michael Reisman articulates in a broader commentary on executive branch obedience, is not, "my country right or wrong," but rather, "a setback ... for my country [caused by disobedience when it violates international law] will actually spell a setback for international law [by undermining government institutions, and catalyzing state breakdown]."[68]

The degree to which this kind of thinking is compatible with the posture adopted at Nuremberg is debatable. On the one hand, in the course of explaining the non-liability of even high-ranking members of the military for the crime of aggression, the NMT in the *High Command* case did identify "rigid discipline" as "necessary for and peculiar to military organization."[69] On the other hand, in the very next paragraph, the tribunal retreated explicitly from the implication that that institutional context could wash obedient officers' hands of guilt, reasoning that disobedience "would have been eminently desirable ... the honourable

66 Benbaji, *supra* note 62, at 59.

67 HUNTINGTON, *supra* note 3, at 73; Vice-Admiral James Bond Stockdale, USN (ret.), *Foreword* to RICHARD A. GABRIEL, TO SERVE WITH HONOR: A TREATISE ON MILITARY ETHICS AND THE WAY OF THE SOLDIER, at xiii, xiv (1982); Gen. Douglas MacArthur, Speech to the Corps of Cadets at the US Military Academy at West Point, NY: Duty, Honor, Country (May 12, 1962).

68 Reisman, *The Quest for World Order*, *supra* note 1, at 374. Although Reisman suggests the application of this principle to all state agents (again, starting from the position that they are already ensconced in institutional roles), the case might be thought strongest for soldiers, given the supreme importance of obedience to military functioning.

69 United States v. von Leeb, 11 TRIALS OF WAR CRIMINALS BEFORE THE NUERNBERG MILITARY TRIBUNALS UNDER CONTROL COUNCIL LAW NO. 10, at 462, 489 (1949).

and righteous thing to do," and terming the officers' obedient participation in the war "morally reprimandable," albeit not a legally established crime.[70] Moreover, for the most senior military leaders in Nazi Germany, of course, the "good soldier" excuse was insufficient even to provide a shield against criminal liability for aggression at the IMT.[71]

Compatibility with Nuremberg aside, claimed role moralities of the kind suggested above demand robust justification independent from that underpinning the institution that defines the role.[72] In this case, the reasons not to provide legal protection to soldiers who disobey on *jus ad bellum* grounds are not reasons to hold that soldiers can wash their hands with obedience when they fight in aggressive wars. Two factors explain the distinction.

First, there is a deep normative difference between inflicting wrongs to achieve a valued end (including upholding a valuable institution) and declining to regulate such wrongs where doing so would be counterproductive. Second, soldiers adopting a maxim of disobedience when confident of a war's illegality would not plausibly pose the institutional risks that a system of legal protection would for those who disobey in illegal wars.

The first major distinction is the difference between inflicting wrongs and failing to regulate them. International law does not permit, much less mandate, the wrongful killing inflicted in an aggressive war. Quite the opposite. That killing is prohibited via the *jus ad bellum* and the criminalization of aggression. States and leaders can be held accountable for it.

[70] *Id.*

[71] On the rejection of the "good soldier" excuse for military leaders, *see Judgment* (Oct. 1, 1946), *in* 22 TRIAL OF THE MAJOR WAR CRIMINALS BEFORE THE INTERNATIONAL MILITARY TRIBUNAL 411, 533–36 (1948). *See also* United States v. Göring et al., Trial Transcript of the Morning Session (Aug. 31, 1946), *in* 22 TRIAL OF THE MAJOR WAR CRIMINALS BEFORE THE INTERNATIONAL MILITARY TRIBUNAL 373, 376–77, 380–81, 385 (1948).

[72] Wasserstrom, *supra* note 7, at 34; Virginia Held, *The Division of Moral Labor and the Role of the Lawyer*, *in* THE GOOD LAWYER 60, 66 (David Luban, ed., 1983); Bernard Williams, *Professional Morality and its Dispositions*, *in id.*, at 259, 262; ARTHUR APPLBAUM, ETHICS FOR ADVERSARIES 111 (2000). Military ethicists recognize the importance of being a good person, over being a good soldier; however, the *jus ad bellum* tends not to feature in their analysis on that point. GABRIEL, *supra* note 67, at 8, 24, 39; TONER, *supra* note 3, at 72; Arthur J. Dyck, *Ethical Bases of the Military Profession*, 10 PARAMETERS 39, 44 (1980). The need for robust justification is particularly acute when the purportedly role-justified action involves the grave violation of other persons. APPLBAUM, *supra* note 72, at 7; Wasserstrom, *supra* note 7, at 37; Jeff McMahan, *The Ethics of Killing in War*, 114 ETHICS 693, 705 (2004).

Similarly, the coercion of soldiers into fighting an illegal war is necessarily wrongful by international law's own lights. It is through that coercion that the state and its leader perpetrate the wrongful violence. At most, international law allows for a general practice of obedience enforcement, including refraining from regulating the specific wrongful coercion imposed on those ordered to fight in an aggressive war.

Per the necessity argument, the most coherent rationale for this failure to regulate is neither endorsement nor permission of the specific coercion in question. Instead, it is that this approach regulates optimally the actors engaged in the killing and violence of illegal wars so as to minimize such killing overall. The idea is that a rule granting soldiers a right to disobey on *jus ad bellum* grounds would exacerbate the infliction of wrongful killing and violence more than it would depress the infliction of such wrongs.

At stake on both sides of that evaluation are commensurate harms inflicted by the various subjects of regulation, not by international law or its agents. In that sense, the law is no more intimately involved in the harms perpetrated under the current regime by those who would have refused to fight under a regime with disobedience protection than it would be in the harms that would be perpetrated by those who would exploit such a regime to wage additional wrongful wars. In either case, other actors perpetrate the wrongs, and the question from the legal point of view is how to regulate in a way that minimizes the incidence of those wrongs.

In contrast, the soldier who fights obediently in an aggressive war inflicts directly the wrongful violence that makes aggression a crime. At best, per the role morality argument above, she does so in order to further a good end – the maintenance of the global security system. However, even assuming that her obedience contributes meaningfully to that end (a point called into question below), it is not at all clear that its pursuit is sufficient to wash her hands of the wrongful violence she inflicts.

Certainly, the claim that it is appropriate to refrain from legal protection for those who refuse to fight does not itself entail that soldiers act blamelessly from that perspective when they obey.[73] Those who suffer the soldier's violence are instrumentalized by her action. Those who suffer wrongful harms that could have been prevented had the law protected

[73] Applbaum, *supra* note 72, at 199.

disobedience are not instrumentalized by the law. The former approach to wrongful human violence is incompatible with the broader normative posture of contemporary international law on the issue.

Under the *jus ad bellum*, states and leaders are banned categorically from waging an illegal war, even if doing so would improve global welfare.[74] As part of the humanization process, the *jus in bello*, too, has become regime focused increasingly on categorical prohibitions. Earlier permissions of belligerent reprisals, sieges, and blockades have been reversed or gutted.[75] Torture and the killing of civilians have been banned and criminalized, even when they might have direct and significant salutary consequences, such as the prevention of a terrorist attack or the accelerated conclusion of a war.[76] Efforts to assert exceptions to these bans have been widely rejected as a matter of law, have been limited anyway to the prevention of imminent and overwhelming catastrophe, and have been depicted, even by their advocates, as lesser evils for which perpetrators would appropriately bear a significant burden or taint.[77]

[74] Draft Articles on Responsibility of States for Internationally Wrongful Acts with Commentaries, Rep. of the Int'l Law Comm'n on the Work of its Fifty-Third Session, U.N. Doc. A/56/10, at 80–84 (2001) (commentaries to art. 25; most significantly, art. 25(1)(b) precludes a necessity justification for a violation of an *erga omnes* norm) [hereinafter Articles on State Responsibility with Commentaries]; *cf.* WALZER, JUW, *supra* note 7, at 243–48.

[75] On the illegality of reprisals, or countermeasures (reciprocal violations of the law in response to breach) that harm the human person – what had previously been considered a crucial mechanism of deterrence prior to the rejection of such instrumentalism under the banner of international law's humanization, *see, for example*, Protocol (I) Additional to the Geneva Conventions of 12 August 1949, and Relating to the Protection of Victims of International Armed Conflicts, arts. 20, 51(6), 52(1), 53(c), 54(4), 55(2), 56(1), 75, June 8, 1977, 1125 U.N.T.S. 3 [hereinafter AP I]; JEAN-MARIE HENCKAERTS & LOUISE DOSWALD-BECK, 1 CUSTOMARY INTERNATIONAL HUMANITARIAN LAW 513–29 (2005) (Rules 145–48); Articles on State Responsibility with commentaries, *supra* note 74, at 131–34 (commentary to art. 50). This rejection of the instrumentalism of reprisals has occurred despite evidence of their efficacy in achieving the objective of improving compliance. *See* James D. Morrow, *When Do States Follow the Laws of War?*, 101 AM. POL. SCI. REV. 559 (2007).

[76] *See* Convention against Torture and Other Cruel, Inhuman or Degrading Treatment or Punishment, art. 2, Feb. 4, 1984, U.N. Doc. A/39/51; AP I, *supra* note 75, art. 51; ICC Statute, *supra* note 11, art. 8.

[77] Advocating exceptions to bans on attacking civilians or engaging in torture, *see* WALZER, JUW, *supra* note 7, at 259–61; Legality of Nuclear Weapons, Advisory Opinion, 1996 I.C.J. Rep. 226 (July 8), para. 105(2)(E); Public Committee against Torture in Israel v. State of Israel [1999] H.C.J. 5100/94 (Isr.), para. 34 [hereinafter *PCATI Torture* Case]. On the question of bearing a moral burden or taint here, *see* WALZER, JUW, *supra* note 7, at 325; Oren Gross, *The Prohibition on Torture and the Limits of the Law*, *in* TORTURE:

In the contexts in which the contemporary international law of war does incorporate and permit instrumentalism with respect to killing and human violence that permission extends only to the unintended, collateral consequences of an attack on a legitimate objective.[78] Even then, such collateral violence is subject to case-specific limits – it must be analyzed in each instance for its proportionality to the military objective and for whether all feasible measures have been taken to ensure its minimization.[79]

The killings and violence that occur in an aggressive war are in no way akin to the exceptional case of permissible collateral damage. They are the immediate objective of the aggressor troops' actions (not a collateral consequence); there is no calculation as to whether participating obediently in that deliberately lethal violence is proportionate and narrowly tailored to the objective of maintaining the global security system; and there is no systemic minimization of the harm inflicted on combatants fighting against aggression.

In short, a role morality that would exonerate the soldier on the basis that her obedience would have salutary long-term institutional consequences assumes a radical consequentialism that lacks support elsewhere in international law's approach to wrongful killing and human violence. If this could be defended at all, the stakes would plainly have to weigh heavily and unambiguously on the direction of obedience. Whatever the

A COLLECTION 229 (Sanford Levinson, ed., 2004); Jean Bethke Elshtain, *Reflection on the Problem of "Dirty Hands", in id.*, at 77. Similarly, the Israeli Supreme Court, although recognizing the use of certain banned interrogation techniques in the case of a ticking bomb scenario to be the lesser evil, nonetheless insisted that those acts remain criminal, and that the individual perpetrator put herself at the mercy of the courts in invoking the necessity defense post hoc. *PCATI Torture* Case, *supra* note 77, paras. 35–38.

[78] This incorporation into the laws of war of a doctrine of double effect approach has itself been subject to moral critique on the grounds that it seems to place too much normative weight on the fact that the civilian deaths are unintended. *See, e.g.*, David Rodin, *Terrorism without Intention*, 114 ETHICS 752 (2004); Nicholas Wheeler, *Dying for Enduring Freedom: Accepting Responsibility for Civilian Casualties in the War against Terrorism*, 16 INT'L REL. 206, 209 (2002) (terming proportionality the "Achilles heel of just war theory").

[79] *See* AP I, *supra* note 75, arts. 51(4–5), 57. Disproportionate attacks can give rise to individual criminal liability. *See, e.g.*, ICC Statute, *supra* note 11, art. 8(2)(b)(iv). However, prosecuting individuals for disproportionate attacks has proven a difficult task. *See, e.g.*, Prosecutor v. Gotovina, Case No. IT-06-90-A, Appeals Judgment, paras. 1–5, 49–84 (Int'l Crim. Trib. for the Former Yugoslavia, Nov. 16, 2012); *id.* (Agius, J., dissenting), paras. 5, 11–14, 19–46.

threshold in that regard, it would be significantly higher than is the threshold for justifying international law's failure to protect those who refuse to fight in illegal wars. For the reasons that follow, the former, more demanding threshold is almost certainly not met.

The core reason provided above to worry that soldiers might systematically misperceive lawful wars as illegal is that their judgment may be distorted by the prospect that refusal to fight in an aggressive war would be protected, thus offering an honorable path out of war's hell. However, in the absence of such protection, there is no reason to believe that soldiers would be motivated to view their wars as illegal. On the contrary, they are likely to be affected exclusively by the countervailing biases rooted in nationalism, acceptance of authority, cognitive bias regarding the decision to deploy, and the prospect of punishment for disobedience.[80] In that context, it is highly likely that soldiers would overestimate significantly the *lawfulness* of their wars, even when the facts point in the opposite direction.

In this context, soldiers who disobey only when confident of their war's illegality would very rarely, if ever, disobey in lawful wars. The worry about distorted judgment – a key premise of the necessity account – simply does not translate to a role morality of obedience. Moreover, in the rare cases in which soldiers do disobey mistakenly when confident of the war's illegality, this is not likely to destroy unit cohesion and trigger disobedience cascades. As discussed above, a key premise of the necessity account is that punishing or ostracizing those who disobey is effective at deterring others from following suit and maintaining unit solidarity among those that remain, thus stemming erroneous disobedience cascades.

If that is right, those who disobey on *jus ad bellum* grounds in a system in which they will face punishment and ostracism for doing so can be confident not only that they are relatively unlikely to be biased towards finding their war to be illegal, but also that if they were to disobey erroneously, that mistake would not likely be amplified through the breakdown of unit cohesion. As with the thousands in the US and UK militaries each year that refuse to fight for any number of reasons, such soldiers' disobedience would have no prospect of protection or vindication.[81] They would be predictably punished and cast out from the group,

[80] *See supra* notes 42–46 and accompanying text.

[81] *Army Desertion Rate Soaring*, CBS News (Nov. 16, 2007) (reporting desertion rates of 4,698 in Fiscal Year 2007 and 3,301 in Fiscal Year 2006), www.cbsnews.com/news/army-desertion-rate-soaring; Sig Christenson, *US Army Desertion Rate at Lowest since*

deterring others and potentially enhancing the cohesion of those that remain. The effect of their disobedience ought not be any bigger than the effect currently triggered whenever soldiers desert for any other reason.

The danger of choice paralysis and the related issues of decision fatigue, and moral distraction might be thought to provide a stronger basis for a role morality of obedience. People are not "frictionless deliberators."[82] There is good reason to believe that both decision-making and self-control deteriorate as individuals make more choices.[83] This raises the prospect that role participants making moral decisions that go beyond their core competence might distract them from performing well on the moral tasks that they could perform well.[84] This risk may be especially acute in combat, given the high risk of choice paralysis there.

To guard against such dangers, Luban advocates a presumptively narrower normative focus according to role, to be overcome only if external considerations are particularly clear and strong.[85] In war, this might mean that soldiers who do not have overwhelmingly clear, unsought, and dispositive reasons to believe their wars to be illegal ought to cabin the *jus ad bellum*, focusing instead on the role values of obedience and compliance with the *jus in bello*.[86] The thought is that

Vietnam, AGENCE FRANCE PRESSE, Nov. 7, 2011(reporting (an unusually low) 1,202 deserting in Fiscal Year 2010, following a sharp economic downturn in the United States). On desertion rates in the British Military, *see* Letter from DCDS Personnel Secretariat, Ministry of Defence, to unknown, Freedom of Information Act: Reference: 20-08-2010-160944-005 (Sept. 13, 2010) (reporting between two and over three thousand deserters per year from the British military during the Iraq War, dropping significantly in 2010), www.gov.uk/government/uploads/system/uploads/attachment_data/file/16803/FOI20082010160944005_AWOL_20002010.pdf. On desertion generally, *see, for example*, ROBERT FANTINA, DESERTION AND THE AMERICAN SOLDIER 1776–2006 (2006).

82 DANIEL MARKOVITS, A MODERN LEGAL ETHICS 141–51 (2010); MICHAEL BRATMAN, INTENTION, PLANS, AND PRACTICAL REASON 28 (1987).

83 *See, e.g.*, Kathleen D. Vohs et al., *Making Choices Impairs Subsequent Self-Control: A Limited-Resource Account of Decision Making, Self-Regulation, and Active Initiative*, 94 J. PERSONALITY & SOC. PSYCH. 883 (2008) (on the fatiguing impact of making choices).

84 *See* Held, *supra* note 72, at 64–65; Janina Dill & Henry Shue, *Limiting the Killing in War: Military Necessity and the St. Petersburg Assumption*, 26 ETHICS & INT'L AFFAIRS 311, 325 (2012).

85 LUBAN, LEHD, *supra* note 46, at 13–14 n.20. *See also* DOROTHY EMMET, RULES, ROLES, AND RELATIONS 147, 181–82 (1966).

86 *Cf.* Dill & Shue, *supra* note 84, at 325; David Luban, *Knowing When Not to Fight*, *in* OXFORD HANDBOOK OF THE ETHICS OF WAR (Helen Frowe & Seth Lazar, eds., forthcoming) [hereinafter Luban, *Knowing When*].

soldiers that do this are likely to perform better morally than if they were to be overstretched by trying to satisfy these demands *and* that of complying with the *jus ad bellum*.

The difficulty with this line of argument is that the dangers of choice paralysis, decision fatigue, and normative distraction apply plausibly only when soldiers contemplate *jus ad bellum* questions during a combat deployment. But many soldiers have time to engage in *jus ad bellum* deliberation prior to, or between, deployments to the combat zone. A soldier who considers the *jus ad bellum* merits of the war in advance, decides whether to deploy, and then cabins the issue once deployed should be no more weakened in her capacities for obedience and *jus in bello* compliance during battle than would be a soldier who ignores the *jus ad bellum* altogether. In cases in which the war's illegality is so manifestly clear as to require no deliberative reflection, the presumptive cabining of the *jus ad bellum* is difficult to justify even during combat deployment.[87]

In contrast, Daniel Markovits argues that moving between a role morality and a universal normative perspective is a recipe for a tragic sense of self.[88] On his view, if an individual accepts the universal background moral principles pursuant to which her institution is justified, she cannot perform a role that requires violation of those principles without her moral integrity suffering gravely. For Markovits, the individual's only way out of this bind is to embrace membership in a distinct role-defined society that defines completely her moral identity and life.[89] By presumption, that alternative normative framework would be fundamentally inconsistent with the very moral principles upon which the institution is premised.[90] Recognizing that this is likely to be almost impossible to achieve under normal conditions, Markovits requires the total normative segregation of the role participant from the morality prevalent in society.[91]

Even accepting its premises, this proposal has debilitating practical and normative problems. As Markovits admits, total normative segregation of the kind he advocates cannot work in our contemporary society.[92] His focus

[87] EMMET, *supra* note 85, at 204. LUBAN, LEHD, *supra* note 46, at 13–14 n. 20; Luban, *Knowing When*, *supra* note 86.

[88] MARKOVITS, *supra* note 82, at 246. *See generally id.* ch. 9.

[89] *Id.*, at 225. *See generally id.* chs. 7–9.

[90] *See, e.g.*, *id.*, at 159, 223–26.

[91] *Id.*, at 223–26. The infeasibility of this for contemporary lawyers is precisely what undermines the tenability of a lawyer's role ethic on his account. *Id.*, at 229–46.

[92] Soldiers are more successfully segregated than lawyers, but fundamental elements of Markovits's challenges to role redescription remain, most notably the diversity of background and community attachments of the personnel and the changing system of rules

is on lawyers, for whom that impossibility is perhaps more obvious, but the point is no less true for today's soldiers. The modern combatant is in constant contact with family and friends outside the force even during war, has regular access to outside media, and must ultimately reintegrate to a non-military community after the war.[93] The rise of remotely operated weapons, which allow soldiers to fight by day and return to their families by night, has further entrenched the impossibility of moral insularity.[94]

Even if total segregation were possible, there is a deeper normative problem here. From a universal normative point of view that justifies the role-defining institution, the role participant's moral outlook is fundamentally mistaken. As such, it is not an outlook that the universal point of view can endorse, much less demand, without instrumentalizing the role participant.

To put this in less abstract terms, international law's treatment of soldiers cannot rely coherently on the notion that those soldiers ought to have rejected the law's moral underpinnings in favor of a contradictory ethical framework. When international law denies protection to soldiers that refuse to inflict the crime-making violence of an aggressive war, the explanation from that point of view cannot be that those soldiers were wrong to agree morally with the legal perspective that that violence is criminally wrongful.

Ultimately, then, although the danger of choice paralysis provides the strongest basis for a role morality defined by obedience and adherence to the *jus in bello*, it can provide that function plausibly only during combat and only when the *jus ad bellum* status of the war is sufficiently uncertain to require real deliberation on the part of the soldier. The notion of a more comprehensive normative segregation is neither feasible, nor internally defensible.

The upshot may be that institutional necessity precludes international law's protection of soldiers when they refuse to fight in aggressive wars,

governing behavior (most notably, the rise of the duty to disobey illegal orders). *Cf.* MARKOVITS, *supra* note 82, at 229–33.

93 On the connection of the soldier to family and friends outside the military even during war, *see, for example*, Lizette Alvarez, *Wartime Soldier, Conflicted Mom*, NY TIMES (Sept. 27, 2009), at A1; Mike Chalmers, *Social Media Allow Military Families a Deeper Connection*, USA TODAY, Nov. 24, 2011. Reintegration has, of course, always been the key challenge for soldiers in this respect. GROSSMAN, *supra* note 48, at 265–66, 273–81. The challenges it poses to the soldier's understanding of her war-time acts may well be an important part of the delayed trauma of having killed in war. *See* Section 1.5 of Chapter 1 above.

94 *See* Section 9.1 of Chapter 9 below.

but that the soldiers who engage in precisely such refusal do the right thing by the law's own lights.[95] This disjuncture is not an impossibility. Unlike its underlying normative posture, the law must take account of the risks of abuse, the danger of creating perverse incentives or moral hazard, and the possibility of shaping culture in a way that is ultimately counter-productive.[96] It must guard against the "migration" of regulated behaviors out of the intended domain.[97] And it cannot respond to contextual particulars with the dexterity of the individuals it regulates.[98]

Even when evaluating their actions with reference to whether the guiding principle could be adopted as a universal maxim (and thus engaging in what might look like the acts of moral legislators), individuals need not consider what kinds of exploitation, miscalculation, or abuse would occur if that maxim were made law.[99] The soldier deciding whether to fight in a war that she judges confidently to be criminally aggressive need only consider her refusal (or participation), the consequences either way, and whether it would be right for others similarly situated to refuse on the same grounds (i.e. to adopt her maxim). She need not consider whether the hypothetical legal protection of her disobedience might encourage others to engage in disobedience that would *deviate* from her maxim.

8.6 The Necessity of Enforced Culpability

Instead of dispelling the dissonance of a regime that criminalizes wrongful war and yet allows the criminalization of those who refuse to kill in its prosecution, this account would accept that dissonance as a jarring

[95] On this phenomenon generally, *see* Larry Alexander, *The Gap*, 14 HARV. J. L. & PUB. POL'Y 695 (1991); LARRY ALEXANDER & EMILY SHERWIN, THE RULE OF RULES: MORALITY, RULES, AND THE DILEMMAS OF LAW (2001).

[96] Deborah L. Rhode, *Institutionalizing Ethics*, 44 CASE W. RES. L. REV. 665, 671 (1994).

[97] Kim Lane Scheppele, *Hypothetical Torture in the "War on Terrorism,"* 1 J. NAT'L SECURITY LAW & POLICY 285, 307–318 (2005).

[98] APPLBAUM, *supra* note 72, at 199.

[99] On a related note, Kutz observes in a discussion of *jus in bello* rules – "if the rules . . . are justified instrumentally, then that fact must be kept from combatants. For a combatant who knows that [the law] is justified on the basis of wholesale calculations of humanitarian advantage will always have reason to ask himself in a given instance whether playing by the rules makes sense, or whether it is a case of what J.J.C. Smart has famously called 'rule-worship.'" Kutz, *Uniforms, supra* note 23, at 167.

institutional necessity. International law depends on states' capacities to force soldiers to act wrongfully by its own lights.

This outcome ought to gnaw at us. It unsettles the comforted view that soldiers who obediently fight in dubious wars are unsullied by what they are forced to do. But it should not surprise. Moral life does not bend to imperatives of convenience or comfort. It leaves remainders.[100] It involves dirty hands.[101] It is affected by luck, and it is not fair.[102] War, in particular, is defined by the tragic dilemmas it poses and the grim choices it demands.[103] If one of those dilemmas is that between upholding a viable long-term international security system and protecting soldiers from being forced to act culpably, it may be that the lesser evil is to empower states to force soldiers to "shoot and cry."[104]

In the context of that necessity, the state fails its soldiers horribly by forcing them to fight in a criminal war, and international law exhibits its weakness in being unable to stand against the use of soldiers as instruments of criminality.[105] But none of this changes the wrongfulness of the

[100] Bernard Williams, *Ethical Consistency*, *in* PROBLEMS OF THE SELF 166, 175 (1973) (arguing that it is a mistake to "eliminate from the scene the *ought* that is not acted upon"). *See also* Thomas E. Hill, Jr., *Moral Dilemmas, Gaps, and Residues: A Kantian Perspective*, *in* MORAL DILEMMAS AND MORAL THEORY 167, 183–87 (H. E. Mason, 1996).

[101] Bernard Williams, *Professional Morality and its Dispositions*, *supra* note 72, at 266; Andreas Eshete, *Does a Lawyer's Character Matter*, *in id.*, at 270, 279–80. On dirty hands generally: Michael Walzer, *Political Action: The Problem of Dirty Hands*, 2 PHILOSOPHY & PUB. AFF. 160 (1973).

[102] *See* Section 4.2 of Chapter 4 above.

[103] Thomas Nagel, *War and Massacre*, 1 PHIL. & PUB. AFF. 123, 144 (1972); David Ben Gurion, *On the Uses and Abuses of Force*, in HARDAN, *supra* note 48, at 14 (war is "a catastrophe not only for the vanquished, but also for the victors . . . values are destroyed"). Walzer accepts that leaders' hands may be dirtied in the course of war when they are required in situations of extreme emergency to engage in tactics such as terror bombing. WALZER, JUW, *supra* note 7, at 323–25. However, he does not accept the view that the soldier's hands may be dirtied by participating in an unjust war. On the contrary, he argues that the soldier's integrity is preserved by pure adherence to the *jus in bello* imperatives of the war convention. WALZER, JUW, *supra* note 7, at 206. *See also* DANIEL S. ZUPAN, WAR, MORALITY, AND AUTONOMY: AN INVESTIGATION INTO JUST WAR THEORY 77–78 (2003).

[104] This turn of phrase is common in the Israeli discourse as applied to the soldier who succumbs to this system in an unlawful war or military occupation, wrongfully in the view of organizations like Yesh G'vul, who make use of the slogan. Yesh G'vul [There is a Border], about, www.yeshgvul.org.il/en/about-2/ (last visited Aug. 1, 2014). The necessity account would hold, in effect, that shooting and crying is precisely what the soldier may be forced to do.

[105] Gerald Postema argues, "if no person can enter a certain profession without jeopardizing his or her moral integrity, then that alone stands as a powerful indictment of the

death and suffering inflicted in such a war and it cannot eliminate the moral burden borne by those who inflict such wrongs. The imposition of the soldier's culpability is just one of the ways her state wrongs her when it forces her to fight a wrongful war.[106]

Unlike the wrong of sending troops to die without good reason, the imposition of this moral harm is not typically recognized.[107] As a necessary implication of taking the law's posture on the *jus ad bellum* seriously, it ought to be. Perhaps the most significant normative remainder of international law's regulation of war is borne by some of the least powerful actors in the international system – the lower-level aggressor troops. In some illegal wars, the burden of killing may be the gravest wrong the state inflicts on its own soldiers.[108]

Quite apart from its significance in disturbing any misplaced comfort regarding the law's posture towards soldiers, this assessment has interpretive implications. Under the laws of war, collateral harm must be

profession. A job no worthy person can accept is a job no worthy society may create. This is not to deny, of course, that it may be a good thing that there be such a job in society, served by unscrupulous or shameless people. [But] we or society in general do not have the right to encourage or exploit the sacrifice of moral integrity." Gerald Postema, *Self-Image, Integrity, and Professional Responsibility, in* THE GOOD LAWYER 294, 290 (David Luban, ed., 1983). It is perhaps in this light that we should understand the considerable ambivalence expressed by Ryan and Reisman about the moral status of those who obey wrongful orders, even as they argue that role obedience may be an institutionally necessary approach. *See* Ryan, *Democratic Duty, supra* note 17, at 40–42; Reisman, *The Quest for World Order, supra* note 1, at 372–73.

106 It is, of course, well understood that institutional imperatives allow the state to treat soldiers in ways that would be indefensible were it not for the overriding necessity of military functioning. Parker v. Levy, 417 US 733, 758 (1974); James Fallows, *Military Efficiency*, ATLANTIC MONTHLY, Aug. 1991, at 21. But the state is not bound to fight wrongful wars. At most, it is bound to maintain a disciplined military. When it does wage a wrongful war, it wrongs its soldiers deeply – not by failing to protect them from being forced to participate, but by waging the wrongful war in the first place in a context in which necessity demands that they be forced to obey and fight.

107 Relatedly, Cheyney Ryan observes, "If a state's right to conscript existed only for just wars, one would assume that conscripting its citizens to fight in an unjust war would be an *additional* aspect of the crime of fighting that war in the first place; but it is not – and I have yet to encounter anyone who has claimed that it should be." Cheyney Ryan, *Moral Equality, Victimhood, and the Sovereignty Symmetry Problem, in* JUST AND UNJUST WARRIORS: THE MORAL AND LEGAL STATUS OF SOLDIERS 131, 143 (David Rodin & Henry Shue, eds., 2008).

108 On the rise of riskless warfare, *see* Section 9.1 of Chapter 9 below. Even in ordinary traditional warfare, many soldiers consider the moral burden of killing to be more profound than the physical risks and scars of battle. *See* Section 1.5 of Chapter 1 above.

recognized, accounted for, and minimized.[109] Drawing on this, not just as a rule of combat, but also as a general principle of law (particularly in this domain) would entail applying it also to moral injuries that the law cannot dismiss as normatively mistaken.[110] Domestically, this would mean thinking more expansively about what society owes its soldiers in light of the full multidimensionality of the burden imposed on them. Internationally, it would mean seeking to protect soldiers from being forced to fight and kill in a criminal war wherever institutional imperatives allow. The final Part of this book begins that work.

8.7 Necessity and Victim Status

Before turning to that discussion, it is worth considering whether necessity could warrant excluding the soldiers who fight against aggression from victim status in ICC proceedings, despite the fact that their deaths and maiming are at the core of what the criminalization of aggression condemns and seeks to prevent. A factor that might be thought to weigh in that direction is the danger that expressing the criminality of the *jus-in-bello*-compliant killing of combatants could undermine the prospects for long-term peace between the warring parties.

The possibility that imperatives of peace and justice can be in tension is recognized in Article 16 of the Rome Statute, which allows the Security Council to defer prosecutions pursuant to its Chapter VII authority to maintain international peace and security.[111] There are multiple ways in which that tension can manifest. The most immediately relevant here is that a singular pursuit of justice could trigger resentment in the

[109] *See* AP I, *supra* note 75, art. 57.

[110] On proportionality as a general principle of international law, *see* Alec Stone Sweet & Giacinto della Cananena, *Proportionality, General Principles of Law, and Investor–State Arbitration*, 46 N.Y.U. J. Int'l L. & Pol. 911, 916–24 (2014); Gebhard Bücheler, Proportionality in Investor–State Arbitration ch. 3 (2015); *cf.* Blum, *Dispensable Lives*, *supra* note 21, at 119, 140–50, 164 (on the interpretive implications of conceiving soldiers' status as targets as rooted in necessity). On the importance (but difficulty) of minimizing the burden borne by role participants, *see* Susan Wolf, *Ethics, Legal Ethics, and the Ethics of Law*, *in* The Good Lawyer, *supra* note 7, at 38, 50; *see* David Luban, Alan Strudler, & David Wasserman, *Moral Responsibility in an Age of Bureaucracy*, 90 Mich. L. Rev. 2348, 2354 (1992).

[111] ICC Statute, *supra* note 11, art. 16. On the other hand, it should be recognized that justice is often seen as a prerequisite of peace. Int'l Law Ass'n, Resolution 2/2010: Declaration of International Law Principles on Reparation for Victims of Armed Conflict, art. 12(1–2) (2010).

community on whose behalf the wrongdoer acted, and potentially catalyze or exacerbate a sense of nationalist grievance that may become the seed of future conflict. Most famously, the so-called "war guilt clause" of the Treaty of Versailles has become emblematic of the danger of overwhelming reparative demands.[112]

Versailles is a classic example of victor's justice, but the danger applies also to independent institutions seeking to dispense impartial justice. When such an institution rules in a way that contradicts the communal narrative of a nation (or other group), the risk is that the ruling will be interpreted not as evidence of the falsity of the nationalist narrative, but as evidence of the institution's illegitimacy or bias. In the worst-case scenario, it may even bolster the nationalist narrative, by creating a sense of grievance around the unfairness of the judgment and perhaps an associated antipathy to international institutions and international law. Under the wrong conditions, the latter result could exacerbate the risk of renewed conflict.

The danger of fanning the flames of a nationalist backlash in this way can arise not just from the imposition of heavy burdens on the state or community (as at Versailles), but potentially even from symbolic attributions of guilt, as when a leader apologizes on behalf of her nation.[113] It is salutary to recall that, even in one of the success stories of this realm, it took many years for German public opinion to fully come to grips with German wrongdoing in World War II.[114] What made the payment of German reparations to Israel domestically palatable in the early years may have been their political value in the circumstances at the time, as much as any widely felt sense of obligation.[115]

[112] Treaty of Peace between the Allied and Associated Powers and Germany, § 231, June 28, 1919, 225 C.T.S. 188. The deleterious impact of the war guilt clause has informed the work of legal authorities since. *See, e.g.*, RAINER HOFMANN & FRANK RIEMANN, INT'L LAW ASS'N COMMITTEE ON COMPENSATION FOR VICTIMS OF WAR, BACKGROUND REPORT: COMPENSATION FOR VICTIMS OF WAR 36–37 (2004); Final Award: Ethiopia's Damages Claim (Eri. v. Eth.), para. 315 (Eri.–Eth. Claims Comm'n 2009).

[113] Jennifer Lind, *The Perils of Apology*, FOREIGN AFF., May/June 2009, at 132; Zohar Kampf & Nava Löwenheim, *Rituals of Apology in the Global Arena*, 43 SECURITY DIALOGUE 43 (2012).

[114] *See, e.g.*, Valentin Rauer, *Symbols in Action: Willy Brandt's Kneefall at the Warsaw Memorial*, *in* SOCIAL PERFORMANCE: SYMBOLIC ACTION, CULTURAL PRAGMATICS, AND RITUAL 257, 263 (Alexander Jeffrey, Giesen Bernhard, & Mast Jason, eds., 2006).

[115] *See, e.g.*, Ariel Colonomos, *German Reparations to the Jews after World War II: A Turning Point in the History of Reparations*, *in* THE HANDBOOK OF REPARATIONS 390, 391–95 (Pablo de Greiff, ed., 2006).

By individualizing guilt, international criminal prosecutions endeavor to take some of the sting out of the process of reckoning with war and atrocity, diverting condemnation away from the nation as a whole and onto specific leaders and perpetrators.[116] However, when those in the dock are taken to be war heroes, or their actions were understood to be part of a widely endorsed national effort, individualization can only go so far.[117] Evaluations of the truth of the ICTY's findings differ wildly according to the degree to which the Tribunal's judgments support the prior narrative of the respondent's ethnic group.[118] Marko Milanović argues that the Tribunal "operates in a bias-driven downward spiral. The more it challenges established narratives, the more likely that it will generate distrust, and hence less likely that its decisions will be believed."[119]

In addition to showing the limits of individualization and the use of international institutions in overcoming the challenges of nationalist myth-making, the ICTY's travails in this respect emphasize that these kinds of concerns are not specific to the *jus ad bellum*. The facts around war crimes, crimes against humanity, and genocide are themselves the subject of nationalist distortion.[120] As such, this is not a problem that can be solved with a tweak in how victims of aggression are recognized at the ICC. It is a broader challenge to the pursuit of international criminal justice.

Nonetheless, aggression does raise unique concerns, both generally and specifically with respect to the issue of victim constituencies. An aggression ruling characterizes each side's war effort as a whole, necessarily contradicting a prominent narrative in the political sphere of the

[116] Gary Jonathan Bass, Stay the Hand of Vengeance 297 (2002); Carsten Stahn, *"Jus ad Bellum," "Jus in Bello" . . . "Jus post Bellum"?: Rethinking the Conception of the Law of Armed Force*, 17 Eur. J. Int'l L. 921, 939–40 (2006).

[117] Marija Ristic, *OSCE Survey: Mladic and Karadzic are Heroes*, Balkan Insight (Feb. 28, 2012), www.balkaninsight.com/en/article/serbs-still-supports-war-crime-defendants.

[118] Marko Milanović, *The Impact of the ICTY on the Former Yugoslavia: An Anticipatory Postmortem*, 110 Am. J. Int'l L. 233 (2016).

[119] Marko Milanović, *Establishing the Facts about Mass Atrocities: Accounting for the Failure of the ICTY to Persuade Target Audiences*, 47 Georgetown J. Int'l L. 1321, 1360 (2016).

[120] Tom Dannenbaum, *The International Criminal Court, Article 79, and Transitional Justice: The Case for an Independent Trust Fund for Victims*, 28 Wis. Int'l L.J. 234, 279–80, 284 (2011). Mark Evans, *At War's End: Time to Turn to Jus Post Bellum?*, *in* Jus Post Bellum: Mapping the Normative Foundations 26, 41 (Carsten Stahn, Jennifer S. Easterday, & Jens Iverson, eds., 2014).

aggressor. This is one reason in favor of limiting such findings to manifest violations of the *jus ad bellum*. The special concern around victim designation arises because combatants killed or injured fighting against aggression would have suffered those harms in the course of trying to kill and maim troops in the aggressor force, pursuant to the very *jus in bello* rules by which they were killed. Recognizing the former harms as criminally wrongful, while dismissing the latter as fully justified has the potential to be incendiary in a state or community not persuaded by the underlying *jus ad bellum* analysis. Even when the *jus ad bellum* analysis is accepted, such an expression could be perceived as implicitly reifying and demonizing soldiers on either side in a way that does not reflect their respective moral deserts, given the factors mitigating most aggressor troops' culpability.[121] From the point of view of the aggressor state's political community, it comes perilously close to identifying soldiers on the other side as crime victims *because* they suffered while trying to kill our innocent brothers, sisters, sons, and daughters. The worry is not just that this would undermine the credibility of the ICC in that community, but that it could stoke the flames of resentment and grievance.

To be clear, this is a speculative concern. Even if there is a good chance that prosecutions and reparations awards do not break through nationalist narratives to become an accepted source of truth, this does not necessarily mean that they will exacerbate conditions sufficiently to raise the probability of renewed violence. Moreover, if an expressive reparative process were to avoid recognizing *jus ad bellum* harms sufficiently, this could play into nationalist myth-making and a sense of grievance on the other side.[122] Seeking to strike a balance between political imperatives

[121] During the controversy over whether President Reagan and Chancellor Kohl would together visit a military cemetery in Bitburg, two local officials wrote an open letter to Kohl emphasizing the lack of culpability of most of the buried soldiers, "The dead who lie at the military cemetery must not, after a cruel selection among the living over 40 years ago, be now made victims of a selection among the fallen, most of them youths." James Markham, *Facing Up to Germany's Past*, NY Times (June 23, 1985).

[122] Duncan Hollis, *Eritrea–Ethiopia Claims Commission Awards Final Damages*, Opinio Juris (Aug. 19, 2009), http://opiniojuris.org/2009/08/19/eritrea-ethiopia-claims-commission-awards-final-damages. Andrea Gattini, *The UN Compensation Commission: Old Rules, New Procedures on War Reparations*, 13 Eur. J. Int'l L. 161, 165 (2002). The same phenomenon can arise when persons are charged with certain *jus in bello* crimes but not others in a context in which a constituency of victims understands the latter to be more important. Prosecutor v. Lubanga (ICC-01/04–01/06), International Center for Transitional Justice, Submission on Reparations Issues, para. 23 (May 10, 2012).

and legal or normative imperatives in this kind of context can leave all sides feeling deeply unsatisfied with the result.[123] Finally, in at least some wars, including particularly those in which the aggressor's nation was not plausibly under threat, the strength of nationalist resistance to contrary narratives from an institution like the ICC may be diminished.[124]

Quite apart from how likely any backlash is, international law and international courts are typically resistant to efforts to distort the application of justice so as to accommodate the demands of peace. This is exemplified by their tendency to reject the validity of amnesties for international crimes.[125] More broadly, the ICTY President asserted recently that it was not the Tribunal's role to facilitate reconciliation in the Balkans, and so it ought not be judged by that metric, but rather by its delivery of truthful judgments.[126] Even Article 16 of the Rome Statute makes the Security Council, and not the ICC, responsible for privileging peace over justice, and allows such privileging only in the form of one-year deferrals.

As such, from the legal point of view, one might think that the speculative danger posed by including combatants as victims may not

[123] *Cf.* Roger P. Alford, *On War as Hell*, 3 Chi. J. Int'l L. 207, 212–13 (2002).

[124] *See supra* Section 6.3 of Chapter 6.

[125] Office of the UN High Commissioner for Human Rights, Rule of Law Tools for Post-Conflict States: Amnesties, U.N. Doc. HR/PUB/09/1 (2009); Prosecutor v. Furundžija, Case No. IT-95-17/1-T, Judgment (Int'l Crim. Trib. for the Former Yugoslavia, Dec. 10, 1998); Prosecutor v. Brima, Case No. SCSL-2004-16-AR72(E), Appeals Chamber, Decision on Challenge to Jurisdiction: Lomé Accord Amnesty (Special Ct. for Sierra Leone Mar. 13, 2004); Fatou Bensouda, Statement of ICC Prosecutor on the Conclusion of the Peace Negotiations between the Government of Colombia and the Revolutionary Armed Forces of Colombia – People's Army, International Criminal Court (Sept. 1, 2016), www.icc-cpi.int//Pages/item.aspx?name=160901-otp-stat-colombia. *See also* Louise Mallinder, *Amnesties and International Criminal Law*, *in* Handbook on International Criminal Law 419 (William A. Schabas & Nadia Bérnaz, eds., 2010) (suggesting that ambiguity remains about the status of amnesties, notwithstanding international criminal law's hostility to them). Similarly, there is hostility to the notion that peace agreements can override reparative rights and obligations related to human rights or humanitarian law violations. Commentary on the Additional Protocols, para. 3649 (Yves Sandoz et al., eds., 1987); Int'l Committee of the Red Cross, *Report on the Protection of War Victims*, 33 Int'l Rev. Red Cross 391, 437–38 (1993); UN Sub-Commission on Human Rights, Rep. of the Special Rapporteur on the Situation of Systematic Rape, Sexual Slavery and Slavery-like Practices during Wartime, §§ 108–09, 112, U.N. Doc. E/CN.4/Sub.2/1998/13 (June 22, 1998). *But see* Hofmann & Riemann, *supra* note 112, at 35–37.

[126] Denis Dzidic, *Hague Tribunal President: "We Offered Truth, Not Reconciliation,"* Balkan Insight (June 21, 2017), www.balkaninsight.com/en/article/hague-tribunal-president-we-offered-truth-not-reconciliation-06-21-2017.

be sufficient to warrant deviating from the correct expression regarding the core victims of the crime. At a minimum, such a deviation would require more robust evidence of the risk than is discussed above.

Nonetheless, that discussion provides prima facie cause for concern. Assuming that the kind of danger outlined above was affirmed by greater empirical study, it would demand being taken very seriously, and perhaps even deviating from a blind pursuit of criminal justice. The criminalization of aggression is a response to the horror of war. The processes around its enforcement cannot operate in a manner oblivious to the danger of facilitating future war.[127]

The question, then, is what the upshot of an affirmation of the risks discussed above would be. To exclude combatants killed by an aggressor force from recognition at the ICC would be to ignore the heart of aggression's criminal wrongfulness. A better way to mitigate the extent to which the victim participation and reparation process may exacerbate nationalist myths, without sacrificing the core message of the criminalization of aggression, would be for the Court to recognize as indirect victims those killed or harmed, after having been coerced or misled into fighting for the aggressor force.

To be clear, as discussed in Chapters 4 and 5, soldiers on the aggressor side are not the core crime victims. However, as also discussed in those chapters, aggressor troops that are genuinely coerced or misled into fighting *are* wronged in a real way by their leaders. In addition to being forced to do wrong, they are also forced or misled into a position in which they are at risk of justified killing and violence, without deserving to be so.

Including such aggressor troops as victims at the ICC would mean reaching beyond the core of the criminal wrong, and adopting an expanded meaning of "indirect" victims in such cases.[128] The wrong they suffer inheres not in the criminal wrong of aggression, but in the coercion or mendacity that causes them to fight. However, as "natural persons who have suffered harm as a result of the commission of [the] crime," they do meet the basic criteria of the ICC Rules of Procedure and

[127] On the idea that it may be required to demand less than one is due in the interests of peace, *see* Larry May, *Jus Post Bellum, Grotius, and Meionexia, in* JUS POST BELLUM: MAPPING THE NORMATIVE FOUNDATIONS 15, 20 (Carsten Stahn, Jennifer S. Easterday, & Jens Iverson, eds., 2014).

[128] Prosecutor v. Lubanga (ICC-01/04-01/06 A A 2 A 3), Judgment on the Appeals against the "Decision Establishing the Principles and Procedures to be Applied to Reparations" of 7 August 2012, paras. 190–91, 196–98 (Mar. 3, 2015).

Evidence.[129] If the interests of peace would be furthered by such recognition, a limited, crime-specific extension in that direction could be warranted.

I have argued elsewhere that a similar rebalancing could be provided in the context of war crimes, crimes against humanity, and genocide cases by the Trust Fund for Victims using its independent authority to pursue assistance projects for those victims whose crimes were not prosecuted at the Court.[130] The scenario here is different, because the only international crime to which harmed and coerced aggressor troops are attached is the aggression. The normative impetus, however, is the same.

So as not to distort excessively the recognition of the core wrong of aggression, the focus of the recognition of soldiers on the aggressor side would need to be on the coercion and mendacity that drove them to fight. Contributions to the trial process could be restricted to those features of their experience, and any symbolic reparation after a conviction ought to focus explicitly on the coercive and mendacious domestic mechanisms that caused them to go to war. This accommodation would go some way to mitigating some of the dangers of an aggression prosecution without thereby overriding the core normative expression of the participation and reparations process in such a case.

[129] ICC R. P. Evid. 85. [130] Dannenbaum, *supra* note 120, at 272–86.

PART III

Respecting Soldiers in Institutions and Doctrine: The Internal Imperative to Reform

9

Shifting Contingencies

The core criminal wrong of aggressive war is the unjustified (and yet *jus-in-bello*-compliant) killing and human violence that it entails. Those harmed or killed by that violence, including soldiers fighting against aggression, as well as civilians caught in the crossfire, are the crime's core victims. Despite academic commentary to the contrary and the potentially distorting precedents of the UNCC and EECC, none of the arguments canvassed in the prior chapters is sufficient to warrant the ICC deviating from that reality in its approach to victim participation and reparations in aggression cases. At most, the imperative of peace may require expanding the scope of indirect victims in an aggression prosecution to include those coerced or misled into fighting on the aggressor side.

At the same time, a combination of duress, ignorance, associative ties, and political duties mean that very few of those who inflict the violence that makes aggression a crime are sufficiently culpable to warrant criminal sanction themselves. The logistical challenges of identifying the few that are, the value of sharpening *jus in bello* incentives for soldiers in war, and the importance of military functioning in lawful wars together provide sufficient reason to grant all lower-level participants blanket protection from liability for the crime of aggression. Aggression is both a crime of human violence and a leadership crime for good reasons.

And yet, from the international legal point of view, lower-level soldiers who struggle to reconcile themselves to having fought in aggressive wars get it right. Given the nature of the first-personal moral perspective and the high culpability threshold for international criminality, this is true even for the majority of aggressor troops who do not deserve to be punished for fighting. Neither the value of *jus in bello* compliance, nor the importance of an obedient military in lawful wars can change this element of the normative structure of war.

Instead, the importance of maintaining military obedience gives the most normatively coherent account of why international law cannot protect soldiers when they refuse to fight for an aggressor force. On that account, soldiers may be forced by law to do wrong by the law's own lights. They are left to bear the normative remainder created by international law's most important weakness.

For a regime that is focused increasingly on human dignity and human values, this is a jarring implication. It also has interpretive consequences. A necessity rationale is contingent on the conditions of the necessity enduring. Even if the account advanced in the previous chapter has been plausible traditionally, fundamental changes in the way wars are being fought suggest that it may no longer be so in all contexts today. This creates an internal imperative to interpret existing law so as to extend certain legal protections to soldiers who refuse to fight in aggressive wars.

9.1 Remotely Fought or Low-Risk Wars

Throughout the period governed by the contemporary laws on the use of force and the conduct of war, there have been belligerents on either side of a war that are removed from the front lines of combat. However, there are now entire wars waged in which all, or almost all, of the troops on one side face no meaningful combat risk. This changes fundamentally how we ought to think about institutional obedience imperatives in the military.

The first major example of such a conflict was NATO's three-month aerial intervention in Kosovo in 1999. Flying at an altitude out of the Yugoslav military's range, the alliance used 1,000 aircraft on 38,000 sorties over 78 days, but suffered no casualties.[1] This striking deviation from the conditions of traditional conflict led NATO Commander, Wesley Clark to comment, "This was not, strictly speaking, a war."[2] It instigated a spate of analyses on the implications of extreme asymmetry, or "risklessness," for the *jus in bello*.[3]

[1] *Facts & Figures*, PBS FRONTLINE: WAR IN EUROPE, www.pbs.org/wgbh/pages/frontline/shows/kosovo/etc/facts.html (last visited Aug. 20, 2014).

[2] Wesley Clark, Press Briefing on the Kosovo Strike Assessment in Brussels, NATO Headquarters (Sept. 16, 1999).

[3] *See, e.g.*, A. V. P. Rogers, *Zero Casualty Warfare*, 837 INT'L REV. RED CROSS 165 (2000); Paul W. Kahn, *The Paradox of Riskless Warfare*, 22 PHILOSOPHY & PUB. POL'Y 2, 2 (2002); Michael Walzer, *Kosovo*, in ARGUING ABOUT WAR 101 (2004); Michael Walzer, *The Triumph of Just War Theory (And the Dangers of Success), in id.*, at 3, 16–17 (2004); MICHAEL IGNATIEFF, VIRTUAL WAR: KOSOVO AND BEYOND 62, 150–55, 161 (2000); David Luban, *Intervention and Civilization*, *in* GLOBAL JUSTICE AND TRANSNATIONAL

Three years after Kosovo, the United States began using unmanned aerial vehicles (drones) in lethal operations for the first time, striking targets in Yemen and Afghanistan.[4] The United States' use of drones in belligerent operations has skyrocketed since, and other states, such as the UK, are following suit.[5] Drones have been used by the United States in a wide range of contexts, from those involving significant US troop deployments (in Iraq and Afghanistan) to those with few if any US troops on the ground (such as in Yemen, Somalia, Pakistan, Mali, and Libya).[6]

The United States views all of these operations through the prism of the law of armed conflict, even when killings are performed remotely and "far" from an "active theater of conflict."[7] Although more ambiguous on this point, the UK has also indicated that compliance with the laws of war would be "sufficient" to underpin the legality of strikes outside the geographic space of an active armed conflict.[8]

POLITICS 79, 82 (Pablo De Greiff & Ciaran Cronin, eds., 2002); Jack M. Beard, *Law and War in the Virtual Era*, 103 AM. J. INT'L L. 409 (2009).

4 *See CIA "Killed al-Qaeda Suspects" in Yemen*, BBC NEWS (Nov. 5, 2002), http://news.bbc.co.uk/2/hi/2402479.stm.

5 *See, e.g.*, Peter Bergen & Katherine Tiedemann, *The Year of the Drone*, FOREIGN POL'Y (Apr. 26, 2010), http://foreignpolicy.com/2010/04/23/the-year-of-the-drone; Sirwan Kajjo & Mehdi Jedinia, *Military Drones Flood War Skies over Syria, Iraq*, VOICE OF AMERICA (May 15, 2016), www.voanews.com/a/military-drones-flood-war-skies-over-syria-and-iraq/3330150.html. On the UK, *see* H. of Lords H. of Commons Joint Comm'n on Human Rights, The Government's Policy on the Use of Drones for Targeted Killing, Second Report of Session 2015–16, HL Paper 141 HC 574 (May 10, 2016) (UK), https://publications.parliament.uk/pa/jt201516/jtselect/jtrights/574/574.pdf. Other unmanned vehicles are proliferating, as is autonomous weaponry. *See, e.g.*, Heather Roff and Richard Moyes, *Meaningful Human Control, Artificial Intelligence and Autonomous Weapons*, Briefing Paper for Delegates at the Convention on Certain Conventional Weapons Meeting of Experts on Lethal Autonomous Weapons Systems (Apr. 15–16, 2016); John Yoo, *Embracing the Machines: Rationalist War and New Weapons Technologies*, 105 CAL. L. REV. 443 (2017).

6 On the operations in Pakistan and Yemen, *see America's Counterterrorism Wars*, NEW AMERICA FOUNDATION, www.newamerica.org/in-depth/americas-counterterrorism-wars (last visited July 4, 2017). On Mali, *see, for example*, Eric Schmitt, *Drones in Niger Reflect New US Tack on Terrorism*, NY TIMES (July 11, 2013), at A3. The United States recently deployed troops to Somalia. *US troops to help Somalia fight al-Shabab*, BBC NEWS (Apr. 14, 2017), www.bbc.com/news/world-africa-39600419.

7 Memorandum for the Attorney General, Applicability of Federal Criminal Laws and the Constitution to Contemplated Lethal Operations against Shaykh Anwar al-Aulaqi, July 16, 2010, at 20, 24, www.aclu.org/files/assets/2014-06-23_barron-memorandum.pdf [hereinafter al-Aulaqi Memo]. *See generally id.*, at 20–30.

8 H. of Lords H. of Commons Joint Comm'n on Human Rights, *supra* note 5, at 3.16–3.19, 3.50–3.55. *See also* the Government's policy on the use of drones for targeted killing: Government Response to the Committee's Second Report of Session 2015–16, Fourth

And yet, even among those adopting this armed conflict framing, there is a view that this form of violent force is different. In 2011, US State Department Legal Adviser Harold Koh reasoned that the lack of risk to US personnel in the Libya operation helped to obviate the need for Congressional authorization under domestic war powers rules, emphasizing,

> [T]he exposure of our armed forces is limited: To date, our operations have not involved US casualties or a threat of significant US casualties. Nor do our current operations involve active exchanges of fire with hostile forces, and members of our military have not been involved in significant armed confrontations or sustained confrontations of any kind with hostile forces.[9]

Whether or not Koh's argument stands as a matter of domestic law, the notable point is that by asserting the need for distinct legal treatment from that applicable to other uses of force, he tried to classify the action as a distinct legal type: a riskless war.[10]

Needless to say, the term "riskless" in this context is one-sided. It is also important to clarify that such operations respond to an alleged threat of violence by the target against some person or group, and those who perform the actions, such as drone operators, are formally legitimate targets under the *jus in bello*.[11] Nonetheless, such operations are distinctive in that participating in the lethal act does not itself place the participant at any personal risk in practice. The attacks are perpetrated remotely, the location of the operator of a given drone is almost certainly

Report of Session 2016–17, HL Paper 49 HC 747, at 16 (Oct. 19, 2016) ("this is a hypothetical question and if this scenario arose as a live issue it would require detailed analysis of the law and all the facts. However, the Government considers that in relation to military operations, the law of war would be likely to be regarded as an important source in considering the applicable principles"), www.publications.parliament.uk/pa/jt201617/jtselect/jtrights/747/74705.htm#_idTextAnchor032.

9 Testimony by Legal Adviser Harold Hongju Koh, US Dep't of State, on Libya and War Powers before the Senate Foreign Relations Committee, June 28, 2011, at 8, www.foreign.senate.gov/imo/media/doc/Koh_Testimony.pdf [hereinafter Koh, Senate Testimony].

10 The position was criticized at the time. *See, e.g.*, Bruce Ackerman, *Legal Acrobatics, Illegal War*, NY Times (June 20, 2011), at A27.

11 *See, e.g.*, al-Aulaqi Memo, *supra* note 7, at 21, 27, 41 (on the alleged threat posed by a drone target); *Interview with Peter Mauer, President of the ICRC: The Use of Armed Drones Must Comply with Laws*, Int'l Committee of the Red Cross (May 10, 2013) (on the target status of drone operators), www.icrc.org/eng/resources/documents/interview/2013/05-10-drone-weapons-ihl.htm.

unknown by the enemy, and her identity is anonymous. She need not live or sleep in a military camp or barracks. As O'Connell puts it, the drone operator "*knows* she will not be attacked. She will go home to her family at the end of the day, coach a soccer game, make dinner, and help with homework."[12] Alongside drones, cyber operations used to inflict human violence share or accentuate many of these features.[13]

What Koh identified in his Congressional testimony, and what many have recognized in academic writing, is that when a state's approach to a particular war creates this "riskless" reality for its troops across the entire war effort, that alone is sufficiently distinctive to warrant separate normative consideration, and possibly different legal treatment.[14] For the purposes of the argument here, the rise of riskless warfare has two significant implications.

First, greater death tolls (or expected death tolls) among a state's own troops raise significantly the justificatory threshold for any government seeking domestic political support for war. In this vein, the ban on images of soldiers' coffins returning from Iraq and Afghanistan was criticized as an attempted prophylactic against rising political opposition to those conflicts.[15] Conversely, a government whose troops bear no immediate risk in a given war is likely to incur less in the way of domestic political scrutiny or cost when it uses force without good reason.[16]

Democratic publics do not necessarily prioritize the *jus ad bellum* in considering whether an action warrants spilling the blood of their co-citizens. However, the justification they demand is likely to include adherence to core *jus ad bellum* principles, like self-defense, whether or not that demand is rooted explicitly in international law.[17] Public

[12] Mary Ellen O'Connell, *Unlawful Killing with Combat Drones*, *in* SHOOTING TO KILL: SOCIO-LEGAL PERSPECTIVES ON THE USE OF LETHAL FORCE 263 (Simon Bronitt, Miriam Gani, & Saskia Hufnagel, eds., 2010) [emphasis added].

[13] For the most comprehensive evaluation of the application of international law to cyber, *see* INTERNATIONAL GROUP OF EXPERTS, TALLINN MANUAL 2.0 ON THE INTERNATIONAL LAW APPLICABLE TO CYBER OPERATIONS (2nd edn 2017).

[14] *See supra* notes 3, 9.

[15] *See, e.g.*, Jeff Jacoby, *Should Photos of Soldiers' Coffins be on the News*, BOSTON GLOBE (Apr. 27, 2004), http://archive.boston.com/news/globe/editorial_opinion/oped/articles/2004/04/27/should_photos_of_soldiers_coffins_be_on_the_news?pg=full; Ann Scott Tyson & Mark Berman, *Pentagon Rethinks its 18-Year Ban on Photos and Videos of Coffins Bearing War Dead Home*, WASHINGTON POST (Feb. 17, 2009), www.washingtonpost.com/wp-dyn/content/article/2009/02/16/AR2009021601480.html.

[16] IGNATIEFF, *supra* note 3, at 143.

[17] The mother of a British soldier who died in Iraq is demanding that Tony Blair and his government be held to account for waging an illegal war. Cole Moreton, *Rose Gentle:*

scrutiny, meanwhile, has the potential to expose mendacity and clarify relevant facts, irrespective of whether it is focused on international law specifically. In the absence of the risk of a significant death toll, the government's *jus ad bellum* claims are less likely to be subject to this level of examination and critique. Waging war, on this view, becomes cheap.[18]

The consequence for soldiers is that risklessness may weaken the case for placing presumptive trust in their own state's *jus ad bellum* claims. At the margins, when the facts publicly available are sufficiently weighty, this may bolster soldiers' confidence that the war is criminal, strengthening the reasons for them to disobey. For others, the fact of risklessness may increase their doubt in the state's claims (and thus the burden of fighting), but not to the point of confidence in the war's criminality.

The second and more important implication of riskless warfare for the analysis here is that the institutional imperative to deny protection to soldiers who refuse to fight in aggressive wars does not apply to riskless wars. The hellish risks of war motivate the bias that might lead to disobedience in lawful wars, underpin the need for tight unit cohesion, and are a key condition of choice paralysis in battle.[19] Thus, in denying a soldier's right to disobey orders to fight in Iraq following the 2003 invasion, the English and Welsh Court of Appeal, focusing principally on unit cohesion, reasoned:

> [O]ther soldiers and colleagues who might also have misgivings about *dangerous* operations can harbour real misgivings about a system that allows particular personnel to avoid *dangerous* duties . . . The service bond is all about the equal sharing of *risk and danger* so such behaviour has real potential to affect operational effectiveness. Service personnel cannot pick and choose what operations and orders they will carry out. To do so would have a corrosive effect on morale and undermine service effectiveness.[20]

Whether or not such reasoning is plausible on its own terms, when fighting means showing up to an office in Nevada, scoping and watching each target for days, and killing persons continents away, the exigencies

Some Mother's Son, INDEPENDENT (Mar. 16, 2008), www.independent.co.uk/news/people/profiles/rose-gentle-some-mothers-son-796622.html.

18 Kahn, *Paradox of Riskless Warfare*, *supra* note 3, at 4.

19 *See* Sections 8.3–8.4 of Chapter 8 above.

20 R v. Michael Peter Lyons [2011] EWCA (Crim) 2808, para. 39 [emphasis added].

underpinning the necessity account lose their force.[21] It is simply not credible to hold that protecting those who refuse to fight in a *criminal* drone war would undermine the state's capacity to wage *lawful* wars, riskless or otherwise.

9.2 The Rise of Private Contractors

A broader challenge to the institutional necessity of allowing states to enforce obedience in illegal wars arises from the dramatic rise in the proportion of participants in contemporary armed conflicts working for private contractors.[22] Britain and the United States used large numbers of such contractors in Iraq and Afghanistan, where some provided key security functions in scenarios predictably leading to engagement in combat.[23]

Unlike soldiers, contractors can quit without facing punishment.[24] The crime of desertion does not apply outside the armed forces.[25] On the necessity account, such contractors ought to be unable to provide an institutional guarantee of efficacy in the hell of war. As such, if major

[21] On the lives of drone operators, *see, for example*, Jane Mayer, *The Predator War*, New Yorker (Oct. 26, 2009), at 36; Nicola Abé, *Dreams in Infrared: The Woes of an American Drone Operator*, Spiegel (Dec. 14, 2012), www.spiegel.de/international/world/pain-continues-after-war-for-american-drone-pilot-a-872726.html.

[22] *See, e.g.*, *In re* KBR, 736 F. Supp. 2d 956, 956 (D. Md. 2010); Hannah Tonkin, State Control over Private Military and Security Companies in Armed Conflict 28–53 (2011); Laura Dickinson, Outsourcing War and Peace: Protecting Public Values in an Era of Privatized Foreign Affairs ch. 2 (2011); Peter W. Singer, Corporate Warriors (2004).

[23] *See, e.g.*, US House Committee on Oversight, Private Military Contractors in Iraq: An Examination of Blackwater's Actions in Fallujah (2007); Jeremy Scahill, *Bush's Shadow Army*, The Nation (Apr. 2, 2007); *Frontline: Private Warriors* (PBS television broadcast, June 21, 2005); James K. Wither, *European Security and Private Military Companies*, PFP Consortium Q. J. 107, 115–17 (Summer, 2005); War on Want, Corporate Mercenaries: The Threat of Private Military and Security Companies 8–9 (2006).

[24] Mateo Taussig-Rubbo, *Outsourcing Sacrifice: The Labor of Private Military Contractors*, 21 Yale J.L. & Humanities 101 (2009).

[25] In the United States, for example, although the UCMJ was amended to allow jurisdiction over civilians accompanying an American military force engaged in contingency operations, the crime of desertion, unlike other UCMJ crimes, is narrowly applicable only to members of "the armed forces." Uniform Code of Military Justice, art. 85, 10 U.S.C., § 885 (2006); Memorandum from Secretary of Defense to Secretaries of the Military Departments, UCMJ Jurisdiction over DoD Civilian Employees, DoD Contractor Personnel, and Other Persons Serving with or Accompanying the Armed Forces Overseas during Declared War and in Contingency Operations (Mar. 10, 2008), https://fas.org/sgp/othergov/dod/gates-ucmj.pdf.

military powers with extensive belligerent experience were truly convinced of the institutional necessity of punishment to maintain functioning, one would not expect to see them turn to contractors or other non-military actors for significant security roles in their wars. And if they were to do so, one would expect dire consequences. Not only would the contractors be ineffective, unit cohesion and commitment in government units could also suffer from the lack of solidarity and reliability from their partners in the fight.

The practice of major military states has confounded both of these expectations. Major military states have employed private contractors in roles ranging from drone operations to battle zone deployments involving extreme risk and a high chance of direct combat.[26] The behaviors of these powers give the lie to claims of a universally applicable "functional imperative" of absolute military obedience.[27]

Prima facie, this calls into question whether allowing their soldiers to disobey in illegal wars would actually undermine the capacity of such states to fight lawful wars effectively. Even under such a system, soldiers would still be subject to greater obedience enforcement mechanisms than would their contractor colleagues (who can disobey without punishment even in lawful wars). Notwithstanding the possible motivated biases discussed in the previous chapter, the need to show that the war is in fact aggressive would be a non-negligible deterrent for any soldier lacking confidence in her judgment of the war's illegality.[28]

Thus far, the use of contractors has been too restricted (in terms of numbers of conflicts and role-types) to debunk thoroughly the empirical premises underpinning the necessity account. However, at a minimum, the use of contractors by major military powers in complex conflict situations suggests that traditional military claims regarding how the institution functions should be interrogated and reexamined.

9.3 The Timing of Disobedience Protection

Even assuming that the empirical premises of the necessity account were to withstand such interrogation, the viability of disobedience protection

[26] *See supra* notes 22–23.

[27] On the "functional imperative" of obedience, *see, for example*, Lt. Col. Kenneth H. Wenker, *Morality and Military Obedience*, AIR UNIV. REV. 82 (1981).

[28] Precisely that phenomenon is apparent already in the context of orders that violate the *jus in bello*.

would still not be limited to riskless wars. With the right limits on timing, protection in wars of mutual risk could be compatible with the institutional obedience imperatives discussed in the previous chapter.

Most obviously, if protections were to apply only to those who disobeyed after an authoritative *jus ad bellum* decision by the Security Council or other competent international authority, the soldier would not need to evaluate the *jus ad bellum* status of the war herself, and there would be no significant migration of disobedience to lawful wars. In this context, the necessity account simply does not obtain. Global security would not be enhanced through maintaining states' capacity to enforce obedience in such circumstances. On the contrary, if anything, it would be bolstered by soldiers disobeying and seeking protection, thus supplementing the various other tools that the international community might use to combat the aggression.[29]

The mechanics of such protection would be straightforward. Although no international *jus ad bellum* authority is itself open to individual petition, any domestic or supranational human rights court could rely on the international authority's *jus ad bellum* assessment in upholding individual disobedience claims. As discussed in the next chapter, when this possibility arises, states have human rights and refugee law duties to open their courts to such claims. They also have an obligation to accept and carry out the Security Council's decisions relating to international peace and security.[30]

Of course, what makes this case straightforward from the institutional necessity perspective is also what makes it extremely rare – the fact that the authoritative *jus ad bellum* decision is issued prior to any soldierly disobedience. However, there is also a more broadly applicable way in which timing can alleviate the institutional imperative not to protect soldiers that refuse. Rather than restricting when the disobedience would occur, this would adjust when its protection and vindication would occur.

The concern about the institutional competence of domestic or human rights courts adjudicating *jus ad bellum* disobedience is most acute when the institution protects disobedience *during* the war. Any court (or other) ruling that the war is unlawful at that moment would likely undermine the state's military effort completely by offering the promise of disobedience protection to those still fighting, motivating disobedience, causing

[29] *See* Section 8.1 of Chapter 8 above. [30] UN Charter, arts. 24–25.

in-theater hesitation, and triggering the breakdown of unit cohesion. Although this would be desirable when the ruling is right, a mistaken ruling could have irreversibly severe consequences.[31]

Suppose, then, that litigation regarding the rights of those who disobey would be delayed until after the war. Would the necessity account still hold in such a scenario? Arguably, yes. A soldier would need to make her own judgment at the moment of disobedience, and that judgment would be distorted by the motivation to exit the war honorably and lawfully. Deliberation on the issue could be a normative distraction, contributing to choice paralysis or poor *jus in bello* decision-making. Those who continue to fight may feel abandoned both by their erstwhile comrades, who would avoid immediate sanction (and have the hope of avoiding future sanction), and by their state, which they might resent for facilitating the painless and straightforward exit of those who refuse.

In short, the delay would create its own problems. Delayed decisions correctly punishing those who refused to fight in lawful wars would not have the impact of deterring imitation and bolstering cohesion among those that remain. As the US Supreme Court has observed, "Court-martial jurisdiction sprang from the belief that within the military ranks there is need for a *prompt, ready-at-hand* means of compelling obedience and order."[32] By this logic, whereas an erroneous judicial decision protecting disobedience during a lawful war would cause graver damage to *that* war effort than would an otherwise identical decision protecting disobedience after the war, a system of delayed litigation would degrade military functioning (to a lesser degree) in a broader range of lawful wars, including those in which the courts ultimately get it right.

However, there may be a way of protecting disobedience that would incorporate both the elements of retrospective protection that prevent an

[31] This is related to the notion that injunctive relief is generally a more invasive judicial intervention in executive branch decision-making than is a subsequent remedial award. *See, e.g.*, Steve Vladeck, *On Justice Kennedy's Flawed and Depressing Narrowing of Constitutional Damages Remedies*, Just Security (June 19, 2017), www.justsecurity.org/42334/justice-kennedys-flawed-depressing-narrowing-constitutional-damages-remedies; Stephen I. Vladeck, Issue Brief: The Bivens Term: Why the Supreme Court Should Reinvigorate Damages Suits against Federal Officer, American Constitution Society (2017), www.acslaw.org/sites/default/files/The_Bivens_Term.pdf. *But see* Ziglar v. Abbasi, 137 S.Ct. 1843 (2017).

[32] United States ex rel. Toth v. Quarles, 350 U.S. 11, 22 (1955). *See also* Letter from Abraham Lincoln to New York Democrats (June 12, 1863), *in* The Political Thought of Abraham Lincoln (Richard Current, ed., 1967).

erroneous judgment from disrupting a lawful war, and the elements of the current system that guard against distorted judgment, choice paralysis, and unit breakdown. This disobedience protection regime would include three safeguards.

First, soldiers who disobey would face immediate punishment during the war, regardless of its legality. Second, to make a claim for disobedience protection, the soldier would need to refuse to participate prior to deployment (or between deployments) and outside the theater of conflict, to turn herself in immediately, and to cite the war's illegality at the time of disobedience.[33] Third, if post-war review were to find the war to have been illegal, any soldier who raised that claim at the time of disobedience would be subject to retrospective exoneration, the clearing of her record, and the lifting of any remaining punishment.

A framework of protection along these lines would avoid many of the pitfalls of alternative disobedience protection regimes. Under the current system, most who desert do so with a view to avoiding capture and punishment altogether. Many, though not all, are successful in that regard.[34] The proposed system would not vindicate such actors retrospectively. Instead, it would grant legal protection only to those who turn themselves in immediately. The certainty and immediacy of the punishment combined with the uncertainty and delay of ultimate vindication would make this form of disobedience attractive only to a limited population. Those attracted to this option would need to be motivated more by legal vindication than by punishment avoidance. They would need to be highly confident that the war is in fact illegal. And it is unlikely that that confidence would be rooted in motivated bias, given that the disobedience would trigger certain and immediate punishment and only uncertain and delayed vindication. If anything, the factors biasing soldiers' judgment in the opposite direction would dominate.

Similarly, the worry about emotional paralysis in the heat of battle would not apply. Once deployed, refusal on *jus ad bellum* grounds would

[33] Especially in wars fought abroad, desertion in theater is already unlikely. Far more common is desertion at home, whether from a barracks or during leave. MARK OSIEL, OBEYING ORDERS 209 (1999) (on the debilitating obstacles to desertion in theater).

[34] On the statistics regarding military punishments for deserters in the UK, *see* Letter from DCDS Personnel Secretariat, Ministry of Defence, to unknown, Freedom of Information Act: Reference: 20-08-2010-160944-005 (Sept. 13, 2010) (reporting between two and over three thousand deserters per year from the British military during the Iraq War, dropping significantly in 2010), www.gov.uk/government/uploads/system/uploads/attachment_data/file/16803/FOI20082010160944005_AWOL_20002010.pdf.

no longer be an option, and would not contaminate the soldier's capacity to focus on the tasks at hand and the *jus in bello*. Indeed, if the protection of *jus ad bellum* disobedience were restricted to out-of-theater refusal, the danger of choice paralysis would likely be far lower than it is already as a consequence of protected and required *jus in bello* disobedience.[35] The latter regime demands the attention of soldiers in the context of combat, including while the bullets are flying, but early concern about its impact on military efficacy has not been borne out.

Finally, the proposed framework would dilute the impact of disobedience on unit cohesion in two ways. First, the fact that disobedience would occur pre-deployment would limit the sense that the unit is being deserted in battle. Second, and more importantly, the immediate punishment of those who disobey would stifle disobedience contagion and could bolster the cohesion of those that remain. The only scenario in which this might not be the case would be one in which there is widespread confidence in the war's illegality. As discussed above, in such contexts, widespread disobedience is both desirable and superior from a human values perspective to many of the alternative methods of countering aggression.

9.4 The Contingency of Necessity

Understanding the current legal posture towards soldiers in aggressor forces as rooted in necessity entails recognizing its delicate empirical contingency. The rise of drones and cyber warfare has thrown the empirical premises into flux; the rise of private contractors has raised a question as to whether those premises obtain even in traditional conflicts; and the possibility of scheduling disobedience, punishment, and protection so as to reduce the threat of breakdown in lawful wars suggests that there may be more room for protection than has typically been acknowledged.

Recognizing this ought both to empower norm entrepreneurs and legal authorities to drive interpretive change in the direction of resolving the regime's normative dissonance, and to invite those and other actors

[35] For the different considerations at play when disobedience occurs away from combat, *cf.* JEFF MCMAHAN, KILLING IN WAR 97–98 (2009); Henry Shue, *Laws of War, Morality, and International Politics*, 26 LEIDEN J. INTL L. 271, 275 n. 14 (2013); OSIEL, *supra* note 33, at 289; Hans Kelsen, *Collective and Individual Responsibility in International Law with Particular Regard to the Punishment of War Criminals*, 31 CAL. L. REV. 530, 556 (1943).

to mobilize for institutional change aimed at restoring the normative coherence and authority of the extant regime, domestically and internationally. Building on the work started in this chapter, the next two chapters begin the conversation about the shape that those doctrinal and institutional changes might take.

9.5 Victim Status

The phenomena described above also have implications for the question of recognizing soldiers killed or harmed fighting aggression as core victims of the crime. In a context of riskless warfare, it is far harder to argue that such recognition would fan the flames of nationalist resentment in the aggressor state. The reason that such victim designation poses a risk above and beyond the finding of aggression itself is that the soldiers granted that status would have gained it through harms suffered in the course of trying to kill the brothers, sisters, sons, and daughters of the aggressor state's people. This is not the case of those killed by drone.

To be sure, the asserted *jus ad bellum* justification of an aggressor state engaged in a drone attack is likely to include a claim that the enemy poses a threat to, or has already attacked, the aggressor, an ally, or a civilian population. However, by finding the leader of that state guilty of aggression, the ICC contradicts precisely that claim. The victim participation and reparation system cannot retreat from that position without sacrificing the integrity of its normative expression. In contrast, in a war of mutual risk, the fact is that soldiers fighting against aggression *do* injure and kill troops on the other side, many of whom are likely to be either minimally culpable, or not at all culpable for the aggression. A victim participation and reparation system that responds to that reality does not retreat from or undermine the core aggression finding.

This spotlights part of why excluding soldiers from the class of recognized crime victims would be the wrong response to worries about triggering a nationalist backlash even in mutually risky wars. The element of that possible backlash that can be accommodated by the ICC without corrupting its core normative message is that there would otherwise be a disproportionate inequity in the treatment of soldiers. The inequity exists because of the undeserved (but justified) harms suffered by those coerced and misled into fighting on the aggressor side, not because there is nothing wrong with the killing and maiming of troops fighting against aggression. Including the former as indirect victims responds to that concern. Excluding soldiers who fight against aggression would not.

The rise of contractors is also relevant to the question of victim status. In the rare cases in which they qualify as "mercenaries," such actors lack the privileges of belligerency.[36] In most cases, however, they are unlikely to fall into that category, because they are nationals or residents of the belligerent state on whose behalf they fight, because they are not motivated "essentially" by private gain, or because they are not compensated "substantially in excess" of the compensation paid to regular troops.[37] In such cases, as long as they comply with the relevant conditions of privileged belligerency, they are protected by international law from domestic criminal punishment for their *jus-in-bello*-compliant acts of violence.

Nonetheless, even when they share a nationality with the state for which they fight, contractors do not have the same relationship with the political community. They are not understood in the same way to be "our" sons, daughters, brothers, and sisters by the members of that community.[38] This may be in part due to a deliberate strategy of states to marginalize contractors from the public consciousness around sacrifice so as to further minimize the political costs of going to war, but there may also be a sense that contractors have not committed in the same way to serve the nation in question unconditionally and exclusively.[39] Whatever the cause, the result of this exclusion from domestic politics is that the exclusion of aggressor contractors from victim status is less likely to feed nationalist myth-making than is the exclusion of aggressor state soldiers.

However, given the inclusion of aggressor soldiers as indirect victims, contractors' exclusion from that status cannot be justified solely on the grounds that they are less central to aggressor's political community. That political context may be why it is important to recognize the former, but once that expanded standard of recognition obtains, it would be arbitrary to exclude contractors on those grounds. If the latter are to be excluded, it must instead be due to the fact that many of the factors that mitigate soldiers' culpability do not apply to contractors. They are not coerced, they do not act out of political obligation, and, having chosen to act through a private employer, it is at least open to question whether they act for associative reasons.

[36] Protocol (I) Additional to the Geneva Conventions of 12 August 1949, and Relating to the Protection of Victims of International Armed Conflicts, art. 47, June 8, 1977, 1125 U.N.T.S. 3.

[37] *Id.* [38] Taussig-Rubbo, *supra* note 24. [39] *See id.* (emphasizing the former).

The one mitigating factor that applies equally to contractors is their likely lack of certainty regarding the *jus ad bellum* status of their war. However, in the absence of coercion, political duties, and associative ties, uncertainty alone ought to weigh strongly in favor of restraint, for all of the reasons discussed in Chapter 5. Presumptively, then, unless contractors can show on an individual basis that misinformation from the aggressor leadership created for them strongly convincing (but mistaken) reasons to believe that the war was lawful, they ought to be excluded from indirect victim status on the grounds that they are not wronged by the harms they suffer in prosecuting an aggressive war.

10

Domestic Implications

The argument thus far has adopted the normative posture of international law. However, this does not limit its interpretive and institutional implications to international law and international institutions. In fact, the failure to recognize the significance of the normative burden of inflicting violence in an aggressive war to domestic law and institutions may be among the most significant lacunae associated with the domestic discourse around when and why we fight.[1]

That discourse tends to focus on a number of issues. Familiar in democratic states is the question of whether the government properly consulted its people and whether it complied with its constitution in deciding to use force on the international stage.[2] Given the blood and treasure required to fight a war, the democratic imperative to have solid domestic authority is strong, and a

[1] *Cf.* Cheyney Ryan, *Moral Equality, Victimhood, and the Sovereignty Symmetry Problem*, *in* Just and Unjust Warriors: The Moral and Legal Status of Soldiers 131, 143 (David Rodin & Henry Shue, eds., 2008).

[2] On the American use of force in Libya in 2011, *see, for example*, Harold Koh played a prominent role arguing that it was not. *See, e.g.*, Testimony by Legal Adviser Harold Hongju Koh, US Dep't of State on Libya and War Powers before the Senate Foreign Relations Committee, June 28, 2011, at 8, www.foreign.senate.gov/imo/media/doc/Koh_Testimony.pdf [hereinafter Koh, Senate Testimony]. Bruce Ackerman and Oona Hathaway penned a series of op-eds arguing that congressional authorization was constitutionally necessary. Bruce Ackerman & Oona Hathaway, *Obama's Illegal War*, Foreign Pol'y (June 1, 2011), http://foreignpolicy.com/2011/06/01/obamas-illegal-war-2; Bruce Ackerman & Oona Hathaway, *Death of the War Powers Act*, Washington Post (May 17, 2011), www.washingtonpost.com/opinions/death-of-the-war-powers-act/2011/05/17/AF3Jh35G_story.html?utm_term=.f241c434f82f; Bruce Ackerman & Oona Hathaway, *The Constitutional Clock is Ticking on Obama's War*, Foreign Pol'y (Apr. 6, 2011), http://foreignpolicy.com/2011/04/06/the-constitutional-clock-is-ticking-on-obamas-war; Bruce Ackerman, *Obama's Unconstitutional War*, Foreign Pol'y (Mar. 24, 2011), http://foreignpolicy.com/2011/03/24/obamas-unconstitutional-war.

government that acts *ultra vires* in this respect perpetrates a significant domestic wrong.[3]

Also familiar is the widely recognized wrong associated with a society sacrificing its troops without good reason. Notwithstanding the prudential case for recognizing those sacrificed in a war of aggression as "indirect victims" of that crime at the ICC, the wrong of unjustified sacrifice is understood and felt primarily in the domestic political sphere. It is an associative failure of the society to properly value its own. Emphasizing the distinction, the domestic discourse around a dubious war is likely to focus primarily on the wrong of sacrificing needlessly the society's own troops, whereas the global condemnation of the same use of force is unlikely to feature that associative wrong at all. Consider in this regard the decision to reserve one third of the seats for Tony Blair's testimony before the Chilcot Inquiry for the families of British soldiers and civilians killed in Iraq.[4] The next of kin of UK persons killed in Iraq were given an opportunity to read the final report prior to its public release.[5] They, more than anyone, were thought to deserve an accounting. The Inquiry's final report noted at the outset that discussions with "families of members of the Armed Forces who died on, or as a result of, military operations in Iraq" and veterans of the war about "the issues on which they considered the Inquiry should focus" were "extremely valuable in shaping the Inquiry's work" and that the Inquiry "sought to address in its Report many of the points that were raised."[6]

These first two dimensions of domestic discourse are, of course, related heavily to one another. One of the reasons for valuing the requirement for democratic authorization is precisely that it is thought to provide

[3] Less commonly discussed, but still very much attached to the question of proper authorization, is the possibility that a lack of constitutional authority could itself create a normative burden for those who fight – a possibility raised by the ongoing litigation on Captain Nathan Smith's request for judicial review of the domestic legal basis for the United States' use of force against the so-called "Islamic State" in Syria. Smith v. Obama, Complaint for Declaratory Relief, paras. 4–7 (D.D.C. 2016), https://law.yale.edu/system/files/documents/pdf/Public_Affairs/smithvobama.pdf.

[4] *Seats Ballot for Tony Blair's Grilling on Iraq War*, BBC News (Jan. 5, 2010).

[5] *Notice to families – details of publication day*, Iraq Inquiry (May 26, 2016), www.iraqinquiry.org.uk/the-inquiry/news-archive/2016/2016-05-26-notice-to-families-details-of-publication-day.

[6] The Report of the Iraq Inquiry HC 264, Introduction, paras. 20–21 (July 6, 2016), *available at* www.iraqinquiry.org.uk/the-report/ [hereinafter Chilcot Report]; *Iraq Inquiry: Full Transcript of Sir John Chilcot's BBC Interview*, BBC News (July 6, 2017) (emphasizing repeatedly the significance of the report to the families), www.bbc.com/news/uk-politics-40510539.

some measure of protection to soldiers against being sent to die without good reason.[7] Nonetheless, the two issues are theoretically distinct, and may diverge in practice. Such divergence is especially likely in states with all-volunteer forces, where the proportion of citizens with ties or potential ties to soldiers may be so low as to undermine majoritarian endorsement as a reliable mechanism for prioritizing soldiers' lives and safety.[8]

A third familiar associative moral concern arises with respect to the treatment of veterans. Here, the idea is that, whatever the cause, having elected to fight, and having sent troops to do so on its behalf, the rest of society thereby takes on a powerful associative obligation to provide those troops with medical and psychiatric care, assistance in social reintegration, and other benefits. Government failure on this dimension can give rise to powerful public outrage.[9]

Significantly, none of these three widely recognized domestic normative concerns regarding waging war is tied inherently to the *jus ad bellum* (in its legal or moral forms). Instead, the animating normative principles are democratic and associative. Each may be violated in a lawful war and all could be upheld in an illegal war. Even the requirement that soldiers

7 The significance of the mortal threat to soldiers in restraining democracies from fighting unnecessary wars has long been one of the core necessary (albeit insufficient) foundations of the liberal democratic peace. *See generally* Immanuel Kant, *Perpetual Peace: A Philosophical Sketch, in* KANT: POLITICAL WRITINGS 93 (Hans Reiss, ed., H. B. Nisbet trans., 1991); MICHAEL DOYLE, LIBERAL PEACE: SELECTED ESSAYS (2011).

8 Precisely this criticism has been leveled against the current system in the United States. *See, e.g.*, Stephen M. Walt, *Is America Addicted to War? The Top 5 Reasons Why We Keep Getting into Foolish Fights*, FOREIGN POL'Y (Apr. 4, 2011), http://foreignpolicy.com/2011/04/04/is-america-addicted-to-war; Andrew J. Bacevich, *Op Ed: The Failure of an All-Volunteer Military*, INTERNATIONAL HERALD TRIBUNE (Jan. 26, 2007).

9 Discussing the scandal, *see* Jordain Carney & Stacy Kaper, *Obama Has Every Reason to Fix the VA. Why Hasn't He?*, NATIONAL JOURNAL (May 14, 2014), www.nationaljournal.com/s/57617; John Dickerson, *Why the VA Scandal Is the Real Outrage*, SLATE (May 20, 2014), www.slate.com/articles/news_and_politics/politics/2014/05/veterans_affairs_scandal_why_the_treatment_of_our_veterans_is_a_genuine.html. Criticizing the relative outrage when veterans do not receive adequate medical care as compared to when others do not receive adequate medical care, *see, for example*, Brian Beutler, *The GOP's Outrageous Health Care Hypocrisy: Vets Aren't the Only People Who Die Awaiting Care*, NEW REPUBLIC (May 27, 2014), https://newrepublic.com/article/117911/gop-veterans-health-care-outrage-doesnt-apply-uninsured-people. On the legal context, *see, for example*, *Symposium: Wounds of War*, 37 NOVA L. REV. (2013) (on the legal and non-legal remedies for US veterans suffering from PTSD); *YLS Clinic Files Nationwide Class Action Lawsuit on Behalf of Vietnam Veterans with PTSD*, YALE LAW SCHOOL (Mar. 3, 2014), https://law.yale.edu/yls-today/news/yls-clinic-files-nationwide-class-action-lawsuit-behalf-vietnam-veterans-ptsd.

be sent to risk their lives only for a worthy cause could be satisfied domestically, despite violating international law, if the war were clearly in the national interest.[10] Democratic peace theorists argue that a government held properly to account by its people will be less likely to wage war against fellow democracies, but this does not extend beyond the community of democratic states, and it is not linked inherently to the *jus ad bellum* as a normative code.[11]

The issue of a war's *jus ad bellum* status is, instead, evaluated from a global normative perspective. The core concerns from that point of view revolve around the justification for inflicting violence on the people and state(s) attacked. In other words, the wrong of an illegal war is inflicted on outsiders with no political or associative connection to the aggressor state or its troops. It seems to occur exclusively on the international plane.

10.1 The Domestic Significance of the *Jus ad Bellum*

Recognizing the burden of fighting for an aggressor force challenges this clean separation between the international and domestic normative planes. The key to transcending that divide is the compound normativity of the burden. Soldiers are wronged by being forced to do wrong. The second wrong in this compound is international; the wrongfulness of the violence the soldier is forced to inflict is determined by the *jus ad bellum* and that violence is perpetrated on outsiders in an international engagement. But the first wrong is domestic; the state and its leaders wrong the soldier through domestic law and domestic instruments of coercion and by exploiting the soldier's associative bonds and sense of domestic political obligation.

In merging these two perspectives, the notion of a burden of fighting for an aggressor force draws domestic attention specifically to the harm a state inflicts on its own soldiers when it demands that they fight a *wrongful* war from a normative perspective applicable to those they kill

[10] Indeed, the "national interest" is often the standard that politicians use when pronouncing in domestic debate on the risks we impose on our troops. To take just one example, in proposing cutting off funding for the Iraq war, Senator Russ Feingold focused not on its *jus ad bellum* status, but identified the core question as whether "putting troops in harm's way" remained "in the Nation's interest." *Iraq*, 153(3) CONG. REC. 4391–92 (Feb. 16, 2007) (statement of Sen. Feingold).

[11] *See, e.g.*, Michael Doyle, *Liberalism and World Politics*, *in* LIBERAL PEACE, *supra* note 4, at 61.

and maim. As discussed in Chapter 2, international law, by definition, provides the only globally applicable normative standard on this issue that is cognizable from the legal perspective. It also replicates commonly accepted standards of wrongfulness across societies, at least in the clear cases. Recognizing the soldier's burden in fighting in a wrongful war means taking seriously as a point of domestic legal and normative concern not just questions of national interest and constitutional authority, but also the question of international legality.

Before turning to what it would mean to take the international legality of going to war seriously in this respect, it is worth pausing to consider one specific situation in which the soldier's burden ought to have a particularly significant role to play in the domestic normative discourse. "Riskless" wars do not raise the associative question of whether *our* troops are being sent to die without adequate reason. Equally, except via the notion of normative burdens, they might be thought to limit considerably the scope of what is owed to *our* veterans. To the extent that democratic endorsement is considered important in significant part because it brings those considerations to bear on the decision to fight, it, too, might be thought to be less than a normative imperative here.[12] In short, by eliminating or weakening each of the key domestic normative checks, remote weapons systems may have made it too easy to go to war.[13]

This ought to be deeply troubling even from a purely domestic perspective, because it ignores one of the profound harms of war – the burden borne by soldiers forced to do wrong. Recognizing that burden spotlights the importance of institutional checks and public scrutiny in riskless war, not simply because it is valuable to uphold international law for its own sake, but because we owe it to our troops, whether or not they face physical risk. As discussed in Chapter 9, this may also be the form of war in which delivering what is due in that sense is most clearly institutionally feasible.

Beyond the context of riskless wars, addressing the burden of fighting in an illegal war confronts the countervailing institutional imperatives

[12] *See* Koh, Senate Testimony, *supra* note 2, at 8; discussion in Section 9.1 of Chapter 9 above.

[13] *See, e.g.*, P. W. Singer, Wired for War 258 (2009); Paul W. Kahn, *The Paradox of Riskless Warfare*, 22 Philosophy & Pub. Pol'y 2, 4 (2002). *But see* Kenneth Anderson, *Efficiency in Bello and ad Bellum – Making the Use of Force Too Easy?*, *in* Targeted Killings: Law and Morality in an Asymmetrical World 374 (Claire Finkelstein, Jens David Ohlin, & Andrew Altman, eds., 2012).

discussed in Chapter 8. The remainder of this chapter explores how to take on that challenge by developing reforms that would limit the coercion that drives soldiers to fight in illegal wars and bolster the soldier's reasons to trust and defer to his state over others, without undermining military functioning in lawful wars.

Limiting coercion would empower at least some to disobey and avoid the burden of participating in the infliction of wrongful death and violence. Bolstering soldiers' reasons for deference would also help to mitigate the normative burden of soldiering. As discussed in Chapter 5, fighting in a legally dubious war is burdensome, even when the soldier is not confident that the war is in fact wrongful and illegal. However, a regime that would protect disobedience whenever the soldier has good reason for doubting the legality of the war, even if the war is in fact lawful, would almost certainly run afoul of the institutional imperatives discussed in Chapter 8. The only way to lessen the burden on such soldiers would be to bolster the soldier's reasons for assessing correctly that such wars are in fact lawful.

A twin focus on coercion and justified deference would underpin three specific changes that ought to be incorporated in one form or another into the domestic institutional and doctrinal structure of any state that takes seriously the burden of soldiering an illegal or seemingly illegal war. Specifically, such states should incorporate: a *jus ad bellum* devil's advocate, a limited retrospective right to disobey orders to fight in illegal wars, and a permanent system of post-war commissions of inquiry. The first and the third would combine to augment the soldier's grounds for deferring to his state over others by institutionalizing the status of the *jus ad bellum* in government decision-making. The second and the third would combine to offer soldiers protection from being forced to fight in illegal wars to the extent compatible with military functioning in lawful wars.

10.2 Deference and the Value of a Devil's Advocate

As discussed previously, the structure and historical context of the *jus ad bellum* are hostile to presumptive deference to one's own state. Most wars are illegal and many militarily active states have a historical record of deceit on *jus-ad-bellum*-relevant facts.[14] Absent specific knowledge about

[14] *See* Section 5.6 of Chapter 5 above.

the war in question, or specific reasons to believe his state is more trustworthy than most on such issues, a soldier's starting presumption should be that his war is illegal. As a result, participating in even some lawful wars is likely to be burdensome. Since the need to protect intelligence sources and methods often precludes publishing primary evidence of the *jus-ad-bellum*-relevant facts, efforts to alleviate that burden ought instead to focus on process.

Publicly evident procedures that would strengthen the influence of the *jus ad bellum* in state decision-making could make it reasonable for those soldiers who lack primary information on the *jus-ad-bellum*-relevant facts to trust their state's claims about those facts. Two institutional steps could advance that objective without changing existing domestic authority structures regarding when and how to use force: a domestic *jus ad bellum* devil's advocate, and permanent provision for a post-war commission of inquiry.

A *jus ad bellum* devil's advocate would serve two objectives.[15] First, it would combat decision-makers' cognitive biases, factual mistakes, and overconfidence on issues relevant to the legal basis for war.[16] Along these lines, some have argued that a failure to subject key intelligence to "red team" or devil's advocate analyses in the build-up to the 2003 invasion of Iraq was a key factor in the errors made in that decision-making process.[17] Second, if properly complemented by a public review body like the post-war commission of inquiry discussed below, a devil's advocate could undermine a leader's capacity after the war to deny awareness of important countervailing information or intelligence weaknesses. This would

[15] On the utility of devil's advocates in foreign policy generally, *see, for example*, ROBERT JERVIS, PERCEPTION AND MISPERCEPTION IN INTERNATIONAL POLITICS 415–17 (1976). David Luban, among others, has argued for such an institution for *jus in bello* purposes in the context of targeted killing. David Luban, *What Would Augustine Do? The President, Drones, and Just War Theory*, BOSTON REV. (June 6, 2012).

[16] JERVIS, PERCEPTION, *supra* note 15, at 417 (explaining why mere diversity without an assigned devil's advocate is often insufficient to combat these dangers). A practice common in intelligence agencies is the "Team A/Team B" process, whereby an outside team is invited to perform an independent alternative analysis of intelligence information, so as to combat biases and groupthink. This can have its own pathologies, particularly if it is used to circumvent primary intelligence that decision-makers do not like. *See, e.g.*, Gordon R. Mitchell, *Team B Intelligence Coups*, 92 Q. J. SPEECH 144 (2006); US SENATE SELECT COMMITTEE ON INTELLIGENCE, SUBCOMMITTEE ON COLLECTION, PRODUCTION, AND QUALITY REPORT: THE NATIONAL INTELLIGENCE ESTIMATES A-B TEAM EPISODE CONCERNING SOVIET STRATEGIC CAPABILITY AND OBJECTIVES (1978).

[17] Robert Jervis, *Reports, Politics, and Intelligence Failures: The Case of Iraq*, 29 J. STRATEGIC STUD. 3, 15–16 (2006).

heighten both the political costs and legal risks of leaders' mendacity on these points.

A domestic institution of this kind ought to be tailored to specific national conditions. Nonetheless, the general contours can be sketched here. Prior to the initiation of any war, the advocate would be asked to review relevant intelligence analysis and prepare a classified adversarial brief for the President or Prime Minister, relevant cabinet members, and security-cleared legislative leaders. The brief would seek to debunk any putative factual predicates for a legal case for war.

Structuring "conflicting cognitive biases" into the system in this way, rather than "seeking 'unbiased' treatment" of the underlying data, would guard against the danger that group-think or related pathologies would produce a single mistaken assessment, without caveats or skepticism, for the decision-maker.[18] An adversarial process would help to ensure that claimed facts that support the legal case for war are queried, would highlight alternative interpretations of those claimed facts, and would expose uncertainties or inconsistencies that may have been glossed over or ignored in the primary intelligence or departmental reports.

The basic value of considering contradictory views as a way of improving compliance with the *jus ad bellum* goes back at least as far as Vitoria, who termed it "obvious" that the prince should "listen to the arguments of opponents" and consult "wise men who can speak with freedom."[19] The challenges are to institutionalize and guarantee the presentation of an effective argument against the war in question, to ensure that the proponent of that contrary case has access to the relevant information, and to design the adversarial system such that the contrary arguments will be taken seriously, rather than dismissed as pro forma and implicitly lacking substantive merit.

The first element of guaranteeing an effective argument against the war would be to define the mandate accordingly, tasking the devil's advocate with the specific function of challenging any official analysis on facts that may underpin the legal basis for war. The second element would be to shield the advocate from institutional capture, so that she could deliver on that mandate. This would entail both depoliticizing her appointment, and, once she has been appointed, separating her office from any government institution or government actor.

[18] Jervis, Perception, *supra* note 15, at 416.

[19] Francisco de Vitoria, *On the Law of War*, *in* Political Writings 295, 307 (Anthony Pagden & Jeremy Lawrance, eds., Cambridge Univ. Press 1991) (1539) (emphasis added).

Optimally, appointment authority would be vested in the nation's supreme judicial organ or the post-war commission of inquiry discussed below. The advocate would be selected from a list of candidates with an expertise in international law, and would have the authority to appoint a small team of lawyers and intelligence analysts to assist in her work. In these respects, the advocate would have some parallels to the now defunct United States Office of the Independent Counsel – an institution charged with the criminal investigation of persons in certain positions close to the US President, so that those investigations would not be under the control of the President, via the Department of Justice.[20] A key problem with the latter office was its perceived overuse, the expansion of investigations beyond their initial remit, the public nature of investigations meaning that their targets were tarnished before any decision or verdict, and consonant efforts by those targets to politicize investigations and undermine the Independent Counsel's credibility.[21] The *jus ad bellum* devil's advocate, in contrast, would have a narrowly defined mandate and less discretion. Moreover, much of her work would take place in the first instance behind closed doors, would not itself imply suspicion of criminality, and would serve primarily to inform the initial decision on going to war and secondarily to inform the post-war commission of inquiry.

Given the relatively sporadic need for her analysis, she would likely maintain a non-governmental career, with a secure and private office for the examination of intelligence and other relevant information when needed. An analogous institution with similar protections exists currently in the form of the UK's Independent Reviewer of Terrorism Legislation. The Reviewer is charged with assessing the operation of the UK's anti-terrorism laws and recommending change through parliamentary and ministerial reports.[22] He is accorded access to highly classified intelligence information to facilitate that role.[23] Indicative of his insulation from the political branches, the Reviewer remains a member of the independent Bar and is based in his own chambers, while retaining a private room and administrative assistance at the Office of Security and

[20] *See, e.g.*, The Independent Counsel Reauthorization Act of 1994, 28 U.S.C. §§ 591–99 (1994). Particularly: *id.*, §§ 592–94.

[21] *See, e.g.*, Julie R. O'Sullivan, *The Independent Counsel Statute: Bad Law, Bad Policy*, 33 Am. Crim. L. Rev. 463 (1996).

[22] David Anderson, *The Independent Review of Terrorism Legislation*, 5 Eur. Hum. Rt. L. Rev. 544 (2011).

[23] *Id.*

Counter-Terrorism for the purposes of intelligence review.[24] Similar structures would make sense for a *jus ad bellum* devil's advocate.

The advocate's brief against the legality of the war would have no binding effect. Her power would come only through the persuasiveness of her analysis. As such, the government would retain its current freedom to use force and wage war. This limit on her power could help to deter political efforts to influence her, although the aforementioned appointment safeguards would remain essential.

Of course, precisely because her authority would be restricted to advising and persuading, there is a risk that she would be ignored. Two features of her mandate would guard against that and strengthen the likelihood that her reports would be considered seriously by decision-makers.

First, the advocate would have access to all of the primary evidence informing the official intelligence analysis in support of the legality of war. More importantly, her office would have the capacity to receive (in full confidence) dissenting or questioning views, interpretations, or additional information from all levels and agencies regarding *jus-ad-bellum*-relevant intelligence. This aspect of the institution would be similar to the US State Department's Dissent Channel, but with broader trans-departmental reach, greater emphasis on classified intelligence, and a narrow *jus ad bellum* focus.[25] This access to primary intelligence would both enable the advocate to bring key information or significant caveats to the attention of senior decision-makers, who otherwise may not receive it, and foil any effort to dismiss her views for lack of expertise.[26]

Second, the devil's advocate would be strengthened immeasurably by being linked to an additional retrospective institution of the kind

[24] *The Reviewer's Role*, Independent Reviewer of Terrorism Legis., https://terrorismlegislationreviewer.independent.gov.uk/about-me (last visited June 30, 2017).

[25] Dissent Channel, 2 US Dep't of State for For. Aff. Manual 070, www.state.gov/documents/organization/84374.pdf. Available to all employees of the Dep't of State and USAID, the dissent channel provides an avenue for lower-level analysts to submit "dissenting and alternative views on substantive foreign policy issues that cannot be communicated in a full and timely manner through regular operating channels and procedures." *Id.*, at 3. The dissenting view is submitted to the Secretary's Policy Planning Staff, which then distributes copies to the Secretary, the Deputy Secretary, the Under Secretary for Political Affairs, the Executive Secretary, and the Chair of the Secretary's Open Forum. *Id.*, at 5.

[26] This primary evidence often does not make it to key executive decision-makers. *See* Section 5.6 of Chapter 5 above.

discussed below. The devil's advocate's reports would be available in full to that commission, which would have the authority to use them in its final report on the war, with the necessary secrecy safeguards. Retrospective engagement with her advice in this form would raise significantly the costs to leaders of dismissing her advice without properly evaluating it at the time of decision. Politically, the exposure of such dismissal could raise questions about whether the leader took sufficiently seriously the sacrifice of blood and treasure that her decision entailed. Legally, the information provided by the devil's advocate could make it harder for the decision-maker to argue that she was not aware of the facts rendering the war manifestly illegal – a key test for criminality.[27]

Although much of the advocate's work during the run-up to war would occur behind the wall of secrecy, it would be a "shallow" secrecy; the institution's existence, design, and role would be widely publicized, its reports would inform the post-war commission's public findings, and they would be provided to security-cleared actors in the legislative and executive branches of government.[28] It could also be appropriate to publish a delayed, declassified summary of her reports after the war, with a view to a further delayed declassification of the full report in due course.

Such declassified summaries of sensitive material are already used in a number of situations. The UK's Independent Reviewer of Terrorism Legislation has full access to classified material and produces public reports based in part on that information that are often critical of the government (although not specifically designed to be adversarial in nature).[29] Similarly, various countries' approaches to adjudicating claims regarding the detention of persons on national security grounds (especially terrorist suspects), require the disclosure of some form of summary of the "gist" or "core" of the evidence against a detainee.[30]

The devil's advocate institution would, of course, be bolstered by the work of existing intra-agency dissent bodies, both through receiving their

[27] *See* ICC, *Elements of Crimes*, ICC-PIOS-LT-03-002/15_Eng, at 30 (2013), www.icc-cpi.int/resource-library/Documents/ElementsOfCrimesEng.pdf.

[28] Any secrecy, in other words, would be shallow, not deep. *Cf.* David Pozen, *Deep Secrecy*, 62 Stan. L. Rev. 257 (2010) (discussing the several dimensions along which secrets vary from deep to shallow and arguing that government secrecy should always be as shallow as possible).

[29] Anderson, *The Independent Review*, *supra* note 23.

[30] Daphne Barak-Erez & Matthew C. Waxman, *Secret Evidence and the Due Process of Terrorist Detentions*, 48 Colum. J. Transnat'l L. 3, 9–18 (2009).

reports, and (if necessary) via the dissent channel mentioned above.[31] However, four features distinguish it from such actors: it would not be internal to any specific department or agency; it would present its work directly to the top decision-makers; it would be focused on the *jus ad bellum*; and it would be connected to an automatic post-war commission of inquiry.[32]

By forestalling errors that may otherwise have been missed, undermining deniability regarding key countervailing *jus ad bellum* evidence, and raising the legal, political, and legacy costs of mendacity, an advocate with these features would augment the soldier's grounds for deferring to his state's *jus ad bellum* assessment. This would reduce the proportion of wars in which it would be unreasonable for him to believe in the lawfulness of the enterprise.

Of course, to the extent it would raise the costs of waging illegal war, such reform is intrinsically desirable from the international legal point of view. However, its virtue in respecting and protecting soldiers as agents involved in a morally burdensome activity is of particular domestic resonance. For the reasons noted above, it would be of heightened significance

[31] In the United States, the Defense Intelligence Agency's devil's advocate or the Department of Homeland Security's "Red Cell" Unit and Alternate Analysis Division, for example could prove important potential allies within those agencies. *See* US Office of the Director of Nat'l Intelligence, ODNI Progress Report: WMD Commission Recommendations (Unclassified) 9 (2006).

[32] Existing adversarial institutions are several. In the United States, the Intelligence Reform and Terrorism Prevention Act required that the Director of National Intelligence "implement a process and assign an individual or entity the responsibility for ensuring that, as appropriate, elements of the intelligence community conduct alternative analysis (commonly referred to as "red team analysis") of the information and conclusions in intelligence products." 50 U.S.C , § 403-1(h)(1)(c). The WMD Commission also demanded greater dissent, redundancy, and alternative analysis in the US intelligence community. Unclassified Version of the Report of the Commission on the Intelligence Capabilities of the United States Regarding Weapons of Mass Destruction 406–07 (2005) [hereinafter WMD Commission Report]. One of the ways this has been implemented is through the creation of an internal devil's advocate in the Defense Intelligence Agency (DIA). US Office of the Director of Nat'l Intelligence, *supra* note 31, at 5. This individual's primary task is to challenge key assumptions on important topics for the agency. Finally, in 1973, after Israel was surprised by an attack by Egypt and Syria, it created the Israel Defense Intelligence (IDI) Revision Department. The Department challenges perceptions held by intelligence analysts, and documents from the head of the Revision Department are sent to the Prime Minister, the Minister of Defense, the Chairman of the Foreign Affairs and Defense Committee, and other key decision-makers. Col. Shmuel Even, *The Revision Process in the Intelligence*, *in* Israel's Silent Defender 309 (Amos Gilboa & Ephraim Lapid, eds., 2012).

in the context of riskless warfare, in which concerns about exposing soldiers to physical threat without warrant have been largely eliminated.

10.3 A Limited Right to Disobey Orders to Fight in Illegal Wars

A second dimension of domestic institutional change would provide soldiers a limited domestic right to refuse to fight in internationally illegal wars, whenever that protection is compatible with military functioning in lawful wars. The imperative to provide such protection is rooted in international law and applies irrespective of constitutional structure. However, diverse domestic political and constitutional constraints on judicial review mean that the will and internal authority to implement such protection would vary significantly across states.

At one end of the spectrum, a broad right to disobey on *jus ad bellum* grounds has already been upheld in Germany. In 2005, the *Bundesverwaltungsgericht* (German Federal Administrative Court, *BVGer*) overturned the conviction of Major Florian Pfaff, who had refused to participate in a military software project because it would be used to support what he considered an illegal war – the US-led invasion of Iraq.[33] Rooting its holding in the German constitutional right to freedom of conscience,[34] the court quashed the conviction and protected Pfaff's disobedience on the grounds that he had "objectively serious legal reservations" to the war.[35] It examined the Security Council Resolutions pursuant to which leading coalition members claimed to be acting, and evaluated, in the alternative, the viability of a self-defense claim under Article 51 of the UN Charter.[36] Rejecting both lines of argument, and emphasizing the international prohibition on aggression, the Court concluded that "the soldier was right in his considerable doubts about the legality of the war against Iraq," and held that "serious doubts" therefore

[33] Deutschland v. N, Bundesverwaltungsgericht, No. 2 WD 12.04, 120 Deutsches Verwaltungsblatt 1455 (June 21, 2005); Ilja Baudisch, Germany v. N Decision No. 2 WD 12.04, 100 AM. J. INT'L L. 911 (2006). The soldier's initial conviction was before the military court (*Truppendienstgericht*), where he was found guilty of deliberate insubordination and demoted from Major to Captain. *Id.*, at 911.

[34] Grundgesetz für die Bundesrepublik Deutschland (German Basic Law [Constitution]), art. 4 (May 23, 1949) (last amended July 29, 2009).

[35] Baudisch, *supra* note 33, at 912.

[36] The key Charter provisions in this instance were: UN Charter, arts. 2(4), 39, 42, 51. The relevant Security Council resolutions were S.C. Res. 1441 (Nov. 8, 2002); S.C. Res. 678 (Nov. 29, 1990); S.C. Res. 687 (1991).

"exist as to whether the supporting actions by Germany were legally permissible."[37] Although refraining from holding explicitly that the invasion of Iraq was in fact illegal, the *BVGer* engaged in a careful and detailed *jus ad bellum* analysis in order to uphold Pfaff's right to disobey, concluding that his legal assessment was "not only sincere, but objectively reasonable."[38]

Bearing the burden of its Nazi legacy, Germany is an anomalous state. It bans aggression in its constitution and its criminal code; it was an early signatory of the ICC's aggression amendments; and domestic judicial review of governmental decisions to participate in war is not uncommon.[39] Moreover, in this particular case, the German population and government were united in opposing the Iraq War, Germany had opposed efforts to secure authorization for the war in both the Security Council and the North Atlantic Council, and the German government had refused to send troops, limiting its contribution to minimal logistical support from outside Iraq's borders.[40]

Although other states have empowered their courts to engage in *jus ad bellum* analysis, these unique features of Germany's relationship to aggression and of Pfaff's case in particular mean that replicating that level of protection elsewhere is politically unlikely.[41] Indeed, if the necessity argument of Chapter 8 holds, it may be dangerous; a generally applicable disobedience protection for soldiers with an "objectively

[37] Baudisch, *supra* note 33, at 914.

[38] *Id.*, at 914–16. Instead it held that the Major's personal belief regarding the illegality of the war was "not only sincere, but objectively reasonable." *Id.*, at 915.

[39] Grundgesetz, *supra* note 34, art. 26; Strafgesetzbuch [StGB] [Penal Code], BUNDESGESETZBLATT [BGBl] I p. 3322, §§ 80, 80a (Ger.) (Nov. 13, 1998); ICC, Press Release: Botswana and Germany ratify amendments on the crime of aggression and article 8, ICC-ASP-20130610-PR916 (June 10, 2013), www.icc-cpi.int/legalAidConsultations?name=pr916; Claus Kreß, *The German Chief Federal Prosecutor's Decision Not to Investigate the Alleged Crime of Preparing Aggression against Iraq*, 2 J. INT'L CRIM. JUSTICE 245, 247–55 (2004). On judicial review of decisions to participate in war (per the requirements of domestic law), consider: Helmut Philipp Aust & Mindia Vashakmadze, *Parliamentary Consent to the Use of German Armed Forces Abroad*, 9 GERMAN L.J. 2223 (2008); German Federal Constitutional Court Press Office, *Organstreit* proceedings brought by the Left parliamentary group on the Bundeswehr deployment in Kosovo unsuccessful: Press Release 122/2009 (Oct. 23, 2009), www.bundesverfassungsgericht.de/SharedDocs/Pressemitteilungen/EN/2009/bvg09-122.html.

[40] Baudisch, *supra* note 33, at 911; *France & Germany Unite against Iraq War*, GUARDIAN (Jan. 22, 2003), www.theguardian.com/world/2003/jan/22/germany.france.

[41] A number of states include aggression in their criminal codes and if the ICC amendment succeeds, others may follow so as to retain domestic primacy. *See* Section 1.1 of Chapter 1 above.

reasonable" objection to their war's legality could threaten military functioning in lawful wars.

Nonetheless, underpinning the *BVGer*'s analysis are accurate premises. Conscience rights must include the right not to be forced to do wrong by the law's own lights. Soldiering can often entail that form of normative burden, and this is true even when the soldier is not certain of illegality. Moreover, that burden attaches to the question of a war's *jus ad bellum* status. Whether or not the court's expansive view of when the right to disobey obtains is viable, the underlying posture of the judgment sets an important precedent and provides a normative resource for those seeking to expand disobedience protection on both the domestic and the international levels.

To the extent the scope of protection provided by the *BVGer* would be institutionally dangerous in more militarily active states, more modest protections could be implemented. The fact of their modesty, however, does not dilute the imperative to provide such protections. On the contrary, if the current regime is indeed rooted in necessity, then there is an internal imperative to implement whatever marginal protection is viable without disrupting military functioning in lawful wars.

For the reasons articulated previously, the rise of riskless warfare presents a particularly fertile opportunity for disobedience protection. In such wars, there is no institutional imperative to preserve rules of total *jus ad bellum* obedience. If institutional necessity is the justification for denying protection in other contexts, protection must be extended in riskless wars.

The obvious practical obstacle to this is that it would require a classification system distinguishing formally between wars of high and low risk to the relevant state's troops. This is not insurmountable. Leaders could be required to formally class their wars as "remotely fought" or "troop-deployed," with the former triggering stronger disobedience rights. The Obama administration's assertion that the low risk level of the Libya intervention obviated the need for congressional approval evinces a belief in the executive branch of a militarily active superpower that a legally consequential classification along these lines is feasible.[42]

The notion of legally different forms of war would hardly be revolutionary. Although the difference between the regimes is narrowing, the

[42] *See supra* Section 9.1 of Chapter 9 above.

applicable regimes of international humanitarian law and war crimes prohibitions hinge already on the classification of a conflict as international or non-international. The divergence is particularly pronounced with respect to the authority to detain or intern, the legal status of certain weapons, and the rules governing population transfers and human shields.[43] And yet, despite the high stakes, various courts, including the Israeli Supreme Court, the UK Supreme Court, the ICJ, and the ICC have ruled on the classification of specific wars, with consequences for states and individuals.[44]

The classification of wars into those that are fought remotely and those involving troop deployment may not even require that level of judicial

[43] *See generally* Jean-Marie Henckaerts & Louise Doswald-Beck, 1 CUSTOMARY INTERNATIONAL HUMANITARIAN LAW (2005) (discussing for each rule of customary international humanitarian law whether it applies in one or both conflict types). Arguing against the ICRC study for a broader difference in rules, *see* John Bellinger & William J. Haynes, *A US Government Response to the International Committee of the Red Cross Study Customary International Humanitarian Law*, 89 INT'L REV. RED CROSS 443, 447 (2007). On the distinction under international criminal law, *see, for example*, Rome Statute of the International Criminal Court, U.N. Doc. A/CONF.183/9, 2187 U.N.T.S. 90, art. 8 (July 17, 1998) (as amended in 2010 by Doc. C.N.651.2010.TREATIES-8); Prosecutor v. Lubanga (ICC-01/04-01/06), para. 539 (Mar. 14, 2012) [hereinafter Lubanga Trial Judgment].

[44] Among the rulings on the classification of an armed conflict, consider Legal Consequences of the Construction of a Wall in the Occupied Palestinian Territory, Advisory Opinion, 2004 I.C.J. 136 (July 9), paras. 89–101; H.C.J. 769/02 Pub. Comm'n against Torture in Isr. v. State of Isr., para. 18 (2006) (Isr.); Armed Activities on the Territory of the Congo (Dem. Rep. Congo v. Uganda), 2005 I.C.J. 168 (Dec. 19), paras. 172–80; Lubanga Trial Judgment, *supra* note 43, paras. 539–67. The United States Supreme Court in *Hamdan* rejected the US government's classification of the war on al-Qa'ida as neither an international nor a non-international armed conflict (since it was not against a state, but was also not internal to the United States). Although declining to rule officially on which classification applied, the Court essentially adopted the non-international armed conflict paradigm with profound consequences for the American detention regime. Hamdan v. Rumsfeld, 548 U.S. 557, 631–32 (2006). Despite the Court's failure to rule explicitly on the classification question, its decision has been interpreted widely as implying that the conflict is non-international. *See, e.g.*, Jelena Pejic, *The Protective Scope of Common Article 3: More than Meets the Eye*, 93 INT'L REV. RED CROSS 1, 7 (2011). Various external authorities have also opined on the classification applicable to the Occupied Palestinian Territories, including, Gaza. Iain Scobbie observes that "During Operation Cast Lead, it appears that a majority of States considered Gaza still to be occupied, despite Israel's disengagement and Hamas' seizure of power in Gaza in June 2007." He notes the expression of this view in Security Council debates and cites the UK, the UN Secretary-General, the Human Rights Council, and the 118-state Non-Aligned movement. Iain Scobbie, *Gaza*, *in* INTERNATIONAL LAW AND THE CLASSIFICATION OF ARMED CONFLICTS 280, 293–94 (Wilmshurst, ed., 2012). The Security Council has, in the past, taken a position on the issue. S.C. Res. 465 (Mar. 1, 1980).

review; popular appraisal may be a sufficient check on mendacity. Whereas the *jus ad bellum* status of a war (and possibly its status as international or non-international) is often ambiguous to those lacking access to intelligence, the issue of whether there are significant military troops deployed to the battlefield is typically less so. Marginal cases could be resolved by setting an explicit threshold for the number of persons on the ground in-theater beyond which the war becomes "troop-deployed."[45] Moreover, even in cases that are ambiguous (because they are close to the margin, or due to a high level of covert actors on the ground), few governments would misclassify a riskless war as "troop-deployed." If anything, the incentive runs strongly in the opposite direction. The remotely fought nature of a war is generally something the government would *want* to assert precisely because minimizing the risks to which its soldiers are subject tends to mitigate political opposition.[46]

Ultimately, then, a domestic classification of wars as either "remotely fought" or "troop-deployed" would be workable. Judicial review of such classification would not be anomalous, but a classification system of that kind should function well even without judicial review. If such a system were implemented, soldiers who refuse to participate in "remotely fought" wars would have a right to have that refusal protected if with reference to the legality of the war.

The process by which that claim would be vindicated would depend on domestic constitutional factors. In states in which *jus ad bellum* judicial review is prohibited, review of the soldier's claimed right to refuse (in addition to any punishment in the event of his defeat) would be delayed and determined by the *jus ad bellum* assessment of the post-war commission of inquiry described below or, at a bare minimum, by an authoritative international ruling in those cases in which one is forthcoming.[47] In states in which judicial review of the *jus ad bellum* is

[45] Even drone operations involve some minimal number of covert actors on the ground, but the fact of these individuals' roles ought not obscure the qualitative distinction between a drone intervention and a land invasion, as recognized in both domestic and international perspectives on the intervention against Libya in 2011. For the Obama administration's domestic posture *see* Koh, Senate Testimony, *supra* note 2, at 8. The qualitative international distinction was at the core of the Security Council authorization for the Libya intervention. S.C. Res. 1973 (2011), para. 4.

[46] *Cf.* Sections 6.1 and 6.3 of Chapter 6 and Section 9.1 of Chapter 9 above.

[47] On the "political question" prohibition of judicial review of the *jus ad bellum*, *see, for example*, Luftig v. McNamara et al., 373 F.2d 664, 665 (D.C. Cir. 1967); Mitchell v. United States, 369 F.2d 323 (2d Cir.1966); Mora v. McNamara, 387 F.2d 862 (D.C. Cir. 1967); United States v. Johnson, 38 C.M.R. 44, 45 (C.M.A. 1967); United States v. Noyd, 40

feasible, the right could be vindicated in a manner similar to that applied by the *BVGer*, except limited to remotely fought wars. Even the occasional mistaken *jus ad bellum* ruling in a riskless war would be unlikely to trigger mass disobedience or cause military breakdown, given that soldiers would have only the right (and not the legal duty) to disobey and given that they would not face any personal threat should they continue to fight.

It may even be that selective conscientious objection rights could be offered in this limited context without undermining functioning in lawful wars. If so, the internal argument given here would provide an additional reason to support such a system, beyond the liberal pluralist reasons that ordinarily underpin demands for selective conscientious objection.[48]

An additional (and more ambitious) domestic reform would extend disobedience rights into traditional troop-deployed conflicts, but with timing restrictions along the lines of those discussed in Chapter 9. In this system, soldiers who refuse to fight on *jus ad bellum* grounds would be punished immediately, but, if they disobey outside the theater of conflict and turn themselves in immediately, they would be eligible for post-war, retrospective exoneration, if the war were found to be illegal.

As discussed previously, this structure would avoid many of the dangers of protecting disobedience. Delaying review of the war's legality would obviate the risk that a mistaken judicial decision would cause a disobedience cascade in a lawful war. Preserving the system of instant discipline and punishment during the war would alleviate the distorting effects of protected disobedience on the judgment and behavior of

C.M.R. 195, 203 (C.M.A. 1969); United States v. Wilson, 41 C.M.R. 100, 101 (C.M.A. 1969); United States v. New, 50 M.J. 729, 739–40 (A. Ct. Crim. App. 1999); United States v. Huet-Vaughn, 43 M.J. 105, 114–15 (1995). *See also* US v. Kabat, 797 F.2d 580, 590 (8th Cir. 1986). On the commission of inquiry, *see infra* Section 10.3. On the possibility of an international authoritative determination, *see* Section 8.2 of Chapter 8 above.

48 Some have argued for selective conscientious rights in "limited wars," and this gained very brief legal traction in the United States before being struck down. TELFORD TAYLOR, NUREMBERG AND VIETNAM: AN AMERICAN TRAGEDY 203–04 (1970); United States v. Sisson, 297 F. Supp. 902 (D. Mass. 1969) (emphasizing the non-existential nature of the war as a reason for expanded conscientious objection rights). Gillette v. United States, 401 U.S. 437 (1971) (denying selective conscientious objection rights). On the concept of "limited" or "low-intensity" war, *see* LOW-INTENSITY WARFARE: COUNTERINSURGENCY, PROINSURGENCY, AND ANTITERRORISM IN THE EIGHTIES (Michael T. Klare & Peter Kornbluh, eds., 1988); US DEPT. ARMY, FIELD MANUAL 100–20: MILITARY OPERATIONS IN LOW INTENSITY CONFLICT (1990). *See also* Bruce Ackerman & Oona Hathaway, *Limited War and the Constitution*, 109 MICH. L. REV. 447 (2011).

soldiers in lawful wars. Restricting the right to disobey to those who refuse to fight while outside the theater of conflict would minimize the negative impact of disobedience on unit cohesion, and remove choice from the paralyzing hell of battle.[49] Protecting only those who turn themselves in immediately would eliminate the opportunistic invocation of the *jus ad bellum* by denying the defense to those who desert for other reasons, even if their wars turn out to be unlawful.

When the war was in fact illegal, retrospective review and protection would recognize that those who refused to fight refrained from what the law must recognize to be wrongful violence. Their refusals would be vindicated and their records would be cleared. Of course, the state would still have wronged them through punishing them during the war. Moreover, those who reasonably believed the war to have been illegal would not be protected at all by this system of retrospective vindication.

However, those shortfalls in protection reflect the enduring institutional necessity of a system of obedience. The framework of retrospective review seeks to balance the value of vindicating and encouraging disobedience in illegal wars against the danger of undermining the general efficacy of the military institution in lawful wars.[50] By its very nature, that balancing entails some sacrifice of optimal protection in order to preserve the institution.

Despite limiting the degree to which soldiers are shielded from criminal sanction, retrospective review along these lines would not be insignificant. Official vindication (even after the end of a criminal sentence) would help to restore the dignity and social respect of those who refuse to do wrong. Deserters from the Nazi wars of aggression worked for decades to have their criminal records overturned following the Allied victory.[51] The same need drives many who have been wrongly accused or tarnished with public assertions of culpability of any kind to go to great lengths to clear their names or the names of dead loved ones.[52] More broadly, this basic human ache for vindication

[49] *Cf.* Section 8.3 of Chapter 8 above.

[50] On balancing the empowerment of individuals to uphold the law and military discipline, *see* Mark Osiel, Obeying Orders 56–57 (1999); Richard De George, *Defining Moral Obligations*, 34 Army 22, 29 (1984).

[51] On the status of Nazi deserters after World War II, *see* Section 1.3 of Chapter 1 above.

[52] Consider, for example, the decades-long (and regularly rebuffed) Hillsborough for Justice Campaign of Liverpudlians seeking to clear the names of their family members after the latter were blamed incorrectly by the police and the media for a football ground crush in which ninety-six of them were killed in 1989. The Report of the Hillsborough

is at the heart of human rights litigation, much of which focuses primarily on demand for official recognition of the wrongs done to the victim, and much less on material compensation, which is typically minimal, if awarded and paid at all.[53]

In operationalizing disobedience protection along these lines, the point on which states are likely to diverge is on the question of which authority would rule retrospectively on the *jus ad bellum*. A judgment or resolution by one of the international *jus ad bellum* authorities would dispose of the issue, and could be the basis for the exoneration of those who disobeyed pursuant to the procedure above.[54] However, in the absence of such a ruling or its imminent prospect, the determination would need to be made domestically. The use of a national institution to reflect on the *jus ad bellum* question would be appropriate in this context precisely because the wrong done to those forced to fight in an illegal war is itself a domestic wrong, perpetrated through domestic law and the domestic instruments of coercion.

Given the stakes, the potentially large number of individual cases, the necessary examination of classified information, the potential complexity of the issues, and constitutional imperatives in many states to keep such issues from the judiciary, it may make sense for such *jus ad bellum* review to be performed not by an ordinary court (or even a supreme court or constitutional court), but by a specialized commission.

INDEPENDENT PANEL (2012), http://hillsborough.independent.gov.uk/repository/report/HIP_report.pdf.

[53] The overriding desire for acknowledgement among those who have suffered human rights violations is manifest in the persistence of human rights litigation even when reparations payments are low or the probability of converting a court-room success into a reparations payment is negligible (and anyway minimal, and plainly inadequate, in the rare cases it is paid). On the importance of official acknowledgement in the aftermath of rights violations, *see* MARTHA MINOW, BETWEEN VENGEANCE AND FORGIVENESS: FACING HISTORY AFTER GENOCIDE AND MASS VIOLENCE 93 (1998); Pablo de Greiff, *Justice and Reparations*, *in* REPARATIONS: INTERDISCIPLINARY INQUIRIES 153, 160–67 (Jon Miller & Rahul Kumar, eds., 2007); Brandon Hamber, *The Dilemmas of Reparations: In Search of a Process-Driven Approach*, *in* OUT OF THE ASHES: REPARATION FOR VICTIMS OF GROSS AND SYSTEMATIC HUMAN RIGHTS VIOLATIONS 135, 142, 149 (K. De Feyter et al., eds., 2005). Advocating the Inter-American Court's focus on satisfaction and rehabilitation, rather than financial payment, Tom Antkowiak, *Remedial Approaches to Human Rights Violations: The Inter-American Court of Human Rights and Beyond*, 46 COLUM. J. TRANS'L L. 351 (2008).

[54] On internationally authoritative rulings, *see* Section 8.2 of Chapter 8 above.

10.4 Reflecting on Why We Fought: Institutionalizing the Post-War Commission of Inquiry

Indeed, an automatic post-war commission of inquiry would be crucial to better respecting the soldier on both the epistemic and the coercive dimensions. Without one, the devil's advocate would be vulnerable to being either ostracized and ignored or captured and impotent. On the issue of disobedience protection, any court tasked with *jus ad bellum* review would lack the relevant legal and intelligence expertise, would be motivated by the need to maintain its political status and authority in its primary legal domains, and may lack constitutional competence to rule on the issue.

The automatic post-war institution of a special commission of inquiry could overcome each of these obstacles. It would also recognize the genuine domestic reasons – exemplified most acutely in the morally strained position of the soldier – to be concerned internally about the lawfulness of the state's external use of force.

The deep domestic controversy around the 2003 invasion of Iraq in a number of states instigated the creation of a number of commissions of inquiry that provide preliminary models for an institution along these lines.[55] Those, however, were ad hoc inquiries, motivated by the political battles and controversies particular to the Iraq invasion. To fulfill its purpose, the commission proposed here must be automatic, guaranteed to investigate the decision to use force irrespective of political controversy, of conflict duration, of national lives lost or risked, or of whether there were known intelligence failures or public lies. It would simply be part of going to war that the decision to do so would subsequently be exposed to intensive *jus ad bellum* examination.

Among recent commissions, the Iraq Inquiry in the UK (also known as the Chilcot Inquiry) was notable for its emphasis on public hearings, including for the interrogation of key decision-makers, and on its insistence on publishing key documents on its website. However, it has been criticized on other fronts. The process took too long (seven years), and was for a long time undermined by the refusal of the government to hand

[55] Chilcot Report, *supra* note 6; Rt. Hon the Lord Butler of Brockwell et al., Review of Intelligence on Weapons of Mass Destruction Report of a Committee of Privy Councillors (2004); US Senate Select Committee on Intelligence, Report: Postwar Findings about Iraq's WMD Programs and Links to Terrorism and How they Compare with Prewar Assessments (2006); WMD Commission Report, *supra* note 32.

over certain key documents regarding cabinet meetings and a phone conversation between Blair and US President George Bush before the invasion.[56] After over three years of intransigence following the Inquiry's final hearings, a compromise on the latter issue was reached whereby a combination of quotations and the "gist" of the documents and conversations were to be published to illuminate the Inquiry's report.[57] Members of the Inquiry were also criticized for being insufficiently skeptical or penetrating in the questions they posed to top decision-makers and others who came before the panel, particularly as regards inconsistencies with documentary evidence.[58]

The biggest missing element of the Iraq Inquiry Report from the perspective of the arguments presented here is its failure to reach a determination on the legality of the war. This was not inevitable. At his inaugural press conference, Sir John Chilcot stated: "We are determined to be thorough, rigorous, fair and frank, to enable us to form impartial and evidence-based judgements on all aspects of the issues, including the arguments about the legality of the conflict."[59] Moreover, the Inquiry heard and received significant evidence and submissions on the war's legality.[60]

However, from the start, Chilcot indicated that the Inquiry would not reach firm conclusions on whether the war was in fact lawful.[61] The final report stayed true to that promise.[62] That said, the Inquiry determined

[56] *See, e.g.*, Richard Norton-Taylor, *Chilcot Inquiry Report will not Reveal Tony Blair's Pledges to George W. Bush*, GUARDIAN (Mar. 12, 2013), www.theguardian.com/world/2013/mar/12/chilcot-inquiry-report-blair-bush.

[57] Letter from Sir John Chilcot to Sir Jeremy Heywood, Cabinet Secretary, The Iraq Inquiry (May, 28 2014), www.iraqinquiry.org.uk/media/185932/2014-05-28-letter-chilcot-to-heywood.pdf.

[58] Bob Marshall-Andrews, *Chilcot: Trial without Tribulation*, GUARDIAN (Jan. 31, 2010), www.theguardian.com/commentisfree/2010/jan/31/chilcot-forensic-failure-cakewalk-blair.

[59] *Transcript of Iraq Inquiry Launch News Conference on 30th of July 2009*, THE IRAQ INQUIRY, July 30, 2009, www.iraqinquiry.org.uk/the-inquiry/news-archive/2009/2009-08-05-transcript/2009-07-30-transcript-of-iraq-inquiry-launch-news-conference-on-30th-of-july-2009/.

[60] *See* CHILCOT REPORT, *supra* note 6, § 5 (in vol. 5); Iraq Inquiry: The Evidence, www.iraqinquiry.org.uk/the-evidence/ (last visited, Aug. 28, 2017).

[61] Andrew Sparrow, *Iraq Inquiry Will not Decide if War was Legal or Illegal*, GUARDIAN (Nov. 23, 2009), www.theguardian.com/politics/blog/2009/nov/23/iraq-inquiry-war-legal-illegal.

[62] Statement by Sir John Chilcot, THE IRAQ INQUIRY, July 6, 2016, www.iraqinquiry.org.uk/media/247010/2016-09-06-sir-john-chilcots-public-statement.pdf. *See also* CHILCOT REPORT, *supra* note 6, Introduction, at 3, 17 (of vol. 1).

that the domestic process leading to the Attorney General's controversial final determination that the war was authorized by the Security Council was "far from satisfactory."[63] Chilcot later said that to describe the process as falling "significantly short" of the appropriate level would be euphemistic.[64] Among its legally significant substantive findings, the Inquiry found that the coalition action was not a last resort in responding to the putative threat posed by Iraq at the time of the invasion; alternative paths remained available.[65] That finding rules out a key factual predicate of even an expansive preemptive self-defense argument.[66] It also arguably weakens the plausibility of the already highly controversial claim that the coalition could act pursuant to Security Council authority, but without a new resolution. However, despite these suggestive findings, the Inquiry stopped short of ruling that the UK's use of force was illegal.

Some have suggested that this outcome was all but determined by the Inquiry's composition, which included five members, none of whom had international law expertise.[67] It may also be a reflection of the tendency of domestic normative discourse to focus on questions of procedural propriety and on the question of whether soldiers' lives were sacrificed for good reason, but not on the *jus ad bellum*. For all of the reasons articulated above, that is a mistaken perspective, but it is not out of synch with the view that leaders wrong their soldiers by forcing them to *die* for an *unworthy* cause, not by forcing them to *kill* in a *wrongful* cause.

The Commission of Inquiry proposed here would build on the Chilcot model of open hearings, publishing key documents, and maximizing transparency (including using the "gist" compromise when absolutely necessary in the interests of national security), but would turn the focus

[63] CHILCOT REPORT, *supra* note 6, § 7, at 621 (of vol. 6).

[64] *Iraq Inquiry: Full Transcript of Sir John Chilcot's BBC Interview*, BBC NEWS, *supra* note 6.

[65] CHILCOT REPORT, *supra* note 6, § 7, at 572, 614 (of vol. 6).

[66] Taking broad approach to pre-emptive self-defense, but still emphasizing the last resort criterion, *see* Jeremy Wright QC MP, British Attorney General, Remarks Delivered at the International Institute for Strategic Studies (Jan. 11, 2017), www.gov.uk/government/uploads/system/uploads/attachment_data/file/583171/170111_Imminence_Speech_.pdf; George Brandis QC, Australian Attorney General, Remarks Delivered at the University of Queensland: Developments in International Law: Self-Defence against Imminent Armed Attack (Apr. 11, 2017).

[67] Afua Hirsch, *Chilcot Inquiry into the Iraq War Incapable of Deciding on Legality*, GUARDIAN (Nov. 23, 2009), www.theguardian.com/uk/2009/nov/23/chilcot-inquiry-iraq-war; Richard Norton-Taylor, *Chilcot Inquiry's Credibility "Is on Edge of an Abyss"*, GUARDIAN (Nov. 14, 2010), www.theguardian.com/uk/2010/nov/14/chilcot-inquiry-iraq-credibility.

more specifically onto the *jus ad bellum*. For the latter purpose, its membership would include international lawyers, as well as military and intelligence experts, and its mandate would include making a ruling on the *jus ad bellum*. In these specific respects, it would be modeled more on the Davids Commission in the Netherlands, the membership of which included a number of leading international law experts, and which reached an unequivocal conclusion that the invasion of Iraq was illegal.[68]

Crucially, the proposed commission's *jus ad bellum* work would link back to the work of the devil's advocate and to that of the institutions involved in disobedience protection. Specifically, it would provide the *jus ad bellum* foundation for the retrospective recognition of the disobedience rights of those who refused to fight in an illegal war. Whether specific individuals satisfy the procedural requirements for lawful disobedience – refusing outside the theater of conflict, and turning themselves in immediately citing the war's illegality – would be adjudicated in ordinary military courts (with a right of appeal), but the prior *jus ad bellum* question would be disposed of by the Commission of Inquiry.

Occurring after the end of a war, the Commission would have access to all relevant intelligence, would receive reports and statements from the devil's advocate, and would have the authority to subpoena participants in the decision-making process for statements before public hearings.[69] When absolutely necessary in the interests of national security, the Inquiry would have the capacity to move to closed hearing, as is done already in various forms in criminal trials and detainee status hearings (in addition to the Chilcot Inquiry compromise).[70] As with documentary

[68] *Report of the Dutch Committee of Inquiry on the War in Iraq: Chapter 8: The Basis in International Law for the Military Intervention in Iraq, translated in* 57 NETHERLANDS INT'L L. REV. 84 (2010). For the original report in Dutch, see RAPPORT COMMISSIE VAN ONDERZOEK BESLUITVORMING IRAK (2010), www.rijksoverheid.nl/documenten/rapporten/2010/01/12/rapport-commissie-davids.

[69] *Cf. Background and Key Documents*, IRAQ INQUIRY, www.iraqinquiry.org.uk/background.aspx.

[70] *Cf.* Justice and Security Act 2013 (c.18), www.legislation.gov.uk/ukpga/2013/18/pdfs/ukpga_20130018_en.pdf?section-18-2 (making provision for closed material proceedings in certain civil litigation in the UK – largely in an effort to balance the right to make human rights claims regarding counter-terrorism state action, especially by intelligence agencies, with the need to maintain the secrecy of sensitive information. Most significantly (and controversially), it provides that evidence may be heard in the absence of the litigant, who is represented by a special advocate who cannot discuss any of the issues that arise with her client). On judicial methods for dealing with sensitive evidence in the United States, *see, for example, Manual for Military Commissions, United States*, MIL.

evidence, the "gist" of any such closed proceedings would be summarized and published in the Commission's final report.

In line with most of the post-Iraq inquiries, the Commission would also examine the decision-making process in the build-up to war.[71] The prospect of the commission engaging in such review would complement the devil's advocate in bolstering the soldier's grounds for deferring to his state's *jus ad bellum* claims before and during the war.

Together, these institutions would preclude deniability for leaders regarding facts countervailing those they emphasize in making the case for war. The leader's awareness of those facts would be evidenced in the devil's advocate's report, and the relevant contents of that report would be published in some form via the commission. The combined effect of these two institutions would be to ensure that the legacies and future political careers of decision-makers would be defined not just by the successes and failures of the war but also by their honesty and their approaches to the war's legality.

This has potency. The taint of association with mendacity, illegality, and perhaps even criminality, in the waging of war can overshadow all else in a leader's legacy. Tony Blair's legacy in Britain is, and always will be, tied fundamentally to the Iraq War. His decision to participate in the US-led coalition has become, in many ways, the defining act of his long premiership. This would probably have been the case in any circumstance, but the nature and force of Iraq's impact on his public standing is a function of the perceived depth

Comm'n R. Evid., § 505(f)(2) (2010) ("any information admitted into evidence . . . shall be provided to the accused." However, there remain strong protections of classified information that is not admitted into evidence. When the accused makes a discovery request for such evidence, the judge may authorize the United States to "delete or withhold specified items," "substitute a summary," or admit relevant facts that the material would tend to prove.); *Manual for Courts-Martial, United States,* Mil. R. Evid., § 505(h)(1–2) (2016) (providing a substantially similar procedure). Section 6 of the Classified Information Procedures Act (CIPA) provides authority for federal courts to hold an *in camera* discussion, outside the presence of the accused, which is placed on the record and sealed, but available for appellate review. Classified Information Procedures Act, Pub. L. 96–456, 94 Stat. 2025 (1980). The point of noting these various manuals and pieces of legislation is only to emphasize that dealing with sensitive information is not something new to legal procedures and there are various tools for dealing with it.

[71] For a comparative discussion of some of the pre-Chilcot inquiries, *see* Jervis, *Reports, supra* note 17.

of his moral culpability – a perception to which the UK's post-war inquiries have contributed.[72]

Knowing in advance of the inevitability of this kind of inquiry would give leaders pause before they march their states to war on false pretenses. Awareness of the functioning of these institutions and the incentives they put in place would strengthen the soldier's grounds for deference to the factual claims of his leaders when they make the case for war. This in turn would grow the number of cases in that state in which it would be reasonable for the soldier to believe his war to be lawful, reducing the burden borne by those who fight, and limiting the number of those likely to disobey in the mistaken belief that the war is illegal.

10.5 Unlawful but Justified

Before turning to international reforms in the next chapter, an important challenge to the argument for the domestic protection of disobedience deserves attention. The notion that international law on the use of force can provide the appropriate moral standard by which domestic institutions would evaluate the wrongfulness of what soldiers are forced to do in war might be thought to depend on the notion that the state in question accepts the normative content of that legal regime.

For the reasons discussed at the start of this chapter, that premise has weight. The use of force regime is the only globally resonant normative framework for waging war and states generally agree as to its content. However, there are situations in which a particular state is not normatively aligned with the content of the *jus ad bellum* as enshrined in the dominant understanding of international law. Such a state may advocate a minority interpretation of the law, or may hold that certain kinds of war are morally just, despite being illegal.

Both postures arise in the interstate discourse on unauthorized humanitarian intervention. The dominant view among states is that such wars are illegal.[73] However, the Netherlands, Belgium, Denmark, and the

[72] On the degree to which the Chilcot Inquiry hearings exposed flaws in Tony Blair's account of the build-up to war, *see, for example*, Philippe Sands, *Chilcot Inquiry: The Bare Facts on Iraq Are There for All to See, Mr. Blair*, GUARDIAN (Jan. 21, 2011), www.theguardian.com/world/2011/jan/21/chilcot-inquiry-iraq-tony-blair.

[73] CHRISTINE GRAY, INTERNATIONAL LAW AND THE USE OF FORCE 47, 51 (3rd edn 2008) (many states have stated explicitly that they regard humanitarian intervention to be

United Kingdom have all asserted the lawfulness of at least some humanitarian uses of force lacking Security Council authorization.[74] Shortly after leaving his post as legal adviser at the US State Department, Harold Koh argued that a unilateral intervention against Syria would be at least plausibly lawful.[75] Others, less convinced of this position, nevertheless view genuinely humanitarian wars as "illegal but legitimate."[76] In that vein, France and Germany defended NATO's use of force in Kosovo, while insisting that it could not be understood as a legal precedent for future action.[77]

A state adopting the "illegal but legitimate" posture could hold that it is appropriate that such wars are illegal, despite being morally justified, as in the account elaborated in Chapter 3. Alternatively, it might hold that international law ought to change to accommodate the action, but recognize that it has not yet done so. The latter form of the "illegal but legitimate position" tends eventually towards asserting a minority

illegal); *Debate Map: Use of Force against Syria*, OXFORD PUB. INT'L L. (Apr. 29, 2014), http://opil.ouplaw.com/page/debate_map_syria/debate-map-use-of-force-against-syria.

74 Jane Stromseth, *Rethinking Humanitarian Intervention: The Case for Incremental Change*, *in* HUMANITARIAN INTERVENTION: ETHICAL, LEGAL, AND POLITICAL DILEMMAS 239–40 (J. L. Holzgrefe & Robert O. Keohane, eds., 2003) (on the Netherlands and Belgium); UK PRIME MINISTER'S OFFICE, CHEMICAL WEAPON USE BY SYRIAN REGIME: UK GOVERNMENT LEGAL POSITION (2013) (providing a recent articulation of the UK position), www.gov.uk/government/publications/chemical-weapon-use-by-syrian-regime-uk-government-legal-position; Statement by H.E. Mr. Niels Helveg Petersen, Minister for Foreign Affairs of Denmark, to United Nations General Assembly 55th Session, General Debate (2000), www.un.org/ga/webcast/statements/denmarkE.htm.

75 Harold Hongju Koh, *Syria and the Law of Humanitarian Intervention (Part II: International Law and the Way Forward)*, JUST SECURITY (Oct. 2, 2013) ("an absolutist [prohibition on non-defensive force absent Security Council authorization] amounts to saying that international law has not progressed since Kosovo ... I believe that under certain highly constrained circumstances (enumerated below), a nation could lawfully use or threaten force for genuinely humanitarian purposes, even absent authorization by a UN Security Council resolution. This was the path the United States and its NATO allies followed in Kosovo in 1999, and that President Obama proposed in Syria last month, before the US-Russian diplomatic initiative took center stage"), www.justsecurity.org/1506/koh-syria-part2/.

76 *See, e.g.*, INDEP. INT'L COMM'N ON KOSOVO, THE KOSOVO REPORT: CONFLICT, INTERNATIONAL RESPONSE, LESSONS LEARNED 4 (2000). Supporting something like this view, *see* THOMAS M. FRANCK, RECOURSE TO FORCE 166–89 (2002). For a commentary on (and criticism of) this perspective, *see* Anthea Roberts, *Legality* v. *Legitimacy: Can Uses of Force be Illegal but Justified?*, *in* HUMAN RIGHTS, INTERVENTION, AND THE USE OF FORCE 179 (Philip Alston & Euan MacDonald, eds., 2008).

77 Stromseth, *supra* note 74, at 239 (quoting Germany's Foreign Minister stating that it "must not become a precedent" and France's saying that it "must remain an isolated case and not constitute a precedent").

interpretation of the law. When states engage in illegal practice with an *opinio juris* that rejects the normative force of the prohibition, they act as the agents of the creation and revision of customary international law.[78] State practice establishing the agreement of the parties can also lead to revised treaty interpretation.[79] Via either of these avenues, states' first step towards making new international law involves breaking international law.[80] Given this blurred line between advocating a legal change and asserting it, the two postures will be addressed together here. The distinct position of a state that asserts that a use of force is morally justified but appropriately illegal is addressed subsequently.

The possibility of jurisgenerative law-breaking is significant in thinking about the domestic response to a soldier who refuses to fight in an illegal war. The state acts unlawfully when it seeks to shift the law through contrary practice. At the same time, international law recognizes the potential long-term legacy of that act as the first (and necessarily illegal) step in what might become a process of collective legal revision.

Given this potential for a form of retrospective legitimacy at the international level, it is difficult, from the domestic legal point of view, to hold that forcing a soldier to fight in such a war is in fact forcing him to do wrong. On the contrary, forcing such soldiers to fight would mean forcing them to do the right thing, according to the state's position on the universally applicable normative standard. There may be an internal imperative for international law to protect disobedient soldiers in such a war, but there is good reason to hold that such an imperative does not extend to the domestic level.

[78] Military and Paramilitary Activities in and against Nicaragua (Nicar. v. US), Judgment, 1986 I.C.J. Rep. 14 (June 27), para. 207 ("Reliance by a State on a novel right or an unprecedented exception to the principle might, if shared in principle by other States, tend towards modification of customary international law"). *See also* Statute of the International Court of Justice, art. 38(1)(a)–(b), June 26, 1945, 3 Bevans 1179, 59 Stat. 1031 (identifying treaties and custom (state practice married with *opinio juris*) as core sources of international law); Anthea Elizabeth Roberts, *Traditional and Modern Approaches to Customary International Law: A Reconciliation*, 95 Am. J. Int'l L. 757, 757 (2001) (discussing different models for the development of custom); Vienna Convention on the Law of Treaties, art. 31(3)(b), May 23, 1969, 1155 U.N.T.S. 331, *in* Treaties and Subsequent Practice (Georg Nolte, ed., 2012) (on the development of treaty law by state practice).

[79] Vienna Convention on the Law of Treaties, art. 31(3)(b).

[80] Roberts, *Legality*, *supra* note 76, 195–98 (on the precedent-setting potential of humanitarian interventions).

To be clear, the fact that the government asserts the lawfulness of a particular war is not itself sufficient to support that conclusion. Rather, the state must assert a generalizable understanding of either the legal standard or the legal standard as it ought to be that deviates from the dominant view among states and other international authorities, but pursuant to which the war would be lawful.

To satisfy this requirement, any exceptional caveat to the soldier's disobedience rights on these grounds should be rooted in a public and detailed declaration of the state's official interpretation of the law.[81] This declaration would set out the relevant reformist *jus ad bellum* doctrine, and would serve as a formal statement of *opinio juris*. Such a declaration could provide the legal standard applicable in the domestic commission of inquiry's review.

This would respect the state's role as a law-creator, and would recognize the internal coherence of a state forcing its soldiers to fight in wars that conform to its own understanding of the appropriate global legal standard. However, by holding the state to that standard, it would remain consistent with a commitment to the rule of law.

A different set of issues arises with respect to states that adopt the form of the "illegal but legitimate" posture on which the war in question is appropriately illegal, but waging it is morally justified. As discussed in Chapter 3, a reason one might hold that such wars should remain illegal is that granting a legal permission broad enough to include them would entail the collateral harm of encouraging or facilitating the waging of unjustified wars to a degree excessive in relation to the value of permitting the action in question and other similarly morally justified wars.[82] In this context, the legal protection of disobedience would be appropriate, even though soldiers would do well (from the domestic point of view) to disobey.

Precisely because cases of moral law-breaking are understood to be highly unusual even by their advocates, those advocates generally insist

[81] *See, e.g.*, Robin Cook, Sec'y of State for Foreign and Commonwealth Affairs, Speech to the American Bar Association in London: Guiding Humanitarian Intervention (July 19, 2000), *in* 71 Brit. Y.B. Int'l L. 646, 647 (2000) [hereinafter Cook, Speech to American Bar Association].

[82] *See, e.g.*, Christine Gray, *supra* note 73, at 52. *But see* Ryan Goodman, *Humanitarian Intervention and Pretexts for War*, 100 Am. J. Int'l L. 107 (2006) (arguing that leaders can become caught in their claimed justifications for war, and that claiming humanitarian intervention is more likely to cause leaders to limit their use of force than would claiming self-defense).

that the legitimacy of law-breaking is dependent on (or at the very least enhanced significantly by) broad buy-in. Such diversity of assent is a prophylactic against the state's self-interested abuse of the humanitarian pretext. Often, this diversity takes the form of multilateral coalition, preferably with regional heterogeneity.[83] The disobedience protection framework described above would instead (or additionally) demand broad *combatant* buy-in prior to deployment when the government claims a moral imperative to wage a war that is appropriately illegal on its own terms.

Although this would threaten the state's capacity to act in such circumstances, the crux of the "illegal but legitimate" concept is that some such weakening of the prospect of genuinely humanitarian wars may be appropriate in order to weaken even further the prospect of pretextual wars. Preserving the soldier's right to disobey in illegal but moral wars contributes appropriately to making it more difficult for the state to engage in moral law-breaking, while placing no legal obstacle in front of soldiers morally persuaded of the cause and thus willing to fight.

It is notable in this respect that many soldiers are keen to fight when the cause is just.[84] And many have a predisposition to believe their own government. Enlistment typically rises in anticipation of war and in its opening stages.[85] Considered against this background, it is difficult to

[83] *See, e.g.*, INT'L COMM'N ON INTERVENTION AND STATE SOVEREIGNTY, THE RESPONSIBILITY TO PROTECT, paras. 6.28–6.40 (2001); *see also* Cook, Speech to American Bar Association, *supra* note 81 ("any use of force should be collective. No individual country can reserve to itself the right to act on behalf of the international community"). *See also* Allen Buchanan & Robert O. Keohane, *Precommitment Regimes for Intervention: Supplementing the Security Council*, 25 ETHICS & INT'L AFF. 41, 52–55 (2011) (discussing the advantages and challenges of a coalition requirement).

[84] The words of a soldier about the start of the Six Day War are not atypical of soldiers before what they believe to be a warranted fight: "The first day we were called up, we all went round with big smiles, slapping each other on the back. I'd even go so far as to say that men actually wanted a war at that point. I think lots of them saw it as an opportunity to prove themselves as soldiers, after they'd done everything for so many years on a sort of 'as if' basis. They thought everyone would get a chance to prove himself now, to put into practice all the stuff they'd spent so much time over in training. Of course, they also shared the general feeling in the country, that the political aspect of the business was justified, and that it was a just war. You had the feeling, long before the call-up, that we were really going off to defend the country." Shimon quoted in AVRAM SHAPIRA, THE SEVENTH DAY: SOLDIERS TALK ABOUT THE SIX-DAY WAR 26 (1970); *see also id.*, at 29.

[85] James Dao, *They Signed Up to Fight*, NY TIMES BLOG: AT WAR (Sept. 6, 2011) (although not experiencing the surge that saw Americans "flock to military recruiting stations" after Pearl Harbor, the attacks of 11 September, which clearly presaged war, did cause enlistment to rise in the ensuing months), www.nytimes.com/2011/09/06/us/sept-11-reckoning/troops.html; JOHN KEEGAN & RICHARD HOLMES, SOLDIERS: A HISTORY OF

imagine a genuinely morally compelling call to arms that would be met with disabling mass disobedience under an institutional system that protects disobedience only under narrow conditions designed to minimize the effects of war's hell on the soldier's decision-making and judgment.[86]

Indeed, it is notable that the threshold for moral law-breaking in the *jus in bello* context is typically set significantly higher than would be the case under the regime proposed here. The most prominent official endorsement of morally violating the *jus in bello* was articulated by the Israeli Supreme Court in 1999, when it ruled that individuals may be criminally liable for engaging in torture, even when doing so is required by urgent necessity (in a so-called "ticking bomb" scenario).[87] The Court held that such soldiers can only hope for the uncertain post hoc mercy of prosecutors or the courts when they engage in such illegal action *even in those rare scenarios in which such illegal action is morally required.*[88] In contrast, the position advanced here would hold only that in the rare case when an appropriately illegal war is nonetheless moral, soldiers ought to fight, but the legal regime cannot coherently deny them the right to refuse.

10.6 Evaluating Reform

Plainly, domestic reforms establishing a devil's advocate, a post-war commission of inquiry, and a limited right to refuse to fight in an illegal war would be insufficient to dispel entirely the normative tension inherent in a legal system in which soldiers can face criminal sanction for refusing to do wrong by the law's own normative lights. However, each of these steps would acknowledge the morally strained position of those soldiers from the legal point of view. Moreover, each would recognize that defending the law's treatment of such soldiers with reference to

Men in Battle 259–61 (1985) (on enthusiasm among young men in anticipation of war).

[86] On soldiers' relative lack of care for their personal security *before* deployment, consider the words of an Israeli soldier on the Six Day War: "Everyone had a terrific feeling of enthusiasm: only let's get out there, get into it all – the unit mustn't miss its turn. Of course *it changed a bit when the first casualties occurred, when the cost of it all began to be felt.*" Shapira, *supra* note 84 (emphasis added).

[87] H.C.J. 5100/94 Pub. Comm'n against Torture in Isr. v. State of Isr. 53(4) PD 817, para. 40 (1999) (Isr.).

[88] *Id.*

institutional necessity entails an internal imperative to do better by those soldiers even when alleviating their burden entirely is not possible.

As war changes and the necessity weakens, the internal case for such reforms grows. The reforms suggested in this chapter are not intended to end the discussion of what it means to take seriously the soldier's burden in domestic law; they are intended to begin it. They chart the key objectives – improving the soldier's reasons to trust his state and alleviating the coercion to fight when the war is wrongful – but they do so recognizing both that there are many routes to improvement along these dimensions, and that states would quite appropriately adopt a range of routes reflecting the diversity of their legal and institutional structures and traditions.

11

An Internal Normative Vision for International Reform

The quirks of the interaction between the domestic and the international levels do not affect the internal imperatives applicable in the latter sphere. The international regime's failure to protect soldiers from being forced to kill in illegal wars is best justified with reference to the global institutional necessity of obedience enforcement in the military. However, as elaborated in Chapter 9, there are gaps in that necessity. Recognizing this opens the door to two forms of disobedience protection at the international level: the provision of refugee status for those who refuse to fight in an illegal war and the elaboration of an international human right not to fight in such wars. Because the imperative to provide these protections is internal to the law's normative underpinnings, this could be achieved through progressive interpretation, and would not require treaty amendment.

Teleological interpretive progression along these lines has been at the core of the "humanization" of international law.[1] In an early landmark ruling exemplifying this phenomenon, the ICTY Appeals Chamber held that a significant portion of the *jus in bello* applicable in international armed conflict had been incorporated via custom into the law governing non-international armed conflicts.[2] The ruling marked a significant doctrinal shift.[3] Treaty law had focused almost exclusively on international armed conflict; protections applicable to non-international conflicts were relatively minimal and had been introduced late in the regime's development.[4]

[1] *See* Sections 2.1–2.2 of Chapter 2 above.

[2] Prosecutor v. Tadić, Case No. IT-94-1-I, Decision on Defence Motion for Interlocutory Appeal on Jurisdiction (Int'l Crim. Trib. for the Former Yugoslavia Oct. 2, 1995) [hereinafter Tadić Interlocutory Decision on Jurisdiction].

[3] Lindsay Moir, The Law of Internal Armed Conflict 136–47 (2002); Christine Byron, *Armed Conflicts: International or Non-International*, 6 J. Conflict & Security L. 63, 64 (2001).

[4] Tadić Interlocutory Decision on Jurisdiction, *supra* note 2, para. 96; Dapo Akande, *Classification of Armed Conflicts: Relevant Legal Concepts*, *in* International Law and the Classification of Armed Conflicts 32, 32–34 (Wilmshurst, ed., 2012).

Although the Appeals Chamber pieced together evidence of state practice and *opinio juris* supporting the application of the *jus in bello* in the latter context, it bolstered that argument significantly with an appeal to the law's normative underpinnings.[5] Specifically, the Chamber reasoned that since World War II,

> a State-sovereignty-oriented approach has been gradually supplanted by a human-being-oriented approach … If international law, while of course duly safeguarding the legitimate interests of States, must gradually turn to the protection of human beings, it is only natural that the aforementioned dichotomy [between international and non-international conflicts] should gradually lose its weight … What is inhumane, and consequently proscribed, in international wars, cannot but be inhumane and inadmissible in civil strife.[6]

Despite its more conservative interpretive posture, the ICJ has also reached for such normative guidance on occasion. It rooted its interpretation of the capacity of states to make and object to reservations to the Genocide Convention in part in the observation that the "complete exclusion from the Convention of one or more States would … detract from the authority of the moral and humanitarian principles which are its basis."[7] On several occasions, it has looked to "elementary considerations of humanity" as an interpretive beacon.[8] That concept helped to underpin the imposition on states of positive duties to protect against wrongful harm – a principle that has become absolutely central to

[5] Tadić Interlocutory Decision on Jurisdiction, *supra* note 2, paras. 100–27. On the significance of the decision in moving the law on this (and thus going beyond what existing state practice and *opinio juris* alone would support), *see supra* note 3. Affirming that methodology, *see* Prosecutor v. Kupreškić, Case No. IT-95-16-T, Judgment, paras. 525–27 (Int'l Crim. Trib. for the Former Yugoslavia, Jan. 14, 2000).

[6] Tadić Interlocutory Decision on Jurisdiction, *supra* note 2, paras. 97, 119.

[7] *Reservations to the Convention on the Prevention and Punishment of the Crime of Genocide*, 1951 I.C.J. Rep. 15, 24 (May 28).

[8] Corfu Channel Case (UK v. Alb.), Judgment, 1949 I.C.J. Rep. 4, 22 (Apr. 9) [hereinafter Corfu Channel Judgment]; Military and Paramilitary Activities in and against Nicaragua (Nicar. v. US), Judgment, 1986 I.C.J. Rep. 14 (June 27), paras. 215, 218, 239. *See also* Jurisdictional Immunities of the State (Ger. v. It.; Greece Intervening) 2012 I.C.J. Rep. (Feb. 3), para. 52. *See also* Matthew Zagor, *Elementary Considerations of Humanity, in* The ICJ and the Evolution of International Law 264 (Karine Bannelier et al., eds., 2012). *See also* Stefan Talmon, *Determining Customary International Law: The ICJ's Methodology between Induction, Deduction and Assertion*, 26 Eur. J. Int'l L. 417, 427 (2015) ("a logical rule requires a smaller pool of state practice and *opinio juris* ").

human rights law, also partly through teleological interpretive creativity.[9]

Helping to justify such interpretive moves is the objective of reconciling the law better to its own normative underpinnings, and thus overcoming normative dissonance within the existing regime. The principle, in Lauterpacht's terms is that "[a] treaty is not concluded in a legal vacuum. It is part of a legal system which, for that very reason, cannot contain rules which are contradictory."[10] Meron writes similarly of an "osmosis" whereby one domain of international law concerned with humanity influences the substantive law of another.[11]

For the reasons discussed below, there are existing resources in human rights and refugee law doctrine to support a right to refuse to fight in an illegal war. The normative account advanced here demands that such doctrinal resources be employed in service of such an interpretation. After exploring interpretive moves in that direction, this chapter closes with a discussion of the best ways to operationalize a reparations regime that would recognize soldiers killed or harmed fighting against aggression and civilians caught in the crossfire as the core victims of the crime.

11.1 From Deserter to Refugee

Refugee law is plainly a key domain within the body of international law focused on and driven by moral concern for the human being.[12] Interpreting it through that "humanized" prism has helped to underpin refugee status for those who refuse to perpetrate atrocities and war crimes. As Cecilia Bailliet observes,

[9] On the ICJ's position on this, *see* Corfu Channel Judgment, *supra* note 8, at 22. On the parallel teleological move in human rights law, see Tom Dannenbaum, *Public Power and Preventive Responsibility*, *in* DISTRIBUTION OF RESPONSIBILITIES IN INTERNATIONAL LAW (André Nollkaemper & Dov Jacobs, eds., 2015); Vassilis P. Tzevelekos, *In Search of Alternative Solutions*, 35 BROOKLYN J. INT'L L. 155, 182 (2010).

[10] Hersch Lauterpacht, *The Limits of the Operation of the Law of War*, 30 BRIT. Y.B. INT'L L. 206, 209 (1953). This reasoning was important to Lauterpacht's support for the IMT's use of the Kellogg–Briand Pact at Nuremberg. *Id.*, at 209–10 n.3.

[11] Theodor Meron, *The Humanization of Humanitarian Law*, 94 AM. J. INT'L L. 239, 244 (2000).

[12] Sepet & Another v. Sec'y State Home Dept. [2003] UKHL 15 (UK) (Lord Bingham of Cornhill), para. 6. This recognition notwithstanding, the House of Lords went on to deny asylum to two Kurdish applicants fleeing orders to participate in Turkish military operations against Kurdish rebels.

> [T]here is an increased emphasis on the rights and duties of individuals to ensure respect for human rights within their nations, and thus there has been a growing recognition of an individual's right of conscientious objection – in particular, in cases where the state is deemed to engage in an illegitimate military action.[13]

So far, the attachment of refugee status to those facing domestic punishment for refusing to do wrong by the law's own lights has not extended as far as those refusing to fight in an illegal war. However, the existing doctrine on the issue is sufficiently open-ended to allow for a progressive interpretation in that direction.

A key resource underpinning the protection of those who refuse to perpetrate *jus in bello* wrongs has been the UNHCR's Handbook on the Refugee Convention, which is widely recognized as an authority on the Convention's interpretation. It starts from the premise that prosecution for refusing to fight does not necessarily constitute the kind of persecution that would underpin refugee status, but that it can be the "sole ground" for refugee status if fighting would contradict "valid reasons of conscience."[14] Elaborating on this possibility, the UNHCR explains,

> It is not enough for a person to be in disagreement with his government regarding the political justification ... Where, however, *the type of military action ... is condemned by the international community as contrary to basic rules of human conduct*, punishment for desertion or draft-evasion could ... in itself be regarded as persecution.[15]

Courts in various countries have held repeatedly in the context of *jus in bello* violations and atrocities that the terms "condemned by the international community" should be taken to include not only actual condemnation by a broad range of states and international organizations in a specific case, but also the implicit condemnation entailed in an

[13] Cecilia M. Bailliet, *Assessing Jus ad Bellum and Jus in Bello within the Refugee Status Determination Process*, 20 Geo. Immigr. L.J. 337, 337–38 (2006).

[14] UN High Commissioner for Refugees [UNHCR], Handbook on Procedures and Criteria for Determining Refugee Status under the 1951 Convention and the 1967 Protocol Relating to the Status of Refugees, paras. 167, 170, U.N. Doc. HCR/IP/4/Eng/REV.1 (1979, reedited 1992). Linking the right to conscientious objection (understood in pacifist terms) and the right to seek asylum, *see* UN Comm'n on Human Rights, Conscientious Objection to Military Service, pmbl., Res. 1998/77, U.N. Doc. E/CN.4/1998/177 (Apr. 22, 1998); UN Office of the High Commissioner for Human Rights, Rep. on Civil and Political Rights, Including the Question of Conscientious Objection to Military Service, U.N. Doc. E/CN.4/2004/55, at 12 (Feb. 16, 2004).

[15] UNHCR, *supra* note 14, para. 171.

action's international illegality.[16] The nature of the wrong entailed in aggressive war is such that it, too, ought to be understood to be a form of military action that is, by its very illegality, "condemned by the international community as contrary to basic rules of human conduct."[17]

There is nothing in the Refugee Convention or the UNHCR Handbook that would preclude extending protection to soldiers who refuse on those grounds. Nor does either the Convention or the Handbook require that such protection be limited to those who would have been criminally liable if they had not disobeyed.[18] As noted above, courts have applied the protection to those fleeing orders to perpetrate *jus in bello* wrongs even when having followed the orders would not have entailed criminal liability. The tests used in such circumstances have focused instead on whether the individual would have been able to "wash his hands of guilt" of the underlying wrong, or whether he "might" have been "associated" with the illegality, had he participated.[19]

The European Union's internally binding directive on the matter is more specific. It recognizes the refugee status of those facing "prosecution or punishment for refusal" to "commit . . . a crime against peace" or to perpetrate "acts contrary to the purposes and principles of the United Nations as set out in the Preamble and Articles 1 and 2 of the Charter of

[16] Zolfagharkhani v. Min. of Employ. & Immigr. [1993] 3 F.C. 540, 554–55 (Can.); Key v. Canada (Min. of Cit. & Immigr.) [2008] F.C. 838 (Can.), para. 21; B v. Sec'y of the State Home Dep't [2003] UKIAT 20 (Potter, L.J.), paras. 42–48; Krotov v. Sec'y of the State Home Dep't [2004] EWCA (Civ.) 69 (U.K.), paras. 26, 29, 39, 51 (Lord Justice Potter); Sepet & Another v. Sec'y State Home Dept. [2001] EWCA (Civ.) 681, *aff'd* [2003] UKHL 15, para. 69. *But see id.*, para. 98 (suggesting that the fact of international condemnation in the particular case matters).

[17] James Hathaway is right to argue that the category includes *jus ad bellum* violations. James C. Hathaway, The Law of Refugee Status 180–81 (1991). However, this is not because such violations involve territorial incursions (as he implies), but because they involve unjustified human violence. Indeed, as discussed in Chapter 3, in some cases, they do not involve any territorial violation at all.

[18] The Convention contains no language on this issue, and the Handbook language says simply: "the type of military action, with which an individual does not wish to be associated, is condemned by the international community as contrary to basic rules of human conduct," but says nothing about whether the individual's *association* with that condemned action must trigger criminal liability. *See* UNHCR, *supra* note 14, para. 171.

[19] Key v. Canada (Min. of Cit. & Immigr.) [2008] F.C. 838 (Can.), para. 279 (citing F.C. 540) (the standard is whether the individual would be able to "wash his hands of guilt"); Krotov v. Sec'y of the State for the Home Dep't [2004] EWCA (Civ.) 69 (UK), para. 117 (the question is whether the individual "might be associated with" the wrongful act). *See generally* the reasoning and cases cited in the *Key* decision. Key v. Canada, F.C. 838, *supra* note 16, paras. 14–29.

the United Nations."[20] Since lower-level troops cannot "commit" a crime against peace, that language might be thought to be less open to their inclusion than is the language of the UNHCR guidance. However, the concept of "acts contrary to the purposes and principles" of the United Nations is more expansive. Illegal wars are clearly contrary to the purposes and principles set out in the preamble and the first two articles of the UN Charter.[21]

On its face, the EU Directive seems to apply the same threshold for actions the performance of which would forever exclude persons from refugee status and actions which, when the individual faces punishment for *refusing* to perform them, would generate refugee status.[22] However, in the interests of consistency with the broader refugee regime and the broader disobedience regime, and in the interests of fairness to soldiers, who would otherwise lack any margin of error even in *jus in bello* contexts, the threshold for protected disobedience in the EU refugee regime ought to be lower than the threshold for disqualifying obedience.[23]

In addition to the interpretive space for *jus ad bellum* disobedience protection in existing refugee law doctrine, there is also a potentially useful, albeit uncertain and isolated precedent for an interpretive shift in that direction. In Al-Maisri v. Canada, the Canadian Federal Court of Appeal granted refugee status to a soldier who was part of the Yemeni contingent sent to assist Saddam's forces in the 1990 invasion and occupation of Kuwait.[24] Overturning the lower ruling, the Court held,

> [T]he Refugee Division misapplied the guidance afforded by paragraph 171 of the UNHCR Handbook, when it ruled that Iraq's invasion of Kuwait was not "condemned by the international community as contrary to basic rules of human conduct" notwithstanding, as it found, that the invasion and occupation of Kuwait was condemned by the United Nations and the annexation of that country by Iraq was declared by that body to be "null and void."[25]

Although the Court did not assess the legality of the Iraqi invasion of Kuwait, the relevant UN condemnations note Iraqi violations of both the

[20] Eur. Parl. & Council Directive 2011/95/EU of 13 December 2011, arts. 9(2)(e), 12(2)., *in* 337 OFFICIAL J. E.U. 9 (2011).

[21] *See* UN Charter, pmbl., arts. 1(1), 2(4).

[22] *Cf.* Directive 2011/95/EU, *supra* note 20, art. 12(2).

[23] *See* Section 1.3 of Chapter 1 above.

[24] Al-Maisri v. Canada (Min. of Employ. & Immigr.) [1995] F.C. 642 (Can.).

[25] *Id.*

jus ad bellum and the *jus in bello*.[26] As noted in Chapter 1, later Canadian jurisprudence failed to build on the opportunity provided by this precedent, and similar applications have failed elsewhere.[27]

If protection for those who refuse to fight in illegal wars is to be developed going forward, it could take a number of forms. The most conservative option would be to provide refugee rights to those refusing to fight in an illegal war only when an internationally competent body has pronounced on the *jus ad bellum*.[28] Protection on those limited grounds is plainly justified by the account of existing law developed above. Given the Security Council's prior resolutions on Iraq's invasion of Kuwait, it is also the form of protection most clearly supported by the Al-Maisri judgment.

The question is whether refugee protection should go beyond that minimum. Opponents of broader protection might argue that in the absence of an international ruling, the receiving state's courts would need to assess the asylum-seeker's claim regarding the *jus ad bellum* status of her state's war. This, the objection might go, would require the receiving state's courts to rule directly on the legality of foreign state action, in violation of *par in parem imperium non habet* – the idea that sovereign equality precludes one state standing in legal judgment of another.[29] Notably in that respect, an understanding annexed to the aggression amendment stipulates that it "shall not be interpreted as creating the right or obligation to exercise domestic jurisdiction with respect to an act of aggression committed by another State."[30]

However, a non-justiciability objection along these lines would be misplaced. The ICC understanding, unlike the 1996 ILC draft, does not assert that the domestic exercise of jurisdiction over aggression by other states is *prohibited*; it merely observes that the Rome Statute has no impact on that question.[31] Moreover, the invocation of *par in parem*

[26] *Id.* For the relevant UN condemnation, *see* S.C. Res. 662 (Aug. 9, 1990) (declaring the invasion and annexation "null and void"); S.C. Res. 674 (Oct. 29, 1990) (condemning hostage taking, mistreatment and violations of the *jus in bello*).

[27] *See* Section 1.3 of Chapter 1 above.

[28] On the competences held by different bodies in this respect, *see* Section 8.2 of Chapter 8, above.

[29] *Cf.* Beth Van Schaack, *Par in Parem Imperium Non Habet*, 10 J. Int'l Crim. Justice 133 (2012).

[30] Assembly of States Parties, Res. RC/Res.6, Annex III, para. 5 (June 11, 2010) [hereinafter ICC Aggression Amendments].

[31] Claus Kreß and Leonie von Holtzendorff, *The Kampala Compromise on the Crime of Aggression*, 8 J. Int'l Crim. Justice 1179, 1216 (2010); Michael Scharf, *Universal*

imperium non habet is unpersuasive here. Domestic courts are already required to determine the legality of foreign conduct in order to discharge their obligations under the Refugee Convention and human rights law.

To gain refugee status, an applicant must be "unable, or owing to [his fear of persecution], unwilling to avail himself of the protection" of his state of nationality.[32] Determining whether that criterion is satisfied typically entails evaluating whether the applicant's home state is either engaged in persecution or failing in its duty to protect the applicant from persecution.[33] This determination, in turn, almost inevitably requires reaching an implicit or explicit judgment on the home state's compliance with international law.[34] Beyond the refugee context, there is developing recognition that human rights law requires domestic courts to rule on the merits of complicity claims against their own states that hinge completely on the wrongdoing of an external state.[35]

It is not obvious why assessing foreign aggression would pose qualitatively unique problems in this respect.[36] In fact, international and regional refugee laws already presume domestic institutions' competence to do precisely that. The UN Convention and EU Directive exclude perpetrators of aggression from refugee status, requiring the receiving state to determine whether there are "serious reasons" for considering that aggression has been committed.[37] The 1969 OAU Convention

Jurisdiction and the Crime of Aggression, 53 Harv. Int'l L.J. 357 (2012). *Cf.* Draft Code of Crimes against the Peace and Security of Mankind with Commentaries, Rep. of the Int'l Law Comm'n on the Work of its Forty-Eighth Session, U.N. Doc. A/51/10, at 27, 30, and art. 8 (1996).

32 Convention Relating to the Status of Refugees, art. 1(A)(2), July 28, 1951, 189 U.N.T.S. 150 (as amended by the Protocol of 1967, 66 U.N.T.S 267) [hereinafter Refugee Convention].

33 Roger O'Keefe, *United Kingdom*, *in* The Crime of Aggression: A Commentary 938, 951 (Claus Kreß & Stefan Barriga, eds., 2016). Providing a normative defense of refugee law's emphasis on state action, *see* Matthew E. Price, *Persecution Complex: Justifying Asylum Law's Preference for Persecuted People*, 47 Harv. Int'l L.J. 413 (2006). *See also infra* note 43.

34 On the state's positive duty to protect individuals in its territory from persecution and other human rights violations, *see, for example* Dannenbaum, *Public Power, supra* note 9.

35 Belhaj v. Straw [2017] U.K.S.C. 3; Al-Nashiri v. Poland, App. No. 28761/11, Eur. Ct. H.R. (2014).

36 It should be borne in mind here that criminal aggression is both a violation of global concern and is limited to cases where the law is clear. O'Keefe, *supra* note 33, at 950–53.

37 Refugee Convention, *supra* note 32, art. 1(F)(a); UNHCR, *supra* note 14, at 149; Eur. Parl. & Council Directive 2011/95/EU, *supra* note 20, arts. 12(2)(a). If this scenario seems far-fetched, consider the case of Rudolf Hess. *Witness Recalls Nazi Rudolf Hess Landing in*

recognizes the refugee status of those fleeing the consequences of aggression.[38] And a *jus ad bellum* determination identical to that applicable in a soldier asylum case would be necessary if a senior official potentially liable for aggression were ever to flee punishment for his refusal to lead an aggressive war.[39]

In that sense, it is simply not credible to rely on the international law principles of sovereign equality or *par in parem imperium non habet* to deny soldiers refugee status when they flee participation in illegal wars. Even if this were not the case, or if domestic law were to preclude the justiciability of *jus ad bellum* questions, it is worth noting that the receiving state's institutions need only find a "well-founded fear" of persecution.[40] As such, in principle they could recognize the refugee status of soldiers fleeing wars that are probably illegal, without ruling that they are – a move similar to that taken by the *BVGer* in the case of Major Pfaff.[41]

Of course, setting a threshold that low might be thought to threaten military functioning in lawful wars for all of the reasons discussed in Chapter 8. However, the threat to military functioning posed by granting

Scotland, BBC NEWS (May 10, 2011) ("On 10 May 1941, Adolf Hitler's deputy Rudolf Hess parachuted into Scotland, landing in a field near Eaglesham. The prominent Nazi had flown solo for nearly 1,000 miles from Bavaria in a Messerschmitt Bf 110, apparently on a peace mission in the days leading up to Germany's invasion of Russia"), www.bbc.com/news/uk-scotland-glasgow-west-13333536. Hess was later prosecuted and convicted of aggression at Nuremberg for his role in the invasions that had already occurred. United States v. Göring et al., Judgment (Oct. 1, 1946), *in* 22 TRIAL OF THE MAJOR WAR CRIMINALS BEFORE THE INTERNATIONAL MILITARY TRIBUNAL 411, 530 (1948).

38 Convention Governing the Specific Aspects of Refugee Problems in Africa, art. 1(2), Sept. 10, 1969, 1001 U.N.T.S. 45.

39 Hinzman v. Canada (Min. of Cit. & Immigr.) [2006] F.C. 420 (Can.), § 151. Here, too, the Hess example is relevant in indicating that such scenarios are not beyond the realms of practical possibility. BBC NEWS, *supra* note 37.

40 Refugee Convention, *supra* note 32, art. 1(A)(2);

41 On the Pfaff case, *see* Section 10.2 of Chapter 10, above. On the standard of certainty applicable in refugee determinations, *see* HATHAWAY, *supra* note 17, at 75–79 (discussing various standards of certainty that have been used in this regard, including: "balance of probabilities," or, more liberally, "good reasons," "plausible danger," "some proof," "reasonable in the circumstances," "real chance," "serious possibility"); Sepet & Another v. Sec'y State Home Dept. [2003] UKHL 15 (U.K.), para. 8 (Lord Bingham of Cornhill) ("refugee status should be accorded [to a soldier who refused, when participating] would or *might* require him to commit atrocities or gross human rights abuses or participate in a conflict condemned by the international community").

foreign refugee protections to fleeing soldiers would be significantly less pointed than would be that posed by analogous domestic protection. Becoming a refugee and leaving one's homeland and most of one's relationships behind involves profound personal costs. Traversing borders to make a claim for asylum can itself be complicated and risky. And an adverse *jus ad bellum* determination in the receiving state would lead to repatriation and criminal sanction.

Consequently, in contrast to the prospect of domestic protection, the availability of refugee protection would likely motivate only those strongly convinced of the war's illegality. Indeed, even if a foreign court were to rule on the *jus ad bellum* and grant asylum during the war, this may not be sufficient to trigger total military collapse. Although tens of thousands of drafted Americans did flee to Canada during the Vietnam War, far greater numbers eschewed that option, despite widespread and deep opposition to the war and Canada's open border policy.[42]

Further mitigating the danger of refugee protection causing military breakdown in lawful wars is the generally applicable rule that review of the substance of asylum applications occurs only if the applicant cannot gain protections in his home state.[43] Applied here, this would mean that if a soldier were to have access domestically to a genuine process of post-war retrospective exoneration of the kind suggested in Chapter 10, this alone would rebut his claim to refugee status abroad, obviating the need for the receiving state's institutions to rule on the *jus ad bellum* dimension of his application. It would only be in the absence of such domestic protections that the relevant authorities in the receiving state would need to engage in any form of *jus ad bellum* evaluation.

Taken together, these factors would limit significantly the danger of mistaken foreign *jus ad bellum* rulings triggering military collapse in lawful wars. But even if these safeguards were deemed insufficient, others could be implemented without denying refugee status in all cases. Most obviously, the recognition of *jus ad bellum* refugee status could be limited

[42] On those who did move to Canada, *see* John Hagan, Northern Passage: American War Resisters in Canada (2001). Tim O'Brien describes his dilemma on this issue thus: "I thought about Canada. I thought about jail. But in the end I could not bear the prospect of rejection: by my family, my country, my friends, my hometown. . . . I was a coward. I went to Vietnam… Each step was an act of the purest self-hatred and self-betrayal . . . ." Tim O'Brien, *The Vietnam in Me*, NY Times Magazine (Oct. 2, 1994). On the widespread opposition to the war, *see, for example*, Murray Polner, No Victory Parades: The Return of the Vietnam Veteran 165 (1971).

[43] *See, e.g.*, Hinzman v. Canada & Hughey v. Canada, 2007 F.C.A. 171 (Can.), para. 41.

to "remotely fought" or "riskless" wars.[44] Outside that context, although the element of immediate punishment in the retrospective protection system discussed in Chapter 10 could not be transferred to the refugee context, the immediate costs of seeking asylum would likely have the same effect. As such, limiting refugee determinations until after the war would likely be sufficient to safeguard against undermining military functioning in troop-deployed conflicts.

In sum, an appropriately tailored system of refugee protection for those who refuse to fight in illegal war would avoid undermining global security, provide disobedience protection to those unprotected at home, and, most importantly, create a significant international incentive for states to institute their own domestic systems of protection. Doctrinal revision in this direction is entirely viable within existing practices of international legal re-interpretation.

11.2 The *Jus ad Bellum* and the Human Rights of Rights Defenders

A second doctrinal shift at the international level would be to recognize the human right not to be forced to fight in illegal wars. Such a right could be added formally through additional protocols to existing international and regional human rights treaties. However, it, too, could be achieved more immediately through a progressive interpretation of the right to freedom of conscience or of the developing doctrines on the right to peace or the rights of rights defenders.

An interpretation of conscience rights in international law along these lines could rely on a similar interpretive theory to that adopted by the *Bundesverwaltungsgericht* on the question of the German constitutional right to conscience in its protection of Florian Pfaff's disobedience.[45] As things stand, most international human rights law authorities recognize a right of conscience that protects absolute pacifists from conscription into mandatory military service.[46] However, the protection has not extended beyond that limited scope. There is neither recognition of a general international human right to selective conscientious objection, nor recognition of a more narrowly tailored human right not to be forced to fight in illegal war.[47]

44 *Cf.* UNHCR, *supra* note 14, para. 168 (an individual "is clearly not a refugee if his only reason for desertion or draft-evasion is his dislike of military service or fear of combat").

45 *See* Section 10.2 of Chapter 10 above.

46 *See* Section 1.3 of Chapter 1 above.

47 *See* Section 2.3 of Chapter 2 above (on what distinguishes this normatively from the question of selective conscientious objection).

It has not always been obvious that this would be the case. The early struggle for international conscientious objection rights gained traction by focusing specifically on the right to refuse to participate in wrongful military action.[48] The General Assembly asserted in 1978 the right to refuse to participate in a military that enforces apartheid.[49] Like the *BVGer* in the Pfaff case, the resolution rooted this right in the right to freedom of conscience.[50] In so doing, it privileged the conscience rights of those who object to complicity in *illegal* action, thus reflecting the legal regime's deep internal imperative not to undermine the moral integrity of those committed to its own normative substance.[51]

Three years later, pursuant to a resolution of the Commission on Human Rights, the Sub-Commission on Discrimination and Protection of Minorities charged two of its members with drafting a report on conscientious objection.[52] Their report adopted the approach advocated here, affirming the General Assembly's position on apartheid and adding the right to refuse to participate in "wars of aggression" or "any other illegal warfare."[53] Indeed, the Report reasoned that "there would be hardly any point" to the *jus ad bellum* established at Nuremberg and in the UN Charter if it were not understood as a normative framework that ought to underpin individuals' fundamental moral commitments.[54] As such, it recognized selective conscientious objection only for soldiers whose militaries were engaged with "some degree of probability" in uses

48 This movement seems to have been forgotten in current debates. *See, e.g.*, Cheyney Ryan, *Moral Equality, Victimhood, and the Sovereignty Symmetry Problem*, *in* JUST AND UNJUST WARRIORS: THE MORAL AND LEGAL STATUS OF SOLDIERS 131, 143 (David Rodin and Henry Shue, eds., 2008), at 143 ("If a state's right to conscript existed only for just wars, one would assume that conscripting its citizens to fight in an unjust war would be an *additional* aspect of the crime of fighting that war in the first place; but it is not - and I have yet to encounter anyone who has claimed that it should be").

49 Status of Persons Refusing Service in Military or Police Forces Used to Enforce Apartheid, G.A. Res. 33/165, para. 1 (Dec. 20, 1978).

50 *Id.*, paras. 2–3.

51 *See* Section 2.3 of Chapter 2 above.

52 Comm'n on Human Rights, Res. 40(XXXVII) (Mar. 12, 1981); Sub-Comm'n on Prevention of Discrimination of Minorities, Res. 14(XXXIV) (Sept. 10, 1981). The UN Comm'n on Human Rights had earlier encouraged individuals to object to their governments' "wars of aggression and colonialist oppression," although it shied away from endorsing international regulation of a right to that effect. UN Comm'n on Human Rights, Rep. on its 27th Session, U.N. Doc. E/4949, at 48 (Feb. 22–Mar. 26, 1971).

53 Asbjørn Eide & Charna L. C. Mubanga-Chipoya, Conscientious Objection to Military Service, U.N. Doc. E/CN.4/Sub.2/1983/30/Rev.1, para. 5 (1985).

54 *Id.*, at para. 28. *See also id.*, at paras. 46–47.

of force that violate national or international law.[55] The Report was widely distributed by the Economic and Social Council, but that was as far as things got on the matter of refusing to fight in illegal wars.[56] The development of jurisprudence on conscience rights since has been marked instead by a narrow and exclusive recognition of the human right of absolute (or pacifist) conscientious objectors to refuse military service.[57]

Fleetingly, a revival of the notion of a right not to be forced to participate in aggressive war looked possible via the developing articulation of a human right to peace. The Human Rights Council's Advisory Committee provided a draft declaration of the right in 2012, which articulated a state obligation to prevent soldiers from "taking part in wars of aggression" and asserted that "[e]veryone has the right to oppose aggression" and other international crimes.[58]

However, these aspects were quickly jettisoned in the first set of revisions proposed by the Chairperson-Rapporteur of the Working Group set up to translate the Advisory Committee's work into a UN Declaration on the Right to Peace.[59] The final version of the Declaration affirmed by the General Assembly in 2016 makes no mention of aggression or any rights associated with it.[60]

A third alternative to the right not to fight in aggressive war would be to root it in the growing body of jurisprudence around the human rights of rights defenders. The 1999 UN Declaration provides that "no one shall be subjected to punishment or adverse action of any kind for refusing" to

[55] *Id.* para. 37. *See also id.* para. 145; Jeremy Kessler, *The Invention of a Human Right*, 44 COLUM. HUM. RTS. L. REV. 753, 773–74 (2013). This built on the arguments of activists and NGOs. *See, e.g.*, Ulrich Herz, The Right to Refuse Military Service and Orders: A Working Paper Prepared for the International Peace Bureau Conference in Reutlingen/Stuttgart, Germany 39 (Aug. 25–30, 1968); Seán MacBride, *A New Dimension to the Legal and Moral Right to Refuse Military Service and Orders*, *in* 1 HUMAN RIGHTS: INTERNATIONAL DOCUMENTS, 1663, 1666–70 (James Avery Joyce, ed., 1978).

[56] Kessler, *supra* note 55, at 775.

[57] For the historical development of the right to conscientious objection following these early claims that there is a right not to fight in illegal wars, *see* generally Kessler, *supra* note 55, at 777–89. The key cases are cited *supra* Section 1.3 of Chapter 1.

[58] Rep. of the Hum. Rts Council Advisory Committee on the Right of Peoples to Peace, U.N. Doc. A/HRC/20/31, §§ 5(2), 7(2) (Apr. 16, 2012).

[59] Office of the High Commissioner, *New Text Prepared by the Chairperson-Rapporteur of the Open-Ended Intergovernmental Working Group on a Draft United Nations Declaration on the Right to Peace* (June 24, 2014), www.ohchr.org/Documents/HRBodies/HRCouncil/WGRightPeace/NV_new_text_Chairperson.pdf.

[60] Declaration on the Right to Peace, G.A. Res. 71/189 (Dec. 19, 2016).

participate "in violating human rights and fundamental freedoms."[61] This captures the internal imperative to protect individuals against being forced by law to do wrong by the law's own lights. On the understanding that the *jus in bello* defines the scope of relevant human rights in armed conflict, soldiers that refuse to follow orders to violate the *jus in bello* are clearly covered by this protection.[62]

The question here is whether the same can be said of those who refuse to follow orders to violate the *jus ad bellum*. On the orthodox account, the answer would be negative; aggression is the rare international crime that does "not implicate human rights violations."[63] On the account presented here, however, that is precisely where the orthodox account goes wrong. The criminalization of aggression provides the otherwise missing criminal law protection of soldiers' and collateral civilians' right to life.[64] Seen in that light, those who refuse to participate in an aggressive war are human rights defenders and worthy of being protected as such.

Ultimately, any one of the rights of conscience, peace, or rights defenders (or some combination thereof) would provide a viable foundation for the development of a right not to fight in illegal wars. The doctrinal hooks exist. Recognizing the normative core of the criminalization of aggression ought to provide the interpretive impetus to exploit them.

One might object at this point that there is something perverse about supplementing the existing prohibition on waging illegal war with a human rights obligation not to force soldiers to fight in such wars. When it decides to fight, the state's leadership either determines that the war is

[61] UN Declaration on the Right and Responsibility of Individuals Groups and Organs of Society to Promote and Protect Universally Recognized Human Rights and Fundamental Freedoms, G.A. Res. 53/144, U.N. Doc. A/RES/53/144, art. 10 (Mar. 8, 1999) [hereinafter UN Declaration on Human Rights Defenders]; *see also* COUNCIL OF EUR., ENSURING PROTECTION – EUROPEAN UNION GUIDELINES ON HUMAN RIGHTS DEFENDERS (2008).

[62] *See* Legality of the Threat or Use of Nuclear Weapons, Advisory Opinion, 1996 I.C.J. Rep. 226, § 25 (July 8).

[63] Iverson, *Contrasting the Normative and Historical Foundations of Transitional Justice and Jus Post Bellum, in* JUS POST BELLUM: MAPPING THE NORMATIVE FOUNDATIONS 80, 96 (C. Stahn, J. S. Easterday, & J. Iverson, eds., 2014); Letter from Aryeh Neier, President, Open Society Institute et al., to Foreign Ministers, Regarding the Crime of Aggression (May 10, 2010), www.opensocietyfoundations.org/sites/default/files/icc-aggression-letter-20100511.pdf [https://perma.cc/G9GX-2FSX]; Amnesty Int'l, *International Criminal Court: Amnesty International's Call for Pledges by States at the 13th Session of the Assembly of States Parties* 5 n. 18 (Oct. 29, 2014).

[64] *See* Section 3.2.2 of Chapter 3 above.

lawful or chooses not to be constrained by international law in that instance.[65] It would be odd if it were simultaneously to respect an international prohibition on punishing soldiers who refuse to fight on the grounds that its war is illegal.[66]

However, that reaction is too simplistic. The provision of an international human right along these lines would trigger obligations not just during the war, but also before and after war. It would make demands on the post-war state *vis-à-vis* the treatment of those who refused to fight during the war; and it would make demands on the pre-war state regarding the institutional constraints it must implement to protect those who might refuse to fight in a future conflict.

Rather than deterring belligerent states from punishing soldiers while engaged in illegal wars, a human right not to fight in illegal wars would provide a useful tool to resisters still serving sentences, facing prosecution, or suffering the consequences of a criminal record after the war and to activists seeking to mobilize for the protection of those who might fight a future war.[67] Cabined in the ways suggested in Chapter 10, such a right could be made compatible with the necessity account of the extant regime. Recognition of this right would also strengthen the case for an unequivocal human rights ban on the death penalty in any war resister case – a ban codified already in ECHR Protocol 13, which has been signed by all but two of the forty-seven states party to the European Convention.[68]

Enshrining the right in international law would also have important institutional consequences. It would give soldiers in states subject to human rights review bodies or courts the possibility of petitioning those

[65] Janina Dill & Henry Shue, *Limiting the Killing in War: Military Necessity and the St. Petersburg Assumption*, 26 Ethics & Int'l Affairs 311, 324 (2012).

[66] UN Secretary General, *Question of Conscientious Objection to Military Service*, para. 29, U.N. Doc. E/CN.4/Sub.2/1983/30 (June 27, 1983); Eide & Mubanga-Chipoya, *supra* note 53, para. 34; Michael Walzer, Obligations: Essays on Disobedience, War, and Citizenship 127, 134 (1970).

[67] On the challenges faced by German deserters following World War II, *see* Section 1.3 of Chapter 1 above.

[68] *See* Protocol No. 13 to the Convention for the Protection of Human Rights and Fundamental Freedoms, concerning the abolition of the death penalty in all circumstances, May 3, 2002, E.T.S. No. 187. The two yet to sign are Azerbaijan and Russia. Armenia has signed but not ratified. On the awkward existing relationship between human rights law and the death penalty, *see, for example*, Christof Heyns, *Report of the Special Rapporteur on Extrajudicial, Summary or Arbitrary Executions*, U.N. Doc. A/67/275 (Aug. 9, 2012); Juan E. Méndez, *Interim Report of the Special Rapporteur on Torture and Other Cruel, Inhuman or Degrading Treatment or Punishment*, U.N. Doc. A/67/279 (Aug. 9, 2012).

institutions when incarcerated for refusing to fight in a wrongful war.[69] Particularly in states in which such individuals would face long sentences or other severe consequences, this could place international pressure on the state to release them and wipe relevant convictions from their records. It is unrealistic to expect that the state would accommodate this during the armed conflict, but it may be more feasible after the war, particularly following a leadership transition.[70]

Providing the international legal mechanisms by which such an outcome might be achieved would better arm these dissenters, and would give post-war leaders domestic political cover for releasing and clearing those imprisoned for refusing to fight. It would provide the international doctrinal nudge that advocates could use to catalyze a norm cascade.[71]

Moreover, it would transform the resister from domestic criminal to international human rights claimant, affecting the cognitive frame within which the soldier acts. It would, in this way, recognize the position that Bill Clinton articulated in a 1969 letter explaining his anguish over the Vietnam draft:

> One of my roommates is a draft resister who is possibly under indictment and may never be able to go home again. He is one of the bravest, best men I know. His country needs men like him more than they know. That he is considered a criminal is an obscenity ... To many of us, it is no longer clear what is service and what is disservice.[72]

The letter came back to haunt Clinton in his first presidential campaign, but it captures an important truth – there *is* an obscenity in criminalizing doing the right thing. That obscenity is exacerbated when the normative premises upon which the "right thing" is defined are those that undergird the law itself. International human rights law stands

[69] On individual complaints mechanisms, see, for example, Alexandra R. Harrington, *Don't Mind the Gap: The Rise of Individual Complaint Mechanisms within International Human Rights Treaties*, 22 DUKE J. COMP. & INT'L L. 153 (2012). On individual access to human rights courts, *see, for example*, Tom Dannenbaum, *Nationality and the International Judge*, 45 CORNELL INT'L L.J. 78, 85–87 (2012).

[70] *Cf.* White House Office of the Press Secretary, Granting Pardon for Violations of the Selective Service Act August 4, 1964 to March 28, 1973 (Jan. 21, 1977).

[71] On the process of such norm cascades, *see, for example*, THE POWER OF HUMAN RIGHTS: INTERNATIONAL NORMS AND DOMESTIC CHANGE (Thomas Risse, Stephen C. Ropp, & Kathryn Sikkink, eds., 1999); THE PERSISTENT POWER OF HUMAN RIGHTS: FROM COMMITMENT TO COMPLIANCE (Thomas Risse, Stephen C. Ropp, & Kathryn Sikkink, eds., 2013).

[72] Letter from William J. Clinton to Colonel Eugene Holmes (Dec. 3, 1969), www.pbs.org/wgbh/pages/frontline/shows/clinton/etc/draftletter.html.

against legal obscenities. It can be productive in eliminating them, and it aims to do just that. But even when its consequences in serving that end are minimal, there is a basic value in taking a stand.

11.3 The Crime of Aggression and the Soldier's Right to Life

The final institutional and doctrinal implication at the international level goes to who is eligible to participate as a victim in aggression proceedings at the ICC and to receive or benefit from the reparations awarded following a conviction. The account presented here would reject the widely held view that the core victim of aggression is the state. It would focus instead on natural persons. However, whereas others have sought to include natural persons as the victims of aggression by expanding the concept of "victim" in the context of aggression prosecutions, the approach taken here would remain true to the principle that the direct victims of an ICC crime ought to be understood as those that suffer the core criminal wrong.[73] The account's capacity to combine adherence to the Court's narrow definition of "direct victim" (as is arguably demanded by the criminal context) with a focus on natural persons (as is arguably inherent in the Court's fundamental connection to the humanization of international law) is a natural consequence of its more coherent fit with international criminal law's broader normative posture.

On the account presented here, those criminally wronged by aggression – those whose rights the crime is framed to protect – are not the attacked states, but the human beings that are the direct objects of aggression's legally unjustified violence and yet unprotected by any other criminal prohibition. As such, the direct victims of aggression are the soldiers killed or harmed fighting against the aggressor force and the civilians killed or harmed in proportionate collateral damage.[74] Their deaths and injuries are what make aggression a crime. Their loved ones

[73] Cf. Section 1.3 in Chapter 1 above.

[74] As noted previously, combatants' right to life is granted narrow protections in the *jus in bello*. *See, for example*, Rome Statute of the International Criminal Court, U.N. Doc. A/CONF.183/9, 2187 U.N.T.S. 90, arts. 8(2)(b)(vi, xi), 8(2)(c), 8(2)(d)(ix) (July 17, 1998) (as amended in 2010 by Doc. C.N.651.2010.TREATIES-8) [hereinafter ICC Statute]. However, that regime does not protect combatants from the illegal and non-defensive violence of an aggressor.

are those with the clearest claim to standing as aggression's indirect victims.[75]

It is this large, but relatively focused, class of persons that ought to be represented in aggression proceedings and targeted with its reparations awards. Notable among those *not* included in this category would be victims of *jus in bello* violations inflicted by the aggressor force, and many of the broader range of harmed persons compensated via the UN Compensation Commission following Iraq's invasion of Kuwait, such as those impacted by the non-fulfillment of contracts that became impossible to complete due to the war.[76]

The exclusion of those harmed by an aggressor's war crimes warrants explanation. Those individuals are, after all, criminally wronged as a foreseeable consequence of the initiation of an illegal war. Indeed, it has sometimes been argued that it is *because* any war comes with war crimes and atrocities that initiating war without justification is criminal.[77] On that view, aggression is a crime because it necessarily entails war crimes. This is a mistake. First, the criminality of an aggressive war does not depend on the occurrence, or even the threat, of war crimes, even though such crimes are likely to occur.[78] Second, defensive force foreseeably involves the likely infliction of war crimes, too, and yet the use of defensive force is entirely legally permissible. Third, and most fundamentally, a key virtue of the unjustified killing account is that it explains aggression's significance by recognizing that it fills what would otherwise be an anomalous gap in the criminality of unjustified killing.[79] That gap is composed, by definition, of those that suffer the *jus-in-bello*-compliant violence of the aggressor force. War crimes are already criminal in another form, and attach to different perpetrators. The criminalization of aggression is not necessary to condemn and punish those wrongs.

Of course, if the war crimes inflicted in an aggressive war are not charged, their victims may never gain standing at the ICC.[80] But this

[75] Prosecutor v. Lubanga (ICC-01/04-01/06 A A 2 A 3), Judgment on the Appeals against the "Decision Establishing the Principles and Procedures to be Applied to Reparations" of 7 August 2012, paras. 190–91, 196–98 (Mar. 3, 2015) [hereinafter Lubanga AC: Reparations Principles].

[76] *Cf.* Section 1.4 in Chapter 1 above.

[77] For a contrary view, *see, for example*, Ferencz, *Epilogue: The Long Journey to Kampala, in* The Crime of Aggression: A Commentary 1501, at 1510 (Claus Kreß and Stefan Barriga, eds., 2016).

[78] Mégret, *supra* note 11, at 1419.

[79] *See* Section 3.2.2 in Chapter 3 above.

[80] Arguing that this is a reason to extend aggression victim status to those harmed by *jus in bello* violations, *see* Erin Pobjie, *Victims of the Crime of Aggression, in* The Crime of Aggression: A Commentary 816, 840 (Claus Kreß & Stefan Barriga, eds., 2016).

problem is not unique to aggression. The Lubanga victims were limited to the conscripted child soldiers, not those harmed by the crimes inflicted foreseeably by those children once conscripted.[81] The failure to charge Lubanga with the latter crimes denied their victims standing and eligibility for reparations.[82] However, the injustice in such situations is the failure to prosecute the other crimes. Expanding who counts as a victim of the crimes that *are* charged would not correct that failure; it would change the standard. As I have argued elsewhere, and as noted above, adjustments to those mistakes are best made through the Trust Fund for Victims' use of its "other resources."[83]

As discussed in Chapter 7, recognizing combatants as among aggression's core victims also departs in another way from the otherwise far broader approaches of the UN Compensation Commission and the Ethiopia Eritrea Claims Commission. Both of those commissions excluded almost all combatant deaths and injuries from compensable *jus ad bellum* damages.[84] It would be a mistake to replicate this exclusion at the ICC. For the reasons elaborated in Chapter 7, the purported rationales for such exclusions do not hold. Excluding those combatants at the ICC would deny official recognition and solidarity to those whose death and suffering is why aggression is a crime.

The harder case is that of aggressor soldiers who fought under significant deception or coercion from their home state, and were killed or harmed doing so. As discussed in Chapters 4 and 5, such soldiers are not the direct crime victims of aggression, because the wrongfulness of the harms inflicted upon them inhere not in the criminality of their state's war, but in the deception or coercion that led them to participate in it. Current doctrine grants "indirect victim" status only to the close relations

[81] Prosecutor v. Lubanga (ICC-01/04-01/06-1813), "Decision on 'Indirect victims,'" paras. 47–54 (Apr. 8 2009). *See also* Section 1.4 in Chapter 1 above.

[82] *Cf.* Valentina Spiga, *Indirect Victims' Participation in the Lubanga Trial*, 8 J. Int'l Crim. Justice. 183 (2010)

[83] *See* Tom Dannenbaum, *The International Criminal Court, Article 79, and Transitional Justice: The Case for an Independent Trust Fund for Victims*, 28 Wis. Int'l L.J. 234, 270–86 (2010).

[84] Final Award: Ethiopia's Damages Claims (Eri. v. Eth.), § 338 (Eri.–Eth. Claims Comm'n 2009). The UNCC allowed a narrow category of claims on behalf of Kuwaiti soldiers killed or injured during the days of and immediately following the invasion, but excluded combatants killed by Iraqi forces once the coalition was engaged. Recommendations Made by the Panel of Commissioners Concerning Individual Claims for Serious Personal Injury or Death (Category B Claims), UNCC Governing Council, U.N. Doc. S/AC.26/1994/1, at 15 (May 26, 1994).

of victims or those who were harmed trying to protect direct victims from the criminal wrong.[85] This helps to maintain a narrow concept of "victim" that is responsive to the criminal context. Plainly, soldiers fighting for the aggressor force do not fall into that category. As such, there are good principled reasons for excluding them from victim status in aggression prosecutions at the ICC.

However, for the reasons outlined in Chapter 8, there may be a pragmatic case for including as "indirect victims" those that were genuinely coerced or deceived into fighting and who were killed or harmed as a result. To do otherwise could exacerbate the very tensions that lead to war in the first place. To the extent the reparative process at the ICC has a transitional justice function, the interest of furthering peace and reconciliation between the warring parties may be sufficient to warrant such an accommodation.

Although this concession would be pragmatic, it would be rooted in the fact that these individuals *do* suffer a genuine, if indirect and contingent, wrong in the course of a criminal aggression. In addition to being wronged by being forced to do wrong, they are also wronged by being forced or deceived into a situation where they may be justifiably harmed or killed. If their inclusion as "indirect victims" on this basis is to avoid distorting fundamentally the basic principles of victim participation, it must be both contingent on and shaped by the coercion and mendacity that are the crux of the wrong they suffered.

With the eligibility criteria for victim status so defined, the key remaining question is how participation and reparations would work in an aggression proceeding. The obvious challenges in that respect are logistical and resource-based. In almost any conceivable aggression, the number of persons qualifying for victim status along the lines defined above would far exceed the number the ICC could grant individual participation rights, particularly given the imperative to safeguard the accused's right to a fair and expeditious trial.[86] Similarly, the financial resources necessary to repair fully all killed or harmed enemy soldiers and all collaterally killed or harmed civilians would far exceed the wealth of any conceivable aggressor state leader. The numbers would only get

[85] Lubanga AC: Reparations Principles, *supra* note 75, paras. 190–91, 196–98.

[86] ICC Statute, *supra* note 74, art. 64(2); Prosecutor v. Katanga and Ngudjolo, ICC-01-/04-01/07, Judgment on Unlawful Detention and Stay of Proceedings, paras. 43–47 (July 12, 2010).

more daunting if the deceived and coerced troops of the leader's own state were to be counted as indirect victims.

Plainly, then, in an aggression prosecution, the victim procedures at the ICC would function in a realm of inadequacy and imperfection. This, however, is hardly unique to aggression. International criminal justice, whether in the context of genocide, crimes against humanity, or most war crimes, is inherently inadequate. To borrow Martha Minow's phrase, there are "no tidy endings" following war or mass atrocity.[87]

Even in relatively narrow war crimes and crimes against humanity cases thus far, the Court has struggled to manage thousands of victims as trial participants.[88] Reparations are no less challenging. Part of the tragedy confronting institutions tasked with awarding reparations in the aftermath of war or atrocity is that the harms are irreparable and the numbers of victims and the diversity of their interests and desires are inevitably overwhelming.[89]

The very premise of the Rome Statute is that this challenging and complex reality is insufficient to warrant retreat from a participation and reparations regime.[90] Nonetheless, these constraints are important in shaping the form that victim participation and reparation must take in aggression and other international criminal proceedings involving mass victimization. They mean that the justice provided must be understood as "rough" or "practical."[91] It may be distorting and unrealistic to think

87 Martha Minow, Between Vengeance and Forgiveness: Facing History after Genocide and Mass Violence 102 (1998).

88 For a critical appraisal, *see* Haslam and Edmunds, *Common Legal Representation at the International Criminal Court*, 12 Int'l Crim. L. Rev. 871 (2012).

89 Brandon Hamber, Transforming Societies after Political Violence: Truth, Reconciliation, and Mental Health 101 (2009); Conor McCarthy, Reparations and Victim Support in the International Criminal Court 73 (2012); Roger P. Alford, *On War as Hell*, 3 Chi. J. Int'l L. 207, 207 (2002); Rainer Hofmann & Frank Riemann, Background Report: Compensation for Victims of War, Int'l Law Ass'n Committee on Compensation for Victims of War 32 (2004). Some war crimes, such as seizing the enemy's property without a justification in military necessity may be reparable via restitution. ICC Statute, *supra* note 74, arts. 8(2)(b)(xiii), 8(2)(e)(xii). However, most involve wrongs the victims of which cannot be made whole.

90 David Donat-Cattin, *Article 68: Protection of Victims and Witnesses and their Participation in the Proceedings*, *in* Commentary on the Rome Statute of the International Criminal Court: Observers' Notes, Article by Article, 1275, 1295 (Otto Triffterer, ed., 2nd edn 2008).

91 Terms of this kind are invoked frequently in the literature on mass claims reparations. *See, e.g.*, John Authers, *Making Good Again: German Compensation for Forced and Slave Laborers*, *in* The Handbook of Reparations 420, 433; Ronald J. Bettauer, *Policy Issues*

about participation and reparation in these contexts in the way one might think of traditional civil litigation.[92] Instead, both the participation and reparations processes are likely to be collective and focused more on rehabilitation and expression than on restitution or compensation. This simply accentuates in aggression proceedings a tendency that is likely to arise in most if not all prosecutions at the Court.[93]

In terms of participation, it means that individual victims would have little if any direct involvement in proceedings, except insofar as they are also witnesses. Instead, a common legal representative would provide the channel through which a group of victims participates in the case.[94] The relevant ICC Chamber may request that a particular collective of victims choose a common legal representative and may request the Registry to choose one if victims cannot agree on one themselves.[95]

Given the particularly large number of victims involved in an aggression prosecution, processing individual victim participation applications, even with a view to assigning them to a particular collective, would be both overwhelming for the Court and potentially exclusionary of those who lack the information or other resources necessary to apply.[96] As such, solutions pursued in earlier ICC cases, such as group applications for victim status or allowing the collective legal representative to channel the views of non-registered victims, where she determines that they

Surrounding the Creation and Operations of the UNCC, *in* WAR REPARATIONS AND THE UN COMPENSATION COMMISSION 9 (Timothy J. Feighery, Christopher S. Gibson, & Trevor M. Rajah, eds., 2015); Francis E. McGovern, *Dispute System Design: The United Nations Compensation Commission*, in *id.*, at 29, 38–39; Hans van Houtte, Hans Das, & Bart Delmartinox, *The United Nations Compensation Commission*, *in* THE HANDBOOK OF REPARATIONS, *supra*, at 321, 341, 368; David D. Caron & Brian Morris, *The UN Compensation Commission: Practical Justice, Not Retribution*, 13 EUR. J. INT'L. L. 183 (2002).

92 Jaime E. Malamud-Goti & Lucas Sebastián Grosman, *Reparations and Civil Litigation*, *in* THE HANDBOOK OF REPARATIONS, *supra* note 91.

93 *See* Haslam & Edmunds, *supra* note 88; Christine Van den Wyngaert, *Victims before International Criminal Courts: Some Views and Concerns of an ICC Trial Judge*, 44 CASE W. RES. J. INT'L L. 475, 480 (2012). For example: Prosecutor v. Katanga & Ngudjolo, ICC-01/04–01/07, Order on the Organisation of Common Legal Representation of Victims, para. 11 (July 22, 2009).

94 Van den Wyngaert, *supra* note 93, at 489.

95 ICC R. P. EVID. 90(2)–(4).

96 *See, e.g.*, Mariana Pena & Gaelle Carayon, *Is the ICC Making the Most of Victim Participation?*, 7 INT'L J. TRANSNAT'L JUSTICE 518 (2013); Assembly of States Parties, Rep. of the Bureau on Victims and Affected Communities and Trust Fund for Victims, ICC-ASP/10/31, at 3 (Nov. 5, 2012).

qualify, may be the only viable paths forward in aggression proceedings.[97]

Following a conviction, the reparative process would also almost certainly be collective. Consistent with the governing framework, collective reparations have been directed through the Trust Fund, which has the authority to proceed with reparative awards whether or not individual victims can be identified, and which may, in the course of providing collective reparations to crime victims, also assist persons not qualifying for that status.[98] Collective repair of this kind may involve providing reparations to a third entity with a view to benefiting the victim class.[99]

Plainly, the functioning of collective representation and the acceptability of collective reparations depend to a certain degree on the cohesion of the collective. In order for collective participation and reparations to proceed in a way that is at least somewhat responsive to the diversity of needs and interests across victims, victims would need to be categorized into different groups, each of which is then represented by its own common legal representative. Precisely this path has been pursued in ICC cases thus far.[100] The categorization of reparations has also been standard in mass claims proceedings.[101]

[97] *See, e.g.*, Prosecutor v. Gbagbo, ICC-02/11-01/11, Decision on Issues Related to the Victims' Application Process, para. 8 (Feb. 6, 2012); Prosecutor v. Gbagbo, ICC-02/11-01/11, Second Decision on Issues Related to the Victims' Application Process (Apr. 5, 2012); Prosecutor v. Ruto and Sang, ICC-01/09-01/11, Decision on Victims' Representation and Participation (Oct. 3, 2012).

[98] Lubanga AC: Reparations Principles, *supra* note 75, paras. 149–67, 212–15; Assembly of States Parties, Regulations of the Trust Fund for Victims, ICC-ASP/4/Res.3 (Dec. 3, 2005), paras. 60–61, 69; ICC R. P. EVID. 97(1), 98(3).

[99] CONOR MCCARTHY, REPARATIONS AND VICTIM SUPPORT IN THE INTERNATIONAL CRIMINAL COURT 255 (2012); Prosecutor v. Lubanga (ICC-01/04-01/06), "Decision Establishing the Principles and Procedures to be Applied to Reparations," para. 197 (Aug. 7, 2012) [hereinafter Lubanga TC: Reparations Principles].

[100] *See, e.g.*, Prosecutor v. Katanga & Ngudjolo Chui, ICC-01/04-01/07- 1328, Order on the Organisation of Common Legal Representation of Victims, paras. 2–4 (July 22, 2009); Prosecutor v. Bemba, ICC-01/05-01/08-1005, Decision on Common Legal Representation of Victims for the Purpose of Trial, para. 16 (Nov. 19, 2010).

[101] *Cf.* Decision Number 2, Claims Categories, Forms and Procedures (Eri. v. Eth.), § A (Eri.-Eth. Claims Comm'n 2004); Michael F. Raboin, *The Provisional Rules for Claims Procedure of the United Nations Compensation Commission: A Practical Approach to Mass Claims Processing, in* THE UNITED NATIONS COMPENSATION COMMISSION 119, 120 (Richard B. Lillich, ed., 1995). *See also* Shuichi Furuya, A Model Statute of an Ad Hoc Compensation Commission: Preliminary Analysis of Some Issues to be Addressed, Paper Submitted to 72nd Conference of the International Law Association in Toronto, at 25–26 (2006).

An example of such categorization in an aggression prosecution might be: (A) loved ones of combatants killed fighting against aggression; (B) loved ones of civilians killed in collateral damage; (C) combatants injured fighting against aggression; (D) civilians injured in collateral damage; and (E) combatants and the families of combatants harmed or killed as a result of having been coerced or deceived into fighting for the aggressor force. The inevitable coarseness of any such categorization creates real challenges to bringing value to victims through the ICC's participatory and reparative processes. As discussed below, if those challenges are to be overcome, the process must be voluntary and victims must feel some sense of ownership over both their interactions with the Court and the reparations that it awards. These requirements are not easily satisfied.

Given the limited resources of individual perpetrators, the vast numbers of victims, and limited capacity of the Trust Fund for Victims as a source of supplementary funding, ICC participation and reparations regime ought to be seen primarily in terms of moral expression.[102] In aggression prosecutions in particular, resource constraints are such that any reparative awards are likely to skew away from restitution or even compensation and towards symbolic reparation and perhaps partial contributions to rehabilitation programs.[103]

Early clarity on this issue is important. If victims are led to believe that reparations will do, or can do, more than is within the realistic capacity of the ICC system, the Court's failure to satisfy those expectations could lead to renewed trauma and an ultimately counter-productive contribution to the victim's struggle to rebuild after war. For the reasons discussed below, the precise contours of reparative projects would need to be driven by the context and the needs and desires of the relevant victim constituencies. Nonetheless, some general comments can be made.

Rehabilitation is a core form of reparation at the ICC and in international human rights law.[104] Reparations projects in this vein could

[102] *See supra* Section 1.4 in Chapter 1. *See also* McCarthy, *supra* note 89, at 61–62, 133 (2012); Redress and Institute for Security Studies (ISS), Victim Participation in Criminal Law Proceedings 17, 19, 23, 25 (2015).

[103] David Donat-Cattin, *Article 75: Reparations to Victims*, in Commentary, *supra* note 90, 1399, 1405.

[104] ICC Statute, *supra* note 74, art. 75; Basic Principles and Guidelines on the Right to a Remedy and Reparation for Victims of Gross Violations of International Human Rights Law and Serious Violations of International Humanitarian Law, G.A. Res. 60/147, U.N. Doc. A/RES/60/147, § 21 (Dec. 16, 2005); Lubanga TC: Reparations Principles, *supra* note 99, paras. 235–36; Prosecutor v. Lubanga (ICC-01/04-01/06 A A 2 A 3 1/97), Appellate

involve the partial funding of medical, psychiatric, and reintegration programs for veterans or collaterally harmed civilians, and various counseling and support programs for bereaved families in either context.[105] As part of the "rough" justice of such a program, the evidentiary threshold for individuals to qualify for such programs would need to be somewhat flexible.[106]

In addition to rehabilitative reparations programs, perhaps the dominant form of reparations in aggression proceedings, given the numbers and resources involved, would be symbolic. This could involve the provision of memorials, commemorations, tributes, and declarations of wrongfulness, as well as formal articulations of facts that might not otherwise make it into the final judgment.[107]

These are forms of the widely recognized reparative category of "satisfaction."[108] Unlike restitution, compensation, and rehabilitation, satisfaction is not listed in Article 75 of the Rome Statute. However, the Lubanga Trial Chamber emphasized that the list in Article 75 is not comprehensive, and that reparations may include a range of symbolic measures.[109] The Appeals Chamber has also emphasized that reparations can have a symbolic value and that they can help to express the accountability of the perpetrator to his victims.[110]

Symbolic reparations may be particularly important in expressing recognition of the wrong suffered by troops on the aggressor side who

Order for Reparations (amended), Annexed to Prosecutor v. Lubanga, Judgment on the Appeals against the "Decision Establishing the Principles and Procedures to Be Applied to Reparations" of 7 August 2012, para. 67 (Mar. 3, 2015) [hereinafter Lubanga AC: Order for Reparations]; McCarthy, *supra* note 89, at 215–16.

105 *Cf.* Lubanga AC: Order for Reparations, *supra* note 104, para. 69; Elizabeth Lira, The Reparations Policy for Human Rights Violations in Chile, De Greiff Handbook 55, 67–71 (on the Program of Reparations and Comprehensive Health Care for Victims of Human Rights Violations (PRAIS) in Chile).

106 *Cf.* Harvey P. Berman, *The Agent Orange Veteran Payment Program*, 53 L. & Contemp. Problems 49, 50 (1990).

107 McCarthy, *supra* note 89, at 174–76, 180–82.

108 *See, e.g.*, Basic Principles and Guidelines on the Right to a Remedy and Reparation, *supra* note 104, § 22; Int'l Law Ass'n, Resolution 2/2010: Declaration of International Law Principles on Reparation for Victims of Armed Conflict, 74th Conference of the International Law Association, The Hague, art. 9 (Aug. 15–20, 2010); Draft Articles on Responsibility of States for Internationally Wrongful Acts with Commentaries, Rep. of the Int'l Law Comm'n on the Work of its Fifty-Third Session, U.N. Doc. A/56/10, art. 37 and commentary (2001).

109 Lubanga TC: Reparations Principles, *supra* note 99, para. 222.

110 Lubanga AC: Reparations Principles, *supra* note 75, paras. 202, 70.

were deceived or coerced by their state into fighting and suffered personal injury or death as a result. Reparations to that constituency could also involve a donation to domestic transparency efforts to explore the process that led up to the decision to go to war, such as the Chilcot Inquiry. The expressive focus in either context must be on the wrongful deceit and coercion of those troops.

More broadly, an exclusive focus on symbolic reparations, although tempting from the perspective of resources, could be counter-productive in recognizing and valuing victims. Symbolic reparations that are not supplemented with more tangible payments or services can be received with some degree of cynicism, when it is felt that these are high-minded, but cheap responses to the real human problems faced by those whose lives have been upended by criminal violence.[111]

The necessarily collectivized nature of victim participation and reparations in aggression proceedings and the likely skew of reparations towards rehabilitation and symbolic reparations entail significant challenges for the victim process in aggression proceedings. While there is no universally preferred form of symbolic reparation, a primary factor in determining any given reparation's capacity to have a positive impact on victims and survivors in given communities is the extent to which those groups and individuals are involved in the processes of defining and realizing the reparative action.

As two observers note, "[G]enuine reparation, and the process of healing ... does not occur through the delivery of the object (for example, a pension, a monument and so on) but through the process that takes place around the object."[112] Victims across contexts express frustration and a further sense of injury when they are dissociated from the process of designing, creating, and developing the memorials that are

[111] Prosecutor v. Lubanga (ICC-01/04–01/06), International Center for Transitional Justice, Submission on Reparations Issues, para. 64 (May 10, 2012); EReshnee Naidu, The Ties that Bind: Strengthening the Links between Memorialisation and Transitional Justice 2 (2006); Ereshnee Naidu, Symbolic Reparations: A Fractured Opportunity 4 (2004); Phuong Pham et al., Iraqi Voices: Attitudes toward Transitional Justice and Social Reconstruction 42 (2004).

[112] Brandon Hamber & Richard Wilson, Symbolic Closure through Memory, Reparation and Revenge in Post-Conflict Societies, 1 J. Hum. Rts. 35, 44 (2002).

putatively directed at them.[113] Conversely, the most effective moral and symbolic reparations are often conceived, driven, and implemented by the community that they are to serve.[114] In some contexts, these processes occur entirely outside any formal reparations procedure and are entirely resourced within the victim community. However, there can be a productive role for the institutions charged with managing reparations, such as the ICC's Trust Fund for Victims, in creating the opportunities for such projects by funding and facilitating the process that victims and survivors then direct, manage, and implement.[115] Recognizing this, the Trust Fund has from the start advocated victim participation in reparative design.[116]

In the context of a collective participation and reparations system, the need for this kind of ownership and participation poses difficult questions. For example, it may be that the families of soldiers killed fighting against aggression – in theory a relatively cohesive group – would differ significantly in their views on key participation and reparations questions. Some may reject the very notion of engaging with the proceeding. Others may wish to participate but differ in their views of what ought to be expressed by the collective legal representative. Following a conviction, different constituencies may diverge on whether reparations are appropriate, on the message or form of any memorial or commemorative expression that would be linked to the wrong of aggression, and on the degree to which they would accept counseling or support from a program funded even in small part from the wealth of the aggressor leader.

This only serves to emphasize that one of the Court's and the Trust Fund's greatest challenges regarding victim proceedings will be balancing the need for victim ownership and participation, the inevitably collective nature of the process, and the diversity of needs and interests even within relatively coherent victim groups. Again, these challenges are inherent to the vast majority of international crimes.[117] Nonetheless, the scope of the

[113] Ereshnee Naidu, The Ties that Bind: Strengthening the Links between Memorialisation and Transitional Justice 9–10 (2006); Ereshnee Naidu, Empowerment through Living Memory: A Community-Centred Model for Memorialisation 6 (2004); Lazarus Kgalema, Symbols of Hope: Monuments as Symbols of Remembrance and Peace in the Process of Reconciliation (1999).

[114] *Id.*; Diana Cammack, *Reparations in Malawi*, *in* The Handbook of Reparations, *supra* note 91, at 241.

[115] *Id.*, at 572. [116] Lubanga TC: Reparations Principles, *supra* note 99, para. 31.

[117] Phuong Pham et al., When the War Ends: A Population-Based Survey on Attitudes about Peace, Justice, and Social Reconstruction in Northern

victim constituencies harmed in an aggressive war makes the issue particularly acute in that context.

As the Court has recognized from the start, one essential element of striking the right balance in this respect is to ensure that the reparations process is consensual; those who reject the process, the outcome, or the very concept must be able to opt out.[118] This is essential given the subject matter; some victims or bereaved families may feel that accepting reparations or engaging with a reparative process would be akin to accepting blood money or doing a disservice to their lost loved ones.[119] Even when they accept a payment or service, they may not accept the description of it as repairing the wrong.[120] Opting out, of course, is more complicated in the context of symbols, like memorials, than it is in the context of the compensatory or rehabilitative modes of reparations. In those contexts, the challenge will likely be to generate as strong a sense of ownership in the process as possible, recognizing that imperfection is inevitable.

The path forward for victim participation and reparations in aggression proceedings is likely to be a rocky one. The scope and diversity of victim constituencies affected, the inevitably inadequate resources of the perpetrator and the Trust Fund, and the challenges associated with designing a process that is responsive to the needs and desires of victims are daunting. The account presented here cannot solve those challenges, many of which will arise in the majority of international criminal proceedings, and not just aggression prosecutions. What it can do is identify the victim constituencies to which the Court's and Fund's attention should be directed in that process – namely, the soldiers and civilians who suffer the unjustified violence of criminal war and who are not protected by any other criminal prohibition.

UGANDA 38 (2007); PHUONG PHAM ET AL., FORGOTTEN VOICES: A POPULATION-BASED SURVEY ON ATTITUDES ABOUT PEACE AND JUSTICE IN NORTHERN UGANDA (2005).

118 Lubanga AC: Reparations Principles, *supra* note 75, paras. 160–62; Lubanga AC: Order for Reparations, *supra* note 104, para. 30.

119 José María Guembe, *Economic Reparations for Grave Human Rights Violations: The Argentinean Experience*, *in* THE HANDBOOK OF REPARATIONS, *supra* note 91, at 21, 25 (the Madres de Plaza de Mayo – Línea Fundadora "contends that economic reparations entail accepting the death of the disappeared"); Ariel Colonomos & Andrea Armstrong, *German Reparations to the Jews after World War II: A Turning Point in the History of Reparations*, *in id.*, at 390, 395–97 (on disputes within Israel on whether to accept German reparations); BRANDON HAMBER, TRANSFORMING SOCIETIES AFTER POLITICAL VIOLENCE: TRUTH, RECONCILIATION, AND MENTAL HEALTH 102, 109 (2009).

120 Colonomos & Armstrong, *supra* note 119, at 393.

Conclusion

It is a mistake to think that soldiers' lives are dispensable from the international legal point of view. Far from being marginalized and ignored, soldiers are at the normative crux of the criminalization of aggression and the contemporary *jus ad bellum*. For those persuaded of the notion that human persons should be the fundamental points of normative concern in war, including many revisionist just war theorists, this ought to be an encouraging finding – international law reflects that position more than moral theorists or lawyers have traditionally recognized. At the same time, this account also illuminates the tragedy of the existing legal posture, and the internal implications of that tragedy for interpretive and institutional reform.

Humanizing our understanding of the *jus ad bellum* means recognizing not just that soldiers are wronged when they are killed by aggressor forces, but also the gravity of what soldiers are asked to do in war. Soldiers forced to fight in aggressive wars are forced by law to do wrong by international law's own lights, and yet they find no sanctuary from that legal coercion. If international law's effort to reflect deep moral values on the use of force is to be taken seriously, the dissonance in this posture is more than simply a question of doctrinal aesthetics. More research is needed to understand the connection between the moral injury associated with inflicting death in war and the grounds for going to war, but the existing evidence indicates that that burden is real. The wrong of being forced to do wrong is one that cannot be dismissed.

From the international legal point of view, the tragedy is that soldiers who feel burdened by fighting in illegal wars get it right. Their felt moral pain cannot be dismissed from that perspective as mistaken or unjustifiably self-abasing. And yet it may be that the best that international law can do is to leave soldiers with that burden in the interests of global security.

Recognizing that as the underlying posture of the existing regime triggers an internal imperative at the international level to interrogate constantly the necessity of that imposition and to limit it wherever possible. This extends to a domestic imperative insofar as international law on the use of force is recognized in that context as the appropriate normative framework for going to war.

Focusing on those imperatives clarifies that under current conditions, there are reforms and interpretive developments that would better respect the moral status of soldiers than the system we have. The proposals along those lines discussed in Part III are aspirational, but they are also tied to existing realities. Processes not entirely unlike the proposed post-war commission of inquiry have occurred already in several states in the aftermath of the Iraq War. Similarly, there are already in existence independent actors with access to classified intelligence whose charge is to provide an adversarial check on the government regarding key matters of national security. The development of domestic and international human rights litigation over the past three decades has shown that normative dissonance internal to the law can both invite litigation and enable significant interpretive change even in the absence of direct state action or consent.

However, although there is reason to believe these changes are possible, there should be no misimpression that they would dispel the tragic position of the soldier from the international legal point of view. Even if each of these reforms were implemented meticulously, much of the normative remainder of international law's core institutional weakness would continue to be borne by men and women in uniform.

Equally, repositioning killed or harmed soldiers and collaterally killed or harmed civilians as the core victims of aggression is essential to properly recognizing the wrongfulness of the harms that those individuals and their loved ones suffer in the course of an illegal war. If the ICC were to fail to do that via its framework of victim participation and reparations, it would replicate the false view that soldiers' lives are in fact dispensable from the international point of view.

Nonetheless, even refocused in the appropriate way, that framework cannot but be woefully inadequate in responding to the wrongs that are its target. Victim participation in aggression proceedings will inevitably be constrained radically. The imperative of a fair and expeditious trial demands as much. Resource limitations will restrict radically the possible reparative response. Moreover, the number and diversity of victims of any conceivable aggression are such that it will be extremely difficult to grant all victims the kind of ownership over the reparative process that is necessary to maximize its benefit.

This conclusion is not sanguine. But nor should it be. War is the site of indescribable human tragedy. If the international legal regime were to have a settled and comfortable posture on war's central participants, it would lack credibility as a normative framework. An international law that takes seriously the moral status of soldiers is an international law that must be in a state of permanent internal moral disquiet, and subject to an ongoing internal imperative to do better whenever exigencies allow. With the criminalization of aggression, those are traits of the international law we have.

The purpose of elaborating a series of institutional reforms in light of this reality is neither to articulate the inevitable normative implications of the arguments that came before, nor to suggest that these are the changes most likely to take hold. Rather it is to identify the kinds of institutional changes that would be responsive to those arguments and the normative impetus behind them. It is intended to start the conversation about what international law owes soldiers on its own normative terms. Ultimately, respecting troops globally, and respecting our troops locally, requires engaging in that conversation without presuming that it can ever be finished.

INDEX

Printed in the USA
CPSIA information can be obtained
at www.ICGtesting.com
LVHW041242081123
763187LV00004B/675

9 781316 620397